FRESH

from a Vegetarian Kitchen

Meredith McCarty

Illustrations by Bernice Kagan

St. Martin's Press

New York

Also by the author:
   American Macrobiotic Cuisine, Avery Publishing Group
   Quick Whole-Grain Sourdough Breads Video, Turning Point Publications

Cover photo: Craig Lord's organic farm, Bayside, California
Photo credit: Neil Gilchrist

Library of Congress Cataloging-in-Publication Data

McCarty, Meredith
      Fresh from a vegetarian kitchen / Meredith McCarty.
         p.   cm.
      Includes index.
      ISBN 0-312-11795-7
      1. Vegetarian cookery.   2. Low-fat diet—Recipes.   3. Menus.

   I. Title.
   TX837.M47   1995
   641.5'636—dc20   94-46272
                                                     CIP

   First St. Martin's Press Edition: April 1995
   10   9   8   7   6   5   4   3   2   1

Dedication

I dedicate this book to my parents, Alfred and Betty James, who encouraged their children's appetites for the best.

I also dedicate this book to my husband, Patrick McCarty, in gratitude for his loving support, his well-timed sense of humor, his discerning appetite, and his expertise at the computer, all of which I've benefited from so much.

Words of Appreciation

The creating of a book is more of a joint venture than I ever would have imagined. I've learned so much in the process and wish to wholeheartedly thank these friends for their efforts:

To my teachers in macrobiotics, a path toward more balanced living: Michio and Aveline Kushi, Shizuko Yamamoto, Herman and Cornellia Aihara, Jacques and Yvette de Langre, and Noboru Muramoto.

To the editors, Susan Stearns and Sandy Rothman; to Bernice Kagan for her artistry; to Neil Gilchrist, cover photographer; and to Jane Lunstrum for her help on the index.

To friends who have joyfully helped prepare, serve, and taste test these meals at the East West Center for Macrobiotics in Eureka, California and the 3 Creeks Macrobiotic Summer Camps: Steve and Donnell Campbell, Karen Bandy, Lynn Montgomery, Cindy Conover, Mary O'Leary, Susie Hand, Randy Brown, Dave Croasdaile, Dan Frye, Gil Friedman, and Hawley Riffenberg.

To fellow cooks Patricia Murray, Carol Connell, Marilyn Wasson, Nancy Rankin, Kristina Turner, Mim Collins-Drewry, Joya Sexton, and Patti Becker.

And to the people who have shared in the natural health education journey over the years—especially Jess and Hazel Moon, Dorothy Gruhlke, Mary Martin, Arlene and Jack Luft, Margaret Brown, Rosemary Bridenbaugh, Bernice Wallace, Tige and Ruth Crane, Pete Kayes, Linda Redfield, Craig Lord, Carolyn Real, Alison Murray, Bob Wunner, Willis Hadley, Brian Musig, Gail Samuelson, Gloria Cavanaugh, Susan Marelich, Frances Alexander, Scott Gavin, Shawn and Margaret Hisatomi, David Guyer, David Edington, Keith Newcomer, Kristine Long, Blake Rankin, Dale Belvin, Rick Turk, Grayce Yamamoto, Pete Pulis, Jenny and Ira Greene, Diana Lynn, Jan and Travie Westlund, George Guthrie, Virginia Hedgecock, Maridell Anderson, Elizabeth Owen, Brooke Sullivan, and Bill Collins.

And to those who keep the good food flowing through our beautiful area, thanks to the staff of the Arcata and First Street Coops, The Tofu Shop, Moonrise Herbs, Eureka Health Foods, TOMO's Japanese Restaurant, Crosswinds Restaurant, The Wildflower Café, and to organic farmers everywhere.

Contents

INTRODUCTION .... i-ii

SOUPS. 1-14
    Miso Soups.................................... 1-8
    Broths.. 8-11
    Stews 11-12
    And More Soups 13

GRAINS, BREADS, AND PASTA............. 15-58
    Brown Rice................................... 16-25
        Varieties of Brown Rice. 16-18
        Rice with Other Grains................ 18-19
        Rice with Vegetables................. 19-25
    Wheat.. 26-51
        Naturally Leavened Bread. 26-33
        Quick Breads. 38-40
        Pasta...Oodles of Noodles. 43-49
        Wheatmeat.............................49
        Couscous.............................50
        Bulgur. 51
    Millet 52
    Corn... 52-54
    Oats... 54
    Barley....................................... 54
    Rye 54
    Buckwheat. 54
    Amaranth 55
    Quinoa. 56-57

SIMPLE TO SUMPTUOUS
VEGETABLE DISHES............................. 59-86
    Quick-Boiled Vegetables. 59-65
    Steamed Vegetables. 66-67
    Simmered Vegetables........................ 67
    Specialty Vegetable Dishes. 68-71
    Simple to Savory Ethnic Sautés. 71-77
    Main Dish Casseroles and Pies. 78-84
    Sea Vegetable Dishes....................... 84-86

SALADS 87-114
    Fresh Vegetable Salads...................... 88-95

Pressed Vegetable Salads...96
Cooked Vegetable Salads. 97-101
Whole Grain and Vegetable Salads.......................101-102
Pasta Salads..103-105
Bean Salads. 105-108
Sea Vegetable Salads. 109-110
Aspics/Gelled Salads. 111-113

SAUCES, SPREADS, AND DRESSINGS. 115-146
Vegetable-Based Sauces, Spreads, and Dressings..116-119
Bean Spreads and Gravy. 120-121
Creamy Tofu Sauces and Dressings......................122-125
Seed or Nut Butter-Based Spreads and Dressings..126-127
Simple, Oil-free Dressings and Sauces. 128
Vinaigrette Dressings.......................................129-132
Marinades. 132-133
Dips. 134-135
Flour-Thickened Gravies.....................................135-136
Table Seasonings. 136-140
Sweet Spreads and Toppings 141-146

BEANS AND SOYFOODS...147-156
Beans..147-150
Soyfoods: Tofu and Tempeh 151-155

PICKLES AND RELISHES...157-170
Pickles...157-165
Relishes..165-166
Commercially Available Japanese Pickles...............166-170

DESSERTS...171-192
Fresh Fruit Desserts...171
Gels and Puddings...172-177
Fresh Fruit Pies...177-181
Pastries 182-186
Cookies 187-190
Candy 190
Ethnic Vegetable Dessert 191

BEVERAGES 193-204
Mild Herb Teas 193-195

Twig Teas 196-197

Grain Teas and "Coffees". 198-199

Cool Summer Drinks 199-200

"Medicinals".. 201-202

Bean and Nut "Milks" 202-203

BREAKFASTS..205-219

Hot Morning Cereals..205-212

Brown Rice for Breakfast 212-213

Dry Cereals 213-215

Waffles 216

Breads and Muffins. 217

Other Breakfast Foods...218-219

APPENDIX

Listing of Recipes by Chapter................................221-231

Quick and Easy Lunch and Dinner Menus.. 233-234

Festive Lunch and Dinner Menus...........................235-237

Picnic Menus. 238

American Regional Menus. 239

Ethnic Menus.. 240-241

Glossary of Food Terms.. 242-246

Resources...247-250

Cooking FRESH...and Fast. 251-253

INDEX 255-262

Introduction

My vegetarian kitchen has bustled with activity since 1977. Times of quiet research and experimentation evolve into group efforts to prepare and serve inspiring meals to visitors at the natural health education center my husband, Patrick, and I direct.

My food background was S.A.D. (Standard American Diet) until 1974 when I was served a meal that changed my life. It was a particularly difficult time when, because of poor lifestyle habits and emotional stress, I had gotten mononucleosis. This is a condition of extremely low energy, a precursor of hypoglycemia and diabetes.

I was invited to dinner at a lovely old farm in the New Hampshire countryside. We walked through the corn patch in the large garden out back before entering the kitchen. I was introduced to the lady cooking at the wood-burning stove...quietly, happily. We continued on to the living room where two young guys were shelling peas in front of the old stone fireplace.

From what I remember dinner consisted of freshly-baked bread, vegetables from the garden, a delicious bean soup, brown rice, and a fresh fruit pie for dessert. It doesn't seem so special now, but for a lady who lived on McDonald's hamburgers or filet mignon, and everything in between, this "real" meal warmed my soul. I smoked heavily then and hardly remember tasting or saying much, but I felt the integrity of the experience to my core.

Those people were conscious in ways that I had not experienced before. They were focused and it seemed as though the food had a lot to do with that. They were more relaxed, playful, and alert than I, and I realized there was much to learn about the basics in life. A year later I joined them in Boston and started my study of macrobiotics.

There are so many reasons to eat in the vegetarian way (full or part time), and so many ways to be a vegetarian. Not satisfied with lacto-ovo vegetarianism (the style which eschews meat, but includes dairy products and eggs), I found that macrobiotics (a basically vegetarian approach to health which in practice often includes fish) had much more to offer.

Macrobiotics is a path of self-discovery which, when applied to eating, means gaining your own understanding of how different foods affect you, rather than following a rigid, unchanging diet. The understanding of balance plus guidelines on proportions based on traditional foods—whole grains and vegetables, with lesser amounts of beans and animal foods, nuts, seeds, and fruit—are ideas which are now substantiated by numerous government and scientific organizations.

One awareness brought to light through macrobiotics that I continue to cherish is the connection between each one of us and the rhythms of nature. Ecological eating, eating seasonally and locally, feels right, and it opens the door to a lifelong study of our place as human beings in the natural world.

I noticed right away that waste is minimal in this approach, and the health benefits were remarkable starting the first week. I have written about the elements of this approach in my first book, *American Macrobiotic Cuisine.*

FRESH is the culmination of 12 years of meal preparation. Every Thursday night, my assistants and I serve a different grain-and-vegetable-based feast for guests at our public dinners. I love the study of fresh foods and have never repeated the same menu twice. Every August we sponsor a week-long summer camp during which our cooking staff of 20 learns to prepare meals for up to 150 campers and visitors, adults and children. Many of the recipes in this book came from these events.

The rest of the year's meals are more simple fare, but are always filled with color and taste. Many of them are shared in this volume as well.

May this recipe book inspire you to *FRESH* ideas and culinary creations.

Meredith McCarty
Eureka, California
August, 1989

Note: The heart-shaped bullets in this text—❤—denote variations on a recipe and serve to separate words in roman from italic typestyle. They do not mark heart-healthy recipes nor my personal favorites.

Soups

Miso soups are so nourishing, they may be served for breakfast, lunch, or dinner. In cold seasons, a bowl of miso soup first thing in the morning sets body and brain in motion with balanced clarity. It even boosts the immune system's ability to ward off colds. In warmer months, a room temperature or slightly cool, clear broth or a puréed summer vegetable soup seasoned with light miso seems appropriate in the cooler evening hours.

The fermented soybean and grain paste called miso is added toward the end of cooking. Miso, as well as natural soy sauce, is a vegetarian source of a rich taste like chicken or beef bouillon.

When taken regularly, miso is known to help remove toxic substances from the body such as radiation, pollution, and nicotine (see *The Book of Miso* by William Shurtleff and Akiko Aoyagi).

There is really no set recipe for miso soups, only the guidelines of including a sea vegetable, root and green leafy vegetables, and, of course, miso at the end. These soups become catchalls for leftover grains and noodles, beans, vegetables, and vegetable cooking broths from the preceding day.

Sea vegetables add the full array of minerals found in the sea (and in the human body) and kombu acts as a flavor enhancer since it contains natural MSG (monosodium glutamate).

The recipes in this section are organized from basic to elaborate soups, broths, and stews. For large amounts, figure 3/4-1 cup soup per serving.

Basic Miso Soup Recipe

Makes 3-4 servings

1 quart (4 cups) water or vegetable cooking
　　broth
6-inch piece wakame or kombu sea
　　vegetable
1/2 cup onion family member (yellow, white,
　　or red onion, leek, green onion, etc.)
1/2 cup root vegetables (carrot, daikon or
　　red radish, turnip, rutabaga, etc.)
1 cup greens (kale, cabbage, collard, water-
　　cress, radish, sunflower sprouts, etc.),
　　thinly sliced and gently packed
Miso to taste, up to 1/4 cup barley, brown
　　rice, or other miso

Place water and sea vegetable in 2-quart pot while you cut the vegetables to similar size and shape. Transfer wakame to cutting board and slice. Return to pot with onion and root vegetables. Bring ingredients to boil and simmer until barely tender, 5-10 minutes depending on size. Add greens and cook until almost done. Remove kombu if used, reserving it for use in another dish. (Kombu may be used 1-3 times as it is too tough to eat after 1 or 2 cookings in soup. When tender, slice and add to soup or vegetables.) Dissolve miso in a little of the hot soup stock and return to pot to simmer very gently 2 minutes more.

Variation: **Good Morning Miso Soup with Mochi** ♥ Mochi is a traditional Japanese food made from a special short grain brown rice known as sweet rice, more glutinous in nature than regular rice. Now made in America, it comes in a large slab which is scored or separated into individual servings. The dry rice cakes are broken along these marks or simply cut with a sharp knife to desired size. Since the rice has been pre-cooked by steaming, and then mashed or pounded into a dense mass before being dried in slabs, it is a quick and easy-to-prepare whole grain food, appropriate for breakfast, lunch, dinner, or snacks. We often have mochi for a quick breakfast as you would toast, with tea or grain "coffee." Cooked by broiling or baking, it puffs up into a stick-to-your-ribs, chewy cake with a crisp crust. Since mochi tends to harden as it cools, it is best served warm.

Mochi may be cooked into soups for just 5 minutes to soften while retaining its shape, or longer, about 10 minutes, so it melts, giving the soup a thicker, creamy texture. It can be broiled or baked for "mochi puffs" to be floated on top of the soup, or cooked and then added to the soup for a

softer texture. Include 4 individual pieces mochi, about 4 ounces.

To broil mochi, place squares on a pan brushed generously with toasted sesame oil. Turn cakes over to coat them lightly for great flavor. Place in broiler until they puff up. Turn over once. In a broiler which is cold when you start, this takes about 10-12 minutes, or 5-6 minutes on each side. In a hot broiler, turn cakes after just 2 minutes to avoid burning, then cook 2 minutes more.

To bake mochi puffs, place on baking sheet to cook at 450° until they puff up, about 10-15 minutes. (At 350° it takes 15-30 minutes, depending on brand.) A toaster oven is handy and energy efficient. Serve warm. (Panfried mochi is soft, but doesn't puff much.) In soup, mochi floats!

Vegetable Soup ♥ Sopa de Verduras

Makes 4-5 servings

Sopa de verduras, literally "soup of vegetables" in Spanish, is as popular and versatile in Mexico and South America as it is in the United States. We met a farmer in Colombia whose Japanese wife brought us some of her corn miso made with the soybeans and grain corn they grew. We used it in this soup as part of a macrobiotic cooking class for their friends and relatives.

3 cups water
6-inch piece kombu sea vegetable
1/4 red onion, thinly sliced
1/4 cup carrots, thinly sliced in half moons
1 small patty pan squash, halved from top to
    bottom, then thinly cut in wedges
1 small yellow crookneck squash, thinly
    sliced in half moons
1 rib celery, thinly sliced
1 large dark green leaf (savoy cabbage, kale,
    collard, etc.), thinly sliced
1/4 cup corn or other miso

Bring water to boil with kombu while you cut the vegetables. Add all the vegetables and when boiling resumes, cook over medium heat until done, about 5 minutes. Dissolve miso in a little of the hot soup stock and add to soup to gently simmer 2 minutes more. Remove kombu and serve.

Patty-pan squash

Peasant's Cabbage Soup

Makes 4 servings

Peasant's cabbage was the name the American colonists gave to kale.

1/2 onion, thinly sliced from top to bottom
1/2 small carrot, thinly sliced in rounds
3-inch piece kombu sea vegetable
3 cups water
2 large leaves kale, about 2 cups, cut length-
    wise along midrib, then thinly crosswise
1/4 cup barley miso

Bring onion, carrot, kombu, and water to boil and simmer covered for 5 minutes. Add kale and cook until vegetables are tender, about 5 minutes more. Dissolve miso in a little of the hot soup broth in a separate bowl and return to soup to cook gently 2 minutes more. Remove kombu and serve.

Corn Miso Soup

Makes 4 servings

1 medium ear corn, about 3/4 cup kernels
3 cups water
3-inch piece wakame sea vegetable
1/2 cup carrots, thinly sliced in flower
    shape
1/2 cup leafy greens (kale, collards,
    mustard, radish, etc.), thinly sliced
1/4 cup corn or another miso

Cut kernels from corn cob. To make corn stock, break cob in half and place in soup pot with water and wakame. Bring to boil, then simmer 10 minutes. Discard cob, cut wakame in small pieces, and return it to pot with vegetables. Return to boil, then slow boil until vegetables are tender, about 5 minutes. Dissolve miso in a little of the hot soup broth and add to pot to simmer very gently in last 2 minutes. If you prefer smooth miso without chunks of soybeans showing, pour the diluted miso through a strainer into soup pot, and press through as much as possible of the remaining mash.

Escarole-Arame Soup

Makes 6 servings

Escarole is a lettuce-like green with a gentle bite. A member of the chicory family like endive, escarole differs from that green leafy vegetable in that it is milder (less bitter) in flavor and its leaves are smooth rather than pointy around the edges.

1 tablespoon arame sea vegetable
1 quart (4 cups) water
1 tablespoon arrowroot powder or kuzu root starch
1/4 cup carrot, thinly sliced in matchsticks
1 cup escarole, thinly sliced and well packed
1/4 cup mung bean sprouts
5 tablespoons white miso

Soak arame in part of the water to cover for 10 minutes. In a separate bowl, place thickener in a little more of the water to cover. Transfer arame to soup pot. Slowly add arame soaking-water to pot, taking care to avoid the last bit where sand may have sunk. Add carrot and remaining water. Bring ingredients to boil, then simmer until tender, about 5 minutes. Add escarole near end of cooking. Dissolve miso in a little of the hot soup stock. Stir thickener to dissolve it. Add miso and thickener to soup with sprouts. Stir well, and simmer gently 2 minutes before serving.

Oriental Vegetable Soup

Makes 4-5 servings

1 quart (4 cups) water
1 carrot, about 1 cup, thinly sliced on the diagonal
1 cup fresh mushrooms (oyster, shiitake, regular, etc.), thinly sliced
1 clove garlic, thinly sliced
1/2 teaspoon unrefined sea salt
1/8 teaspoon white pepper
2 tablespoons brown rice vinegar
2 tablespoons arrowroot powder or kuzu root starch
1 cup Chinese cabbage, bok choy, or watercress, thinly sliced
8 snow peas
3 tablespoons white miso
1/4 cup Chinese parsley (cilantro), coarsely chopped
1 sheet nori seaweed, cut with scissors into bite-size squares or triangles
2 teaspoons natural soy sauce
1/4 teaspoon toasted sesame oil or hot chili oil (optional)

In a 3-quart pot, bring to boil water with carrot, mushrooms, garlic, salt, and pepper. Cook over medium-low heat until carrot is almost tender, about 5 minutes.

In a small bowl, pour vinegar over thickener and let sit.

Add Chinese cabbage and peas to pot and cook until crisp-tender, about 2 minutes. Dissolve miso in a little of the hot soup stock. Stir thickener to completely dissolve.

Add both miso and kuzu to soup with other remaining ingredients. Stir and cook about 2 minutes more. Serve immediately for bright color.

Variation: Add fresh corn kernels in season.

Cream of Celery Soup

Makes 4 servings

This quick and easy soup has a pretty, pale green color and a light, smooth texture.

4 cups celery, about 1/2 bunch, stalks cut
  in 1/2-inch chunks
1 onion, cut in 1/2-inch chunks
1 clove garlic
2 cups water
1/4 cup white miso
1 tablespoon arrowroot powder or kuzu root
  starch
2 tablespoons cool water
Carrot, grated, or watercress sprigs, or
  celery leaves, for garnish

Place first four ingredients in pressure cooker or pot and cook by pressure or boiling until soft, just 3 minutes in pressure cooker. Transfer mixture to blender and purée with miso until smooth. Return purée to pot. Mix thickener with cool water, add to pot, and heat to boiling, stirring until soup thickens, in 1-2 minutes. Garnish to serve.

Summer Squash Soup

Makes 5 servings

4 cups yellow summer squash, cut lengthwise, then in 1-inch slices crosswise
2 cups water (to barely cover squash)
6-inch piece kombu sea vegetable
3 tablespoons light miso such as white or
  corn miso
1 clove garlic, chopped
1 teaspoon fresh dill weed or basil, or 1/2
  teaspoon dry
1 tablespoon arrowroot powder or kuzu root
  starch

2 tablespoons cool water
Fresh herb sprigs (dill or basil), or flower-cut
  carrots, steamed, and green onion tops,
  thinly sliced for garnish

Bring first 3 ingredients to boil, then slow boil covered until soft, about 5 minutes. Remove kombu. Transfer mixture to blender, add miso, garlic, and herb, and purée until creamy. Mix thickener and cool water and add to soup. Heat through, stirring until soup becomes thick and smooth, about 1-2 minutes more. Garnish to serve.

Cucumber Soup

Makes 6-7 servings

1/2 cup brown rice flour
1 quart (4 cups) water
6-inch piece kombu sea vegetable
2 cups cucumbers, cut in 1/2-inch slices,
  except 6-7 very thin slices, set aside for
  garnish
1/2 cup green onion, sliced
2 tablespoons fresh dill weed or 1 table
  spoon dried
6 tablespoons white miso

Make a paste of flour and enough of the water to cover and set aside.
  In soup pot, bring water to boil with kombu. Remove kombu, add flour paste, vegetables, and dill, and stir well. Return to boil, then simmer until vegetables are soft, about 10 minutes. Watch for soup frothing over upon boiling, and keep lid ajar. Dissolve miso in a little of the hot soup liquid and return to pot in last 3 minutes of cooking.
  Purée ingredients until creamy smooth. Serve garnished with thin cucumber slices.

Soup Paysanne

Makes 5 servings

This is a healthful version of an Italian countryside soup.

1/2 carrot
1/2 onion
1 rib celery
1 clove garlic
1/2 cup peas, green beans, and/or corn, in
    season, or 1 cup kale
1/4 cup cooked brown rice
1/2 cup *Italian Red Sauce* (see page 117)
3-inch piece kombu sea vegetable
3 cups water
1/4 cup corn or barley miso
1 heaping tablespoon parsley, minced, for
    garnish

Slice vegetables thinly.

Place all ingredients in soup pot except kale (if used), miso, and parsley. Bring to boil, then simmer covered over low heat until vegetables are soft, about 10-15 minutes. If using kale, add it in last 5-10 minutes of cooking.

In a small bowl, dissolve miso in a little of the hot soup stock. Return it to soup to cook gently in last 2 minutes. Garnish to serve.

Variations: **Mexican Vegetable Soup with Cornmeal Dumplings (or Hominy)** ❤ Prepare soup as above, substituting 10 cornmeal dumplings (recipe follows) or 1/2 cup hominy (see page 52) for rice. Add dumplings in last few minutes to heat through.

Cornmeal Dumplings:

Makes 12

1/8 teaspoon unrefined sea salt
1/2 cup water
1 cup yellow cornmeal
1 quart water to cook dumplings

To make dumplings, bring salted water to boil and add to cornmeal. Boiling water softens the meal and makes for a more cohesive dough. Mix well. Form into 1 1/2-inch balls with moistened hands, and flatten. Add to boiling water and slow-boil until dumplings are done in the middle, 10-30 minutes. Drain.

Note: The Hopi Indians make small blue cornmeal dumplings called blue marbles and serve them in the cooking broth. Shaped in balls into which indentations are pressed with the thumb, the dumplings can become Hopi thumbprint bread.

Variations: **Mexican Vegetable Soup with Wheatballs** ❤ **Sopa Juliana con Albondigas** Follow *Soup Paysanne* recipe, but omit basil in red sauce. Add 1/2 cup cooked wheatballs (see recipe on page 49) and 2 fresh mint leaves, minced (optional), in last 5 minutes of cooking.

Mexican Clear Broth Soup with Vegetables ❤ **Caldo** is one of two types of soup made in Mexico, the other being the *sopas* which are made very thick with vegetables, rice, and noodles. Follow *Soup Paysanne* recipe, including kale and omitting rice and red sauce. Add 1 tablespoon cilantro (fresh coriander leaves, also called Chinese parsley), chopped, along with miso, and garnish each serving with a sprig of cilantro.

Hominy Soup ❤ Pozole

Makes 2 servings

A soup like this Spanish-American one warmed us one chilly morning in a Mexican marketplace. We were intrigued by the whole grain corn kernels. Here, light miso substitutes for pork and chicken stock.

Pozole (or posol) is also the name for a drink made of cornmeal, water, and sugar.

1 cup hominy (see page 52)
2 cups hominy cooking broth or water
1/2 cup mushrooms, thinly sliced
1 clove garlic, sliced
1/2 teaspoon oregano
2-3 tablespoons light miso
1 tablespoon fresh coriander (cilantro or
    Chinese parsley), thinly sliced; and 2
    sprigs for garnish
1 tablespoon red wine vinegar or lemon juice
Few grains chili pepper powder

When preparing hominy, add more water than usual for second cooking to make enough broth for the soup.

Bring first 5 ingredients to boil and simmer until mushrooms soften, about 3 minutes. In a small bowl, dissolve miso in a little of the soup broth. Add with cilantro, vinegar, and chili to soup and cook gently 3 minutes more. Garnish.

Variation: A 15-ounce can of hominy contains 1 1/2 cups hominy and 1 cup salted water/cooking broth. If you choose to use canned hominy, include less miso in the recipe.

Chickpea-Lentil Soup ❤ Haraira (Moroccan)

Makes 5 servings

A rich bean and vegetable soup, haraira is eaten every day at sundown during the fasting month of Ramadan in Morocco. The eggs and tomatoes have been omitted, and miso replaces the flavors from meat and salt. I was delighted to learn the Moroccans use "seagreens" in their cooking. Chickpea miso, sometimes called chickpeaso, seems appropriate here. A good source is South River Miso Company (see Resources).

1/2 cup chickpeas
1/4 cup lentils
Water to cook beans plus 5 cups
1/4 cup whole-wheat flour
6-inch piece kombu or wakame sea
    vegetable
2 tablespoons pasta (whole wheat ribbons,
    spaghetti, etc.)
1/2 red onion, diced small
1 rib celery, diced small
1 teaspoon ground coriander seeds and/or 2
    tablespoons fresh coriander leaves,
    finely chopped
1/4 cup light miso such as chickpea miso
1 tablespoon lemon juice
1/4 cup parsley, finely chopped
Lemon, thinly sliced in half moons for
    garnish

Sort through and rinse beans. Dissolve flour in 1/4 cup of the water and set aside. In pressure cooker, bring beans to boil in remaining 4 3/4 cups water, then slow boil 5 minutes, uncovered. Add sea vegetable and pressure-cook for 45 minutes.

If using spaghetti, break it in 2-inch pieces. When pressure subsides, remove sea vegetable and dice small. Return it to pot with onion, celery, flour-water mixture, noodles, and ground coriander if used. Resume boiling, then simmer until ingredients are tender, about 10 minutes. Dissolve miso in a little of the hot soup broth, and add it to pot with lemon juice, fresh coriander if used, and parsley. Simmer very gently 2 minutes more. Garnish with lemon slices to serve.

The Stone Soup Story

Served at church and other potluck gatherings around the country, stone soup has a history with as many variations as there are tellers. The main theme is that soldiers (some say Roman) in olden times arrived in an unfamiliar town without food or money. They lit a fire, set their soup pot on it, and put stones inside. When passersby asked what they were doing, they replied: "Making stone soup. It's delicious, if we only had a carrot..." And with that the villagers would go and get whatever basic ingredients they had on hand. Before long, the soup really did become delicious nourishment for the hungry travellers.

The moral for our soup creations is to be open to playing with whatever edibles are on hand, little bits of this and that. Like any traditional peasant soup, such a creation is sure to satisfy.

Broths

Consommé

Makes 3-4 servings

A consommé is a French soup based on seasoned meat stock. This vegetarian version features a vegetable-soy sauce broth with a wonderful rich flavor.

1 quart (4 cups) vegetable cooking broth or water
4 dried shiitake mushrooms
6-inch piece kombu sea vegetable
Soy sauce to taste, up to 3 tablespoons
1 tablespoon chives or green onion tops, finely sliced, for garnish

Bring stock or water to boil with mushrooms and kombu, and simmer covered for about 10 minutes. Strain out mushrooms and kombu and reserve for future use. Add soy sauce to stock and cook over low heat 2 minutes more. Garnish to serve.

Vegetable Cutout Consommé

Makes 4 servings

1 quart (4 cups) water
3-inch piece kombu sea vegetable
2 tablespoons pickled plum (umeboshi) vinegar
1 small carrot, or part carrot, turnip, rutabaga, or kohlrabi (carrot thinly sliced on the diagonal, others in rounds)
1 tablespoon natural soy sauce
1 tablespoon Japanese sweet rice cooking wine (mirin), optional

1 tablespoon chives or green onions, thinly sliced

Bring to boil water, kombu, and ume vinegar. Add vegetables and simmer until crisp-tender, but still colorful, about 5 minutes. Transfer to cutting board to cut in shapes with tiny hors d'oeuvres or canapé cutters. Include both inner and outer cut-outs in soup. Add cutouts and remaining ingredients to pot and cook another minute to blend flavors. Remove kombu, reserving it for future use. Serve.

Variation: Add 1/2 teaspoon powdered American white or Japanese green horseradish (wasabi).

Vegetable Cutout Soup

Makes 4 servings

1 quart (4 cups) water or mild-tasting vegetable broth
6-inch piece kombu sea vegetable
2 dried shiitake mushrooms
2 slices butternut squash, 1/4-inch thick, center portion cut out with cookie cutter design such as star or heart shape, both inner and outer portions used in soup
1/4-1/2 cup small, whole-wheat shell pasta (or other shapes such as alphabets, veggie elbow macaroni, or sesame-rice spirals)

2 tablespoons natural soy sauce
1 green onion, thinly sliced on the diagonal

Bring water to boil with kombu and mushrooms, then simmer covered for 10 minutes. Remove them from broth, setting kombu aside, and thinly slicing mushroom tops, discarding the stems. Return tops to pot with squash cutouts and pasta, and slow-boil until almost tender, about 5 minutes. Add soy sauce and green onions in last 2 minutes of cooking.

For large amounts, so as not to break or lose the ingredients in the bottom of the pot, boil squash and pasta in a separate pan in just enough of the broth to cover. Place them in individual serving bowls and pour hot soup over to serve.

Light Lemon-Miso Broth with Garlic Toasts

Makes 3-4 servings

1 quart (4 cups) water or vegetable broth
4 dried shiitake mushrooms
3-inch piece kombu sea vegetable
1 tablespoon arrowroot powder or kuzu root starch
1/4 cup white or light miso
1 tablespoon lemon juice
1 green onion or 1 tablespoon chives, very thinly sliced in long diagonals

Garlic Toasts:

Makes 4-8

1 large garlic clove, minced
1 tablespoon olive oil
4 slices whole-grain bread

Bring water to boil with mushrooms and kombu and simmer until mushrooms are soft, 10-15 minutes.

To prepare toasts, preheat oven to 400°.

In serrated mortar (suribachi), mash garlic with oil to form a paste.

Cut bread into shapes with cookie cutters. Brush garlic paste onto 1 side of the bread and transfer to baking sheet. Bake until golden, about 7 minutes.

With a flat strainer, transfer mushrooms and kombu to bowl and set aside for future use. Dissolve arrowroot in just enough hot soup broth to cover or kuzu in just enough cool water to cover. Add to pot and return to boil, stirring for a slightly thicker soup consistency. Add miso and lemon juice to a little of the hot soup broth. Stir to dissolve miso and add to pot to cook 2 minutes more, without boiling. Just before serving, stir in green onions or chives. (Color is lost if green onions sit in soup broth for any length of time.)

To serve, float toasts atop each soup.

For large amounts, make garlic oil in food processor. Set processor in motion, then drop in garlic and drizzle in oil.

Make bread crumbs from leftover crusts by whirring them in food processor. Toast crumbs in 350° oven until golden, 5-10 minutes, stirring once.

Variation: **Olive Toasts** ❤ To prepare olive paste, first remove pits from 6 olives. Mash pulp with garlic, olive oil, and 1/4 teaspoon oregano.

Hot and Sour Soup

Makes 3 servings

1 tablespoon arrowroot powder or kuzu root starch
1 teaspoon brown rice vinegar
3 cups water
10 dried tree ear mushrooms (called *mo-er*)
1/4 rib celery
1-inch piece carrot
1 green onion
1/4-inch slice tofu
1/2 teaspoon unrefined sea salt
1 tablespoon natural soy sauce
Dash white pepper

Place kuzu and vinegar in a small bowl with 1/4 cup of the water and set aside. Simmer dried mushrooms in remaining 2 3/4 cups water for 10 minutes.

Cut vegetables in thin slivers and tofu slightly thicker so it holds together.

Strain mushrooms from cooking broth. Discard the last bit of broth which may contain a few particles of sand. Cut mushrooms in thin slices.

Return to pot broth, mushrooms, vegetables, tofu, and seasonings. Cook until vegetables are soft, about 5 minutes. Stir thickener mixture and add to soup. Turn heat up and stir until soup thickens somewhat, about 1 minute.

Variation: Add a dash of sesame oil flavored with red pepper at the end.

Other broth recipes:

Buckwheat Noodles in Dipping Broth (see page 44)
Sushi Dipping Sauce (see page 23)

Stews

African Skillie Stew

Makes 4 servings

Stews, along with soups and sauces, are staple menu items all over Africa, served along with a basic carbohydrate food such as boiled rice. Most of the time stews contain no meat, chicken, or fish. A simple one consists of only an onion and one green vegetable. More ingredients, such as other vegetables, beans, peanuts (called groundnuts) or peanut butter, are added in proportion to the fertility of the soil and the affluence of the family. Flavors are sharpened by the addition of onions and red hot pepper. However, in many parts of East Africa red pepper is not considered good for children.

This recipe is inspired by several others from West, South, and Central Africa. I've cut down on the large quantities of oil and seasonings, and on the hours recommended to cook the stew. Miso substitutes for salt. When serving the complete African menu (see page 241), for moderation and distinct flavors, include hot pepper in only one dish. You may want to delete it from this stew since its peanut-miso gravy is already richly satisfying.

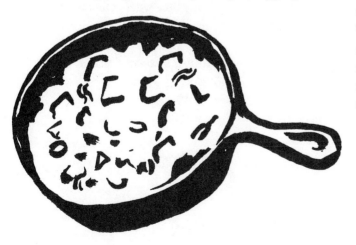

1 tablespoon peanut oil or another variety
1 onion, diced small
1 turnip, diced small
1 cup winter squash (buttercup, acorn, butternut, or delicata), diced small, skin left on, or summer squash in the warm months
1 cup water
3 tablespoons peanut butter
2 tablespoons barley miso or other variety
1/4 teaspoon turmeric (optional)
1/8 teaspoon crushed red pepper, or to taste (optional)
4 cups greens (kale, collard, or cabbage), diced, gently packed

Heat oil in skillet and add onion to sauté briefly. Add turnip and squash and 1/2 cup water. Stir, cover, and simmer over medium-low heat until barely tender, about 10 minutes.

Mix together remaining 1/2 cup water with peanut butter, miso, turmeric, and pepper. A wire whisk is helpful.

Add greens and peanut butter mixture, stir, and cover to cook until greens are done and a sauce forms, about 8 minutes more. Stir once or twice. Serve the stew in the skillet.

For large amounts, cut oil and liquid for cooking vegetables by half. To retain the bright color of the greens, boil them separately, drain, and set aside. Bring peanut butter mixture to boil in a separate pot and cook uncovered until it thickens, for several minutes. When vegetables are done, drain most of the liquid if needed, and add greens and gravy. Stir well to serve.

Biscuit-Topped Savory Stew

Makes 4-6 servings or 8 cups

Thanks to Steve and Donnell Campbell of Bethalto, Illinois for this natural foods version of a favorite stew enjoyed by mid-westerners.

Vegetables:

1 tablespoon corn oil
1 onion, diced in 1-inch cubes
4 green onions, finely sliced, whites kept
    separate from greens
2 carrots, cut in 1/4-inch rounds
1/4 pound mushrooms, trimmed and halved
    or quartered
1 clove garlic, minced
1 teaspoon basil
1 teaspoon oregano
1 teaspoon thyme
Kernels of 1 ear corn
3 cups broccoli, tops cut in small flowerets,
    edible portion of stems cut in half
    lengthwise, then in 1/4-inch sections
    crosswise
1 1/2 cups daikon radish, cut in half length-
    wise, then in 1/4-inch slices crosswise
2 ribs celery, sliced in 1/2-inch sections
2 tablespoons natural soy sauce
3/4 cup water
1/4 cup cooking wine or sake (optional)

Gravy:

2 tablespoons corn oil
5 tablespoons whole-wheat flour
1 1/4 cups water
2 tablespoons natural soy sauce
1 tablespoon brown rice vinegar
Chili powder blend to taste, about 1 1/2
    teaspoons

To prepare vegetables, heat oil in a large skillet or pot and sauté until almost tender onion, white parts of green onions, carrot, mushrooms, garlic, and herbs. Add remaining vegetables, soy sauce, water, and cooking wine or sake. Turn heat up, and when liquid starts to boil, cover to simmer until vegetables are tender, about 10 minutes. Stir occasionally.

Preheat oven to 425°.

Make gravy by heating oil in 1-quart saucepan and stirring in flour until evenly blended and heated through, about 1 minute. Gradually add water, stirring constantly with a wire whisk to avoid lumping. Whisk in remaining ingredients and cook over medium-low heat until thick and bubbly, about 5 minutes.

Pour gravy over the vegetables, add green onion tops, and gently stir. Immediately transfer hot mixture to 2-quart casserole dish.

Make biscuit dough (see page 40). Place dough shapes on top of casserole. Bake until casserole ingredients are bubbling and biscuits are golden, about 15 minutes. Allow casserole to cool for 15 minutes before serving for texture to firm up somewhat.

For large amounts boil carrots, broccoli, daikon, and celery in a separate pot to keep their colors distinct and the texture crisp-tender. Cut liquid for sautéing the other vegetables to 1/4 cup. Mix with other ingredients before baking or serving.

Variation: **Hearty Harvest Stew** ❤
Omit biscuits and baking. Add 2 cups wheatmeat (see page 49), cut in bite-size pieces.

And More Soups...

Fresh Pea Soup with Mint

Makes 4 servings

Popular in South Africa as well as Europe and North America, this bright green spring-through-fall soup is a refreshing change from winter's dried split pea version.

3 cups English peas, freshly shucked, or
    edible pod varieties (sugar snap or snow
    peas), strings removed
1 onion, diced
2 cups water
2 teaspoons mint leaves, dried, or 2 table-
    spoons fresh
1 1/2 teaspoons unrefined sea salt
Fresh mint or parsley sprigs for garnish

Bring all ingredients to boil, except garnish, and cook over medium heat until soft, about 5 minutes. Blend. Strain soup if you use edible pod varieties, pressing as much as possible through strainer. Garnish to serve.

Sauerkraut Soup

Makes 6 servings

Cabbage soups, made with either fresh or pickled cabbage, are among Russia's favorites. The preferred winter version, called schee, is made with sauerkraut. This variation looks exactly like the tomato broth original, and with the tart, slightly acidic taste of the kraut, it's doubtful anyone would recognize its carrot-beet origin. Made with fresh cabbage in place of kraut, the soup is known as Lazy Schee.

1 cup dried mushrooms (shiitake work
    nicely)
1 bay leaf
1 quart water
1 tablespoon corn oil
1 onion, chopped
2 tablespoons whole-wheat flour
1 cup sauerkraut, drained
1 cup *Red Sauce* (see page 117)
1/4 cup *Tofu "Sour Cream"* (see page 122) for
    topping

To prepare stock, bring mushrooms, bay leaf, and water to boil, then slow boil covered until mushrooms are soft, about 20 minutes. Discard bay leaf. Remove mushrooms and set aside for another dish such as *Stroganoff* (see page 77) which accompanies this soup in the Russian menu (see page 241). Measure stock to be sure you have 3 cups, and add water if necessary.

Sauté onion until tender. Sprinkle flour over cooked onion and mix well. Add mushroom stock with kraut and red sauce. Bring to boil, then simmer covered to blend flavors, about 5 minutes more. Garnish with a heaping teaspoon of tofu "sour cream."

Grains, Breads, and Pasta

The wide variety of whole grains offered to us by nature is truly amazing. Each has its own special qualities which are enhanced with cooking. Starting with several varieties of rice and many forms of preparing it, this chapter proceeds to all the foods based on wheat: naturally-leavened breads, corn-breads (including tequezquite-leavened corn-bread), quick breads, pasta dishes, wheat-meat, bulgur, and couscous. Millet, corn (including homemade hominy and masa), and quinoa, a newly discovered ancient grain of the Incas, round out the section.

Salt is known historically to render whole grains more digestible. It alkalinizes the grain by adding minerals. For variety, add a small piece of kombu sea vegetable instead.

Brown Rice

For the best flavors and textures, short and medium grain rices, and sweet brown rices may be either pressure-cooked or boiled, but long grain rice varieties should be boiled rather than pressure-cooked.

The general ratio of water to rice is 1 1/4 to 1 1/2 times the amount of rice for pressure-cooking (depending on the kind of cooker), or 1 1/2 to 2 times the amount of rice for pot cooking (less for amounts over 1 cup rice).

Whereas 1 cup dry short grain rice usually makes 2 servings, the same amount of long grain rice makes 3 servings.

Short or Medium Grain Brown Rice

Makes 4-6 servings or 5 - 6 1/2 cups short grain rice, less with pressure-cooking, more with boiling

2 cups short or medium grain brown rice
2 1/2 - 3 cups water (less for pressure-cooking, more for boiling)
A pinch to 1/4 teaspoon sea salt (up to 1/8 teaspoon per cup rice)

Short or medium grain rices may be cooked by boiling or pressure-cooking. Pressure-cooking is especially nice in the cooler times of the year for a more condensed, warming grain dish, as well as the best-tasting rice. Boil more often during the summer for lighter rice. Nine cups short grain rice is the maximum amount to put in a 5-quart pressure cooker.

(*Note:* 1 cup rice is too small an amount to pressure-cook, and so is best boiled in a 1-quart saucepan with 2 cups water. Makes 2 1/3 - 3 cups.)

Rinse rice by swishing it around in water to cover generously in pressure cooker or 2-quart pot. Drain through strainer. Add measured amount of water and salt. Water measures about 1/2 inch above rice in pressure cooker, 3/4 inch above rice in pot.

If time allows, let short grain rice soak one to several hours before cooking. This step is optional but does lend a softer quality to the rice.

Bring to pressure or boil. Place flame spreader under pressure cooker and cook over medium-low heat. You should be able to hear the gentle hiss of the pressure cooker. Time for 45-60 minutes. Some natural foods restaurants serve rice which is chewy and sticky, indicating it's undercooked. Allow pressure to come down naturally, or more quickly by running cool water over top of cooker. When pressure gauge can be lifted easily without hissing, it's all right to open cooker.

For boiling, place spreader under pot after 1/2 hour of cooking. Time for 1 hour total.

For large amounts, bring to boil 1 1/4 times volume of water as rice. Add rinsed rice and cook as above.

Transfer cooked rice to serving bowl by spreading out large spoonfuls at a time to aerate rice, or fluff it with a fork. This ensures a light texture as the rice cools. Cover with a cloth or mat. Leave rice at room temperature for up to 3 days. For best texture and taste, refrigerate only if temperature in kitchen is hot.

Reheat rice with a little water in a pot or steamer basket, or sauté it alone, with onions, or a variety of vegetables.

Long Grain Brown Rice

Makes 5-6 servings or 5 cups

Figure 1/4-1/3 cup dry long grain rice per serving when including noodles, bread, or another grain dish at the same meal.

3 cups water (1 1/2 times the volume of dry rice)
A pinch to 1/4 teaspoon sea salt
2 cups long grain brown rice

For the fluffiest long grain rice, in a 2-quart pot bring water and salt to boil, then add rinsed rice. When boiling resumes, turn heat low. Place flame spreader under pot after 1/2 hour of cooking and time for 1/2 hour more, or a total of 1 hour.

For extra flavor, dry-roast rinsed rice in an unoiled skillet until it is dry, slightly golden, and mildly fragrant. Cook as above.

For 1 cup rice, figure 1 1/2 - 2 cups water.

Variations: **Brown Basmati Rice** ♥ *A special long grain rice from the Himalayan foothills of northern India, basmati rice is now grown in this country as well. A variety grown in Texas is called Texmati. One organic source is Southern Brown Rice (see Resources). Known for its fragrant nature, basmati has a slightly buttery aroma. Although a lighter version has been called "unrefined" or "naturally white without milling," brown basmati is the kind to choose.*

Cook brown basmati rice like long grain brown rice.

Wild Rice ♥ Figure 1 cup rice to 2 cups water. Proceed as above. No flame spreader needed.

Shaped Rice ♥ Lightly oil a small bowl and pack in cooked rice. Tap rice onto serving plates. West Africans are known to do this with their long grain red rice, but it works for any variety, whether hot or at room temperature.

Quick-Cooking Brown Rice

Makes 2 servings or 2 - 2 1/2 cups

On those rare occasions (!?) when you're hungry and haven't prepared a grain dish ahead of time, rice which cooks in 5-20 minutes brings tasty relief. The texture is pleasingly light and fluffy.

Two kinds of quick-cooking rice are available, one made with rolled grains and the other with the kernels intact. The former has a nicer flavor and cooks more quickly. The process for the rolled kind involves flaking and/or soaking or pressure-steaming the whole grains, after which they are partially dried, roasted, and flattened with a roller and dried completely.

A pinch up to 1/8 teaspoon unrefined sea salt
1-1 1/2 cups water, less for rolled rice flakes, more for kernels
1 cup quick-cooking brown rice

Since this rice is already precooked, there is no need to rinse it.

Bring salted water to boil in a 1-quart saucepan. Add rice and stir to level it. When boiling resumes, turn heat low and cover to cook until liquid is completely absorbed and rice is light and fluffy, 8-20 minutes, less for flakes, more for kernels. (I find the 5-minute variety takes 8 minutes.) Transfer to serving bowl by fluffing with a fork.

For large amounts of flaked rice, increase ingredients proportionately and proceed as stated.

Baked Rice

Makes 6 servings

Hiroshi Hayashi, master chef, created this dish. He felt that Americans would enjoy rice sautéd in a little oil from their country's native grain, corn, and then cooked by baking, the method so often used in the early pioneer days.

Corn oil
2 cups short grain brown rice
1 quart water
A pinch up to 1/4 teaspoon unrefined sea
    salt

Preheat oven to 350°. Brush bottom and sides of ovenproof pot with corn oil. (Cast iron is nice to use here as it retains heat evenly, so the rice is cooked well from all sides.)

Rinse rice and drain. Heat oiled pot on top of stove, and add rice to sauté for several minutes. Add water and salt and bring to boil, or bring salted water to boil in a separate pot and add to rice. Cover and place pot in oven to bake for 1 hour.

Variations: Rice may be dry-roasted to eliminate oil.

Sauté onion, garlic, and/or other vegetables before adding rice.

Rice with Other Grains

Brown Rice and Barley

Makes 5 servings

There are several varieties of barley: whole grain barley with just the hull removed (hulled barley); barley with the bran layers removed (the most familiar form called pearled barley); and Oriental pearl barley (a different grain with a unique taste).

1 1/2 cups short grain brown rice
1/2 cup barley, any variety
3 cups water
A pinch up to 1/4 teaspoon unrefined sea
    salt

Pressure-cook according to directions on page 16.

Bulgur Rice

A delicious combination with a nice texture whether boiled or pressure-cooked.

Prepare according to recipe on page 16, substituting bulgur for half of rice (equal amounts of each).

Long Grain with Wehani Red Rice

Wehani rice is a rust-colored long grain rice produced on the Lundberg Brothers' Wehah Farms in Richvale, California (see Resources). The name is a composite of the beginning letters of each of the Lundberg brothers' names. The kernel is larger than long grain brown rice. (Wehani looks a lot like Chinese red rice, a rare variety my husband and I purchased there, but the grains are larger and firmer.) I enjoy it in combination with long grain rice rather than on its own. Wehani is a fragrant grain and its firm texture and earthy color accent long grain rice nicely.

Substitute Wehani rice for 1/4 the volume of long grain brown rice in the recipe on page 17.

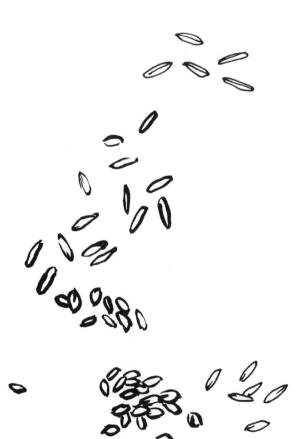

Rice with Vegetables

Rice with Mixed Vegetable Sauce

Makes 4-6 servings

This classic Chinese-style vegetable sauce includes much of summer's bounty. Vary ingredients to enjoy nature's harvest throughout the entire year.

6 cups cooked brown rice

Mixed Vegetable Sauce:

Makes 4 1/2 cups

3 cups water
3-inch piece kombu sea vegetable
1 carrot, diced small
1 onion (yellow, white, or red), diced small
1/2 cup green beans or yellow wax beans and/or whole snow or sugar snap peas, thinly sliced to size of other vegetables
1/2 cup green summer squash (zucchini or patty pan), diced small
1/2 cup yellow summer squash, diced small
4 red radishes or 1/4 cup red bell pepper, diced small
1/4 cup arrowroot powder or kuzu root starch
1/4 cup cool water
4-6 tablespoons natural soy sauce
1 teaspoon ginger, freshly grated
1/4 cup almonds, toasted
1/4 cup green onion, sliced for garnish

To prepare sauce, in a 2-quart pot, bring water to boil with kombu. Add carrot, onion, and green beans and cook about 5 minutes. Add remaining vegetables and cook until tender, about 5 minutes more. Transfer vegetables to colander and set kombu aside.

Measure to see that 2 cups broth remains and add a little water if necessary. In a small bowl, place thickener in cool water to cover and set aside. Bring broth to boil with soy sauce and ginger. Stir thickener to dissolve and add to hot stock, stirring until mixture turns saucy and shiny, about 1 minute.

Mix sauce with vegetables and almonds. To serve, spread 1 - 1 1/2 cups rice on plate and pour 3/4-1 cup sauce over rice. Garnish with a sprinkling of green onions.

Variations: Add 1/2 pound prepared tofu or tempeh, cubed. Add 1/2 cup arame to cook with vegetables.

Rice with Fresh Greens

Makes 4-6 servings or 5 - 6 1/2 cups

2 cups brown rice, any variety
1/2 cup fresh soft greens (watercress, green onion tops, parsley, bok choy, Chinese cabbage, lettuce, escarole, or endive), or cooked hardy greens (kale, collards, mustard greens, etc.), thinly sliced or diced

Cook rice according to recipes on pages 16 and 17. Place alternating layers of hot rice and fresh or cooked greens in serving bowl. Soft greens wilt as they are slightly cooked by the heat of the rice. Their bright green colors and fresh flavors are retained.

Variations: To further enhance flavor, include fresh green herbs in their seasons such as Chinese parsley (also called cilantro or fresh coriander), basil, dill, or green shiso leaves.

Although they are not considered greens, include other green vegetables, parboiled or steamed, and thinly sliced, such as green beans or peas.

Red Herb Rice

For information about red shiso leaves, see page 168.

Add 1 1/2 tablespoons wet shiso leaves, or 1 1/2 teaspoons dry powdered shiso leaves per cup uncooked short grain brown rice, and pressure cook according to directions on page 16.

To make this dish with 2 cups cooked rice, place 1/4 cup water and 1 tablespoon wet shiso or 1 teaspoon dry shiso leaves, minced, in a small saucepan. Lay rice on top and cook until heated through, then toss to serve.

Ume Plum Rice with Red Radish, Italian Broadleaf Parsley, and Red Herb Sprinkles

Makes 3-5 servings or 5 cups

A great way to use up those pickled plum (umeboshi) pits, and to enjoy flavor and mineral variation from the usual unrefined sea salt. Tossed with blanched and raw vegetables, this rice dish serves as a light summer salad.

4 cups *Ume Plum Rice* (recipe follows)
1 cup red radish, thinly sliced in rounds or quartered lengthwise
Water to quick-boil or steam radishes
Up to 2 tablespoons powdered red shiso leaves, to taste
1/2 cup Italian broadleaf parsley, leaves left whole, stems discarded, or regular parsley, leaves coarsely chopped, stems minced

Ume Plum Rice:

Makes 5 - 6 1/2 cups

2 cups short grain brown rice
2 1/2 - 3 cups water
4 pickled plum (umeboshi) pits, or flesh of 2
   plums, or 1 tablespoon plum paste

Cook rice according to recipe on page 16. Discard pits.

Quick-boil or steam radishes in water until hot flavor is gone, but color is still vibrant, about 2 minutes. Drain.

Transfer rice to bowl to cool. Gradually add shiso powder to taste and fold in vegetables.

Easy Rice Pilaf

Makes 6 servings

Pilaf or pilau is a dish made of seasoned rice often flavored with meat broth. This pilaf is so savory, it serves well for festive gourmet meals.

1 tablespoon oil (sesame, olive, corn, etc.)
1 onion, diced small
3 cups water
2 cups long grain brown rice
3 tablespoons natural soy sauce
1 large sprig parsley for garnish

Heat oil and sauté onion briefly. Meanwhile, bring water to boil in a separate pot. Add rinsed rice to onion and stir well, then add boiling water and soy sauce. Return to boil, cover and cook over low flame for 1 hour. (No flame spreader is necessary as onion and oil add extra liquid to dish.) Transfer pilaf to serving bowl and garnish to serve.

For large amounts, decrease oil by half.

Calculate volume of water at 1 1/4 cups per cup dry rice, and figure 1 tablespoon soy sauce per cup water.

Rice with Fresh Corn and Pumpkin Seeds

Makes 6 servings

2 cups brown rice, any kind
3 cups water
2 cups corn kernels
A pinch up to 1/4 teaspoon unrefined sea
   salt
6 tablespoons pumpkin seeds, toasted and
   sprinkled with soy sauce (see page 136)

Boil all ingredients except seeds according to directions on page 17. Toss with seeds to serve.

Long Grain-Wehani Rice Blend with Fresh Corn

Makes 4-7 servings or 5 1/2 - 7 cups

3 cups water
1 tablespoon natural soy sauce
1 3/4 cups long grain brown rice
1/4 cup Wehani Rice (see page 19)
1/2 cup corn kernels

In a 2-quart pot, bring water to boil with soy sauce. Add rinsed rices and corn. When boiling resumes, turn heat low to cook covered for 1 hour. Place flame spreader under pot after 1/2 hour.

Variation: **Country Wild Rice Blend with Fresh Corn** ❤ Substitute Country Wild Rice Blend available from Southern Brown Rice for both long grain and Wehani rices. This organic blend grown by the Hogue family in Arkansas (see Resources) contains basmati rice, Arkansas Red Rice, and Minnesota Wild Rice. It makes a great holiday rice pilaf with the addition of sautéd onion, garlic, and herbs.

Ranch Rice

Makes 4 servings

1/2 cup fresh corn kernels or hominy (see page 52)
1/4 cup fresh peas or green onion tops, thinly sliced
1/4 cup carrots, diced small
1 tablespoon fresh dill weed, minced, or 1 teaspoon dried
1/4 cup water
4 cups hot, cooked brown rice
1/4 cup sunflower seeds, toasted and sprinkled with soy sauce (see page 136)

Simmer vegetables and dill weed in water until tender, about 5 minutes. Gently toss vegetables with rice and seeds to serve.

Summer Sushi

Makes 2 rolls

Sushi is a Japanese word for fermented or vinegared (su) rice (shi). Originally made with fermented fish, sushi is now composed of rice which is usually seasoned with vinegar and a little sweetener, and a wide variety of flavorful vegetables, as well as fish. Sushi wrapped in nori seaweed comes in cylindrical shapes, varying in size from 1-3 inches in diameter.

Smaller rolls called hosomaki *may contain just one ingredient. The larger rolls, called* futomaki, *contain up to 6 ingredients. This recipe falls somewhere in between.*

The 4 sushi recipes in this book make 2 rolls each, or 2-4 servings. For large amounts, cut rolls in 6 pieces each and figure that rolls make 3 servings or 4 slices per person.

2 cups pressure-cooked short grain brown rice, room temperature, packed
1 teaspoon brown rice vinegar (optional)
1 teaspoon sweet rice cooking wine (mirin), brown rice syrup, or pure maple syrup (optional)
2 sheets nori seaweed

Filling:

1/2 teaspoon *Japanese Horseradish Paste (Wasabi),* recipe follows (optional)
1 cup water
2 green beans or 6 sugar snap peas, trimmed
1 small yellow summer squash, outer portion cut in 1/2-inch strips
1/4 red bell pepper, cut in 1/2-inch strips
2 large pickled plums (umeboshi), pits set aside for future use, or 1 tablespoon pickled plum paste
1 tablespoon amazake daikon pickles (see Resources), thinly sliced (optional)
1/4 teaspoon black or brown sesame seeds for garnish

Japanese Horseradish Paste (Wasabi):

Makes 2 teaspoons

Good Japanese horseradish paste (wasabi) is

naturally green in color and contains 60% pure Japanese horseradish and 40% regular horse-radish. Check the label.

1 tablespoon dried Japanese horseradish
    powder (wasabi)
1 teaspoon water

To prepare rice, sprinkle it with rice vinegar and sweetener and toss gently.

To make horseradish paste, mix powder with water. When preparing large amounts ahead of time, store in covered container so paste doesn't dry out.

If nori does not come already toasted (packaged sheets which are folded as opposed to flat indicate nori has not been toasted), toast it by placing 2 sheets shiny sides together and waving them over a hot burner until color changes from purple to green and sheets become slightly brittle, about 30 seconds.

To prepare filling, bring water to boil and quick-boil vegetables until crisp-tender, about 3 minutes. Drain and set aside to cool.

Place a bowl of cool water next to your work area to keep hands moist while making sushi, and to moisten far end of nori for sealing sushi after ingredients are assembled. (Add vinegar or lemon juice to water for added flavor.)

To assemble sushi, lay nori sheet horizontally on bamboo sushi mat, shiny side down. Moisten hands, and transfer 1 cup rice to nori sheet. Press with fingers to spread rice over nori to edges on 3 sides and to within 1 inch of the far edge.

Spread umeboshi plums, about 1 1/2 teaspoons per roll, over rice in a horizontal line on end nearest you. Spread horseradish, about 1/4 teaspoon per roll, in a line next to the plum paste. Place filling ingredients, except black sesame seeds, over these seasonings.

Moisten the top end of nori. Roll up fairly tightly from end nearest you, pressing with sushi mat while rolling, but trying not to touch the rice with your fingers or the mat. Press to seal nori. Place sushi on cutting board, seam-side-down. With a sharp knife, swiftly cut each roll into 6 rounds. Wipe knife clean with a damp sponge or cloth for ease in cutting. Serve garnished with black sesame seeds.

Cucumber-Rice Rolls

Makes 2 rolls

2 sheets nori seaweed, toasted
1/2 teaspoon Japanese horseradish paste
    (wasabi)
2 teaspoons pickled plum (umeboshi) paste
2 cups pressure-cooked short grain brown
    rice, room temperature, packed
2 or 4 long, thin strips carrot (or other color-
    ful vegetables in season such as yellow
    summer squash or sweet red pepper)
Water
1/2 medium cucumber (peeled if not organic
    or if waxed or bitter in flavor, seeded only
    if seeds are large), thinly sliced length-
    wise in strips
2 teaspoons sesame seeds, toasted

Dipping Sauce:

Makes 2 tablespoons
1 tablespoon natural soy sauce
1 tablespoon water or Japanese sweet rice
    cooking wine (mirin)

To toast nori, prepare wasabi, or to assemble sushi, see preceding recipe. Make the following additions: Cook carrot strips in water to cover until tender, about 5 minutes. (Cook yellow squash or sweet red pepper just 2 minutes.) Assemble sushi including seeds in filling.

To prepare dip sauce, simply mix ingredients.

Variations: **Inside-out Sushi** ♥ For a unique effect, after pressing rice on nori, turn nori over onto a moistened cloth with a smooth surface (not terry cloth). Transfer cloth to sushi mat. Spread and lay filling ingredients on nori side, then roll sushi up with rice on outside and filling on inside.

Half-size Sushi Rolls ♥ For thinner sushi rolls, cut nori in half widthwise and include 1/3 the ingredients.

Romaine-Rice Rolls

Makes 2 rolls

Romaine lettuce makes a nice dark green filling for sushi. It's fun to have myriad ways of preparing greens we usually reserve for salads.

1 quart (4 cups) water
2 or 4 long, thin strips carrot (or other color-
      ful vegetables in season, such as yellow
      summer squash or sweet red pepper)
1/2 head romaine lettuce, halved again
      lengthwise
2 sheets nori seaweed, toasted
2 teaspoons pickled plum (umeboshi) paste
2 cups pressure-cooked short grain brown
      rice, room temperature, packed
Prepared sushi condiments (2 teaspoons
      sushi ginger and 2 tablespoons sushi
      daikon—see Resources), very thinly
      sliced, optional

To prepare vegetables, bring water to boil. Cook carrot until tender, about 5 minutes, and transfer to plate to cool. (Cook yellow summer squash and/or sweet red pepper strips about 2 minutes.) Cook romaine until done, about 3 minutes. Drain, reserving broth for soup. Let cool, then squeeze out excess liquid.

To assemble sushi, spread umeboshi paste across rice and sprinkle sushi seasonings over it, then lay romaine and carrot over seasonings. Roll up and slice to serve, with dip sauce from preceding recipe.

California Rolls

Makes 2 rolls

These were unknown in Japan until they were created in California sushi bars. They usually contain crab, or, as in our local Japanese restaurant, shrimp (also called a Mendocino Roll). Avocado is not eaten regularly in a low-fat approach to health because of its high fat content, equivalent to cream cheese, but as a favorite California food it seems appropriate served on occasion. Select ripe avocados which are slightly firm rather than mushy.

The best way to learn how to make sushi is to watch the masters perform their craft at the sushi bars in Japanese restaurants, or take a cooking class and try it yourself with the help of an experienced teacher.

1-2 teaspoons brown rice vinegar
2 cups pressure-cooked short grain brown
      rice, room temperature, packed

2 sheets nori seaweed, toasted

2 teaspoons pickled plum (umeboshi) paste

1/2 teaspoon Japanese horseradish paste
    (wasabi), see recipe on page 22

4 slices avocado, about 1-inch thick at
    widest point

4 long slices cucumber (peeled if waxed or
    bitter-tasting only), seeded, and cut
    lengthwise in 1/4-inch wide julienne
    strips, or 1/2 cup alfalfa sprouts

1 teaspoon sesame seeds, toasted, for
    garnish

Gently mix vinegar into rice. Toast nori (see directions on page 23).

Spread umeboshi and horseradish pastes in parallel lines along bottom edge of rice. Lay avocado and cucumber slices (or sprouts) over pastes. Cut each sushi in 4 to 6 equal slices. Prepare dip sauce from recipe on page 23. Garnish.

Jambalaya

Makes 6 servings

Jambalaya is a Spanish Cajun or Creole rice and vegetable dish. In this version, a light miso-sea vegetable stock substitutes for chicken stock. The chicken and sausage fat have been omitted and the spices mellowed out.

1 tablespoon sesame oil

4 cups onion, diced

1 cup green pepper, diced

1 tablespoon garlic, chopped fine

2 cups long grain brown rice

1 teaspoon thyme

1/8 teaspoon chili powder

1/16 teaspoon cayenne

1/16 teaspoon ground cloves

1/16 teaspoon black pepper

3 cups water

3-inch piece kombu sea vegetable

1 bay leaf

1/4 cup light miso

1 tablespoon parsley, minced for garnish

Heat oil and sauté vegetables about 5 minutes. Rinse and drain rice, and add to vegetables with seasonings. Sauté 5 minutes more.

Bring water to boil with kombu and bay leaf and simmer 2 minutes. Add a little hot broth to miso in a small bowl and stir well to dissolve miso, then add to stock. Remove sea vegetable and bay leaf from stock, and return stock to boil. Pour stock over rice and vegetables.

Bring mixture to boil, then simmer covered for 1 hour. To serve, mix gently as vegetables rise to surface with cooking. Garnish with parsley.

For large amounts, cook rice and vegetables separately. Cook rice in stock. Sauté onions first, then add other vegetables and seasonings and cook covered until tender. Combine rice and vegetables and serve.

Other rice recipes:

Vegetable Fried Rice (page 48)

*Easy Dinner Rice with Summer Vegetable
    Sauce* (page 46)

Soft Breakfast Rice (page 212)

Whole Rice Cream (page 212)

Rice Cream (page 207)

Steamed Rice (page 213)

Grain-Bean-Seed Cereal ❤ Kokkoh (page
    209)

Mochi Waffles (page 217)

Good Morning Miso Soup with Mochi (page 2)

Wheat

Naturally Leavened Bread

Bread is the basic grain food for people of European ancestry as it has always been a staple in Europe, and then in this country via immigration. It's easier to serve fresh-baked whole-grain bread to newcomers to natural foods than a bowl of miso soup and brown rice. I've come to enjoy and feel a need for brown rice almost every day, but bread, and then noodles, hold a similar value.

Home-baked bread is truly a gift from the heart. Sharing bread with family and friends is a tradition of warmth and closeness. The words "company" and "companion" are from the Latin "com-pan-io" meaning one who shares bread (pan).

History

Bread's history goes back more than 5,000 years. Archaeological remains show Stone Age Europeans mixed crushed grains with water and cooked them on flat stones producing the forerunner of unleavened flat breads. Whole-grain bread is still the main food in many European countries.

The Bread Museum in Ulm, West Germany is unique. Besides the archives containing copies of just about everything written on bread, it has art works and artifacts pertaining to bread in history, and samples of bread from around the world. Because most American bread is all the same shape and questionable as to nutritive value, none is on display.

The museum offers scientific support that bread made from whole-grain flour, and not from refined white flour from which the germ and bran have been removed, is better for health. According to an article in *The Chicago Tribune*, the museum says most packaged bread is "a true enemy of the people" because "it is a foodless food," and white bread is "white death."

The Egyptians first leavened bread around 2300 B.C. They saw that leaving a mixture of flour and water uncovered for several days causes it to bubble and expand, and that if this is mixed with fresh dough and allowed to stand for a few hours before baking, a light, sweet bread results. They also learned that a small amount of raised dough removed before baking can be used to repeat the process a few days later.

Natural leavening remained the basis of Western bread baking for the next 4,200 years, until the 20th century. From late medieval times, bakers were highly trained and skilled craftsmen.

The work of scientists like Justus von Liebig (the founder of modern nutritional science) and Louis Pasteur led to the discovery and identification of the microorganisms that are responsible for the fermentation process. One of these, the single celled yeast species *Saccharomyces cerevisiae*, was isolated and cultured. Used by itself it was found to cause a very rapid, uniform, and predictable raising of dough. Yeasted bread was born.

The initial advantage of this type of bread was mainly to the baker....

Gradually, steadily, it displaced traditional naturally leavened bread so that today, even in France, 'the nation of bread,' it is very difficult to find even white flour naturally leavened bread. We have come to think of yeasted bread as the true bread of history. But no civilization has been nourished on it.

–from "A Return to Real Bread" by Ronald E. Kotzsch, *East West*, July 1984, excerpted by permission

Quality

Naturally leavened bread is truly "bread for the world." It all begins with the starter, a simple mixture of fermented flour and water. To it is added more flour and water, and then a little salt, to form the dough. After a short period of time, just 3-6 hours or the same time it takes some yeasted breads to rise, the dough is ready to be baked into loaves of health-enriching whole-grain bread.

The fermented quality of naturally leavened bread likens it to other fermented foods—fine wines, beers, and pickles such as sauerkraut, brine, and Oriental rice bran. Enzymes develop during aging which are not lost in baking since the center of the bread remains at a lower temperature than the crust. The long proofing allows the fermenting agents to break down the bran, made of cellulose, releasing nutrients into the dough. Complex carbohydrates are broken down into more digestible forms, simpler sugars or monosaccharides. Proteins are broken down into amino acids.

These processes of predigestion enable us to absorb nutrients more easily and cannot be achieved with yeast which is a false leaven. European experts explain that yeast actually diminishes vitamins and other nutrients in the grain.

It's the fermentation, partly from lactobacillus, that makes eating good quality bread an aid to the digestion of all complex carbohydrates including other grains, beans, and vegetables. It helps restore the functioning of the digestive tract, resulting in proper assimilation and elimination.

This is a brown bread which truly is the "staff of life" as it helps to strengthen the immune system. Jacques de Langre, director of the Grain and Salt Society in Magalia, California, states that: "The natural leavening agents provide a better strain of bacteria to the human system than the lactobacillus acidophilus which is derived from cow's milk. These bacteria help control candida albicans. On the other hand, baker's yeast is a pro-candida organism."

The difference between naturally leavened bread and commercial sourdough (or yeasted bread) is that the former rises naturally over time by the action of yeasts (actually a variety of microorganisms such as fungi and molds) which are drawn to the starter from the air in the particular environment. In commercial sourdough bread, yeast is always added to the flour with the sourdough starter. The characteristic sour flavor indicates that the starter and/or the bread dough has been allowed to ferment too long. During this time, the beneficial lactic acid turns into acidic acid as is found in vinegar. Acidic acid has a higher acid content and a lower pH, and may be harmful to the mucus lining of the intestines.

The ingredient label on the famous San Francisco Sourdough Bread, the "Original Fisherman's Wharf Bread," reads "enriched flour, water, and salt." The Sourdough Garlic Bread made by the same company contains enriched flour (bleached flour, malted barley flour, niacin, iron, thiamin, mononitrate, riboflavin), water, salt, yeast and yeast nutrients (calcium sulfate, amonium chloride, and potassium bromate), and vegetable shortening in the spread (palm, soy-bean and/or cottonseed oil).

I called Parisian Bakeries to find out if yeast is always used in their starter. The baker said there is "a little yeast, 1/12 - 1/20 the usual amount, put in to loosen up the dough and get it to start to rise." He added that it depends on the weather each day, and that more yeast is added if it's very cold.

In my experience, sourdough is a slow riser only if too little of it is used.

Even the otherwise wonderful books, *The Laurel's Kitchen Bread Book* and *The Tassajara Bread Book,* include yeast in their sourdough bread recipes. The former does have a good detailed description of the complicated, traditional yeast-free bread called "desem."

Both have recipes for yeast-free breads made without even sourdough starter (as do I in *American Macrobiotic Cuisine*), but for many people the rising time is too long and the results unreliable. The loaves often turn out like "flour bricks," described by Ron Kotzsch, a writer with a sense of humor: "The late, but unlamented macrobiotic Ohsawa loaves of the '60s...while not particularly good eating, saw extended service as doorstops and bludgeons."

Yeasted breads are risen very quickly by a refined yeast strain which is manufactured in a laboratory under controlled conditions. The quick rise or explosion of starch cells has been likened to the pattern made by cancer cells multiplying. The process has been related to that illness, as a probable cause, by concerned people including research scientists and bakers in Europe.

Quoting Kotzsch again: "According to French researcher Jean Claude Vincent, the bio-electrical energy of the dough also is identical to that of cancer cells. In contrast, the starch cells of naturally leavened bread expand and swell like ripe fruit. In his book *Checkmate to Cancer* the German researcher Dr. Johannes Kuhle asserts that yeasted bread is a cause of cancer and that naturally leavened bread is an inhibitor. Kuhle's work has been carried on by Dr. Max Wahren of the Swiss Association of Master Bakers. Author of over 30 books on the subject, Wahren is a leader in the movement to promote traditional bread."

In addition, the phytic acid in grains needs to be 90% neutralized in order for the minerals, concentrated in the bran, to be absorbed. Kotzsch says: "According to the experiments of R. Hauspy of the Lima Factory in St. Maartens, Belgium, phytin can be neutralized by baking or by natural bacterial action. In naturally leavened bread the combination eliminates all phytin, while in yeasted bread about 90% remains."

The natural leaven method of bread-making is quick and easy. Very little kneading is called for—about 100 times in all—compared with directions for kneading 10-20 minutes or 300-600 times by other techniques. With this method, the starter does all the work during the rising time. It takes just about 10 minutes of hands-on work to pull the loaves together.

Jacques de Langre is considered the father of natural leaven breadmaking for many of us in this country. Nancy Crowell of Seattle, Washington is a student of his who teaches the method with clarity and enthusiasm. Both produce beautiful bread, and have inspired and guided this cook.

Ingredients

Because bread is a basic food, only the finest of ingredients should be used...the highest quality flour, water, and salt.

Whole-wheat flour, made from stone-ground, organic hard wheat berries is the main ingredient. Hard spring wheat is generally higher in gluten and therefore rising power than hard winter wheat. Part of each kind may be combined. You may choose to include half organic unbleached white flour if your bread comes out heavy because you have access only to low-gluten whole-grain flour.

Store-bought flour makes good bread, but freshly ground is best, flavorwise, nutritionally, and for the lightest texture. Five pounds of wheat berries yield 16-17 cups of flour.

Water should be purified or tested clean, even in the countryside where giardia and other bacteria may contaminate natural spring water. (The Multi-Pure system with its solid carbon block filter is superior to granulated carbon filters. See Resources.) Distilled water should not be used since it contains no minerals or taste.

Salt should be unrefined sea salt. The ones listed in Resources differ greatly from the usual sea salt in that they are usually hand-harvested, and are not stripped of the trace elements and full array of minerals found in the sea and in human blood.

Regular sea salt is the same as commercial salt without the added ingredients (including sugar and anti-caking agents). It is devoid of all nutrients except sodium chloride. The price is dramatically different, $2-$4.50 per pound for unrefined sea salt versus 20¢ for commercial salt, but it's worth it.

In bread making, active fermentation occurs when friendly bacteria thrive on the essential trace elements in nutrient-rich flour and fully mineralized salt.

If using damp, coarse, light grey Celtic salt, grind it in a serrated mortar (suribachi) with a pestle before use. Or lightly dry-roast salt first, then grind it in an electric or hand-powered grain mill or a food processor.

Basic Cookware

Oven thermometer
Oven mitts or an old-fashioned wooden "oven rack puller" to remove pans from oven without burning your hands, wrists, or arms
Apron
Bread pans: tinned steel, clay, stainless steel, or glass. Tinned steel is the kind used by professional bakers and I prefer it too. Line glass pans with parchment paper to prevent sticking.
Pastry brush to oil pans
1- and/or 2-quart measuring cups
Cotton terry cloth to cover dough
2 mixing bowls, one to make bread, one to feed starter during first rising; size depends on number of loaves
2-quart or 1-gallon jar for storing starter
Cooling rack
Kitchen scale for weighing dough (optional)
Serrated mortar (suribachi) and wooden pestle, or a mill or food processor for grinding large salt crystals (optional)
Bread knife

The Starter

2 cups whole-wheat flour
1 1/2 cups water

Mix flour and water with your fingers and transfer it to a glass jar or earthenware crock so it is not more than 2/3 full. (Do not store starter in a metal container as a chemical reaction may take place.) Cover with a cotton cloth. Place jar in a cool area, such as a cool kitchen, outside in the shade, or near a window or door. Everyday add 1/4 cup water, then 1/3 cup flour to the mixture. To do this, transfer starter to a bowl. Thoroughly wash out the jar. (It's important to keep the jar clean so undesirable elements are not allowed to enter the starter. Follow this step each time you feed it.)

In the bowl, add water to starter and gently mix together with fingers, then work in flour. Another reason for taking the starter out of the jar and mixing it in a bowl is to incorporate fresh air, a process known as oxidation. Return refreshed starter to jar. Do this every day for 6 days. (Makes 3 cups starter. By this time, you'll need a 1 1/2- to 2-quart jar.) On the 7th day, the starter is ready. Cover tightly with a lid and refrigerate until ready to use or feed.

Always make sure you have 1 cup starter on hand. Whenever you feed it, give it 12 hours to digest the flour and water and to develop before use. Starter should be somewhat bubbly to promote rising action in the bread. It should have a slightly fruity-sour smell. Even though the smell is slightly sour, the bread won't be. The texture should be thick enough to pick up in your hand without it running through your fingers like water or a thin batter, pourable but also somewhat handleable. As flour textures vary, this criterion is more important than exact measurements. Of course, the best way to experience breadmaking is to take a class where you can actually see, smell, feel, and taste both the starter and the dough in varying stages.

The starter needs attention every 7-10 days. For the freshest tasting bread, feed it the day before you make bread. (If you feed it less than 12 hours before use, the new flour will neutralize the leavening capacity of the starter somewhat.) If you let it go longer, and it turns sour and grey, pour off the grey liquid that collects on top. Feed starter twice at 12-hour intervals. When it's bubbly and has risen in the jar, it's signaling that it's active.

The more watery a starter is, the more likely it is to turn sour. If you don't want to tend it as often, feed it less water in proportion to flour so consistency is thicker, i.e. 1/2 cup water to 1 cup flour. If you are not going to use the starter every 7-10 days, give or throw away some before you replenish it.

In the beginning, feed the starter small amounts, say 2 cups each time. When a starter is quite old and active (the fermentation develops quickly), you can add more flour than usual to neutralize the bubbles, and therefore also the sourness or acidity (i.e., an equal amount of flour as starter such as 5 cups starter: 5 cups flour and 2 1/2 - 3 3/4 cups water). Even with these large amounts of flour, you'll see the starter will be ready to make bread the next day. Return starter to refrigerator shortly after feeding, especially if the temperature is warm or hot.

One of my teachers, Nancy Crowell, says, "With proper care and attention, your starter should yield you a lifetime of loaves." Her starter was 2 1/2 years old when she shared some with each student, including this one, in June of 1988. It is not necessarily easier to obtain well-risen bread when you begin with someone else's properly developed starter. A new one is effective right away. I usually feed my starter and bake bread once a week.

To travel with your starter, add enough flour to make it into a dry dough—1/2-1 cup flour to 1 cup starter. Minimizing the water cuts down on fermentation, thus avoiding a jar of starter which bubbles over en route! When you reach your destination, refresh the starter with more water and some fresh flour.

Naturally Leavened Bread ♥ *Basic Recipe*

Makes 8 2-pound loaves

12 cups starter
8 cups purified water
3 tablespoons unrefined sea salt
24 cups whole-wheat bread flour

Makes 4 loaves

6 cups starter
4 cups purified water
4 teaspoons unrefined sea salt
12 cups whole-wheat bread flour

Makes 2 loaves

3 cups starter
2 cups purified water
2 teaspoons unrefined sea salt
6 cups whole-wheat bread flour

Makes 1 loaf

1 1/2 cups starter
1 cup purified water
1 teaspoon unrefined sea salt
3 cups whole-wheat bread flour

Place starter in a mixing bowl and cover with the water. With your hands, mash starter in water to release the natural gases from fermentation in the starter. Stir in salt and any other ingredients such as cooked grains, raisins, nuts, or seasonings. Add the flour.

With your hands or a wooden spoon, or in a dough mixer, briefly mix ingredients together to form a moist dough. If needed, add more flour to proper consistency (not too sticky nor too dry). Too much flour added after this time, i.e. after the 2-hour rising period or just before baking, doesn't have time to leaven properly, and may taste raw.

Knead in the bowl 25-50 times. Fold dough over onto itself, towards you, with your active hand while turning the bowl or dough 1/4 turn between kneads with your less active hand. Or turn dough out onto floured surface to knead. Return dough to bowl.

Clean off your hands. Moisten a cotton cloth by saturating it with water and wringing it out, and cover dough with it.

First rising: Allow to rise about 2 hours.

Rising times are flexible and with practice you'll sense when it's appropriate to proceed to the next step. Leavening happens faster in warm weather, in a warm kitchen, and near a full moon. Overrisen bread is light, but it has lots of air holes and tastes sour. If for some reason you need to leave for an extended period of time, to avoid overrising, bread dough may be refrigerated until ready to proceed—preferably before the first rising period, or very briefly thereafter.

Shaping the loaves: With moistened hands, divide dough in 1, 2, 4, or 8 equal portions, about 2 pounds or 3 cups each. There's no need to punch or treat the dough roughly as you would yeasted bread dough. For standard loaves, you may choose to roll dough in a sausage shape, slightly depressed in the middle, so that when bread is baked the top will be level instead of risen.

Transfer loaves to lightly-oiled bread pans. (Sesame, corn, canola, or olive oil works well.) **Be sure pans are no more than half full.** Cover pans with a dampened cloth to prevent crusting over.

Second rising: **Allow to sit until dough is fully risen and soft (it has spread out in pans)**, 1/2-4 hours. Air bubbles may show on the surface. Make air vent slashes on top of loaves with a razor blade or sharp knife held at an angle, if desired.

Baking: There are two ways to bake the bread. The first is to preheat the oven to 400°. Put loaves in oven on the lower rack nearer the source of heat if only one rack is being used. Bake for 20 minutes. Lower heat to 350° and continue to bake until loaves are fully risen and golden in color, another 20-40 minutes, less with baguette pans. Baking time is 40-60 minutes altogether.

The other baking method is to start with a cold oven set at 400°. Turn temperature to 350° after 1/2 hour and bake until done.

Either way, the practice of spraying the loaves with a mister filled with water or vinegar, once just before placing the loaves in the oven and twice during baking, adds moisture to the air in the oven, giving the crust a rich golden sheen without egg whites. However, an easier method is to brush loaves with oil and return them to the oven for the last 5 minutes of baking.

Loaves are done when they are golden brown and sound hollow when given a sharp rap on the bottom. If loaves need further baking, return them to oven either in or out of the pans.

Immediately remove bread from pans. Let them cool on wire rack(s) or on oven racks with the oven off and the door wide open. Or set them on ends as you see French baguettes in bakeries and shops, tilted against the sides of a basket.

For best texture, allow bread to cool before slicing—at least 2 hours. Figure one standard loaf yields 16 slices.

This kind of bread keeps extremely well. According to Kuhle, the healthful properties of the bread reach their peak in 5 and up to 10 days. Store loaves in the traditional plain, unpainted wooden box, or in paper, waxed paper, or cellophane bags (see Resources) in a cool place unrefrigerated for about a week. Or store in cellophane or plastic bags in the refrigerator for about 2 weeks. Plastic bags are not recommended for use outside of the refrigerator because they don't allow the bread to breathe, causing it to sweat and mold easily. Bread freezes well.

Enjoy bread as is, steamed, or toasted. The more you chew bread, the better it tastes. Saliva in the mouth aids the digestion of grains. Try eating bread as a meditation, chewing each mouthful 30-50 times.

To clean new pans, soak in water for 1/2 hour or so. Over time they become seasoned; the bread can be easily removed, and the pans simply stacked.

Steamed Bread

Steaming is the best way to refresh bread which is somewhat dried out. Steamed bread seems as though it came right out of the oven, soft and spongy. Cut loaves in slices or wedges depending on shape. A round loaf lends itself to the easily hand-held wedge shape. Steam briefly, about 2 minutes after water comes to boil, to soften and warm up. Or, if steamer is large enough, steam whole loaf, then cut individual portions. A Chinese bamboo steamer works well.

Croutons

Makes 1 1/4 - 2 cups

2 tablespoons oil (sesame [plain or toasted], olive, etc.)
2 cups whole grain bread, cut in 1/2- to 1-inch cubes

Preheat oven to 350°.

In an oiled skillet, heat oil and add bread cubes. Stir so all oil is absorbed. If bread is very dried out, add 1-2 tablespoons water to pan and cover to steam for 2 minutes. Transfer bread to oven (either place ovenproof skillet in oven or transfer sautéd bread cubes to baking sheet and place in oven). Bake for 10-15 minutes. Or continue to cook on stovetop, stirring often. Croutons harden somewhat as they cool.

Garlic Toasts

Makes 4-8

1 large clove garlic, minced
1 tablespoon olive oil
4 slices whole-grain bread

Preheat oven to 400°.

Mash garlic with oil to form a paste.

Cut bread into shapes with cookie cutters. Brush garlic paste onto 1 side of the bread and transfer to baking sheet. Bake until golden, about 7 minutes.

Sourdough Sesame Bread

For 1 loaf (see page 31), add 1/2 cup toasted sesame seeds to starter-water-salt mixture before adding flour. Reserve a few seeds to sprinkle on top of loaf. For variation, include a few black sesame seeds for garnish.

Onion Bread, Onion-Herb Bread or Muffins

For 1 loaf (see page 31), sauté 1 onion, diced small, in 1 tablespoon oil (plain or toasted sesame, olive, etc.). For herb loaves, add 1 tablespoon dry or 2 tablespoons fresh herbs. Three nice combinations are thyme, chervil, and tarragon; oregano, basil, chives, and parsley; or the French combination called Herbes de Provence (tarragon, chervil, savory, sage, marjoram, thyme, parsley, basil, and sometimes lavender).

Stretch dough out to 1-inch thick rectangle. Sprinkle onions and herbs over dough and roll it up. Form into loaf or muffins (see the following recipe).

Muffins

One loaf worth of dough (see page 31) may be shaped into 12 balls (1/3 cup or 3 ounces each) and placed in oiled muffin pans to bake 15-18 minutes. For mini-muffins, divide balls in half, or weigh out at 1 1/2 ounces each, for 2 dozen muffins. Small cast-iron muffin pans with scallop, heart, or animal shapes are fun to use. When dough is spread out in pan, it's ready to bake.

For day-old muffins, steam them briefly to warm them and give them a soft texture and a shiny surface.

Variations: **Carrot-Nut Muffins** ❤ Add 1 cup grated carrot, 1/2 cup walnuts, toasted and chopped, and 1 tablespoon dry dill weed or 2 tablespoons fresh dill, minced, to starter mixture before adding flour.

Fruit 'n Nut Muffins ❤ Substitute apple juice for water. Mix juice with starter, then stir in 3/4 cup currants or raisins, or grated apple or pear, or dried fruit, soaked until reconstituted, and chopped; 1/2 cup nuts, toasted and crushed; and 1 teaspoon each cinnamon and vanilla. Add flour and knead as usual. Bake 15-18 minutes. Makes 14.

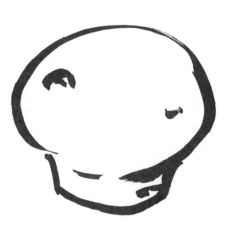

Country French Bread ❤ Baguettes
Crusty Italian Bread

Makes 2 loaves

For the most fun, visit a kitchen shop and purchase several French and/or Italian pans (called "batard" pans in French) for bread as good as you'll find in any boulangerie in Paris. Baguette pans create a longer and thinner shape than the Italian pans do. Oil pans well and sprinkle with cornmeal for Italian bread.

On a lightly floured surface, shape 1 1/4 - 1 1/2 pounds dough (see page 31) for baguettes and 2 pounds dough for Italian loaves in long sausage shapes. Calculate length to 1 inch shorter than pan on both ends. Moisten hands to keep from sticking, if necessary. Or roll dough out to a thin (1/2 to 1 inch thick) rectangular shape and roll up from the long end to shape.

You may wish to roll each loaf over 2 tablespoons toasted sesame seeds spread on the table. (This variation has the best flavor and is easiest to roll out, but seeds must be pre-toasted as no further toasting takes place in baking.)

Transfer dough to pan seam-side-down. Allow to rise and spread out in the pan, covered with a damp cloth. If you like, slash each loaf 4 or 5 times with a sharp knife at an angle on the diagonal, or snip dough with scissors. Bake about 40 minutes total.

For a great spread for French bread, see *Lentil Paté* on page 120.

Variations: **Small Sandwich Baguettes ❤ Petit Pain** Popular throughout much of Europe. Divide dough in 1/2-pound sections and shape as for baguettes. Bake 2 in each baguette pan.

New Orleans-Style French Bread ❤ Join 2 portions of dough for one long, thin baguette. Bake on a sheet of aluminum foil or parchment paper set diagonally in oven for loaves "up to 9 feet in length." (The commercial oven I use extends just 2 1/2 feet?!)

Seeded French Bread ❤ *This loaf won both First Place and the Consumer's Choice Award in the Harvest Bread Bake-off sponsored by the North Coast Bakery in Arcata, California.*

Combine 2 tablespoons toasted sesame seeds with 1 tablespoon poppy seeds, 2 teaspoons cumin and/or caraway seeds, and 1 teaspoon mustard seeds. Roll dough over seeds when shaping loaf.

Garlic Bread ❤ For 1 loaf, grind together in serrated mortar or small blender container: 1/4 cup olive oil, 4 large cloves garlic (minced if using a mortar), and 1/4 teaspoon sea salt. Makes a little more than 1/4 cup. Slice Italian bread in half lengthwise or in individual slices. Spread garlic oil on. Bake about 20 minutes at 350° or broil about 5 minutes.

Anise-Scented Barley Bread (Moroccan)

Makes 2 loaves

In Morocco, bread is important as a food and as an implement for grasping other foods and swirling them in a gravy or stew. Somewhat heavy-textured, these chewy, round loaves are baked in shared neighborhood ovens and cut into wedges to serve, often spread with almond butter.

Simple, unleavened flatbreads made from millet, wheat, or barley, the staple grain crops of Morocco, are eaten by wandering Arab tribesmen in the pre-Sahara and outlying oases. The Tuareg people of the Sahara have the custom of sanctifying meetings with strangers by sharing bread, saying "By bread and salt we are united."

Follow the recipe for one loaf on page 31, substituting 1 cup barley flour for wheat. When ready to shape dough, add 1 tablespoon anise seeds. Form into 2 round shapes and transfer to pie pans which have been lightly oiled and sprinkled with cornmeal. Sprinkle surfaces with 1 teaspoon toasted sesame seeds. Allow to rise as usual, then bake until done.

Black Bread

Makes 1 loaf

Also called Russian or German Rye or Dark Pumpernickel, this loaf is quite delicious—moist, chewy, and slightly sweet—especially when made with freshly ground rye flour.

Rye flour is naturally darker than wheat flour, but molasses, cocoa powder, unsweetened chocolate, or caramel coloring is commonly used to darken commercial rye bread.

Proceed as for standard naturally leavened bread (see page 31), substituting rye flour for wheat, and decreasing volume of water to 1/2 cup. Since rye contains less gluten than wheat, knead dough longer to fully develop the elasticity. Form 1 standard loaf or a round shape by placing ball of dough in oiled pie pan to rise. Bake for 1 hour. After cooling, cut in slices or wedges to serve.

Variations: Black Bread is an all-rye bread, but rye bread may be made with some whole-wheat flour as well, such as 1/4 or 1/2 wheat.

Although there is whole-wheat flour in the starter, you may want to experiment with making rye "sours" (sourdough starter) for people allergic to wheat.

When honored guests arrive at a Russian home, the host and hostess go out to meet them at the door carrying a platter with a loaf of bread and a little mound of salt. "Hleb ee sol," bread and salt, are symbolic words of hospitality in Russia. They mean that although the house may be able to offer nothing more than bread and salt, the guests are welcome to share whatever there is to eat.

The platter with the offering of bread is presented with a snow-white cloth under the bread. The salt is on the family's very best dish of silver, glass, or china. The host and hostess bow low, from the waist. They say, "Dobro pojalovat."— "Welcome with good will." The guest then cuts a slice from the loaf, dips it in the salt, and eats it.

Newlyweds are installed in their first home with the same ritual of the bread and the salt, offered in this case by the parents or elderly relatives of the bride and groom. When the newly married couple goes visiting, at the threshold of each home they visit they are greeted with the "hleb ee sol" salutation.

--from an out-of-print Russian cookbook

Shaped Breads

To make loaves which you shape yourself instead of placing them in a container such as a bread or pie pan, proceed as in basic recipe on page 31. Be sure to work in enough extra flour so dough holds its shape. Too much flour added at the end of the rising time, just before baking, makes for a heavier loaf because the new flour hasn't had enough time to leaven.

Cover dough with a damp cloth to proof until dough is ready. "Ready" means texture of dough has lightened up. When pulled back, dough shows long threads of gluten (the elastic part of the wheat) or air bubbles. This occurs in 3-6 hours.

Add a little more flour if necessary to shape dough according to the following variations. The final rising (or proofing) time is reduced to just 15-30 minutes.

Green Onion Flat Bread

Makes 2 loaves or 8-12 servings

During a month of travel following my husband's studies at the Shanghai College of Traditional Chinese Medicine, we were surprised to find this whole-wheat bread being sold on a train station platform near Xian in central China.

Add 3 tablespoons toasted sesame oil, 1/2 cup green onions, thinly sliced, and 1 tablespoon sesame seeds, toasted, to recipe for 1 loaf of dough (see page 31).

Knead onions into dough. Divide dough into 2 balls and roll out to form 3/4-inch thick, round flat loaves. Place sesame seeds on the surface of loaves and press them into surface with rolling pin to make smooth. Final-proof loaves on corn-oiled baking sheet for 1/2 hour, and bake for 1/2 hour.

Pita Pocket Bread

Makes 6 loaves

Also known as Middle Eastern bread, Syrian flat bread, or Bible bread, pita resembles a thick chapati with a hollow center. After puffing quickly in a hot oven, the bread falls slightly when removed from the oven and allowed to cool, forming the pocket.

Store-bought pocket breads are often dried out from having been frozen, and they tend to tear easily. Steam them for about 1 minute to render them soft and pliable.

When 1 loaf worth of dough (see page 31) is spongy, divide into 6 balls and roll out on floured surface to 1/4-inch thick rounds, 6 inches in diameter.

Generously sprinkle 3 baking sheets with 1/4 cup each corn flour, cornmeal, or toasted sesame seeds, or line sheets with parchment paper. Final-proof 15 minutes while you preheat the oven to 450°. Do not reduce temperature. Transfer bread to oven and watch them puff up in about 5-8 minutes (loaves may overcook in 10 minutes). Great steamed the next day!

Pita may also be made in a skillet, but the percentage that puff up is less. Set flame high so cornmeal smokes lightly in skillet. Add pita and cook until golden and slightly stiff on the bottom, and bubbles appear on top, about 2 minutes. Flip bread over to cook 2 minutes more.

Freeform-Style Country French Bread and Crusty Italian Bread

To form long loaves without a special pan, figure 1 1/2 pounds dough per loaf (see page 31). Roll dough back and forth on the table with outstretched palms until shape is more or less uniform in diameter. Lightly oil baking sheet, or sprinkle sheet with coarse cornmeal for Italian bread, and place loaf seam-side-down on baking sheet. Allow to final-proof 15 minutes, then cut 3 or more diagonal slashes on the surface of the dough with knife or scissors, if desired. Bake.

Breadsticks

Make 1 loaf's volume of dough (see page 31). Figure 1 ounce dough per small stick, or 2 ounces for large ones. Roll dough out and allow to rise 15 minutes, then bake about 20 minutes, turning once during baking. Makes 16-32 sticks.

Variation: **Sesame Breadsticks** ❤ Roll breadstick dough shapes over toasted sesame seeds.

Mexi-Sticks ❤ Add 3 cloves garlic, minced, 1 1/2 teaspoons oregano, and 3/4 teaspoon cumin seeds or powder to starter-water-salt mixture before adding flour.

Quick Breads

Skillet Cornbread

Makes 9-12 servings

Unlike some of the recipes in early New England cookbooks with names like Barefoot Bread or Church of God Cornbread, the special qualities of this quick bread are the lack of dairy products and eggs in a grain dish that is both light and attractive.

One secret of delicious cornbread is using freshly-ground cornmeal; 2 cups whole grain corn yields 3 cups meal. To enhance the flavor of store-bought cornmeal, roast it in a dry skillet until a pleasant aroma rises, about 5 minutes, stirring often.

1 1/2 cups cornmeal
1 1/2 cups whole-wheat pastry flour, or half organic, unbleached white flour
1 1/2 tablespoons non-aluminum baking powder
1 teaspoon unrefined sea salt
1/3 cup light canola oil, or part corn or sunflower oil
1/3 cup sweetener—brown rice syrup (see page 171), barley malt, and/or pure maple syrup
Up to 2 cups Edensoymilk; or 1 3/4 cups Rice Dream "milk," or 2 1/2 cups plain amazake

Preheat oven to 400°. Liberally brush with oil a medium-size cast-iron skillet (or an ovenproof pan such as a standard 8-inch square baking dish). Preheat pan in oven for 5 minutes while you prepare the batter, not long enough for oil to smoke.

Mix dry ingredients. Gently whisk in remaining ingredients. Batter should be thin and pourable. Transfer batter to hot skillet and bake until bread tests done, 30-40 minutes.

Variation: **Carrot Cornbread** ❤ For a colorful addition with a slightly sweeter taste, add 1 cup grated carrots.

Carry dat load on your head
De Lord will bless your good corn bread
　　　　　—early New England cookbook

Tequezquite-leavened Cornbread, Corn Sticks, and Mini-Muffins

Makes 1 loaf cornbread (8-12 servings),
16 corn sticks, or 18 mini-muffins

Native Americans traditionally processed cornbreads with "culinary ash." The ash softened the grain fiber. It is now known that it also imparts minerals such as calcium, potassium, magnesium, and other trace elements to the bread, and makes amino acids more available to the body. They soaked the ashes in boiling water until the water cooled, just as is done in this recipe.

Tequezquite (teck-e-SKEE-tay) comes from the Indian word "tequixquitl" which means "stone-like thing." Found in several lakes in Mexico, it has been used for centuries by the indigenous people there for cooking, as a source of salt, as an antacid, for skin ailments, and as a hair conditioner. It is a compound of salts and sodium carbonates created by the decomposition of volcanic rock and the biological action of microalgae.

Tequezquite comes in the form of powdered, grey clay. It is dissolved and boiled in water. When the solids settle to the bottom, and the solution has cooled, only the liquid is used as a leavening agent in place of baking soda or powder. It brings out the flavor and color of grain corn and makes it softer. (I unsuccessfully experimented with using it as a leavening agent for whole-wheat pastry flour baked goods.)

No salt is included as the leavening is also a good source of minerals including salt. (Analysis shows tequezquite contains 86.99% clay, organic matter, etc., and 13.01% salts [Na2CO3 + NaH 2CO3, NaCl, K Cl, and Na2SO4]).

Tequezquite darkens the breads a little and has a wonderful, earthy flavor. As a leavening agent, it gives a slight rise and a cake-like crumb. This cornbread is dense compared to baking powder and egg breads, but very delicious.

Corn stick pans and small cast-iron muffin tins are worthwhile investments for the homey feeling they impart to anything prepared in them. They are the best choice for tequezquite baking as they produce a quite light bread. (Corn sticks are also called corn pones and corn cakes.)

Thanks to Goldmine Natural Foods (see Resources) and to Nancy Crowell, cooking teacher in Seattle, Washington, for help in learning how to use tequezquite.

1 cup water
2 tablespoons tequezquite natural leavening
　　agent (2 teaspoons per cup flour)
2 cups cornmeal, yellow or blue
1 cup whole-wheat pastry flour
1 cup soymilk
3 tablespoons corn oil
3 tablespoons brown rice syrup

In a small saucepan, bring water and te-quezquite to boil. Stir, turn heat off, and remove pan from stove so sediment settles completely and water is lukewarm to touch, about 1/2 hour.

Preheat oven to 400°.

Mix flours well. Carefully pour off liquid from tequezquite, taking care not to include sediment which should be discarded (or saved for the garden). Makes 2/3 - 3/4 cup liquid. Add liquid to soymilk with oil and syrup. Stir. Add to dry ingredients and whisk into a batter. Makes about 3 cups.

Generously brush with corn oil a 9-inch cast-iron skillet, 8-inch square baking dish, or small cast-iron muffin or corn stick pans. Place in hot oven to heat oil, but don't allow it to smoke, about 5 minutes (an optional step). Fill quickly and return to oven to bake until done, about 15-18 minutes for muffins and corn sticks, 1/2 hour for cornbread. Immediately turn muffins or corn sticks out onto cooling rack. To clean pans, soak in hot water without detergent (which would re-move the seasoning), then scrub gently.

Breads are great steamed the next day.

Variation: Double recipe to make a larg-er cornbread (2 inches thick). Bake 35-40 minutes.

Biscuits

Makes 8-12

Since pioneer times, biscuits have been popu-lar for their speedy preparation. For a quick Sunday brunch or holiday food, try them served with a sweet or savory spread. Soy-milk causes biscuits to rise more fully than either juice or water.

2 cups whole-wheat pastry flour or up to
    half organic, unbleached white flour
1 tablespoon non-aluminum baking powder
1/2 teaspoon unrefined sea salt
3/4 cup soymilk
1/4-1/3 cup canola or part corn oil

Preheat oven to 400°.

Mix the dry ingredients. Stir in the oil, then the soymilk. Knead briefly. Dough should be soft (on the moist side) and smooth. Add a little more flour if necessary. On a floured surface or on one sprinkled with cornmeal, roll dough to 1/2-inch thick-ness. Cut dough in 2-inch rounds and transfer to a lightly-oiled baking sheet. Bake until golden on the underside, 8-10 minutes.

For a shinier surface, brush tops with oil in last 5 minutes of baking.

Variations: For whimsy's sake, cut rolled biscuits in cookie cutter shapes. One of my favorites is hearts which come in 3 sizes.

For **Toasted Sesame Biscuits** ♥ add 1/2 cup sesame seeds, toasted, to dry ingre-dients.

For **Dropped Biscuits** ♥ as opposed to rolled, add more soymilk, about 1 cup total. Drop by large spoonfuls onto oiled baking sheet.

Chapatis

Makes 8

Chapatis are unleavened whole wheat flat breads which are a lot of fun to make. They are the most common form of bread served in India where most people prefer the time-honored finger-and-bread scoop method to fork and spoon. Most Indians dip their chapatis in the staple bean sauce, soup, or gravy called dahl. Chapatis are also relied on by the long-lived Hunza people of Pakistan.

In Mexico, where they are known as wheat tortillas (tortillas de harina), these flat-breads are used to make burritos and tostadas. We found them covered with sesame seeds in Mexico City, with a hole formed near the edge for stringing and hanging. In Africa, millet chapatis are a staple.

Originally made with only flour and water, today's healthful commercial versions usually contain a little vegetable oil and salt. Traditionally cooked on both sides on a hot, dry griddle and then tossed over hot coals or an open flame, they are also known as Open Flame Bread.

2 cups whole-wheat bread flour
2/3 cup water

Mix flour and water, then knead about 50 times to form a smooth dough. Let dough rest about 15 minutes covered with a damp cloth.

Divide dough into 8 balls of equal size. Roll dough out to form 1/8-inch thick circle, about 6 inches in diameter. To do this, flatten each ball, then roll across it, once away from you, once toward you. Turn dough over and move it 1/4 turn, then roll again. Shapes become rounder as you progress.

Just before serving time, heat a dry skillet over medium heat, about 3 minutes. Quickly brown chapatis by toasting about 1 minute on each side. Then place chapati directly on the burner over the flame for about 10 seconds each side and watch it puff up. Serve hot off the fire or wrap in a natural fiber cloth to retain heat.

Tortillas

Most commonly made from corn, the traditional staple grain, tortillas were used by the American Indians long before the Spanish Conquest in 1524. Tortillas are the national bread of Mexico where corn accounts for half the total volume of food consumed. They are enjoyed in parts of Central and South America as well. Thin, round, unleavened flat breads, they can be made from wheat as well. East Indians enjoy the whole-wheat version known as chapatis (see preceding recipe).

American Indians prepared corn in 2 ways: grinding the whole dry kernels into meal or boiling them in an alkaline lye solution made with wood ashes. Without the boiling solution, corn takes 2 days of soaking and cooking to soften the extremely tough outer layer. The cooked grain, called hominy, is chewy and slightly sweet. Lime or baking soda have also been used to soften the hulls, but hominy made from ash is highest in nutrition according to Hopi Cookery. Apparently the other softening agents take off too much of the bran, causing the germ to fall apart.

The type of corn available in most natural food stores is dent corn (notice the tiny dent in the fat end). Flint corn, used by the Indians, is harder to find, but superior in flavor. It comes in beautiful bright colors of blue, yellow, and red, or combinations. The red loses its color when cooked.

In Mexico, masa is made from finely ground dried hominy to which water and salt are added and the resulting dough pressed or rolled by hand or machine. Today, soft yellow corn tortillas are still patted by hand by Indian women in restaurants, or while kneeling on straw mats in the marketplaces. They are cooked on hot dry griddles which rest on rocks surrounding the fire, or on gas griddles in many homes, Indian and non-Indian alike.

In the southern United States, broken pieces of dried hominy are known as hominy grits or just grits. The dried hominy is cracked coarsely in a flour mill to be cooked for porridge.

Today's natural foods cook may use a pressure cooker to cook the corn, and a hand-operated steel mill to grind the cooked corn into a smooth dough. Electric mills and stone grinders do not work, the latter because liquid seeps into and clogs the stones, ruining them. A food processor works but the texture is not as smooth as with the steel mill.

Use masa to make tamales, arepas, and dumplings in addition to tortillas. See recipes for Tofu Enchiladas and Bean Burritos on pages 82 and 150 respectively.

Makes 3-4

1 cup corn dough *masa* (see page 52)
Corn oil to brush pan

Divide dough into 3 or 4 balls of equal size. Press in one of 2 ways: between palms or between 2 sheets of waxed paper with a flat plate, rolling pin, or in a tortilla press. For tortilla press, cut waxed paper and place one piece in press. Place ball of dough slightly nearer the hinge as dough spreads away from it. Place another sheet of waxed paper on top of dough and press. Stack tortillas with waxed paper in between until ready to cook

and serve.

Lightly brush a skillet with corn oil and heat over medium-low flame. Cook each tortilla for about 1-3 minutes on each side, brushing a tiny amount of corn oil on skillet between tortillas if skillet is dry. Turn tortillas with a spatula to avoid sticking. Wrap them in a natural fiber cloth, or in festive Mexican tortilla bags or straw tortilla hats, to keep warm.

To refresh tortillas (homemade or store-bought) and render them soft and warm, steam briefly, 30 seconds to 2 minutes, less for store-bought as they tend to be thinner and more delicate.

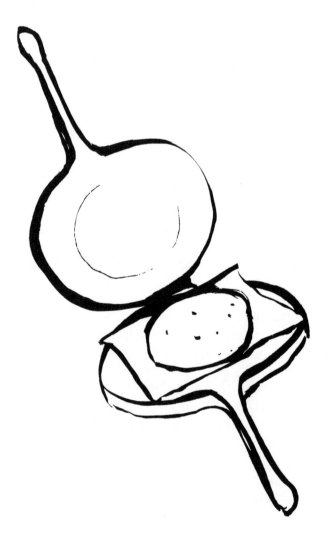

Pasta...Oodles of Noodles

These irresistible pasta and vegetable dishes, some with luscious toppings, are worth repeating time and time again. Fast-cooking and dairy-free, they quickly become staples for lunch or dinner. Noodle dishes may be served hot or cool, plain, or with a broth, sauce, or dressing. Be flexible in adapting the ingredients to the changing seasons.

Try any of the wide variety of Italian-American pastas from spaghetti to cork-screw pasta called *fusilli*. Be sure to sample the popular Japanese varieties such as thick buckwheat *soba* (made from buckwheat flour alone or with varying amounts of whole-wheat flour), whole-wheat or brown rice *udon* (looks like whole-grain fettucini), or thin whole-wheat *somen* (looks like spaghetti), or the buckwheat noodles such as *jinenjo soba* with wild mountain yam, *cha soba* with green tea, or *yomogi soba* with green mugwort herb.

Note: Cooking pasta or noodles in a generous volume of water, i.e. for 1/2 pound of pasta, 2 quarts (8 cups) water, eliminates the need to add cold water at intervals during cooking.

Spaghetti and Wheatballs

Makes 3-4 servings

Italian Red Sauce (recipe follows)
Pasta (recipe follows)
9-12 *Wheatballs* (see page 49)
1/4 cup parsley, finely chopped for garnish

Italian Red Sauce:

Makes 1 3/4 - 2 1/2 cups

1 bay leaf
1 small beet, about 1/4 cup or 1 ounce, diced small
3/4 pound carrots (or winter squash or pumpkin), 2 1/4 - 3 cups, cut in 1/2-inch slices
1 1/2 cups water (1/2 cup to cook vegetables, up to 1 cup to add for proper texture)
1 teaspoon *each* dried oregano and basil
1/4 cup miso, soy sauce, or sauerkraut juice

Pasta:

Makes 4 1/2 cups

2 quarts (8 cups) water
1/2 pound whole-wheat spaghetti or whole-wheat somen noodles

To make sauce, place bay leaf on bottom of pressure cooker, and add vegetables and 1/2 cup water. Bring to pressure and cook 5 minutes. Discard bay leaf and purée ingredients with seasonings in blender or food processor. Add remaining water gradually to achieve a saucy texture. For large volumes, simply increase amounts proportionately.

To prepare pasta, bring water to boil, add pasta and cook until tender, 5-10 minutes for somen, 10-20 minutes for spaghetti. Drain.

To serve, pour sauce over individual servings of spaghetti. Place 3 wheatballs on top and sprinkle parsley over all.

Variations: **Carrot Marinara Sauce** ♥ Heat 1 tablespoon olive oil in skillet and sauté until tender 1 onion, diced; 2 cloves garlic, minced; and 1 cup mushrooms (3 ounces), sliced. Add sauce to vegetables and cook covered 10 minutes more to blend flavors. Makes 3 cups.

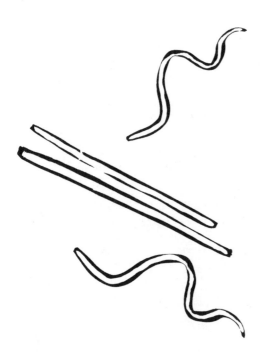

Buckwheat Noodles with Dipping Broth

Makes 2-6 servings

In Japan, noodles are consumed almost every day. Buckwheat noodles (soba) *and wheat noodles* (udon) *are served hot or chilled depending on the weather. They are served in a savory stock or with a stronger dipping broth on the side, also made hot or cool depending on the season. It's called zaru soba, zaru referring to the bamboo mat on which cool buckwheat noodles may be served.*

Noodles:

Makes 4 1/2 cups
2 quarts (8 cups) water
1/2 pound buckwheat noodles (packages
   ranging from 7-8.8 ounces are fine)

Dipping Broth:

Makes 1 3/4 cups
2 cups water
3-inch piece kombu sea vegetable
3-4 tablespoons natural soy sauce

1/2 teaspoon ginger, freshly grated, or
   Japanese horseradish paste (wasabi)

To cook noodles, bring water to boil in a 3 1/2- to 4-quart pot. Add noodles and cook until done, about 8 minutes. Strain and serve immediately or, for later use or to serve at room temperature or chilled, run noodles under cold water to keep them from becoming sticky. Noodle broth is not usually used in the dipping broth because of its murky color. However, if noodles are made from organic flour, the broth is nutrient-rich and may be used in home cooking.

To make dipping broth, bring water and kombu to boil and simmer 5 minutes. Remove sea vegetable and set aside for later use. Add soy sauce and ginger to broth and simmer 1 minute more before serving. Serve broth in separate bowls for dipping, or pour directly over deep bowls of noodles.

For a main dish, figure 1 1/2 cups noodles with 1/2 cup broth, topped with 1 tablespoon each grated daikon (white radish), thinly sliced green onion, and 1/2 teaspoon nori flakes. For small side dish servings, figure 1 cup noodles in a small bowl topped with 1/4 cup broth.

Variations: **Summer Soba** ❤ Rinse noodles in cold water and drain. Chill broth to serve.

Use other kinds of noodles such as whole-wheat udon which makes 4 1/2 - 6 cups in about 12-15 minutes. Allow both noodles and broth to cool to room temperature or chill to serve during the heat of summer.

A variety of flavors come from adding other ingredients to the basic kombu stock (*dashi*): Cook 2 dry mushrooms 15 minutes, discard hard stems, and add enough water to equal 2 cups after cooking. Add 2-4 tablespoons sweetener such as brown rice syrup or sweet rice cooking wine (*mirin*), and/or 1 tablespoon lemon juice.

To further enhance taste, serve side dishes of 1/4 cup green onions, finely sliced on the diagonal, 1/2 cup grated daikon, plain or seasoned nori sea vegetable strips, finely cut, or 1-2 tablespoons nori flakes and 1-2 tablespoons toasted sesame seeds to be sprinkled on top of the noodles.

Noodles with Season's Savory Vegetable Sauce

Makes 3-4 servings

Noodles:

Makes about 3 1/4 - 6 cups, less with somen, more with udon

2 quarts (8 cups) water
1/2 pound (8 ounces) any kind whole-grain noodles

Vegetables:

2 quarts (8 cups) water
1 onion (yellow, white, or red, or equivalent amount leeks, halved lengthwise to clean between leaves, or green onions), thinly sliced
1 carrot (or all or part other root vegetables) halved lengthwise, each half thinly cut in diagonals
4 cups broccoli, tops separated into flowerets, hard outer portion of stems peeled and discarded, insides thinly sliced in diagonals, or other green vegetable(s) such as Brussels sprouts, bok choy, cabbage, kale, and/or watercress, cut in bite-size pieces, or large sprouts such as sunflower, mung, or soybean

Season's Savory Vegetable Sauce:

Makes 2 2/3 cups

2 cups vegetable cooking broth or water
3-inch piece kombu sea vegetable
4-6 tablespoons natural soy sauce
1/4 cup arrowroot powder or kuzu root starch (about 2 tablespoons per cup liquid)
1/4 cup cool water

Optional sauce ingredients—Add 1 or more of the following:

2 shiitake mushrooms
1 large clove garlic, minced
1 teaspoon ginger, freshly grated, or ginger juice (ginger root grated and squeezed)
2 teaspoons red shiso leaf, freshly chopped, or 1 teaspoon, powdered
1 teaspoon green nori flakes
1/4 cup nuts or seeds (almonds or pumkin or sunflower seeds), toasted
1/2 pound prepared tempeh or tofu (see recipes pages 153 and 151), or green beans or peas (snow, sugar snap, or English)

Bring water for both noodles and vegetables to boil in separate pots. Meanwhile, cut vegetables. Cook noodles until done, tender but firm, about 5-15 minutes depending on kind. Drain and run under cool water to prevent sticking if not serving immediately.

To cook vegetables, add all of them, except softer greens if used, to boiling water and cook until just tender, about 5-8 minutes. (If dry shiitake mushrooms are included, soak 10 minutes then cook with vegetables, cutting off and discarding hard stem after cooking.) Add softer greens to pot during last 2 minutes of cooking time. Drain, reserving broth for sauce.

To prepare sauce, place broth and kombu in saucepan, with optional ingredients if desired, and bring to boil. Turn heat low and remove kombu. Thoroughly dissolve thickener in cool water, and add it to pot. Stir until mixture becomes shiny and thick, about 1 minute.

To serve, gently mix noodles with vegetables (adding nuts, seeds, or prepared tempeh or tofu at this point) and pour sauce over all.

Variations: **Easy Dinner Rice with Summer Vegetable Sauce** ❤ Substitute 3-6 cups cooked rice (or other grains) for noodles. To celebrate the colorful excitement of summer, include sweet corn, carrot, red radish, broc-coli, red onion, yellow summer squash, fresh green beans or peas. Cut vegetables in similar sizes and shapes.

If including tempeh in dish, add 1 tablespoon wet mustard to sauce.

Noodle Sushi

Makes 3 rolls

Although any whole-grain noodles may be used, thin whole-grain Asian noodles or spaghetti are easiest to roll up. Thicker varieties will have to be rolled up more tightly.

Pickled ginger, gari in Japanese, adds a zesty zing to whole-grain noodle- or rice-and-vegetable rolls (sushi). Macrobiotic quality sushi ginger, unlike the commercial type, doesn't contain artificial flavoring, coloring agents, sugar, or preservatives. Only fresh ginger root with rice vinegar, cider vinegar, ume vinegar, shiso leaves, and sea salt make up this delicious condiment.

2 quarts (8 cups) water
1 carrot, cut lengthwise in thin strips
2 cups dark greens (watercress, kale, etc.) or
    1 cup cucumber, slivered lengthwise
1/2 pound whole-grain noodles (thin
    Japanese buckwheat noodles [soba], thin

wheat noodles [somen], thicker rice or
    wheat noodles [udon], or whole-wheat
    spaghetti
3 sheets nori sea vegetable, toasted
1-1 1/2 tablespoons pickled plum paste
1 teaspoon *Japanese Horseradish Paste*
    (Wasabi), recipe follows
2 teaspoons marinated sushi ginger (or 1
    tablespoon marinated sushi daikon—see
    Resources), slivered

Japanese Horseradish Paste (Wasabi):
Makes 2 teaspoons
1 tablespoon Japanese horseradish (wasabi)
    powder
1 teaspoon water

Dipping Sauce (optional):

1 1/2 tablespoons natural soy sauce
1 1/2 tablespoons water

Bring water to boil in a 3 1/2- or 4-quart pot. Add carrots and cook until tender, about 5 minutes. Transfer to towel to dry. If included, add whole greens to hot broth and press them down so they are completely submerged. Cook until tender, 2-5 minutes, less for watercress, more for cabbage family greens. Spread greens on a kitchen towel and pat dry.

When boiling resumes, add noodles and cook until tender, 5-15 minutes depending on variety. Drain and immediately run cold water over noodles to stop cooking process and make texture firm. Drain noodles, spread them on a towel, and pat dry. Measure 3-4 cups for use in this dish and set the rest aside. Makes 3 1/4 - 6 cups.

To prepare wasabi, mix ingredients. When preparing large amounts ahead of time, store in covered container so paste doesn't dry out.

To assemble sushi, place nori horizontally on sushi mat and lay 1 - 1 1/2 cups noodles on nori, spreading them to sides of nori, leaving 2 inches of space at the far end and 1 inch at the end nearest you. (It doesn't matter if noodles are arranged in any specific fashion, such as horizontally.) Place several strips carrot and greens or cucumber across mid-section. Spread 1/3 each plum paste, wasabi, and ginger over nori at end nearest you. Moisten far end of nori, roll sushi tightly, and squeeze roll to seal the end. With a sharp knife, cut sushi roll in 6-8 equal pieces.

Mix dipping sauce ingredients and serve.

Vegetable Fried Noodles

Makes 3-6 servings or 7-8 cups

Inspired by the Vegetable Chow Mein in Chinese restaurants, this dish (as well as the variation, Vegetable Fried Rice) is a great choice for a quick and easy one-dish meal. Whole-wheat spaghetti or Japanese whole-wheat somen noodles are exactly like the ones served in the open-air markets in China. Unlike Chop Suey which is said to be a dish of leftover odds and ends invented in San Francisco, Chow Mein is an authentic Chinese dish.

Noodles:

Makes 4-5 cups, less of spaghetti, more of somen

2 quarts (8 cups) water
8 ounces whole-grain spaghetti or somen
    noodles, broken in half

Vegetables and Seasonings:

2 tablespoons toasted sesame oil (or half
    regular sesame oil)
1 onion, thinly sliced

1 carrot, thinly cut in matchsticks
2 cups green onions, cut in 2 1/2-inch sec-
    tions, whites separated from greens
1 teaspoon ginger, peeled and freshly grated
1/4 cup natural soy sauce
2 cups cabbage, thinly sliced in 2 1/2-inch
    lengths, well packed
1 cup celery, about 2 ribs, thinly sliced on
    the diagonal

Bring water to boil and cook noodles until done, 5-6 minutes for somen and 20 minutes for spaghetti. Drain and pour cool water over noodles to prevent them from becoming too soft.

To prepare vegetables, in a large skillet heat oil and briefly sauté onion, carrot, and whites of green onion. Mix ginger with soy sauce and add half to skillet. Cover and cook over medium-low heat until almost tender, about 5 minutes more. Add cabbage and celery, stir, and cover to cook until done, about 5 minutes. Add noodles to vegetables with green onion tops and remaining ginger-soy sauce mixture. Gently stir to mix ingredients well and cover to heat through, about 2 minutes more, stirring occasionally.

Variations: Substitute other suitable vegetables such as bok choy, Chinese cabbage, watercress, broccoli or cauliflower, green beans, mushrooms, or mung or soybean sprouts. Add 1 cup slivered wheatmeat (see page 49), or tofu cutlets (see page 151), thinly sliced, and 2 cloves garlic, minced.

Vegetable Fried Rice ♥ Substitute 4 cups cooked brown rice for noodles. Cut vegetables in small dice and add up to 1/2 cup water mixed with a tablespoon of soy sauce only if needed to freshen rice.

For a simplified version with great taste, include 4 cups rice with 1 cup wheatmeat (see page 49), diced small, and 6 green onions, thinly sliced. Sauté green onions and wheatmeat until onions are soft, about 3 minutes. Add rice and drizzle up to 2 tablespoons of the ginger-soy mixture over rice. Stir well and serve.

Quick and Easy Noodle-Vegetable Delight

Makes 3-4 servings

A very appealing, simple dressing completes this one-dish meal which may be served hot, or cool as a salad. The dressing is a favorite on raw or cooked vegetable salads as well.

2 quarts (8 cups) water
1 onion (yellow, white, or red, or equivalent
    amount leeks, halved lengthwise to
    clean between leaves, or green onions),
    thinly sliced
1 carrot (or all or part other root vegetable),
    thinly sliced on the diagonal or in
    matchsticks
2-4 cups broccoli, tops cut into flowerets,
    hard outer portion of stems peeled and
    discarded, insides sliced in 2-inch
    lengths, 1/4-inch thick or matchsticks
1/2 pound (8 ounces) whole-grain noodles,
    your choice
1/4-1/2 cup dry sea palm, arame, or hijiki
    sea vegetables (optional)
2 cups water to soak and cook sea
    vegetables

Toasted Sesame Vinaigrette:

2 tablespoons toasted sesame oil
2-4 tablespoons pickled plum (umeboshi)
    vinegar or natural soy sauce, to taste

Bring to boil just 1 pot (2 quarts) water. Boil vegetables, and with a flat strainer transfer them to a bowl. Add noodles to hot broth and return to boil to cook until done.

If including sea vegetables, soak until reconstituted, about 10 minutes, then cook in soak water (or fresh water if a milder flavor is desired) until tender, 5-15 minutes, less for arame, more for sea palm and hijiki. Drain, reserving broth.

Prepare dressing by combining ingredients.

Gradually mix dressing with noodles to strength desired, then gently toss with vegetables to serve.

Variations: For very large amounts, boil vegetables and noodles in separate pots. Keep dressing well-whisked and add it gradually to taste. Less is required. Place vegetables on top of individual portions of seasoned noodles to avoid crushing vegetables.

For a simpler version, include just 2 cups slivered (thin matchstick-cut) carrots and 1 cup green onions, thinly sliced in long diagonals. After cooking carrots, add green onions to cook just 10 seconds.

Substitute olive oil for toasted sesame oil.

Add 1-2 tablespoons sweetener (brown rice syrup, pure maple syrup, or sweet rice cooking wine [mirin]) to dressing.

Other pasta recipes:

Lasagna (page 83)
Pasta Primavera (page 103)
Hot Italian Pasta Salad (page 104)
Arame-Cucumber-Noodle Salad (page 104)
Gelled Corn Pasta Salad (page 111)

Wheatmeat *(Seitan)*

Makes 1 - 1 1/2 cups or 9-12 wheatballs

Dough:

2 cups whole-wheat bread flour (finely
    ground hard red spring wheat is best)
1 cup warm water

Cooking Broth:

1 cup water
2 tablespoons natural soy sauce
3-inch piece kombu sea vegetable
1 bay leaf
1 clove garlic, minced

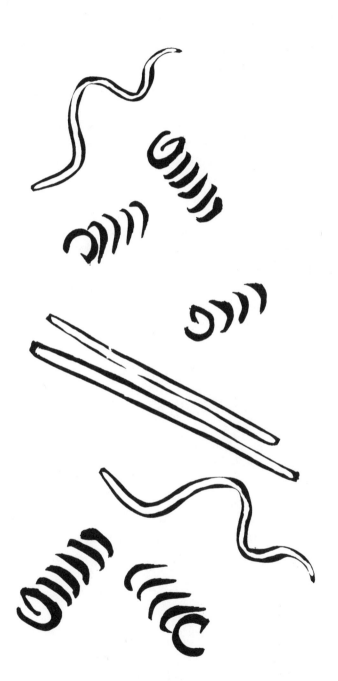

Prepare dough by mixing flour and water in a large bowl, then kneading or stirring the wet dough until smooth and elastic, about 50 times. (Although dough is quite moist, kneading is possible if you work quickly and moisten your hands.)

Cover dough with warm water for 15 minutes. Wash dough gently, then more vigorously, kneading and stretching it under the water so the white starch and brown bran flakes come out into the water, leaving the stretchy, protein-rich gluten. Feel for gritty parts where bran is still incorporated in the mass. Change water 2 or 3 times, alternating warm, then cool water, until it stays almost clear. This process takes 10-15 minutes.

To prepare cooking broth, bring ingredients to a rolling boil. Tear off 1-inch pieces of dough or simply separate dough in 9-12 equal portions. Add to boiling stock, then keep broth at moderate boil to cook until flavor permeates dough, 15 minutes or longer. Store wheatmeat in the refrigerator with its broth.

Recipes using wheatmeat:

Spaghetti and Wheatballs (page 43)
Early American Scrapple (page 218)
Mexican Vegetable Soup with Wheatballs
    (page 6)
Moroccan Couscous (recipe on this page)

parsley

Couscous

Couscous is a traditional Moroccan (North African) grain dish made from coarsely ground and steamed durum wheat semolina. It cooks instantly for serving in a hurry. It is usually served with a gravy-like stew poured over it.

Most couscous is refined. (Both bran and germ are removed leaving only the starchy center portion of the wheat kernel.) Now an organic whole-wheat couscous is available. It cooks up just as light and fluffy in 5 minutes.

Couscous

Makes 3-6 servings or 3-4 cups

2 cups water
1 teaspoon-1 tablespoon natural soy sauce
    for added flavor, or a few grains sea salt
1 cup couscous (12-oz. pkg.=1 1/2-2 cups)

In a small pot, bring water and soy sauce or salt to a rolling boil. Add couscous and stir to level as mixture returns to boil. For whole-grain couscous, cook for 5 minutes. For refined couscous, immediately remove pot from heat, cover, and let sit for 10 minutes. With either kind, fluff with a fork onto serving platter.

Variation: **Moroccan Couscous** ♥ In a 2-quart pot, heat 1 tablespoon olive oil and sauté 1/2 cup onion, diced small, until soft. Meanwhile, bring water to boil for couscous. Add 1 cup diced wheatmeat (see page 49) and 1/8 teaspoon crushed saffron threads to onion. When water boils, add it with couscous to onion mixture. When boiling resumes, remove pot from heat, cover, and let sit for 10 minutes. Makes 4 cups.

Bulgur

Bulgur with Fresh Corn and Pumpkin Seeds

Makes 7-9 servings or 7 cups

This quick and easy summertime recipe was inspired by Jackie Pukel in the Macrobiotic Foundation of Florida's newsletter, Joy of Life: "For when it's an effort to cook, and more of an effort to write 'em down!" Mother of 5, Jackie suggests serving the grain dish with steamed kale, watercress, or broccoli, and a sheet of nori seaweed, toasted and crushed or cut.

3 cups water or mild-tasting vegetable broth
1 tablespoon natural soy sauce
2 cups bulgur wheat
Kernels from 2 ears corn
1/4 cup pumpkin seeds, toasted
1/4 cup parsley or green onions, thinly
　　sliced for garnish

Bring water and soy sauce to boil. Add bulgur, then corn kernels. When boiling resumes, turn heat down to cook covered for 15-20 minutes. Transfer to bowl by fluffing with a fork. Sprinkle with pumpkin seeds and parsley to serve.

Variation: **Cracked Wheat** ❤ Though not as light as bulgur, cracked wheat may be substituted. Cracked wheat is coarsely ground wheat which has been sifted. Include 1 1/2 - 2 times the amount of water for cracked wheat, less for fluffier grain, more for softer. Prepare as above.

Other bulgur recipes:

Bulgur-Rice (page 18)
Quinoa with Bulgur (page 57)
Bulgur Wheat Salad ❤ Tabouli (page 102)

Millet

Baked Millet Kasha (Russian)

Makes 7-10 servings or 7 cups

In Russia, any baked cereal dish is known as kasha, such as buckwheat, barley, and corn.

Up to 1/4 teaspoon unrefined sea salt
4 cups water
2 cups millet

Preheat oven to 400°. Bring salted water to boil in a 2-quart ovenproof pot. Rinse and drain millet and add to pot. When water resumes boiling, cover and transfer to oven to bake for 1/2 hour.

Variation: Toast millet dry or in a little oil before boiling.

Other millet recipes:

Soft Millet Morning Cereal (page 208)
African Millet Meal Porridge (page 53)
Millet "Mashed Potatoes" with Country Gravy (page 74)
Millet "Mashed Potato" Casserole (page 74)

millet

Corn

Homemade Hominy and Masa

Makes about 6 cups hominy, about 4 cups masa, and 2 cups hominy tea

2 cups whole dry corn
8 cups water (4 cups for soaking and first cooking with ashes, 4 cups for second cooking)
1/2 cup sifted wood ashes

Wood ashes should be made from clean hardwood, free of paint and preservatives, and from a fire started with natural materials such as leaves or dry brush instead of newspaper, which contains chemicals. Ash from different woods vary in degrees of alkalinity, and so its effectiveness in softening the hull will vary. When ashes cool, sift to store in covered container.

Soak corn overnight in a stainless steel pressure cooker with 4 cups water. (Stainless steel cookware is preferred over aluminum, especially in this case. The lye in the wood ash reacts strongly with aluminum to produce hydrogen gas, which is both flammable and explosive.)

In the morning, tie up measured amount of ashes in 2 thickness of cheesecloth and add to pot. Squeeze bag to permeate water with ashes. Bring to pressure and cook for 1 hour. Check corn at this time to see if hulls have loosened and corn is soft. If not, return to pressure to cook 1/2 hour more, or add 1/4 cup more ashes and water to cook longer.

If corn has softened, remove bag, drain liquid (good for the garden), and carefully rinse the corn until the water is completely clear. Rub the corn between your palms under water to loosen the hulls. Return corn to pressure with 4 cups fresh water and cook 1/2-1 hour more (less if corn is soft, more if still rather hard).

Strain out and reserve hominy broth from the final cooking to serve as a tea or in soups. Use hominy as is (see *Hominy Soup* [Pozole] recipe on page 7) or grind cooked corn in a steel mill to make masa. (See *Tortillas* recipe on page 41 for more information on making masa and one way to use it.) Grinding the corn in a steel mill is most easily done with a friend, as each of you can take turns grinding or pressing the kernels down into the hopper. A wooden pestle is helpful. Knead dough very briefly to form a cohesive dough.

Variation: **Whole Corn Thumbprint Dumplings** ♥ Form masa into 1-inch balls. Press thumb in center to make indentation and add to soups or stews just long enough to heat through.

Cornmeal Mush ♥ Fufu (African)

Makes 2-3 servings

Corn or maize was introduced into Africa, by way of the American Indians, by Spanish pioneers who planted it everywhere. It sustained the new settlers, along with Africa's indigenous grain, millet.

Roasted corn flour is known as mealie meal *to Central and South Africans, and as* ablemanu *to the West Africans. Both cornmeal mush and millet meal porridge are known as* foo foo *or* fufu *in West Africa,* ugali *in East Africa,* nshima *by the Zambians in Central Africa, and* putu *by the South Africans.*

Both cereals should be quite stiff when turned out of the pan, like polenta. In Africa, each person tears off walnut-sized balls and dips them into a stew or sauce. This practice is shared by the Hopi Indians in this country who call the dish *huzusuki.*

It's interesting to note that millet is still the staple ingredient in the national porridge of South Africa despite the introduction of corn.

Once I used fresh-ground red Indian corn in this dish. Since the inner portion is yellow and white just like yellow corn, the cereal turned out to be tri-colored with red specks accentuating the dish. The sweet grain corn taste is very satisfying.

1 cup corn flour or meal, lightly toasted
2 1/4 cups water
1/8 teaspoon unrefined sea salt

In a saucepan, soak flour in water overnight. Add sea salt and bring to boil, stirring occasionally to avoid sticking. (A wire whisk is helpful.) Place flame spreader under pot and cook covered over low heat for 1/2 hour, stirring occasionally. Allow to cool for at least 15 minutes to 1/2 hour, then transfer to a small wooden cutting board, plate, or bowl to serve.

For larger amounts, soak flour in just enough of the measured water to cover. When ready to cook bring remaining water to boil, add soaked mush and cook as usual.

Variations: **African Millet Meal Porridge** ♥ Substitute toasted millet flour for corn and proceed as above, increasing water to 2 1/2 cups.

Hopi Finger Bread ♥ Usually served with stews and eaten with the fingers. I've added salt and sage for flavor. Prepare as above, substituting blue cornmeal for yellow or white. Increase salt to 1/2 teaspoon and add 1 tablespoon fresh sage, minced, or 1 teaspoon dried. Transfer gruel to an oiled pie pan or 8-inch square baking dish and allow to set about 1/2 hour before serving. To use leftovers, slice and fry on both sides until crisp like *Scrapple* (see page 218). Makes 6-10 servings (less as major grain dish) or 4 cups.

Other corn recipes:

Corn 'n Amaranth Morning Cereal (page 208)
3-Grain Cereal (page 209)
Breakfast Grits (page 209)
Early American Scrapple (page 218)
Mexican Vegetable Soup with Cornmeal Dumplings (page 6)
Alison's Skillet Cornbread (page 38)
Carrot Cornbread (page 39)
Tequezquite-Leavened Cornbread, Cornsticks, and Mini-Muffins (page 39)
Tortillas (page 41)
Gelled Corn Pasta Salad (page 111)
Strawberry Shortcake, Blueberry and other *Corncake* recipes (page 184)
Latin American Squash in Hot Cinnamon Syrup (page 191)

Oats

Recipes featuring oats:

Oatmeal with Rice (page 211)
Oatmeal with Raisins (page 211)
Oatmeal with Granola, Trail Mix, or Muesli (page 211)
Hot Muesli Morning Cereal, Summer Muesli, and Cool Muesli (page 211)

Barley

Recipes featuring barley:

Tibetan Barley Cereal Tsampa (page 207)
Barley and Sweet Corn Salad (page 101)

Rye

Recipes featuring rye:

Rye and Wheat Cereal (page 207)
Black Bread (page 36)

Buckwheat

Recipes featuring buckwheat:

Buckwheat Noodles with Dipping Broth (page 44)

Amaranth

Grain amaranth was as important to the ancient Aztecs as corn and beans. Recently rediscovered, it is hailed as "the grain of the future" by agricultural researchers because of its nutritional superiority to all other cereals. Like quinoa, amaranth is hardier than corn or wheat. When combined with other whole grains, the new mixture becomes a complete protein the body can utilize more efficiently than soybeans or milk. (Amaranth contains lysine, the essential amino acid lacking in other grains.) Amaranth contains about 16% protein (compared with 13% is most wheats, 9% in corn, and 8% in rice), and is rich in vitamins A and C, and the minerals calcium and iron.

Amaranth has been selected as one of 4 cereal crops from among 400 with promising economic value by the National Academy of Sciences. The various types are adaptable to a wide range of growing conditions, from the wet tropics to semi-arid lands and from sea level to 10,000-foot mountains. Its drought-, heat-, and pest-resistant nature makes it an ideal crop for Third World countries as well as the U.S.

Cortez and the Spanish conquerors banned the cultivation of amaranth, because of its use in ceremonies involving human sacrifice, as part of the destruction of the Aztec empire in 1521. But enough seed survived and a few small farmers in Mexico and Central and South America still grow it today, where it is considered "Indian food."

Some time after Columbus, the seeds found their way to Asia where they are especially popular among farmers in the foothills of the Himalayas. In India, amaranth is known as "seed sent by God." (*San Francisco Chronicle*, "A Superfood from the Aztecs," by Jane E. Brody, October 28, 1984.)

Unlike grain plants with their narrow-leaved grasses, amaranth is a very tall, broad-leaved plant with huge seed heads containing up to half a million seeds per plant. Flowers range from purple to orange, red, and gold.

The leaves resemble spinach in flavor, but surpass other greens as a source of protein, calcium, and iron. Called vegetable amaranth, they are already popular in Greece and West Africa. (Pigweed is a wild edible variety of amaranth commonly found in this country.)

Today, Thailand, Kenya, and some South American countries have set up amaranth research stations. There are 20 farmers in the U.S. growing the crop, in addition to the work being done at the Rodale Research Center in Kutztown, Pennsylvania. One grower, New Waves of Grain Amaranth Company, was a source for this information.

I find amaranth to have a distinct flavor all its own, unrelated to any of the other grains. It is smaller in size than sesame seed. Boiled, its texture is gelatinous; dry-roasted, some kernels pop; but my favorite way to use amaranth is as flour, in combination with other flours. Used thusly, it adds a refreshing new taste to crackers, breads, and hot breakfast cereals.

Recipes featuring amaranth:

Whole Wheat 'n Amaranth Cereal (page 207)
Corn and Amaranth Morning Cereal (page 208)

Quinoa

Quinoa, pronounced keen-wa, is another ancient grain which is becoming popular in this country. It has been cultivated in the Andes Mountains of South America since at least 3000 B.C. and was known as "the mother grain" by the Incas who grew it along with corn and potatoes.

Like amaranth, the sacred grain of the Aztecs, quinoa production was suppressed by the Spanish during the conquest in the 16th century. However, peasants in the more remote areas continued to grow it; it remains a staple of millions of descendants of the Incan empire in Ecuador, Peru, Bolivia, Colombia, Argentina, and Chile.

According to *Newsweek* (December 11, 1984), although quinoa is presently dismissed by the upper classes in those countries as "Indian food," it is being researched as a potential super-food to feed the world. China is investigating some of the 2,000 strains.

Renewed interest in quinoa comes from its outstanding qualities. Easily grown under adverse weather and soil conditions, it is hardier than corn or wheat. It contains more protein than any other grain and the protein is complete. It is also a relatively good source of calcium, iron, phosphorus, vitamin E, and some of the B vitamins.

Quinoa is not a true cereal grain but is actually the fruit of the Chenopodium family which includes lamb's quarters. Its small seeds are similar to millet in shape but the appearance, taste, and texture are unique. The tan-colored seeds turn translucent with cooking and have a little white band, called the germ ring, encircling each kernel.

The first quinoa crop to be grown outside of South America was started in the Colorado Rockies in 1982 and is now appearing in natural foods stores across the country. I find quinoa to be a delightful culinary experience. It's delicious, satisfying, and yet so very light. It's also quick and easy to prepare, taking just 15 minutes, like bulgur.

For more information, contact the Quinoa Corporation, or see the fascinating article by Rebecca Theurer Wood, "Quinoa: Tale of a Food Survivor," which appeared in the April 1985 issue of *East West.*

Quinoa

Makes 4 cups

1 1/2 cups water
1 teaspoon-1 tablespoon natural soy sauce
1 cup quinoa

In a 1-quart saucepan, bring water to boil with soy sauce. Rinse quinoa thoroughly. Drain, then add to boiling stock. Stir to level. When boiling resumes, turn heat low to simmer until water is completely absorbed and grain is light and fluffy, about 15 minutes. Grains turn from tan to translucent. Transfer grain to serving bowl by fluffing with a fork.

Quinoa with Bulgur

Makes 3 cups or 3-4 servings

This grain dish is a great flavor combination!

1 1/2 cups water
1 teaspoon natural soy sauce
1/2 cup quinoa
1/2 cup bulgur

To prepare, follow directions in preceding recipe.

For larger volumes, increase ingredients proportionately.

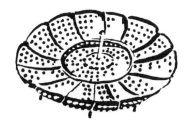

Simple to Sumptuous Vegetable Dishes

With textures ranging from crispy to creamy, brightly colored vegetables fulfill the need for foods which are light and refreshing. An abundant variety and sufficient quantity in the daily diet can help reduce cravings for sweets.

Vegetable cookery is a major focus in a good cook's repertoire. It is thus essential to learn to prepare them in all their variety— greens (for their upward/uplifting/expanded energy, and higher calcium and vitamin C contents than milk or fruit respectively), root vegetables (for their grounding energy), and sea vegetables (the most highly mineralized food source on the planet).

Simple vegetable dishes balance a meal in which other foods are more elaborately prepared with seasonings or oil. Steaming (cooking above boiling water), simmering (cooking in a small amount of boiling water), and quick-boiling/parboiling/ blanching (cooking completely immersed in boiling water) are fast, easy techniques which produce bright, clear, and clean-tasting vegetables. Flavors may be enhanced for further variety with simple dressings, or with a sprinkling of toasted seeds or nuts.

Basic Recipe for Oil-Free, Quick-Boiled/ Parboiled/Blanched Greens (or Combined Vegetables)

Makes about 3-6 servings (volume varies with type of greens, see chart on page 62)

Three different words describe the same quick-and-easy method of cooking greens or vegetable medleys so they are bright and tender. Greens may be cooked whole and cut afterward, or cut before cooking. Used in ethnic cooking worldwide, this method, plus cutting them after they have tenderized and shrunk in size, comes specifically from the Japanese cooking style called ohitashi. Although spinach or watercress is often featured in Japanese vegetable cookery, any greens shine when prepared this way, from the fresh, gentle taste of kale to the pleasantly bitter flavor of escarole.

The important things are not to overcook the greens and to use the broth! It makes a delicious beverage in place of tea or water, may be used to cook other vegetables, or used as a delicious liquid base for soups, sauces, or morning cereals such as oatmeal.

(Taste cooking broth to be sure flavor is mild; mustard and turnip greens, escarole and endive often give off a bitter flavor.) At the very least, use it to water house or garden plants.

See the variation for Quick-Boiled Greens with 1-, 2-, or 3-Taste Dressings *for a variety of delicious seasonings to expand eating pleasure. See the volume chart for greens following this recipe for estimating exact amounts.*

1/2 teaspoon unrefined sea salt (1/4 tea-
　　spoon per quart water), optional
2 quarts (8 cups) water
2 quarts (8 cups) greens
　　(hardy ones such as kale, collards,
　　mustard, cabbage, bok choy, or broc-
　　coli;
　　or soft greens such as Chinese cab-
　　bage/nappa, endive, escarole, or water-
　　cress); greens left whole, folded in half
　　and stuffed into measuring cup;
　　or ends trimmed, stems thinly sliced,
　　leaves halved or quartered lengthwise,
　　folded over to stack, then cut crosswise
　　in thin slices or in 1- to 3-inch sections

Bring (salted) water to boil in a 3 1/2- or 4-quart pot while you prepare and rinse the greens. Discard wilted, spoiled, or yellow parts of leaves. Add whole greens to boiling water and press down to completely sub-merge.

Cook until tender but bright green in color, 30 seconds to 5 minutes after adding greens to pot, less for blanching soft greens (30 seconds for soft crisp greens; or just 2 minutes for parboiling escarole or endive; about 3 minutes for bok choy, Chinese cabbage, and watercress); more for hardy greens (kale, collards, mustard, and green or red cabbage). Drain in strainer or colander, reserving broth for future use. (For small amounts, lifting greens from water is easy with a flat mesh strainer.)

Allow vegetables to cool naturally, or run them under cool water. Gently squeeze out excess liquid and cut in thin or thick (1-3 inches wide) slices. (One way to do this is to stack leaves with stem ends arranged together in the same direction. Roll up green into tubes to squeeze and slice.) Fluff up greens if compacted and serve, plain or dressed.

For large amounts, cut water by half or more and cook greens in several batches. This way you'll have less broth with a stronger flavor. Figure 1/2-1 cup cooked greens per serving. Greens pack down as they sit. If not serving right away, make more than you think you'll need, at least 1 cup cooked per serving.

Variations: **Blanched Cabbage with Escarole, Endive, and Carrot** ❤ *The pleasing bitter quality of escarole and endive is nicely balanced with the cabbage's milder taste. A pretty color combination as well.*

Prepare greens as above, substituting 1/4 total volume with endive and escarole. Include 1 medium-large carrot, thinly sliced in diagonals, half diagonals, or matchsticks. Cook all together until tender, about 5 minutes. Serve plain or dressed.

Blanched Chinese Cabbage and Red Onions ❤ Cut 1 red onion in thin slices, crescents, or rounds. If greens have been cut before cooking, cook onion with greens. Otherwise cook onion separately, then toss together.

Blanched Mustard Greens and Bean Sprouts ❤ Include 2 cups large sprouts such as mung bean or soybean. After greens have been cooked and drained, return water to boil. Add sprouts and cook about 30 seconds. Drain. Toss with greens.

Collard Greens with Toasted Pumpkin Seeds ❤ Include collard greens. After cooking, toss with 1/4 cup toasted pumpkin seeds which have been sprinkled with soy sauce (see page 136).

Season's Greens with Kernel Corn ❤ *Kernel corn is the name used in Colonial times to describe sweet corn off the cob.*

Include the kernels from 2 ears of corn. Cook corn with greens, or separately to serve vegetables side-by-side.

Kale

Collards

Mustard Greens

Bok Choy

Dandelion Greens

Cooking Greens

Type of Greens	1 lb. Raw in Cups	Same Volume Cooked
Kale	12-16 cups	2 1/2-4 cups
Mustard greens	8-14 cups	2-4 cups
Collard greens	12 cups	3-6 cups
Bok choy	7-9 cups	3 cups
Green cabbage	6 1/2 cups	4 cups
Red cabbage	5 cups	4 cups
Chinese cabbage/Nappa	8 cups	3 cups
Broccoli	4-6 cups	4 cups
Watercress	12 cups	4 cups
Endive	14 cups	2 1/2 cups
Escarole	12 cups	2 cups
Spinach	16 cups	1 1/2 cups

This chart is meant as a help when planning meals for large groups of people. The chart shows the volume cooked for a pound of each kind of greens. I usually plan 1/3-1/2 cup cooked greens per serving if a salad or another cooked green vegetable (as part of another dish such as a soup, stew, quiche, pasta salad, etc.) is to be served at the same meal. Figure 1/2-1 cup if it is the only green vegetable at the meal.

Greens are sold by the bunch or by the head. Often, but not always, bunches are weighed out to 1/2 or 1 pound each, but it's best to weigh them out yourself when buying by weight. The chart makes purchases easy.

Different cutting techniques cause yields to vary greatly. For the chart, most greens were rinsed, stacked in bunches, stem ends trimmed, stems very thinly sliced, leaves halved (or for very large greens, quartered) lengthwise, folded over to stack, and cut in 1-inch slices crosswise. They were then gently packed into the measuring cup.

All greens were added to 2 quarts (8 cups) boiling water in a 3 1/2- or 4-quart pot and pressed to completely submerge. They were cooked covered for 3-5 minutes, less for tender greens such as Chinese cabbage, watercress, endive, and escarole, more for the other, hardier greens. Broccoli is included as it is a green vegetable, albeit not a leafy green. Broccoli tops were separated into flowerets, edible portion of stems thinly sliced. Cabbages were thinly sliced including the core.

Recipes for Swiss chard, spinach, and beet greens do not appear in this book. Their high oxalic acid content which is known to bind calcium, preventing its absorption and possibly causing kidney stones, makes them less desirable than other greens for daily use. Other greens to enjoy are romaine and other lettuces; those from turnips; daikon and red radishes; carrot tops; and dandelion greens.

Quick-Boiled Greens (Or Other Vegetables) with 1-, 2-, or 3-Taste Dressings

Make delicious oil-free dressings with pickled plum (umeboshi) vinegar, brown rice vinegar, citrus juices (lemon, lime, and orange juices), soy sauce, tamari (wheat-free soy sauce), miso, or sweeteners such as Japanese sweet rice cooking wine (mirin), brown rice syrup, barley malt syrup, or pure maple syrup. To enhance flavors further, add flavorful oils such as olive or toasted sesame, and seasonings such as ginger, garlic, fresh or dried herbs, mustard, or horseradish.

Figure dressing ingredients at 1-2 teaspoons per cup cooked vegetables. To begin, combine equal parts of 2 dressing ingredients, then change amounts for subtle flavor variations according to taste.

Dressings for Greens and Other Vegetables

1-Taste Dressings

Choose one.

Pickled plum (umeboshi) vinegar
Vinegar (brown rice; apple cider; or balsamic or wine vinegar for Italian dishes)
Citrus juices (lemon, lime, or orange)
Natural soy sauce
Tamari (wheat-free soy sauce)
Miso (dilute in cooking broth)

2-Taste Dressings

Choose one combination.

Oil-Free:

Pickled plum (umeboshi) vinegar & brown rice vinegar
Ume vinegar & citrus juice
Ume vinegar & soy sauce or tamari or miso
Soy sauce or tamari or miso & brown rice vinegar
Soy sauce or tamari or miso & citrus juice
Soy sauce or tamari or miso & Japanese sweet rice cooking wine (mirin)

With oil:

Ume vinegar & toasted sesame oil or olive oil
Soy sauce or tamari & toasted sesame oil or olive oil

3-Taste Dressings

Add toasted sesame oil or olive oil and/or sweetener (brown rice syrup, malted barley syrup, pure maple syrup, or mirin to 1- or 2-Taste Dressings.

Veggie Sticks

Makes 4 servings

Veggie sticks make great crunchy snacks served raw or quick-boiled.

1 carrot, cut in quarters lengthwise, then in 4-inch lengths crosswise
8 sugar snap peas or 12 snow peas, or 8 green or yellow wax beans, threads or stem ends discarded
1 rib celery, halved lengthwise, then cut in 4-inch lengths crosswise
1/2 small cucumber or equivalent amount burpless Armenian cucumber or 1 lemon cuke, cut in 4-inch lengths crosswise, then in eighths lengthwise
1 cup water to blanch vegetables, if desired

Serve as is, or quick-boil carrot and peas or beans, and celery if desired, until crisp-tender, about 1 minute.

Blanched Broccoli, Carrot, and Summer Squash

Makes 4 servings or 4 1/2 cups

A beautiful spectrum of summer and early fall garden colors are combined in this very simple vegetable dish. When serving firm vegetables such as these, which hold their shape with cooking, figure 1 cup per serving.

1/4 teaspoon unrefined sea salt (optional)
1 quart (4 cups) water
1 carrot, sliced in 1/4-inch thick diagonals
2 cups broccoli, cut in 3-inch long, bite-size flowerets

1 cup yellow summer squash (scallopini, golden zucchini, or crookneck), scallopini cut in wedges 1-inch across at widest point, others cut in 1/2-inch rounds
1 cup green summer squash (patty pan or zucchini), patty pan cut in wedges 1-inch across at widest point, zucchini cut in 1/2-inch rounds

Bring (salted) water to boil in 3-quart pot. Add carrot and cook about 3 minutes, then add broccoli and squash and cook 5 minutes more. Drain, reserving broth for future use. Serve plain or dressed.

For large amounts, boil vegetables separately to be sure cooking time is proper for each vegetable.

Blanched Greens with Carrots and Shiitake Mushrooms

Makes 4 servings or 4 cups

2 quarts (8 cups) water
1 large carrot, thinly sliced in diagonals
8 cups Chinese cabbage or bok choy, whole head quartered lengthwise, then cut in 1-inch slices crosswise, cabbage core thinly sliced
4 cooked shiitake mushrooms from *Light Lemon-Miso Broth* (see recipe on page 9), hard stem portions discarded, tops thinly sliced

Bring water to boil in a 3 1/2- or 4-quart pot Add carrot and cook about 3 minutes. Add greens to pot and continue to cook until crisp-tender, about 3 minutes more. Drain, reserving broth for use in soup or as stock for cooking grains.

To serve, simply toss vegetables together. Dress if desired.

For large amounts, cut water by 1/2 or more and cook in several batches. Soft greens such as these are often done just when boiling resumes.

Corn on the Cob with Pickled Plum (Umeboshi)

For irresistible, cholesterol- and fat-free corn on the cob with a flavor which rivals butter and salt, try rubbing with the beautiful bright red Japanese plum called umeboshi. Ume (for short) has been pickled in salt and is known for its medicinal qualities as well as its fine flavor. This sounds strange at first, but is really delicious!

To prepare corn, husk and scrub with vegetable brush to remove silk. Add to boiling water to cook until tender, about 3-7 minutes, less for very fresh, tender corn. Figure 1/3-1 plum per person depending on size, or tear plums in quarters or halves to serve with fresh-cooked corn.

Corn Baked in the Husk

For a rich, fresh corn flavor, try baking un-husked corn on the cob. Preheat oven to 400°. Bake until kernels inside are soft, about 1/2 hour. Nutrients are retained or sealed in as the corn cooks in its own juices. This method also makes corn silk very easy to remove. Allow to cool briefly, then discard husks to serve.

For flavor variation, brush with a mixture of 1 tablespoon umeboshi vinegar and 1 teaspoon corn oil. This is enough for 2-3 ears.

umeboshi plums

Steamed Vegetables

Steaming is another way to prepare simple, clean-tasting vegetables, free of salt, oil, or seasoning. Especially nice in the summertime, they satisfy the need for the light taste year-round. They may be dressed with any of the dressings or sauces in that section.

Steamers come in a variety of forms. The stainless steel, fold-up variety available in most hardware/kitchen stores fits inside a pot to hold the vegetables above the water. The Chinese bamboo steamer basket fits over a pan of water which is slightly larger at the rim than the basket to prevent burning over high heat. Some pots are specifically made with holes in the bottom for steaming over another pot of water.

Basic Steamed Vegetables Recipe

Rinse or scrub vegetables and cut them in similar shapes and size (wedges, slivers, chunks, cubes, rounds, etc.). Figure 1 - 1 1/2 cups firm vegetables or 1 1/2 - 3 cups greens (before cooking) per serving. Place in steamer over water, cover and bring to boil. Steam until done, 5 minutes or more depending on size and variety of vegetable. Serve plain or dressed.

Steamed Cabbage Wedges

Figure 1 cabbage serves 12 to 16. Cut bottom stem off and discard any imperfect outer leaves. Cut cabbage in half from top to bottom. Cut each half in wedges, including a little stem in each slice to hold leaves together. Steam until tender, about 5 minutes.

Simply Steamed Vegetables with Ume Vinegar

Makes 4 servings or 4 cups

Any seasonal vegetables may be substituted for this colorful summer and fall combination.

1 cup yellow summer squash, thinly sliced in half moons
1 cup patty pan squash, halved from top to bottom, then thinly sliced in wedges
1 cup kohlrabi, halved and thinly sliced in half moons
1 cup purple cabbage, thinly sliced
1/2 cup carrot, thinly sliced in half moons
1 tablespoon pickled plum (ume) vinegar (3/4 teaspoon per cup vegetables)

Steam vegetables until tender, 5-7 minutes. Transfer to serving bowl, dress, and gently toss.

Broccoli and Cauliflower with Ume-Rice Vinegar Dressing and Toasted Sesame Seeds

Makes 3-4 servings

Water to steam
2 cups broccoli, hard bottom stem portion
  discarded, stem cut in thin diagonals,
  top separated in bite-size flowerets
2 cups cauliflower, stem thinly sliced, top
  separated in bite-size flowerets

Ume-Rice Vinegar Dressing:
Makes 2 tablespoons
1 tablespoon pickled plum (umeboshi)
  vinegar
1 tablespoon brown rice vinegar
1/2 teaspoon sesame seeds, toasted

Prepare vegetables according to *Basic Steamed Vegetables Recipe* on preceding page. Mix dressing ingredients. Drain vegetables, transfer to serving bowl, and dress to serve. Avoid stirring, and possibly breaking vegetables.

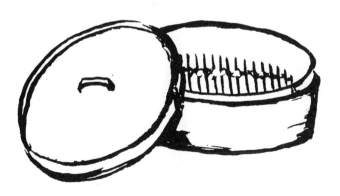

Simmered Vegetables

Known by many as steaming, simmering is actually done without a steamer, as the vegetables cook in a small amount of liquid.

To cut down on oil, substitute a little water for the oil in a sautéd vegetable dish. This is known as the water-sauté technique and, of course, is the same as simmering.

Red and Green Shiso Cabbage

Makes 4 servings

1/4 cup water (to cover pan by 1/8 inch)
1 tablespoon red shiso leaf, minced or
  powdered
2 cups red cabbage, about 1/4 small-
  medium head, sliced
2 cups green cabbage, about 1/4 small-
  medium head, sliced

In a 2-quart pan place water and shiso leaf, then the red cabbage, and then the green cabbage on top. This way the red color doesn't spread to color the green. Bring to boil, cover, and simmer until done, 8-10 minutes. Stir to mix just before serving.

For large amounts, barely cover bottom of pan with water, about 1/2 inch, since so much liquid comes out of the cabbage.

Note: Drizzling vinegar over red cabbage revives its color from dull purple to a bright purple-pink. Figure either 1 tablespoon brown rice vinegar or 2 tablespoons umeboshi vinegar per pound cabbage.

Variation: **Shiso-Simmered Kohlrabi**
♥ *Often ignored, kohlrabi has a pretty, light green color and a refreshing flavor. A member of the cabbage family, it is just as versatile and deserves attention during the summer and fall months when it is in season.*

Instead of cabbage, include 4 cups kohlrabi bulbs and greens (bulbs peeled only if difficult to cut), bulbs and greens thinly sliced (rounds, half- or quarter-moons, or slivers). Cover bottom of pan 1-inch deep in water, add shiso and kohlrabi, and cook as before. Makes 4-6 servings.

Specialty Vegetable Dishes

Vegetable Crudités with Creamy Mustard Dip

Makes 4 servings

Vegetable crudités are crunchy, raw or lightly cooked vegetables which are served as finger foods. The brief cooking maximizes flavor and color. Served with a bowl of dip, they are often accompanied by crackers and chips on hors d'oeuvres or appetizer platters.

More artful presentations range from containers such as hollowed-out pumpkins, squashes, or red and green cabbages, to baskets, trays, and wooden or earthenware bowls. Great served at a picnic or party, any colorful combination of vegetables pleases. As Martha Stewart points out in Entertaining *(Clarkson N. Potter, Inc., New York, 1982), "Crudités are not just a haphazard bowl of cut-up carrot and celery sticks; they are closer to a good still life, an artful edible exhibit."*

2 cups water
1 cup red radish
1 cup daikon radish
1 cup carrot
1 cup string beans and/or yellow wax beans
1 cup kohlrabi or broccoli

Creamy Mustard Dip/Basic Dip Recipe:
Makes 1 cup

1/2 pound tofu, fresh
1 tablespoon pickled plum (umeboshi) vinegar

1 tablespoon brown rice vinegar
1 tablespoon wet mustard
Water, only if necessary to blend (start with
    1 tablespoon)

To prepare vegetables, cut them in similar, easy-to-hold shapes, about 3 inches in length and 1/4-inch wide. Bring water to boil and cook separately until crisp-tender, about 3-5 minutes, less for radishes, more for string beans and kohlrabi. Drain. To serve cool, run under cold water or place in refrigerator. However, vegetables may be served warm or at room temperature as well.

To make dip, boil or steam whole block of tofu for 2 minutes and drain. Blend until creamy smooth with remaining ingredients.

Arrange vegetables nicely on serving platter with dip in a container in the center or at the side.

Dip variations: Substitute soy sauce for ume vinegar and lemon juice for rice vinegar. Omit mustard and substitute other seasonings such as onion, garlic, fresh or dry herbs, horseradish, ginger, etc. To make into salad dressings, add 1/4-1/2 cup water and taste to see if you need to adjust seasonings. Try the *Creamy Dill Dressing* (see page 124), or *Tofu "Sour Cream"* (see page 122) or *Thousand Island Dressing* (see page 125) made with less water. Some spreads also may be used successfully as dips with the addition of a little water.

Spring Crudité Platter ❤ Include snow or sugar snap peas, asparagus spears, and carrots. Figure 4 peas, 3 asparagus, and 1/4 large carrot per serving. Remove and discard strings from peas. Snap asparagus as far down to the bottom of the stem as possible, discarding hard bottom portion. Cut carrots in half lengthwise, then in 1/4-inch diagonals. Boil peas just 1/2-1 minute,

asparagus about 3 minutes, and carrots for 5.

Other vegetable possibilities: cauliflower; green, red, yellow, or white onions; green, red, or orange sweet pepper strips; turnip; rutabaga; parsnips; celery and cucumber (the last 2 served raw).

Vegetables with Italian Herb Paste ❤ Pesto

Makes 4 servings

Italian Herb Paste (Pesto):
                Makes 1 - 1 1/4 cups
Pesto is an Italian herb paste based on fresh basil. The word pesto translates to mean pounded in Italian. Traditionally ground together in a mortar and pestle, modern recipes call for blending in a blender or food processor with equally delicious results.

Even without cheese and just half the oil used in most recipes, this version doesn't sacrifice pesto's irresistible flavor. A must during the summer and early fall when basil is fresh, it serves as a topping for pasta, rice, cooked vegetables, salad, or in soup.

2 cups fresh basil, about 3/4-1 bunch,
    stems and any discolored leaves dis-
    carded, gently packed
2 large cloves garlic, chopped
1/2 cup walnuts or pine nuts, lightly
    toasted
2 tablespoons extra virgin olive oil
1/2 teaspoon unrefined sea salt
1 tablespoon natural soy sauce
Up to 1/4 cup water

Vegetables:

1 medium carrot, cut in 1 1/2-inch pieces
    across, then in 1/4-inch slices length-
    wise
1 medium red onion, halved from top to
    bottom, then cut in 1/4-inch slices or
    crescents
1 1/2 cups cauliflower, separated into bite-
    size flowerets, stems and core cut in
    1/4-inch slices
1 1/2 cups broccoli, tops separated into bite-
    size flowerets, edible portion of stems
    cut like carrots, hard skin discarded
1 cup green beans (or peas with edible
    pods), ends discarded, beans cut in
    thirds, about 1/4 pound

To prepare pesto, blend ingredients until
smooth.

   To prepare vegetables, quick-boil (about
5 minutes) or steam (about 8-15 minutes)
until done. Vegetables may be cooked together except green beans which may take
longer. Gently mix vegetables to distribute
colors evenly. Spoon a dollop of pesto atop
each serving or mix 1/2 cup into vegetables
in serving bowl, reserving a few undressed
vegetables to place on top for color clarity.

   Variation: **Winter Pesto** ❤ Substitute
fresh parsley for fresh basil and include
about 1/4 cup dried basil in the total volume.

   Should this pesto sit long and the dry
herb absorb moisture, add a little more water or oil for texture desired.

Acorn Squash Cups filled with White Bean Chili

Makes 4 servings

2 small acorn squash, cut in half through
    the middle, seeds removed, ends cut off
    to make flat surface for serving
3 cups *Chili Beans* (see recipe on page 148)
1 tablespoon parsley, chopped for garnish

To cook squash, boil in water to cover or
steam until done, 20 minutes or more. Or
for richer flavor, bake squash. Preheat oven
to 450°. Place hollowed-out side down on
baking sheet and bake until squash is easily
pierced, about 20-30 minutes.

   To serve, fill squash cups generously
with chili beans and garnish with parsley.
You may want to cut one squash cup in half
for smaller portions.

Patty Pan Squash with Sesame-Onion Sauce

Makes 4-8 servings

4 medium or 8 small patty pan summer
    squash (also called scallop or saucer
    squash when light green, scallopini
    when dark green, and yellow or sun-
    burst scallopini when yellow), ends
    trimmed
Water to cover squash

Sesame-Onion Sauce:

Makes 2/3 cup

1/2 onion, cut in 1/2-inch dice
1/4 cup water
2 tablespoons sesame butter

1 tablespoon natural soy sauce
1 tablespoon parsley, minced for garnish

Bring squash in water to boil. Cook until easily pierced with a small sharp knife, about 15 minutes.

To make sauce, place onion and water in small saucepan and bring to boil. Slow-boil until soft, about 10 minutes. Add sesame butter and soy sauce and stir well. For large amounts, cook onions in water to barely cover. If sauce is watery, cook uncovered to thicken.

To hollow out squash for stuffing, transfer squash to cutting board and cut a circle on top to where scallops begin. Scoop out inside portion to about halfway through squash and fill with sauce.

Transfer filled squashes to oven-proof pan. Broil until top is browned, about 5-10 minutes. (For amounts too large to fit in the broiler, bake squash to brown.) Very large squash may be halved to serve (after baking) if smaller portions are desired. Garnish.

Variations: Sesame-Onion Sauce is good on kasha, rice, and noodles. Add a little more water for pourable texture.

Nutty Miso Stuffed Patty Pan ❤ For an even simpler dish which is quicker to prepare, omit onion. When ready to make filling, simply whisk together 1/4 cup of your choice of nut butter, 1 tablespoon miso, and 1/4 cup hot squash cooking broth. Add broth gradually to desired consistency. Include a few chopped nuts in sauce for added texture. Makes 1/2 cup.

Kale

Simple to Savory Ethnic Sautés

Basic Onion Family-Greens Sauté Recipe

Makes about 3-6 servings
(volume varies with type of greens)

When cooked greens are mixed with sautéd onions and seasoned, as Europeans do, a richer dish is created.

1 tablespoon flavorful oil (olive or toasted sesame)
1 onion (yellow, white, or red, or 2 leek whites, or 4 green onions [scallions], or 8 shallots), thinly sliced
1 tablespoon natural soy sauce or 1/2 teaspoon unrefined sea salt, or half of each

Quick-boil or steam greens according to basic recipes on pages 60 and 66. While greens cook, in a small skillet heat oil and sauté onion until tender, about 5 minutes. Add cooked greens, stir well, sprinkle with soy sauce and/or salt, and stir again. Serve.

For large amounts, decrease water by at least half and boil greens in several batches. This way you're left with less, but stronger-flavored, broth.

Variations: **Shallot-Kale Sauté** ❤ Substitute shallots for onion, and include kale as greens. Sauté shallots until tender, about 3 minutes, and proceed as above. Yields 3 cups.

Shallot-Savoy Sauté ❤ Include savoy cabbage with core, thinly sliced. Yields 4 cups.

Season's Greens Sautéd with Fresh Mushrooms ❤ Substitute 1 cup your choice of fresh mushrooms (3 ounces standard white mushrooms), thinly sliced, for onion family member, or cook mushrooms along with onion.

Garlic-Greens Sauté ❤ Substitute 4 cloves regular or elephant garlic, thinly sliced, for onions.

Garlic-Mushroom-Greens Sauté ❤ Include garlic and mushrooms from previous variations.

Onions and Greens (Native American)

Makes 6-8 servings or 6 cups

Having learned that onions and greens are a popular dish with some Native Americans, but not having come across a recipe, I offer this simple but tasty version. Pumpkin seed oil adds a particularly special, rich flavor

1 tablespoon sunflower, pumpkin seed, or
    corn oil
1 onion, cut in 1/4-inch slices from top to
    bottom
1/2 head savoy or other cabbage, 8 cups
    gently packed or about 1 1/2 pounds,
    cut in half from top to bottom, core re-
    moved and thinly sliced, cabbage cut in
    1/4-inch slices crosswise
1/4 teaspoon unrefined sea salt
1/2 cup water
2 cups kale or other dark greens, thinly
    sliced; or watercress or sunflower
    sprouts, cut in 2-inch lengths, ends
    trimmed off sprouts

In a large skillet or 3-quart pot, heat oil and sauté onions until partially soft, about 5 minutes over medium-low heat. Add cabbage and stir, then sprinkle with salt and add water. Bring to boil over high heat, then slow-boil covered until almost done, about 5 minutes. Add kale, stir, and cook until tender, about 5 minutes, or add watercress or sprouts, stir, and cook about 2 minutes more.

For large amounts, sauté onions and sprinkle them with salt. Omit water. Quick-boil greens with water to cover, drain, and add to sautéd onions to serve. Figure 3/4 cup per serving.

Yellow Summer Squash Sauté

Makes 2-3 servings or 2 1/2 cups

This vegetable dish is beautiful served along-side a brightly colored cooked greens dish or a salad.

2 teaspoons oil (sesame, plain or toasted, or olive)
1 onion, cut in 1/2-inch rounds or slices
2 yellow zucchini or crookneck, or 3 yellow scallopini squashes, about 3/4 pound, cut in 1/2-inch rounds or wedges
1/8 teaspoon unrefined sea salt
1/4 cup water

Heat oil in skillet. Add onion and sauté until barely tender, about 5 minutes. Add squash. Sprinkle with salt, add water, and cover to cook until tender, about 10 minutes. Water should be gone when vegetables are done.

For large amounts, so as not to mash tender squash, sauté onions alone, sprinkling them with sea salt. Quick-boil squash separately. Drain. Add to onions and mix.

Green Vegetable Gumbo (Southern)

Serves 4-6, less without, more with okra

Gumbo is the African word for okra. Filé is a powder made from dried sassafras leaves, discovered by the Choctaw Indians. In wealthy Southern homes of the past the cooks were blacks whose ancestors contributed some of the earliest important Creole dishes such as gumbo, now considered indigenous to New Orleans. Most gumbos are thickened with either okra or filé, except Green Gumbo. This stew-like vegetable dish is an unusual type which originally contained no meat and is thickened with flour. Once a Lenten dish, legend has it that you make as many friends as the number of different greens you put in. Okra is added optionally as it is often unavailable. Serve over boiled long grain brown rice or as a side dish.

In general, Southern gumbos, jamba-layas (see page 25), and stews all begin with a roux which is simply a mixture of fat and flour browned slowly. Small amounts of unrefined vegetable oil and whole-grain flour give the same rich texture and taste.

2 quarts (8 cups) water
2 quarts (8 cups) mixed greens (collard, mustard, turnip, radish greens, green cabbage, watercress, green onions, parsley, or carrot tops), folded in half and stuffed into measuring cup
6 okra (optional)
1 tablespoon sesame oil
1 cup onion, thinly sliced from top to bottom
1/4 cup whole-wheat flour
1/2 teaspoon unrefined sea salt
1/2 teaspoon celery seeds

Bring water to boil. Add whole greens and okra and cook until bright green and just tender, about 3 minutes. Drain and reserve liquid. Finely slice vegetables.

Heat oil and sauté onion until soft. Sprinkle with flour and stir well. Layer greens and seasonings on top. Add 1/2 cup cooking broth, bring to boil, then slow-boil covered until liquid forms sauce, about 5 minutes.

For larger amounts, boil the greens in half the water or less, in several batches if necessary. Decrease amount of broth added for sauce to 1/3 cup (i.e., for 6 times recipe, add 2 cups cooking broth).

Millet "Mashed Potatoes" with Country Gravy

Makes 5 servings

This version of an old macrobiotic favorite looks like mashed potatoes with a pleasing flavor and texture all its own. See page 117 for an explanation to the question, "Why not use potatoes as an everyday vegetable?"

Millet "Mashed Potatoes":

Makes 3 3/4 - 5 1/2 cups

1 cup millet
1 tablespoon sunflower oil (or other kind)
1 onion, coarsely chopped
2 cups cauliflower, about 1/2 pound, coarsely chopped, well packed
2 - 2 1/2 cups water, less for pressure cooking, more for boiling
1/2 teaspoon unrefined sea salt

Country Gravy:

Makes 12 servings or 1 1/2 cups

Sunflower oil and an herbed, soy-flavored stock lend their rich flavors as welcome replacements for the usual high-fat gravy ingredients, meat drippings and bouillon.

2 tablespoons sunflower oil (or other kind)
1/3 cup whole-wheat pastry flour
2 cups cool water
1 tablespoon natural soy sauce
1 teaspoon unrefined sea salt
1 tablespoon fresh sage, minced, or 1 1/2 teaspoons dried, crushed
2 tablespoons parsley, minced

Rinse and drain millet. In pressure cooker or pot, heat oil and sauté onion briefly. Add millet and continue to sauté. Add remaining ingredients, cover, and bring to pressure or boil. Turn heat low to pressure-cook for 15 minutes or boil for 1/2 hour. No flame spreader needed.

To prepare gravy, in a skillet or saucepan heat oil, add flour, and stir until oil is completely absorbed. Set pan aside to cool, about 15 minutes. Mix remaining ingredients except parsley and gradually add liquid to flour, stirring with a wire whisk to avoid lumping. (Gravy should be no more than 1 inch deep in pan in order for it to cook in this brief amount of time.) When all liquid is added, bring mixture to boil, stirring occasionally. Lower heat to simmer uncovered until desired consistency is reached, 10-15 minutes. Stir in parsley in last 2 minutes of cooking. (For larger amounts, increase ingredients proportionately, but allow more time for cooking, about 1/2 hour for 4X recipe.)

When millet is done, while still hot, purée mixture in food processor or Foley Food Mill (also known as a ricer) until smooth, or mash ingredients well. Transfer to serving bowl and allow to sit for about 10-15 minutes before serving for texture to firm up to proper consistency. Serve with gravy poured over or at the side.

Variation: **Millet "Mashed Potato" Casserole** ♥ Preheat oven to 350°. Prepare as above reserving 1 teaspoon oil, then transfer mixture to corn-oiled pie pan or casserole dish. Smooth surface. Mix remaining 1 teaspoon oil with 1 tablespoon soy sauce and drizzle it over top. Bake for 1/2 hour. Let sit 15 minutes before serving. Makes 9 servings.

Chinese Mixed Vegetables in Brown Sauce

Makes 3 servings or 3 cups

This dish uses almost all the types of vegetables we saw in the outdoor market in Shanghai in late November.

3 dried shiitake mushrooms
Water to cover shiitake
1 teaspoon-1 tablespoon sesame oil
1 onion, cut in 1/4-inch slices
1 small carrot, cut in 1/8-inch diagonals
1 rib celery, cut in 1/4-inch diagonals
2-inch piece daikon radish or turnip, daikon cut in 1/4-inch diagonals, turnip cut in half, each half cut in 1/4-inch diagonals
1 cup broccoli, edible stem portion cut in 1/4-inch diagonals, head separated in small flowerets
1/2 cup cauliflower, stem cut in 1/4-inch slices, head separated in small flowerets

Brown Sauce:

Makes 1 cup

1 cup mushroom cooking broth and/or water
1/4 cup whole-wheat flour
3 tablespoons natural soy sauce

Boil dried mushrooms in water to cover generously until soft, 15-20 minutes. Drain, reserving liquid to use in sauce. When mushrooms have cooled somewhat, cut off and discard hard stems, and cut caps in halves or quarters.

Heat oil and sauté onion briefly, then add carrot, cover and cook until slightly done, several minutes. Add other vegetables and cover to cook over medium-low heat until crispy-soft in texture, about 10 minutes more.

Make sauce by mixing ingredients in a small saucepan. Place over high heat and stir with a wire whisk until sauce thickens, then simmer uncovered 5 minutes more. Pour sauce over vegetables and mushrooms and mix gently to serve.

This recipe works well for large groups by simply increasing all ingredients proportionately. Pour a little sauce over each serving instead of trying to stir large volumes of vegetables with sauce and possibly breaking them.

Seasoned Vegetables ♥ Tagine (Moroccan)

Makes 3-4 servings

Tagines are vegetable dishes which are simmered long and slow in a glazed earthenware pot. This version is quicker and simpler, and very delicious.

1 tablespoon extra virgin olive oil
2 large cloves garlic, minced
2 cups cauliflower, separated in small
    flowerets
1 cup pumpkin or winter squash (substitute
    summer squash in its season), cut in
    1-inch chunks
1/2 teaspoon unrefined sea salt
3/4 cup water
1/2 teaspoon cumin
1/4 teaspoon oregano
1/4 teaspoon basil
2 cups cabbage, cut in 1-inch squares
1/8 teaspoon paprika for garnish
2 tablespoons green onion tops, cut in 1-
    inch pieces for garnish

Heat oil and sauté garlic briefly. Add cauliflower and pumpkin or squash. Dissolve salt in half the water and pour over vegetables. Stir, cover, and cook over medium-low heat until vegetables are barely tender, about 7 minutes.

Mix cumin, oregano, and basil in remaining water. Stir vegetables, add cabbage and seasoned water. Cover and continue to cook until vegetables are soft with a light, gravy-like broth, about 10-15 minutes, less with summer squash, more with winter squash. Serve vegetables with broth. Garnish with paprika and green onions.

For large amounts, to preserve color and texture, cook squash first, then add cabbage. Substitute broccoli for half the cauliflower and boil both before adding them at the end.

Vegetables, North Indian Style

Makes 4 servings

1 tablespoon sesame oil
2 teaspoons coriander
1 teaspoon cumin
1/2 teaspoon turmeric
1/2 teaspoon unrefined sea salt
4 1/4 cups water
2 onions, cut in 1/2-inch slices
12 mushrooms, cut in 1/2-inch slices
1 carrot, cut in 1/2-inch rounds
2 cups summer squash or cauliflower,
    squash cut in 1/2-inch rounds (quar-
    tered lengthwise first if large), cauliflow-
    er separated into large flowerets, then
    stems cut in 1/2-inch slices lengthwise
    up through flowerets
4 cups mustard greens, folded in half and
    stuffed into measuring cup

Heat oil, add seasonings and sauté, then add 1/4 cup water and stir well. Add onions and cook until they soften somewhat, then add mushrooms, carrots, and cauliflower if used. Stir, cover, and simmer over medium-low heat until almost done, stirring occasionally, about 15 minutes.

Meanwhile, boil whole mustard greens in 4 cups water until almost done, about 3 minutes. Drain and slice.

Add squash to vegetables and cook several minutes, then add greens and heat through to serve.

For large amounts, halve water for both greens and other vegetables.

Stroganoff (Russian)

Makes 4 servings or 4 cups

First made for a Russian Count Stroganoff in the 1880s, this version of the classic Russian dish includes onions, mushrooms, and wheatmeat or tempeh. It's a good example of how to substitute for beef, butter, sour cream (one of the characteristic features of Russian cooking) and yogurt. According to one Russian source, the secret of the sauce is the mustard.

Wild, edible mushrooms are eagerly, if not wildly, sought in Russia. Since they are most likely dried for winter use, we've included that kind here, although fresh mushrooms work well, too, at double the volume.

The Russian cookbooks I consulted recommended serving stroganoff over fresh boiled rice or as a side dish, but it's also great served over whole-grain ribbon noodles, bulgur wheat, whole-wheat bread or toast, or any baked grain dish which the Russians call kasha.

1 tablespoon corn oil

1 large onion, cut in 1/2-inch slices

1 cup dried shiitake mushrooms, cooked, stems discarded, and cut in 1/2-inch slices (see *Sauerkraut Soup* recipe on page 13) or 2 cups fresh mushrooms, sliced

6 tablespoons whole-wheat flour

2 cups water

1/4 cup natural soy sauce

1 cup *Wheatmeat* (see recipe on page 49), cut in thin strips

1/2 cup *Tofu "Sour Cream"* (see recipe on page 122)

1 teaspoon wet mustard

1/4 cup fresh dill or parsley, minced for garnish

Heat oil and sauté onion (and fresh mushrooms if included) until soft. Sprinkle flour over onions and stir in well. Mix water and soy sauce and add to onions with cooked dried mushrooms and wheatmeat. Bring to boil, stirring with a flat-bottomed wooden spoon to prevent flour from sticking. Turn flame low and simmer 10 minutes, covered, stirring occasionally. Turn heat off.

Mix tofu "sour cream" with mustard and add to pot when it has cooled down just slightly, after about 5 minutes. Garnish to serve.

For large amounts, whisk together until smooth flour, water, and soy sauce. Add this mixture to onions and stir to make a gravy. Proceed to add mushrooms and wheatmeat.

Variations: **Tempeh Stroganoff ♥** Substitute tempeh for wheatmeat. Cut an 8-ounce package of tempeh in 1/3-inch slices and prepare according to *Tempeh Cutlet* recipe on page 153. Add tempeh just before serving to retain its shape.

For a simplified version without the wheatmeat or tempeh, just substitute more onions. For large groups, when you don't want to go through the effort of making a lot of wheatmeat, cut volume in half to 1/2 cup and increase onions to 2 large. Increase all ingredients proportionately.

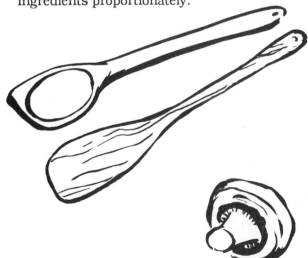

Main Dish Casseroles and Pies

Mixed Baked Squash, Southern Style

Makes 3 servings

Heavy tofu "cream" with herbs substitutes well for the dairy cream used in the original version of this southern recipe.

3 cups mixed summer and winter squash (yellow, patty pan, and acorn), hard seeds removed and squash cut in bite-size chunks
Heavy Tofu "Cream" with Herbs (recipe follows)
1 tablespoon green onion tops, sliced for garnish

Heavy Tofu "Cream" with Herbs:

Makes 1/2 cup

2 ounces tofu, fresh, about 1/3 cup
1 teaspoon natural soy sauce
1/8 teaspoon each rosemary and coriander
3 tablespoons water

Preheat oven to 450°.

Oil a 1-quart casserole or baking dish. Mix squash chunks and transfer to casserole.

Prepare tofu "cream" by blending ingredients until smooth. Pour over squash. Cover dish to bake until squash is tender, about 40 minutes. Uncover and return to oven until top is nicely browned, about 10 minutes more. Garnish to serve.

Vegetable Pot Pie

Makes 8 servings

Stock:

1 quart water
1 tablespoon natural soy sauce
1 teaspoon corn oil
1 teaspoon thyme

Vegetables:

1 onion
1/2 carrot
1/2 turnip, rutabaga, or parsnip
1/4 head green cabbage
1/2 cup peas, if edible pod variety, cut in 1-inch slices (optional, in season)
1 cup *Wheatmeat* (see recipe on page 49)

Gravy:

Makes a little more than 1 cup
1 cup hot stock
1/3 cup whole-wheat pastry flour
2 tablespoons natural soy sauce

Top Cutout Crust:

3/4 cup whole-wheat pastry flour
1/4 cup corn flour or meal
1/8 teaspoon unrefined sea salt
2 tablespoons light vegetable oil
1/4 cup warm stock
1/8 teaspoon thyme

Bring stock ingredients to boil. Preheat oven to 350°.

Cut vegetables and wheatmeat into 1-inch chunks. Add root vegetables to boiling stock and when boiling resumes, turn heat down to slow-boil for 5 minutes. Add cabbage and peas and cook 5 minutes more. Strain out vegetables and measure stock.

To make gravy, return 1 cup hot stock to pot and add flour and soy sauce. Stir with wire whisk over high heat until mixture becomes smooth and thick, in 1-2 minutes. Pour gravy over vegetables, add wheatmeat chunks, and mix well. Transfer to lightly-oiled pie pan.

Make top crust by mixing dry ingredients. Add oil, then warm stock. Mix well, knead briefly to form a cohesive ball, and roll out to a thin round. Sprinkle thyme over surface and press it in with a rolling pin. To make a decorative air vent, cut a hole in the center of the dough with a cookie cutter. Lay pastry on top of pie filling and tuck edges under all the way around. Poke holes on top only if you haven't used the cookie cutter.

Bake for 1/2 hour.

For large amounts, increase ingredients proportionately.

Variation: Omit wheatmeat and substitute another 1/2 carrot and turnip.

Garden Vegetable Pie in Pistachio Pastry

Makes 8 servings

Vegetables and Nuts for Filling:

1 cup onion, cut in 1/2-inch dice
1 cup carrot, cut in 1/2-inch dice
2 cups broccoli, tops separated into flowerets
2 cups cauliflower, separated into flowerets
1/2 cup pistachio nuts, toasted and coarsely chopped (1 cup in their shells yields 1/2 cup nuts; salted nuts are fine here)

Pistachio Gravy for Filling:

Makes 2 cups

3 tablespoons pistachio nut butter
2 cloves garlic, chopped
1 teaspoon each cumin and oregano, or 2 teaspoons dill
3 tablespoons natural soy sauce
3/4 cup whole-wheat pastry flour, or up to half the volume of organic, unbleached white flour
2 cups vegetable broth or part water

Pistachio Pastry (Double Crust Pastry):

3 cups whole-wheat pastry flour, or up to half organic, unbleached white flour
1/2 cup pistachio nuts, toasted and finely-ground (makes 1/4 cup nut meal)
1/2 teaspoon sea salt
1/2 cup light vegetable oil (canola oil or part corn oil)
1/2-1 cup water

Preheat oven to 400°.

Steam vegetables until tender, about 7 minutes.

To make gravy, purée ingredients in a food processor or blender, adding water gradually. Transfer to a 2-quart saucepan. Simmer until a bit thicker than normal, about 5 minutes, stirring occasionally with a wire whisk.

To prepare pastry, mix flour with nut meal and salt. Work in oil, then add enough water to form a smooth dough. Roll half the dough out thin between sheets of waxed paper. Dust bottom sheet and dough with flour. Line a lightly-oiled 9-inch pie pan with dough.

Gently mix vegetables with nuts and gravy and transfer to pie. Roll out other half of dough, cut out shapes with a cookie cutter (one heart shape in the middle is nice), and lay pastry over filling. Roll out extra dough for crackers.

Bake until quite golden, 30-45 minutes. Brush surface with oil in last 5 minutes of baking. Before serving, let pie cool for about an hour for gravy to set up.

Variations: Substitute other vegetables, nuts, and nut butter for the ones listed, for instance almonds or hazelnuts.

Corn-Bean Pie

Makes 10-12 servings

I often use our own local Humboldt County speckled bayo beans, an heirloom variety, in this recipe. Originally brought to the U. S. by the Spanish, bayo beans have thrived in the moist climate of northern California for a hundred years. The miners made them their staple protein food along with the animals they hunted. The succulent wild greens they ate with them are still called miner's lettuce.

Speckled bayo beans are organically grown and packed by Warren Creek Farm (see Resources). Since they are an odd-shaped bean for the modern harvester, the growers use an old-fashioned model. They're so carefully cleaned, one rarely finds a stone among them.

Filling:

2 cups small red beans (not azukis), or
    pinto, kidney, or speckled bayo beans
7 cups water (4 cups to soak, 3 cups to
    cook)
6-inch piece kombu sea vegetable
1 cup fresh corn kernels, 1-2 ears
2 green onions, cut in 1/2-inch slices
1/4 cup natural soy sauce

Cornmeal Crust:

3/4 cup cornmeal
3/4 cup whole-wheat pastry flour
1/4 teaspoon unrefined sea salt
1/4 cup light vegetable oil (canola or part
    corn)
1/4-1/3 cup water

To prepare filling, sort through, rinse, then soak beans overnight or about 8 hours in 4 cups water. Drain off water, saving it for house or garden plants. Transfer beans to pressure cooker with 3 cups fresh water. Bring to boil uncovered and allow to slow-boil for 5 minutes. Add sea vegetable, cover, and bring to pressure. Cook over low heat for 1 hour.

Mash beans and sea vegetable or stir them vigorously with a wire whisk until half are creamed. Add remaining filling ingredients and cook uncovered over medium heat just 2 minutes more. Let cool 15 minutes before filling pie.

Preheat oven to 350°.

To prepare crust, mix dry ingredients. Add oil, then water. Stir, then knead to form a smooth dough, adding a little more flour if necessary. (Remember that a slightly moist dough is easier to work with than a slightly dry one.) Roll dough out on lightly-floured surface and transfer to lightly-oiled pie pan. Shape edges.

Transfer filling to crust and bake for 1/2 hour. Allow to cool to lukewarm for filling to gel, at least 1 hour.

For 2 or more pies, simply multiply ingredients proportionately, but calculate cooking water by measuring it to barely cover beans by just 1/2 inch. If you do make beans with too much liquid, pour some off before mashing beans, reserving it for soup broth, or add whole-wheat flour, about 1/2 cup per pie.

Fresh Corn Soufflé

Makes 4 servings

The word soufflé means breath, an appropriate name when you consider the puffiness endures for only a short moment. Usually based on cream sauce or butter and milk with egg yolks and whipped whites, this version, with its lovely golden crust, results in a delicious, low-fat, cholesterol-free dish without a single egg or dairy product. Like tofu quiches, dairy-free soufflés are light and fancy, and even easier to make because they don't require a crust. Indeed, any tofu soufflé can be served as a quiche (with the addition of a pie crust) and vice versa. Or if it's not quite as high as an egg soufflé, you may feel more comfortable calling it a "crustless quiche."

A very special lunch or brunch favorite, fresh corn soufflé is the perfect menu item for a summer solstice or an autumn equinox celebration. Round out the meal with a whole-grain dish and/or bread, and a cooked vegetable dish and/or a salad.

1 pound tofu, fresh, about 2 cups mashed and well packed
Kernels from 3 medium ears corn
Up to 1/2 cup water, only if necessary to blend
1 teaspoon unrefined sea salt (if corn is sweet), or 2 tablespoons umeboshi paste (for added flavor)
1/4 cup fresh basil or dill weed, finely chopped, or 1 tablespoon dried
1/2 cup green onions or chives (or garlic chives), finely chopped

Preheat oven to 400°.

Purée together tofu, corn, water, and salt (or umeboshi paste and dry herb, if included). Fold in green onions or chives and fresh herb and mix well. Transfer to lightly-oiled, ovenproof bowl, pie pan, or soufflé dish of 1-quart capacity. Smooth surface and bake until surface is bright golden yellow in color, 40 minutes to 1 hour. Allow to cool 1/2-1 hour before serving.

French Onion Quiche ❤ Quiche Alsacienne

Makes 8 servings

Dairy-free quiches are fancy, but very simple to prepare. They are ideal served with a whole grain and a vegetable or salad. Tofu quiches are custard-like pies with a light, eggy texture, made without eggs, cheese, cream, or milk.

Quiche Alsacienne is always made with sautéed onions. This recipe was transformed from one in The Joy of Cooking. *My new version was featured in the food section of the* San Francisco Chronicle.

Filling:

Makes 3 cups

1 tablespoon sesame oil
2 medium onions, diced small or thinly sliced
1/2 teaspoon unrefined sea salt
1 pound tofu, fresh
1 tablespoon tarragon leaves, dried, or 2 tablespoons fresh
1 tablespoon natural soy sauce
1/8 teaspoon turmeric
Water to blend smooth, 1/4-1 cup

Basic Single Crust Pastry:

1 1/2 cups whole-wheat pastry flour
1/4 teaspoon unrefined sea salt
1/4 cup light vegetable oil (canola or part corn oil)
1/4 cup water

To prepare filling, heat oil and add onions. Sprinkle with salt and sauté until completely soft and golden, about 15 minutes. (Onions do not soften further with baking.) Add a tablespoon of water and cover during last 5 minutes. Stir occasionally.

Meanwhile, blend other ingredients until creamy smooth, gradually adding water or the liquid from cooking the onions. Stir cooked onions into tofu purée.

Preheat oven to 400°. To prepare pie dough, mix dry ingredients, then add oil and water. Knead briefly to form a smooth dough. Roll dough out between sheets of waxed paper and transfer to corn-oiled pie pan. Trim edges to 1/2 inch over rim and crimp or shape them. Roll out extra dough to make crackers.

Transfer filling to pastry and smooth surface. Bake until top is quite golden, 1/2 hour or more. Allow to set at room temperature, about 1/2 hour before serving.

Variations: **Red Onion Quiche** ❤ Red onions lose most of their color with cooking, but their flavor is definitely sweeter than most yellow onions. Substitute red onions, olive oil, and basil leaves, or half the volume of fines herbes, for equivalent ingredients above. Add a few grains of black pepper.

Tofu Enchiladas

Makes 3-6 servings

Thanks for Linda Redfield for tasty collaboration on this recipe. Freezing and thawing the tofu gives it a meatier consistency.

Tofu Filling
Adobe Sauce
Tofu "Cheese" Sauce Topping or 1 cup soy "mozarella cheese" (I prefer SoyaKass), grated

6 corn tortillas
1/4 cup parsley, thinly sliced

Tofu Filling:

2 tablespoons extra virgin olive oil
1/2 pound tofu, frozen overnight, thawed and squeezed, crumbled
2 cloves garlic, sliced
9 black olives, sliced
1 1/2 teaspoons chili powder
2 teaspoons natural soy sauce
1/2 cup green onions, thinly sliced

Adobe Sauce:
Makes a little more than 3 cups
3 cups *Red Sauce* (see recipe on page 117) or tomato sauce
1 1/2 tablespoons apple cider vinegar
1/3 cup onion, coarsely chopped
3 cloves garlic, coarsely chopped
1 1/2 teaspoons cilantro (fresh coriander or Chinese parsley), optional
1 1/2 teaspoons chili powder
3/4 teaspoon unrefined sea salt

Tofu "Cheese" Sauce Topping:
Makes a little more than 1 cup
1/2 pound tofu, fresh
1 tablespoon apple cider vinegar
2 cloves garlic
1/2 teaspoon unrefined sea salt
Water to blend, about 2 tablespoons

To prepare tofu filling, heat oil and sauté ingredients briefly, adding green onions last. To prepare adobe sauce and tofu "cheese" sauce, blend ingredients until smooth.

Preheat oven to 400°. Steam tortillas until soft to prevent breakage, about 1 minute after water comes to boil.

Spread 1 cup adobe sauce to lightly cover bottom of standard 8-inch square baking dish or equivalent. To assemble enchiladas, fill each tortilla and top with a dollop of adobe sauce. Fold sides over filling, then place enchiladas in baking dish seam-side-down next to each other. Completely cover enchiladas with remaining adobe sauce, then spoon tofu "cheese" sauce (or sprinkle soy "cheese") over all. Cover and bake for 1/2 hour. Uncover and return to oven to brown surface, about 10-15 minutes more. Garnish with parsley to serve.

Lasagna

Makes 8-9 servings

This luscious Italian casserole is based on whole-grain pasta with a seasoned tofu "cheese" sauce and a vegetable sauce based on carrots and beets instead of tomatoes. Italian Red Sauce resembles tomato sauce in texture, appearance, and even flavor. (For an explanation of why to substitute for tomatoes, see page 117.) Italian White Sauce really satisfies the desire for dairy foods, especially cheese, and for rich Italian flavors.

2 1/2 - 3 cups *Italian Red Sauce* (recipe follows)
3 cups *Italian White Sauce* (recipe follows)
4 quarts (16 cups) water
1/2 pound whole-wheat lasagna noodles, broken in thirds
2 tablespoons parsley, minced for garnish

Italian Red Sauce:

Makes 2 1/2 - 3 1/2 cups

1 pound (3 cups) carrots and/or winter squash, thinly sliced
1 small-medium beet, thinly sliced
1 1/2 cups water
1 bay leaf
2-4 tablespoons natural soy sauce, miso, umeboshi vinegar, or sauerkraut juice
1 1/2 teaspoons each basil and oregano

Italian White Sauce:

Makes 3-4 cups

1-2 tablespoons extra virgin olive oil
2 large onions, thinly sliced
Water
4 large cloves garlic, finely sliced
1 pound tofu, fresh
2 tablespoons natural soy sauce
1 teaspoon unrefined sea salt
1 tablespoon each basil and oregano

Carrots and/or sweet winter squashes such as sweetmeat or buttercup have the best flavors for the red sauce. (This is a nice way to use pumpkin, but the flavor is milder.)

To prepare red sauce, pressure-cook vegetables in 1/2 cup water with bay leaf for 5 minutes. Discard bay leaf and transfer ingredients to processor, blender, or food mill with seasonings. Purée until smooth adding more water to texture desired, about 1 cup. There is no need to remove the skin from soft-skinned squashes (or pumpkins), but do so for those with dark green or hard skins, after cooking. To double recipe, keep water at 1/2 cup. For larger volumes, figure 1 cup water.

To make white sauce, heat oil in a large skillet and sauté onions briefly. Add 2 tablespoons water and cook, stirring occasionally, until onions are almost soft, about 5 minutes. Add garlic, crumble tofu over garlic, and add remaining ingredients. Cover to cook for about 5 minutes more. Purée ingredients until creamy smooth, adding water to texture desired, perhaps 1/2 cup. Or blend just half the mixture for a chunkier effect.

To cook noodles, in a large pot (5 quart capacity) bring water to a rolling boil, add noodles and boil until soft yet firm or al dente, about 15-20 minutes. Pour off water and run noodles under cool water. Drain and set aside until you are ready to assemble lasagna.

Preheat oven to 350°.

To assemble lasagna, spread red sauce over the bottom of a standard 8-inch square baking dish. Layer one thickness of lasagna noodles over sauce, side-by-side, cutting off any extra from ends. Follow pasta with white sauce. Repeat this order (red sauce-pasta-white sauce-pasta) ending with red sauce. In all, there will be 4 layers of pasta, 3 of red sauce, and 2 of white sauce.

Bake casserole for 1/2 hour. Garnish with parsley to serve.

Note: For large groups, noodles may be used uncooked. Be sure the top layer of red sauce is thick enough that noodles are completely submerged. Bake covered for 45 minutes, then uncovered for 15 minutes more.

Buon Appetito!

Other main dish casserole recipes:

Millet "Mashed Potato" Casserole (see page 74)
Biscuit-Topped Savory Stew (see page 12)

Sea Vegetable Dishes

Green Beans and Arame

Makes 4 servings or 2 1/4 cups

1/2 cup arame sea vegetable, well packed
1 cup water
2 cups green beans (1/2 pound), ends snipped off, beans sliced in 1 1/2-inch sections
1 tablespoon natural soy sauce

Soak arame in water for 10 minutes. With fingers, transfer sea vegetable to cooking pot. Gently pour half soak water over arame, taking care not to disturb bottom portion where sand may collect, although this is rare with arame. Place beans on top of sea vegetable and bring to boil. Cover to simmer until beans are crisp-tender, 8-10 minutes. Pour off any remaining broth, add soy sauce, and stir to serve.

Arame with Chives

Makes 4 servings

1 cup arame sea vegetable, well packed
2 cups water
1/4 cup chives (or green onions), cut in 1-inch pieces
2 teaspoons pickled plum (umeboshi) vinegar or other dressing
Chive flowers for garnish (optional)

Soak arame in water for 10 minutes. Transfer with fingers to a small saucepan and pour soak water over arame, discarding last bit. Bring to boil, then simmer covered until tender, about 3 minutes. Drain, reserving broth for house or garden plants.

Toss arame with chives and drizzle with ume vinegar to serve.

For large amounts, include only enough soak water to cover arame by 2 inches.

Hijiki with Fresh Corn

Makes 3-4 servings

An easy, pretty, and very tasty summer land and sea vegetable dish.

1/4 cup hijiki sea vegetable, well packed
1 cup water
2 cups fresh corn kernels
1 tablespoon natural soy sauce

Soak hijiki in water until soft, about 20 minutes. Pick up hijiki with fingers and transfer to small cooking pot, then pour over most of soaking water.

Bring hijiki to boil, then simmer until almost done, about 5 minutes. Or try the no-soak method: Bring hijiki to boil and turn heat to medium-low to simmer until tender, 20-40 minutes.

Pour off most of cooking broth and save for plants. Add corn and soy sauce and cook until corn is soft, about 5 minutes more. Stir once.

Sesame Hijiki

Makes 3-4 servings or 1 cup

1/2 cup hijiki seaweed, gently packed
2 cups water
1/2-1 teaspoon toasted sesame oil

1 teaspoon natural soy sauce
1 teaspoon sesame seeds, toasted

Soak hijiki until reconstituted and tender, about 20 minutes. In a small saucepan, heat oil. With fingers, lift hijiki from soak water and transfer to pan to sauté briefly. (Any sand will sink to bottom of soak water.) Gently add enough soaking liquid to barely cover hijiki, and cover to cook until hijiki is soft and water is almost completely gone, about 15-20 minutes. Add soy sauce, stir, and cover to cook several minutes more. Toss with seeds to serve.

Variation: **Sesame Hijiki with 3-Taste Dressing** ❤ Proceed as above adding 2 teaspoons mirin and 1 teaspoon brown rice vinegar to hijiki with soy sauce.

Hijiki-Vegetable Sauté with Tempeh

Makes 6 servings

1/2 cup hijiki sea vegetable, well packed
2 cups water
1 teaspoon-1 tablespoon sesame oil (optional)
1 cup onion, thinly sliced
1 cup carrot, thinly sliced in matchsticks (or julienne)
8-ounce package tempeh, cut in 1/2-inch slices
2 tablespoons natural soy sauce
2 tablespoons parsley or green onion tops, cut in 2-inch lengths

Soak hijiki in water until reconstituted, about 20 minutes.

In a large skillet, heat oil and sauté onion and carrot briefly. Push vegetables to side of pan, and transfer hijiki to pan. Place vegetables and tempeh on top of hijiki. (If oil is omitted, simply layer hijiki, then raw onion and carrot, then tempeh in pan.) Pour over hijiki soak water to a depth of 1/2 inch. Take care to avoid using the last bit of water where sand or other particles may have settled. Cover and bring to boil, then turn heat to medium-low to slow-boil until done, about 15 minutes. Broth should be almost gone by now, but if not, pour it off and reserve for future use. Add soy sauce and parsley or green onion tops and cook a couple of minutes more, uncovered.

Hijiki

Salads

A Word on Dressings...

The dressings in this book call for less oil (and therefore, less fat) than usual because good quality oils display far more flavor and body than highly refined oils. All the dressings go well with cooked vegetables as well as salads—and some pressed salads—and some enhance simple pasta or whole grain dishes. Let all dressings sit several minutes for flavors to blend. Taste dressings before serving to adjust seasonings if desired.

Directions in the recipes for creamy tofu dressings call for boiling or steaming the tofu for 2 minutes before use. This is a step I omit when I know and trust the source —e.g., our local tofu shop. But for tofu that may have travelled a long way and perhaps sat in the market for several days, the quick cooking serves as a refreshing and sanitizing agent.

For people who prefer oil-free dressings or who are on oil-restricted diets, serve vinaigrettes at the side. Give them a choice of a simple dressing based on pickled plum (umeboshi) vinegar, or citrus juice or brown rice vinegar combined with soy sauce. Sesame salt is another flavorful alternative for whole grain and pasta salads.

Fresh Vegetable Salads

Serving sizes vary for the salads in this chapter. A small portion of about 1 cup is served directly on the dinner plate, while a larger portion of about 2 cups is served in a separate salad bowl. All salad greens should be rinsed by swishing them in a bowl of purified water. Dry them in a salad spinner or with a towel. See the chapter on sauces for a categorized listing of dressings.

Salad with Apple Cider Vinaigrette

Makes 2-4 servings

1/2 head green leaf lettuce, torn in large
    bite-size pieces
8 leaves small, tart salad greens (watercress, radicchio [red chicory], or arugula [also called roquette or rocket]) or 2 large tart greens (escarole or endive), cut in large bite-size pieces
1/4 cup red cabbage, very thinly sliced

Apple Cider Vinaigrette:
Makes 1/2 cup
1/4 cup apple cider vinegar
2 tablespoons apple cider or apple juice
2 tablespoons mild oil (sesame, almond, walnut, etc.)
1/2 teaspoon unrefined sea salt
1/8 teaspoon black pepper

Mix dressing ingredients and set aside to blend flavors.
    Toss salad ingredients with dressing to serve.

Salad with Ranch Dressing

Makes 4 servings

Thanks to Steve and Donnell Campbell of Bethalto, Illinois for their creative version of a salad enjoyed in the Midwest. Tofu replaces buttermilk and mayonnaise. Very popular! (Dressing is delicious on rice as well.)

8 cups lettuce, torn in bite-size pieces
1 cup *Ranch Dressing* (recipe follows)

Ranch Dressing:
Makes about 1 1/2 cups
1/2 pound tofu, 1 cup mashed, fresh
2 tablespoons green onion, finely sliced
2 teaspoons parsley, minced
1 teaspoon dill weed, dried, or 2 teaspoons
    fresh, chopped
1 clove garlic, pressed or sliced
2 tablespoons lemon juice
1 tablespoon natural soy sauce
1 tablespoon extra virgin olive oil
2 teaspoons pickled plum (umeboshi) paste
2 teaspoons brown rice vinegar
1/4 teaspoon white pepper
1/3-2/3 cup water

To prepare dressing, if tofu is not completely fresh, boil or steam whole block of tofu for 2 minutes. Drain and allow to cool. Blend all ingredients until smooth in food processor or blender, adding water to proper consistency.

Garden Salad with Dulse and Tahini-Lime Dressing

Makes 3-6 servings

The colors and flavors in red leaf lettuce and dulse complement each other nicely.

1/2 cup dulse sea vegetable, about 1/4
    ounce, gently packed
1 cup water
1 small head red leaf lettuce, about 4 cups,
    torn in bite-size pieces
Edible flowers (calendula, borage, nastur-
    tium, violet, etc.) or other colorful salad
    ingredients

Tahini-Lime Dressing:

Makes a little more than 1/2 cup

1/4 cup sesame tahini, toasted
2 tablespoons lime juice
1 tablespoon pickled plum (umeboshi)
    vinegar
1 teaspoon garlic, chopped
1/4 cup water

To prepare dressing, simply blend ingredients until smooth.

Soak dulse in water until reconstituted, 2 or 3 minutes. Drain and gently squeeze, reserving liquid for later use in soup. Tear dulse in bite-size pieces. Place lettuce in individual bowls, topped with dulse and flowers. Dress to serve.

Garden Vegetable Salad with Walnut-Miso Dressing

Makes 4-8 servings

1/6 bunch broccoli, tops separated into tiny
    flowerets
1/6 head cauliflower, tops separated into
    tiny flowerets
1/3 carrot, thinly sliced in flower shapes
1/2 head iceberg or green leaf lettuce, torn
    in bite-size pieces
1/4 bunch red radishes, thinly sliced in
    rounds, greens set aside for future use
    if fresh
1/4 pound tofu, medium to firm style (not
    soft), cut in 1/2-inch cubes
1 cup *Walnut-Miso Dressing* (recipe follows)

Walnut-Miso Dressing:

Makes a little more than 1 1/2 cups

1 cup walnuts, lightly toasted (makes 1/2
    cup walnut butter)
1/4 cup white miso
2 tablespoons lemon juice or brown rice
    vinegar, or part each
1 cup water

Figure 3 pieces of each vegetable and about 6 pieces tofu per serving. Steam or boil vegetables, except lettuce and radish, with tofu until done, about 5 minutes. Place lettuce in individual salad bowls and arrange vegetables and tofu on top.

To prepare dressing, combine ingredients in blender or food processor and blend until smooth.

For large amounts of dressing, add water gradually to desired consistency. It will require less than a proportionately increased amount.

Garden Patch Salad with Creamy Herb (Dill) Dressing

Makes 4-8 servings

This salad features a hint of arugula, the gourmet green which was known in colonial gardens as rocket, noted for its peppery flavor.

There is no cheese or sour cream as in the standard version of this dressing. Great served over boiled or steamed vegetables such as broccoli and cauliflower.

1 head butter lettuce, about 7 ounces or 7
    cups, gently packed, torn in bite-size
    pieces
4 leaves arugula, torn in bite-size pieces
1/2 cup alfalfa sprouts

Creamy Herb (Dill) Dressing:
                    Makes 1 1/4 - 1 1/2 cups
1/2 pound tofu, fresh
1 tablespoon pickled plum (umeboshi)
    vinegar
1 tablespoon brown rice vinegar
1 tablespoon dill weed, dried, or 1/4 cup
    fresh, minced
1/3-1/2 cup water (start with less, to tex-
    ture desired)

Toss salad greens with sprouts.
    To prepare dressing, boil or steam whole block of tofu for 2 minutes. Drain and allow to cool. Blend ingredients until smooth. Dressing thickens as it sits.

    Variations: For an **Herb Dip** ❤ simply add less water.
    Another nice herbal combination in place of dill is 1/4 teaspoon thyme, crushed,

1/8 teaspoon rosemary, powdered, and 1 tablespoon fresh parsley, minced.

Green Salad with Creamy Cilantro Vinaigrette

Makes 4-8 servings

1 head red leaf lettuce, torn in bite-size
    pieces
1/4 cup carrot, grated
6 tablespoons *Creamy Cilantro Vinaigrette*
    (recipe follows)

Creamy Cilantro Vinaigrette:
                    Makes 1/2 cup
6 tablespoons sesame oil
2 tablespoons apple cider vinegar
2 tablespoons cilantro (fresh coriander or
    Chinese parsley), coarsely chopped
1/2 teaspoon sea salt

To prepare dressing, blend ingredients until frothy. Toss salad ingredients and dress to serve. This dressing is best prepared just before serving as ingredients separate and cilantro loses its pretty green color with time.

Tossed Green Salad with Orange-Shiso Dressing

Makes 4-8 servings

1 head bibb lettuce (or butter or Boston let-
    tuces), rinsed and torn in bite-size

pieces
Chinese cabbage, half amount of lettuce, cut
in 1-inch squares
1/4 cup red cabbage, very thinly sliced

Orange-Shiso Dressing:

Makes a little more than 3/4 cup

*Shiso leaves are added to umeboshi plums in
the pickling process to turn the plums red and
add flavor. This combination makes for a delicious zesty taste, perfect for salad dressings.
Use the shiso that comes with the plums for
this recipe.*

1/2 cup orange juice
1/3 cup sesame tahini, toasted
1 - 1 1/2 tablespoons pickled plum (umeboshi) vinegar (start with less)
2 teaspoons red shiso leaves, finely chopped

To prepare dressing, simply blend ingredients until smooth.
Toss greens and dress to serve.

Mixed Green Salad with Toasted Sesame Dressing

Makes 2-4 servings

4 cups mixed salad greens (green leaf and
romaine, or others), torn in bite-size
pieces
4-inch piece cucumber, thinly sliced in
rounds
1/2 cup carrot, daikon, and/or red radish,
grated
1/2 cup *Croutons* (see page 33)

Toasted Sesame Dressing:
Makes 2 tablespoons

This 3-taste dressing is a favorite.

1 tablespoon toasted sesame oil
1 1/2 teaspoons natural soy sauce
1 1/2 teaspoons lemon juice or brown rice
vinegar

Mix greens with other vegetables. Sprinkle
croutons over top of salad.
To prepare dressing, simply mix ingredients. Dress to serve.

Mixed Green-Sprout Salad with Thousand Island Dressing

Makes 6-12 servings

1/2 head green leaf lettuce, torn in bite-size
pieces
1/2 head romaine lettuce, torn in bite-size
pieces
1 cup alfalfa sprouts, about 2 ounces
1/4 bunch red radishes, thinly sliced in
rounds, greens set aside for future use
if fresh

Thousand Island Dressing:
Makes about 1 1/2 cups
1/2 pound tofu, fresh
2 tablespoons *Red Sauce* (recipe follows)
2 tablespoons brown rice vinegar
2 tablespoons natural soy sauce
2 tablespoons brown rice syrup
1 tablespoon sesame oil
1 tablespoon onion, chopped
2 tablespoons dill pickle, finely chopped

Red Sauce:
Makes 1/2 cup
1/2 cup carrot, finely sliced
2 tablespoons beet, finely chopped
1/2 cup water

To prepare dressing, boil or steam whole block of tofu for 2 minutes if not completely fresh. Drain, and allow to cool.

Prepare red sauce by boiling ingredients in a small saucepan until soft, about 5 minutes, then purée in small container of blender. (A small amount such as this won't purée in a food processor.) Place all dressing ingredients except dill pickle in food processor or blender to purée until smooth, then fold in pickle.

Toss salad ingredients together, and spoon-pour dressing over top to serve.

Salad with Sweet Poppy Seed Dressing

Makes 3-4 servings

This land and sea vegetable salad comes with an especially popular dressing.

1/4 cup dry dulse, pulled apart and gently packed to measure
1/2 head green leaf lettuce, torn in bite-size pieces
1/2 cup combination of 2 kinds of sprouts (large ones such as mung, soybean, or sunflower, and/or small ones such as daikon radish or alfalfa)
1/2 cup cucumber, thinly sliced in rounds
2 tablespoons red onion, very thinly sliced in rounds
2 tablespoons celery, thinly sliced on the diagonal
1/4-1/3 cup *Sweet Poppy Seed Dressing* (recipe follows)

Sweet Poppy Seed Dressing:

Makes little less than 1/2 cup

This is a great creamy-style vinaigrette dressing.

1 teaspoon poppy seeds
1/4 cup sesame oil
2 tablespoons brown rice vinegar
1 tablespoon maple syrup or 2 tablespoons brown rice syrup or mirin
1 teaspoon onion
1/4 teaspoon dry mustard powder
1/4 teaspoon unrefined sea salt

To prepare dulse for salad, simply soak in water to cover for 1 minute and squeeze out excess liquid. Mix salad ingredients, reserving dulse to place on top.

To prepare dressing, blend ingredients. (If including brown rice syrup as sweetener, when necessary heat jar in small pot of water so syrup softens and dissolves easily when mixed.) Stir again just before serving.

For a prettier presentation, especially when serving larger amounts, place lettuce on individual plates or in salad bowls, then sprinkle sprouts and other ingredients on top.

Chinese Cabbage and Watercress Salad with Japanese Plum Dressing

Makes 3-6 servings

Fantastic light salads can be created with soft green leaf vegetables other than lettuce, such as bok choy and Chinese cabbage. Their colors and flavors are heightened with small amounts of the stronger soft greens—watercress, endive, escarole, or chicory—or with sprouts or parsley. Because of its high oxalic acid content (which prevents absorption of calcium in the body), I use spinach infrequently as a salad green.

This zesty dressing is great on steamed vegetables as well as salads. For a sauce with less bite, cook several minutes to neutralize the raw onion taste.

4 cups Chinese cabbage, about 1/2 pound, quartered lengthwise and finely sliced crosswise
1 cup watercress, cut in 1-inch pieces
2 tablespoons sunflower seeds, toasted and sprinkled with soy sauce (see page 136)
3/4 cup *Japanese Plum Dressing* (recipe follows)

Japanese Plum Dressing:
Makes a little more than 1 cup
2 tablespoons pickled plum (umeboshi) paste
1/2 cup almond or sesame butter
2 tablespoons onion, coarsely chopped
Water to texture desired—start with 1 cup

Toss salad greens with seeds.

To prepare dressing, blend ingredients until smooth. Pour dressing over individual portions.

Variation: **Bok Choy-Alfalfa Sprout Salad** ❤ Substitute bok choy and alfalfa sprouts for Chinese cabbage and watercress, and 1/4 cup toasted pecans for seeds.

Creamy Cucumber Salad ❤ Raita

Makes 4 servings

Raitas are East Indian salads, usually made with yogurt, vegetables, and seasonings. Their creamy, cooling qualities are meant to cleanse and soothe the palate between bites of more highly spiced dishes. This delicious version is made with tofu.

3-inch piece cucumber, quartered lengthwise, then thinly sliced crosswise

Indian-Style Tofu "Yogurt":
Makes 1 cup
1/2 pound tofu, about 1 cup, fresh
2 tablespoons brown rice vinegar
1 teaspoon cumin powder
1/2 teaspoon unrefined sea salt
1/4 cup water

To make Indian-style tofu "yogurt," boil or steam whole tofu for 2 minutes. Drain, allow to cool, then crumble tofu into blender with other ingredients and purée until creamy smooth.

To prepare raita, simply stir cucumber into "yogurt."

Variation: **Plain Tofu "Yogurt"** ❤ Omit cumin powder.

These recipes have the flavor and consistency of yogurt, but without the milk sugar and fat. Tofu "yogurt" is not fermented as yogurt is. The lactobacillus which exists in yogurt is contained in other fermented foods such as pickles and miso, the fermented bean paste used often in soups and in some dressings and sauces.

Marinated Cucumbers and Onions ❤
Bread and Butter Pickles

Makes 10 servings or 2 1/2 cups

Thanks to Steve and Donnell Campbell for this healthy version of a typical Midwestern pickled salad. Very tasty with a pleasingly mild sweet-and-sour flavor.

1 tablespoon unrefined sea salt
3 cups water
1 cucumber, thinly sliced in rounds
1 onion, thinly sliced in rounds, rounds
    separated

Sweet and Sour Dressing:

1/4 cup brown rice syrup
1/4 cup brown rice vinegar
1/2 cup water

Bring salted water to boil, then pour it over cucumber and onion to sit until onions have lost their bite and are translucent, about 2 1/2 - 3 hours.

At end of soaking time, place dressing ingredients in small saucepan and heat together to dissolve the sweetener. Drain pickles and pour warm dressing over them. Let stand to absorb flavors, at least until mixture has cooled, before serving. Flavor heightens over time.

Salsa Salad

Makes 9 servings or 4 1/2 cups

This very colorful and flavorful salad makes use of the wonderful carrot-beet sauce as a choice in place of the usual tomato sauce. (See page 117 for more information.)

1 1/2 cups cucumber
1 cup each celery and green pepper
1/2 cup each green onion and parsley
2 1/2 cups *Seasoned Red Sauce*
2 tablespoons extra virgin olive oil
Butter lettuce leaves for serving

Seasoned Red Sauce:
                Makes 3 1/2 - 4 cups
2 1/2 cups *Red Sauce* (see recipe on page
    117), or tomato sauce
1/2 cup apple cider vinegar
Water to texture desired; start with 1/4-1/2
    cup
1 tablespoon cilantro (fresh coriander), finely
    chopped
1 1/2 teaspoons unrefined sea salt
1 teaspoon cumin
1 teaspoon oregano
1/16 teaspoon cayenne red pepper powder
    or 1/2 teaspoon crushed red pepper
4 cloves garlic, finely chopped

Dice vegetables in 1/2-inch chunks. Mix with sauce and oil. Allow to set for flavors to meld, then taste to adjust seasonings.

Serve 1/2-cup portions on individual lettuce leaves.

Hard Bread Salad ❤ Panzanella

Makes 2-4 servings

2 slices stale whole-wheat bread, cut in
    1-inch cubes
1/2 head red leaf lettuce, torn in bite-size
    pieces
1/2 small bunch red radishes, or part
    cucumber, thinly sliced in rounds
1/2 small red onion, thinly sliced in rounds
2 tablespoons parsley, thinly sliced

Italian Herb Dressing:

Makes 1/4 cup

2 tablespoons extra virgin olive oil
2 tablespoons red wine vinegar
1/4 teaspoon unrefined sea salt
1/4 teaspoon oregano
1/8 teaspoon rosemary, powdered

Mix dressing first to blend flavors.
    Sprinkle hard bread with cool water to
soften. Mix salad ingredients and toss with
dressing just before serving.

Variation: Although this Italian salad is
usually made with 3-day-old bread, fresh
bread works well too. Simply omit sprinkling
bread with water.

Pressed Vegetable Salads

Quick Pressed Salad with Light Lemon-Rice Vinegar Dressing

Makes 2 cups or 8 servings

Pressed vegetable salads may be pressed with a weight on a plate or in a pickle press, a clear plastic container with a screw-down lid. A pickle press makes the process quick and easy, and fascinating to watch. Made in Japan, they come in a variety of sizes. This salad fits nicely in the 2-quart press. 7 1/2 cups raw vegetables become 2 cups in 1 hour as the liquid is squeezed out and the fiber is slightly broken down, rendering the vegetables more digestible, but still fresh and crispy—somewhere between cooked and raw.

1/2 head soft lettuce (butter or green leaf), thinly sliced
1/2 head romaine lettuce, thinly sliced
1/2 cup carrot, grated
1/2 cup daikon radish, grated
Sea salt—1/4-1/2 teaspoon per cup vegetables

Light Lemon-Rice Vinegar Dressing:
Makes 2 tablespoons
1 tablespoon lemon juice
1 tablespoon brown rice vinegar

Toss lettuces with carrot and radish. Sprinkle salt over salad ingredients and work in by rubbing between palms. Press until liquid covers vegetables, about 1 hour. Drain and discard salty liquid. Fluff up vegetables. Mix dressing ingredients and pour over salad to serve.

Nappa Cabbage and Red Radish Pressed Salad

Makes 4-5 servings or about 1 1/2 cups

This one's so light while bursting with color and flavor.

4 cups nappa (Chinese) cabbage, quartered lengthwise
1 cup watercress or green onion
1/4 cup red radish, including their greens if bright green
1/4 cup carrot, grated on large holes of grater
Fresh dill, cilantro, or basil, to taste
Sea salt—1/4-1/2 teaspoon per cup vegetables
Vinegar or citrus juice for dressing

Thinly slice vegetables and herbs. Mix with salt and press until submerged in liquid, about an hour. Season and fluff vegetables to serve.

Variations: Substitute red onion, thinly sliced, for red radish, and carrots, cut in thin matchsticks. Or in summertime, substitute green and/or red sweet pepper. Just before serving add 1 tablespoon seeds or nuts, toasted and chopped.

Cooked Vegetable Salads

Choose ingredients with an eye for color. Boiled salads (also known as cooked, hot, warm, or winter salads) may be simple, with ingredients such as broccoli with carrot or cauliflower. When you have more time, plan one dark green vegetable (kale, watercress, mustard, or bok choy), one light green (regular, savoy, or Chinese cabbage), always carrot for its joyful clarity, and another root vegetable (parsnip, rutabaga, or daikon radish). Other vegetables add dimension in their season such as purple cabbage; red radish; sweet red, orange, or yellow bell peppers; fresh corn; or green peas.

Boil vegetables separately until you know their cooking times, or when you want to serve them in separate mounds for composed salads. Combine vegetables which cook in the same amount of time or are to be mixed together.

Hot Slaw

Makes 5 servings

6 cups cabbage, thinly sliced
1/2 cup celery, thinly sliced
1/3 cup carrot, grated
1/4 cup water
1 cup *Tofu "Mayonnaise" Dressing No. 2* (recipe follows)
1 tablespoon green onion tops or chives, thinly sliced for garnish
Chive flowers for garnish (optional)

Tofu "Mayonnaise" Dressing No. 2:
Makes 1 1/4 cups

1/2 pound tofu, fresh
2 tablespoons lemon juice
2 tablespoons brown rice syrup
1 tablespoon brown rice vinegar
1 tablespoon oil (olive, sunflower, sesame, etc.)
1 teaspoon unrefined sea salt
1/4 teaspoon dry mustard powder or 1 teaspoon wet mustard
2 tablespoons water
1/4 teaspoon celery, caraway, or dill seeds

To make dressing, boil or steam whole block of tofu for 2 minutes. Drain, allow to cool, and blend until smooth with all other ingredients. For large amounts, omit water, adding it gradually, and only if necessary for blending.

Simmer vegetables, except green onion tops or chives, in water until tender, about 5 minutes. Stir occasionally. Drain and mix with 1 cup dressing, then sprinkle with green onion or chives (and chive flowers) to serve.

Variation: Arrange slaw on 1 large or several small cabbage leaves.

Chef's Salad with Carrot-Sesame Dressing

Makes 4 servings

The idea for this composed salad comes from the Souen Macrobiotic Restaurants in New York City.

6 cups water
2 cups broccoli, separated into large flowerets with stem to 3 inches in length
2 cups cauliflower, separated into large flowerets with stem to 3 inches in length
1 large carrot, cut in 3-inch lengths, then in 1/2-inch sticks
1/2 bulb kohlrabi, cut like carrot
2 ribs celery, halved lengthwise, then cut in 3-inch lengths crosswise
1 small head green and/or red leaf lettuce, torn in bite-size pieces
1 small cucumber, cut in 1/2-inch diagonal slices
8 whole sprigs watercress

Carrot-Sesame Dressing:

Makes 2 cups

2 cups water or vegetable cooking broth
2 cups carrots, sliced in 1/2-inch rounds
2 tablespoons sesame butter
2 tablespoons natural soy sauce

To prepare vegetables, bring water to boil in 3-quart saucepan. Add broccoli, cauliflower, carrots, and kohlrabi at the same time. Cook until crisp-tender, about 5 minutes, adding celery in last 2 minutes. Drain, reserving broth, and spread vegetables out to cool.

To make dressing, bring water or broth to boil in a 2-quart saucepan with carrots and cook until tender, 5-8 minutes. Transfer carrots to food processor with 1 cup cooking broth, sesame butter, and soy sauce. Purée until smooth. Allow to cool.

To assemble salad, arrange vegetables in individual salad bowls in separate groups placed side-by-side. Pour 1/2 cup dressing across center of salad to serve.

Variation: Substitute 12 sugar snap or snow peas, or 8 red radishes, halved, for kohlrabi. Cook peas with other vegetables and add radishes in last minute of cooking.

Cooked Vegetable Salad with Tofu "Sour Cream" Dressing

Makes 4-8 servings

This Russian-style salad, or "salat," features a combination of cooked and raw vegetables which is said to be more popular than raw ones alone.

1 cup each carrot, turnip, and rutabaga, cut in thin slices of similar size and shape
1/2 cup water
1 small head green lettuce (green leaf, bibb, etc.), torn in bite-size pieces
1 small cucumber, thinly sliced (optional)
1/4 cup red radishes, thinly sliced (greens reserved for future use if fresh)
1 green onion, thinly sliced

Tofu "Sour Cream" Dressing:

Makes 2/3 cup

1/2 cup *Tofu "Sour Cream"* (recipe follows)
2 tablespoons water
1 tablespoon natural soy sauce
1 tablespoon apple cider vinegar (or brown rice vinegar)

2 teaspoons extra virgin olive oil

1/8 teaspoon black pepper

Tofu "Sour Cream":

Makes 2 cups

1 pound tofu, fresh

2 tablespoons apple cider vinegar

1 tablespoon natural soy sauce

1/2 teaspoon unrefined sea salt

To prepare tofu "sour cream" for dressing, boil or steam whole block of tofu for 2 minutes. Drain and allow to cool, then blend with other ingredients until creamy smooth. To prepare dressing, mix those ingredients well.

   To prepare vegetables, cook carrot, turnip, and rutabaga with water until tender, stirring occasionally. Drain, allow to cool, then mix with other salad ingredients. Dress and serve.

Moroccan Carrot Salad

Makes 6 servings

A favorite! For this boiled salad, be sure to select quality olives, those without the preservative ferrous gluconate (to stabilize color) found in most canned varieties.

3 large carrots, 1 pound or 4 1/4 cups, sliced in half-moons, 1/4-inch thick

1 large clove garlic, chopped

Water

6 black olives, pits discarded

2 tablespoons parsley, minced

Gingered Vinaigrette Dressing:

Makes 3 tablespoons

1 tablespoon wine vinegar

1 tablespoon brown rice vinegar

2 teaspoons sesame oil

1 teaspoon fresh ginger, peeled and grated

1/4 teaspoon unrefined sea salt

Mix dressing ingredients and let sit several minutes.

   Boil carrots with garlic in water to cover until tender, about 5 minutes. Drain and toss with olives, parsley, and dressing.

Cooked Vegetable Salad with Parisian Parsley Dressing

Makes 6 servings

This recipe is adaptable to the changing seasons by substituting different vegetables as they appear in market or garden. This springtime version has spectacular color variation. The vegetable cooking broth may be used in soups and consommés.

Vegetables:

2 quarts (8 cups) water

1 cup Brussels sprouts, quartered lengthwise

1 pound asparagus, about 2 cups, cut in 2 1/2-inch lengths, tough bottom part of stems discarded

1 carrot, halved lengthwise, then cut diagonally

1 rutabaga, halved lengthwise, then cut diagonally

1 cup daikon radish, halved lengthwise, then cut diagonally

1 cup red radish, about 3/4 bunch, quartered lengthwise

Parisian Parsley Dressing:

Makes 1/3 cup

3 tablespoons lemon juice, freshly squeezed
1 1/2 - 2 tablespoons extra virgin olive oil
1 clove garlic, minced
1/2 teaspoon parsley, minced
1/2 teaspoon unrefined sea salt

Prepare dressing by combining ingredients, and set aside to blend flavors.

Bring water to boil while you rinse and cut the vegetables. Add vegetables and boil, partially covered, until done, about 7 minutes. Drain, reserving broth for use in another dish.

Dress to serve, hot or cool.

Variation: Include leeks or red onion when not including other onion entrées in the menu.

Vegetables Vinaigrette
♥ *Boiled Vegetable Salad with Tangy Orange Dressing*

Makes 4-6 servings or 6 cups

This and other boiled vegetable salads lend themselves to an endless variety of vinaigrette dressings.

3/4 teaspoon unrefined sea salt
1 1/2 quarts (6 cups) water
1 carrot, cut in half lengthwise, then in 1/4-inch thick diagonals
3 cups broccoli, cut in 3-inch lengths starting from flowering end, flowerets separated, edible portion of stem sliced like carrots

8 green or purple beans or edible pea pods (sugar snap or snow peas), stem ends cut off and discarded, peas threaded
8 yellow wax beans, stem ends cut off and discarded
1 small-medium yellow summer squash or golden zucchini or yellow scallopini (also called sunburst squash), zucchini cut in 1/4-inch rounds, scallopini cut in wedges 1/2-inch thick at widest point
4 red radishes, halved
4-6 leaves red leaf lettuce, whole or shredded, for serving
6 tablespoons any vinaigrette dressing (see pages 129-132)

Tangy Orange Dressing:

Makes 6 tablespoons
Thanks to Lynn Montgomery for this tasty recipe.

2 tablespoons orange juice
1 teaspoon orange peel, freshly grated
2 tablespoons brown rice vinegar

1 tablespoon safflower oil
1 tablespoon sesame oil
1/4 teaspoon unrefined sea salt

Mix dressing ingredients and allow to sit for flavors to meld.

In a 3-quart pot, bring salted water to boil. Add carrot, broccoli stems, and beans. Cook about 3 minutes, then add flowerets and cook about 2 minutes more. Add squash and radishes and cook until crisp-tender and bright in color, 2-3 minutes more. Transfer to colander to cool, or serve hot. Reserve broth for future use.

Gently mix vegetables to artfully distribute colors, adding dressing as you go. Serve each portion on a lettuce leaf or shredded lettuce.

Variation: **Gingery Orange Dressing** ♥
Add the juice of 1 tablespoon ginger, freshly grated, to the above ingredients.

Whole-Grain and Vegetable Salads

Basic Grain and Vegetable Salad ♥
Barley and Sweet Corn Salad

Makes 6-8 servings or 5 cups

The barley found in most food stores (natural or regular supermarkets) is not a whole grain. The outer layers have been removed during 6 "pearlings," hence the name pearl(ed) barley. Many nutrients are lost during the process including almost all the fiber, and over half the protein, fat, and minerals. Just the starchy part of the grain remains. Look for and request American-grown whole grain barley (also called hulled barley), and use pearled barley on occasion for variety.

Oriental pearl barley is another kind of barley which is a whole grain. It is delicious in this recipe, substituted for part or all of the regular barley.

Brightly colored vegetables add pizzazz to this nutritious summer salad. Use the recipe to design others with different grains, vegetables, and dressing ingredients.

4 cups cooked barley, gently packed (recipe follows)
Kernels from 2 medium ears corn, about 1 1/2 cups
1/2 cup carrot, diced small
1/2 cup red sweet pepper or red radish, diced small

1/2 cup broccoli flowerets, separated in
    small sections
1 rib celery, diced small
1/2 cup cucumber, green onion, or parsley,
    diced small

Dilled 3-Taste Dressing:
                                          Makes 1/2 cup
3 tablespoons pickled plum (umeboshi)
    vinegar
3 tablespoons brown rice vinegar
2 tablespoons sesame oil
1 tablespoon fresh dill, minced, or 1 tea-
    spoon dry

Barley:
                                    Makes 3 1/2 - 4 cups
1 cup barley (regular pearled barley or Ori-
    ental pearl barley)
1/8 teaspoon unrefined sea salt
3 cups water

To prepare barley, rinse and drain it. Bring
to boil in salted water, then turn heat low to
simmer for 1 hour (no flame spreader necessary). Transfer to bowl to cool, fluffing with a
fork. With Oriental pearl barley, drain off
any liquid which remains after cooking. For
larger amounts, such as 3 cups barley, figure water to cover barley by 1 inch.

To prepare dressing, simply mix ingredients. Dill weed retains its color even when
dressing is mixed hours ahead of time.

To prepare vegetables, steam corn, carrot, red pepper or radish, broccoli, and celery until tender, about 6 minutes after water
comes to a rolling boil. Allow to cool.

Mix barley, vegetables, and dressing.
Serve as is or on individual lettuce leaves.

Variations: Substitute fresh coriander
for dill.
Rice and Sweet Corn Salad ❤ Substitute cooked brown rice for barley.

Bulgur Wheat Salad ❤ Tabouli

Makes 6-9 servings or 3 1/2 cups

*Pronounced ta-boo'-lee, this Middle Eastern
(Lebanese) salad is an earthy blend of
cracked wheat (precooked and dried) and
vegetables, delicately seasoned. Although
some people simply soak the bulgur in boiling
water, I like to cook it briefly for a softer, fluffier texture.*

1/2 teaspoon unrefined sea salt
1 1/2 cups water
1 cup bulgur wheat
1 cup cucumber, diced small (optional)
1 small ripe tomato, diced
1/2 cup parsley, finely sliced
1/2 cup green onion, finely sliced
Lettuce leaves for serving (optional)

Lemon-Garlic-Mint Dressing:
                                  Makes 6-7 tablespoons
1/4-1/3 cup lemon juice, to taste (start with
    less)
2 tablespoons extra virgin olive oil
1 clove garlic, minced
1 tablespoon fresh mint leaves, minced

In a small saucepan, bring salted water to
boil. Add bulgur to pot. When boiling resumes, turn heat low to cook covered until
tender, 10-15 minutes. No flame spreader
necessary. Transfer to a large bowl by fluffing with a fork, and allow to cool.

To prepare dressing, mix ingredients
well. Gently mix bulgur with vegetables and
dressing. Serve as is or on individual lettuce
leaves.

To increase volume (as for 10 times this
recipe) multiply ingredients proportionately,
except water which should be measured to 1
inch above bulgur.

Pasta Salads

Pasta Primavera

Makes 5 servings or 10 cups

Primavera is the Italian word for spring, "prima" meaning first and "vera" meaning green. The first vegetables of springtime are highlighted in this pasta and steamed vegetable salad. However, seasonal vegetables may be substituted for year-round enjoyment. Green beans and fresh corn kernels are nice additions in the summer.

1/2 pound asparagus, about 1 1/2 cups
1/2 pound broccoli, about 3 cups
1/2 carrot
1/2 stalk celery
1/2 cup whole sugar snap or snow pea pods, threads removed, or English peas, shucked
2 quarts (8 cups) water
1/2 cup mushrooms, sliced
1/2 small red onion, thinly sliced in rings
1 tablespoon nori sea vegetable flakes
1 tablespoon parsley, minced
1/2 pound whole-grain pasta (corkscrew or spirals, small shells, ribbons, spaghetti, or green spinach pasta, or green mugwort soba [Japanese buckwheat noodles])

Italian Herb Dressing No. 2:

Makes 1/2 cup

1/4 cup extra virgin olive oil
1/4 cup red wine vinegar or apple cider vinegar, or slightly less balsamic vinegar
2 cloves garlic, minced
1 tablespoon dry basil, or 2 tablespoons fresh, minced (or a combination of Italian herbs—basil, oregano, and rosemary)
1 teaspoon unrefined sea salt

Mix dressing ingredients and set aside.

Snap off and discard hard bottom portion of asparagus. Cut asparagus, broccoli, carrot, and celery in 2-inch lengths, then cut broccoli, carrot, and celery in 1/4-inch slices lengthwise, leaving broccoli flowerets whole.

In a 3-quart pot, bring water to boil and cook vegetables except last 3 until done, about 5 minutes. Transfer to bowl to cool. Add 1 cup more water and when boiling resumes, add pasta and cook until done, 8-20 minutes, depending on kind. Rinse under cool water and drain. Makes 4 cups.

Toss dressing ingredients with pasta and vegetables. Garnish with raw onion rings, nori, and parsley.

Variations: Add marinated and sliced tofu or tempeh cutlets, or cooked beans, and/or cooked sea vegetables such as arame, hijiki, or sea palm to the salad.

Arame-Cucumber-Noodle Salad with Shiso Leaf Dressing

Makes 4 servings

The dressing for this salad is flavored with shiso leaf, the red herb which is pickled with the salted plums (umeboshi). It comes with the plums or in a separate package, already dried and powdered. Whole-wheat (or brown rice) udon noodles look like fettucini.

1/2 cup arame sea vegetable
2 cups water
8-ounce package whole-wheat udon noodles, or other variety
2 quarts (8 cups) water
1 medium cucumber, or part yellow lemon cucumber, thinly sliced in rounds, then in strips if desired
4 red radishes, thinly sliced in rounds, then in strips if desired

Shiso Leaf Dressing:

Makes 6 tablespoons
1/4 cup pickled plum (umeboshi) vinegar
2 tablespoons toasted sesame oil
1 tablespoon red shiso leaves, chopped, or dried and powdered

Quickly rinse and drain arame, then bring to boil with 2 cups water. Cook over low heat until tender, about 10 minutes. Drain, reserving broth for soup stock, or as food for house or garden plants.

Cook noodles in 2 quarts water until done, drain, and rinse under cool water.

Mix dressing ingredients and toss with noodles and vegetables to serve.

Dressing variations: Substitute 2 tablespoons soy sauce for umeboshi vinegar.

Substitute brown rice vinegar or citrus juice for part of umeboshi vinegar.

Hot Italian Pasta Salad

Makes 3-6 servings or 6 cups

Bright red and green colors highlight this tantalizing dish. Even though red onions tend to lose their color with cooking, adding vinegar near the end of cooking brings it back.

When designing this recipe, I tried whole-wheat mushroom pasta, but because we couldn't taste the mushrooms and it didn't hold together well, I don't recommend it.

2 quarts (8 cups) water
2 cups broccoli, cut in flowerets, sliced in long sections for serving with spaghetti, or short and small for serving with shells
1/4 cup peas, about 3 ounces in pods
1/2 pound pasta (whole-wheat spaghetti, small or medium-sized shells, or spirals [some are a combination of whole-wheat, soy, and rice flours])
2 tablespoons extra virgin olive oil
1 red onion, thinly sliced in rounds

4 cloves garlic, thinly sliced
1 teaspoon unrefined sea salt
2 tablespoons red wine vinegar
1 cup whole basil leaves
8 black olives, pitted and sliced

Bring water to boil in 3-quart saucepan. Add broccoli and peas and cook until tender, about 5 minutes. Remove vegetables from broth and set aside to cool, or cover drained vegetables with a loose cotton cloth to retain some heat. When boiling resumes, add pasta and cook until done. Drain and run cool water over pasta.

In a medium-large skillet, heat oil. Add onion and garlic. Sprinkle on salt, stir well, and cook until tender, about 10 minutes. Add vinegar and basil and cover to cook until basil is wilted but still very bright in color, about 2 minutes more. Turn heat off. Add cooked pasta and stir gently to distribute flavors evenly, then carefully fold in vegetables and black olives.

Other pasta salad recipes:

Quick and Easy Noodle-Vegetable Delight
    (see page 48)
Macaroni Salad (see page 108)
Gelled Corn Pasta Salad (see page 111)

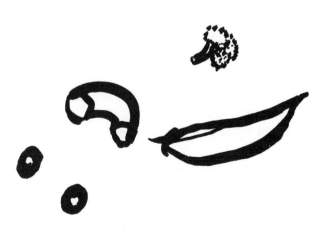

Bean Salads

Marinated Lentil and Wild Land and Sea Greens Salad

Makes 6 servings or about 3 cups

2 1/2 cups cooked lentils (recipe follows)
1 tablespoon nori sea vegetable flakes
1/2 cup edible wild greens (miner's lettuce, chickweed, watercress, dandelion, etc.), leaf sections cut in 1-inch pieces, bitter varieties such as dandelion finely sliced
Water
1 stalk celery, quartered lengthwise and thinly sliced crosswise
2 green onions or 1/4 cup chives, finely sliced, or red onion, finely diced
2 tablespoons parsley, minced
6 leaves lettuce for serving (red leaf is nice)
Edible flowers (chive, nasturtium, borage, violets, etc.), if available, for garnish

Lentils:

Makes a little less than 2 1/2 cups

1 cup lentils
1 quart water
3-inch piece kombu sea vegetable
1 bay leaf

Marinade:

Makes little more than 3/4 cup

1/2 cup brown rice vinegar
1/4 cup extra virgin olive oil
2 cloves garlic, minced
4 teaspoons wet mustard

1/2 teaspoon lemon peel, freshly grated
1/2 teaspoon unrefined sea salt

Whisk marinade ingredients and set aside to blend flavors.

To prepare lentils, sort through dry lentils and rinse in a bowl of water. Pour off any which float to the surface along with rinse water. Place lentils in a 2-quart pot with remaining ingredients and bring to boil, then simmer with lid set slightly ajar until lentils are tender, but not mushy, and still retain their shapes, about 20-30 minutes. Drain, remove kombu and bay leaf, and transfer lentils to a bowl to cool. When in a hurry, run cold water over lentils to cool them quickly. Drain, add marinade and set aside at least 15 minutes, or until ready to serve. For larger amounts, figure 1/2 cup less water per recipe increase to cook lentils.

Packaged Japanese nori flakes are available. To prepare your own nori flakes, pull apart and spread dried wild nori on baking sheet to bake at 350° until color changes slightly and nori is crushable when cool, about 5 minutes. Overcooking causes a bitter flavor. Crush into flakes with hands, or into a powder by whirring in a food processor or blender. One-half ounce (half a 1-ounce package) yields a little less than 1/2 cup flakes.

Just before serving, pour off some of the marinade. Toss lentils with other salad ingredients. Serve on individual lettuce leaves. Garnish with edible flowers.

Variations: **Marinated Lentil Salad in Pita** ❤ Serve salad in pita pocket bread. Cut 3 pitas in half, then steam to soften. (Do not cut pitas after steaming or they will stick shut.) Tuck lettuce leaf in each pita half followed by 1/2 cup salad.

For a simpler salad, substitute more green onions and parsley for wild greens.

Fiesta Bean Salad

Makes 4-10 servings or 6 cups

Thanks to Donnell and Steve Campbell of Bethalto, Illinois for this vibrant bean and vegetable salad, ideal for the summer and early fall seasons.

2 cups cooked kidney beans (recipe follows)
2 cups cooked chickpeas (recipe follows)
2 cups fresh corn kernels (2 large ears)
1/2 cup red and/or green bell pepper, diced small
1/2 cup parsley or green onions, finely sliced, or red onion, diced small (for color balance if using green bell pepper)
4-10 lettuce leaves for serving

Sweet Mustard-Dill Dressing:

Makes a little more than 1/2 cup

1/4 cup brown rice vinegar
2 tablespoons sesame oil
2 tablespoons pure maple syrup
1 tablespoon natural soy sauce
1 tablespoon dried dill weed or 2 tablespoons fresh, minced
2 teaspoons wet mustard

Beans:

Makes 2 1/2 cups kidney beans or 2 3/4 cups chickpeas

1 cup kidney beans or chickpeas (garbanzo beans)
4 cups water (2 cups to soak, 2 cups to cook)
3-inch piece kombu sea vegetable

To prepare beans, sort through, then rinse beans. Soak each kind separately in 2 cups water each for 8 hours or overnight. Drain, reserving liquid for house or garden plants. Cook each with 2 cups fresh water and 3-inch piece kombu.

Since the beans must retain their shapes for use in salad, cooking time is shorter than usual, about 1/2 hour for both. I like to boil the kidney beans (in a 2-quart pot) as they are likely to turn mushy quickly and must be watched closely. Chickpeas may be pressure-cooked.

Mix dressing ingredients and set aside to blend flavors.

Steam corn until tender, about 5 minutes, and set aside to cool.

When beans are done, drain them immediately, reserving broth and kombu for use in soup. If kidney beans are covered with a little of the mashed inner portion, quickly swish them in cold water to make surface shiny. Set aside to cool.

To assemble salad, mix all ingredients, then dress to serve right away or to marinate. Serve on individual lettuce leaves or in a bowl with lettuce leaves tucked in around the outer edge.

For cooking large amounts, figure water to cover beans by 2 inches. Figure portions at 3/4-1 cup per serving.

Mandarin Summer Salad

Makes 6 servings or 5 cups

1 quart (4 cups) water
1 cup mung bean sprouts
1/2 cup green onions, cut in 1/2-inch
    slices, whites kept separate from greens
1 pound tofu, fresh, firm
1/2 cup bell pepper (red, yellow, and/or
    green), diced in 1/2-inch pieces

1/2 cup celery, diced in 1/2-inch pieces
1/2 cup peanuts, toasted
6 butter (or bibb or Boston) lettuce leaves

Gingered Lemon-Soy Dressing:
Makes 5 tablespoons
3 tablespoons natural soy sauce
2 tablespoons lemon juice or rice vinegar, or
    1 tablespoon of each
2 tablespoons water
1 teaspoon toasted sesame oil
1 teaspoon ginger, peeled and grated

In a 2-quart pot, bring water to boil. Blanch sprouts and white part of green onions for 30 seconds. Scoop out with flat strainer. When boiling resumes, add whole block of tofu and cook for 2 minutes. Drain and allow to cool.

Mix dressing ingredients.

Cut tofu in 1/2-inch cubes. Gently toss with other ingredients and dressing. Serve on individual lettuce leaves or in a bowl with lettuce tucked in around the outer edge.

Tempeh Salad

Makes 4-5 servings or 3 cups

This salad resembles chicken salad. Serve as is, on a bed of lettuce, or as a sandwich filling or topping for rice cakes. The dressing may be used with other salads as well, such as macaroni salad or cole slaw. Sunchokes add a clean, crunchy quality similar to water chestnuts.

8 ounces tempeh, cut in 1/2-inch cubes,
    about 1 1/2 cups
Water to steam tempeh
1 rib celery, sliced in half lengthwise, then
    thinly crosswise
2 tablespoons red onion, finely chopped

2 tablespoons parsley, finely chopped
2 tablespoons Jerusalem artichokes (sunchokes), peeled and finely chopped (optional, in season)
2 tablespoons carrot, grated (optional)
4-5 lettuce leaves (green leaf is nice here)

Tofu "Mayonnaise" Dressing:

Makes little more than 1 cup

1 cup *Tofu "Mayonnaise"* (recipe follows)
2 tablespoons dill pickle, finely chopped
2 teaspoons wet mustard
1-2 cloves garlic, minced

Tofu "Mayonnaise":

Makes 1 1/4 cups
Tofu "mayonnaise" substitutes well for regular mayonnaise as an ingredient in sandwiches and salads. Containing no eggs and very little oil, this wholesome version is very low in fat and calories, with no cholesterol. Lasts up to 3 weeks refrigerated.

1/2 pound tofu, fresh, soft or firm
2 tablespoons lemon juice, or 1 tablespoon each lemon juice and brown rice vinegar
2 tablespoons extra virgin olive oil
1/2-1 teaspoon unrefined sea salt
1 teaspoon wet mustard
1/8 teaspoon turmeric

Water to blend to smooth consistency, about 2-4 tablespoons

Cut, and then steam tempeh for 10 minutes while you cut the vegetables and prepare the dressing. Reserve lettuce leaves for serving.

To make tofu "mayonnaise," combine ingredients in food processor or blender and purée until creamy smooth. If tofu needs refreshing (see introductory note on page 87), boil in water to cover for 2 minutes, drain, and allow to cool.

To make dressing, simply combine ingredients. As "mayo" thickens in the refrigerator, whisk in a little more oil or water to regain smooth texture.

To assemble salad, gently toss ingredients. Serve on individual lettuce leaves.

Variations: **Curried Tempeh Salad ❤**
Use only lemon juice in tofu "mayonnaise" and add 1 teaspoon curry powder, or 1/2 teaspoon each curry and cumin powders, to dressing.

Macaroni Salad ❤ Lovingly known as macro-roni salad to some....Substitute 1 1/2 - 2 cups cooked macaroni for steamed tempeh and proceed as above. Cook 1/2 pound corn, whole-wheat, or veggie elbow macaroni in 2 quarts (8 cups) water. Makes 3 cups. Stir corn macaroni once after it comes to boil to prevent sticking, and cook about 8 minutes.

Tempeh
Salad

Sea Vegetable Salads

Mim's Arame Salad

Thanks to Mim Collins, mother, psychotherapist, and macrobiotic cooking teacher in Seattle, for this delicious dish with great color contrast among the black, white, and green ingredients.

Makes 4-6 servings or 3 1/2 cups

1 1/2 cups arame sea vegetable (about 1 ounce)
3 1/2 cups water
1 head cauliflower, separated into small flowerets
1 cup snow peas, threads removed, peas cut in half on the diagonal

3-Taste Dressing:

Makes little more than 1/2 cup

1/3 cup lemon juice
3 tablespoons natural soy sauce
1 tablespoon sesame oil

Soak arame in 3 cups water for 10 minutes. Place remaining 1/2 cup water and cauliflower in saucepan and bring to boil, then simmer covered until barely tender, about 5 minutes. Add snow peas, cook 2 minutes longer, then turn heat off and let sit covered to steam for 5 minutes.

Transfer arame to another saucepan. Add just enough of the soaking liquid to barely cover arame and bring to boil. Simmer covered for 10 minutes.

Mix dressing ingredients. Drain both arame and vegetables and mix together with dressing. Pour off dressing after 1 minute (5 tablespoons remain). Serve.

Hijiki, Corn, and Tofu Salad

Makes 5-7 servings or 5 cups

Thanks to Kristina Turner, author of The Self-Healing Cookbook *(Earthtones Press, 1987) for the original version of this creative salad.*

Hijiki:

Makes 2 cups

1 cup hijiki seaweed, about 1 1/2 ounces
2 cups water

Other ingredients:

Kernels of 2 large ears yellow corn
1/4 pound tofu, fresh and firm, cut in 1/2-inch cubes
2 green onions, thinly sliced
4 leaves lettuce, about 4 cups, thinly sliced
1 tablespoon sesame seeds, toasted

Japanese Vinaigrette Dressing:

Makes 1/2 cup

1/4 cup brown rice vinegar
2 tablespoons natural soy sauce
1 tablespoon Japanese sweet rice cooking wine (mirin)
2 teaspoons toasted sesame oil

Rinse hijiki by swishing in a bowl of cool water. Drain. Bring to boil with measured amount water in 1-quart saucepan, then simmer covered until tender, about 1/2 hour. Drain, reserving broth for soup, or for house or garden plants. Cut hijiki in bite-size pieces if strands are very long.

To prepare salad, steam corn and tofu until corn is tender, 5-7 minutes. When cool, gently mix with hiziki and green onion.

Mix dressing ingredients and toss with other ingredients. Serve on a bed of shredded lettuce and sprinkle sesame seeds over top.

Variation: For a dressing which is lighter in color, and therefore allows tofu to maintain its whiteness, substitute 1 tablespoon pickled plum (ume) vinegar for 1 tablespoon soy sauce.

Sea Palm-Sprout Salad

Makes 4-6 servings or 2 cups

Sea palm grows only on the west coast of North America. It is fast becoming a popular sea vegetable for its mild, delicious flavor and easy preparation.

4 cups water (2 cups to cook sprouts, 2 cups to cook sea palm)
2 cups mung bean sprouts

1/2 cup sea palm, about 1/2 ounce, well packed
1 green onion, thinly sliced

2-Taste Dressing:

Makes 2 tablespoons
1 tablespoon brown rice vinegar or lemon juice
1 tablespoon natural soy sauce

Bring 2 cups water to boil in a 2-quart saucepan. Add sprouts and parboil for 1 minute. Drain and transfer to strainer to cool. In the same pot, bring the remaining 2 cups water to boil, add sea palm and simmer until tender, about 1/2 hour. Drain, reserving broth for soup or house or garden plants. Allow sea palm to cool briefly and cut in 2-inch lengths.

Toss sea palm and sprouts with green onion to distribute colors well.

Mix dressing ingredients. Dress and serve.

Other sea vegetable salads:

Arame-Cucumber-Noodle Salad (see page 104)

Aspics/Gelled Salads

Aspics can be works of art. Fresh, colorful vegetables suspended in a tasty broth, they are refreshing, light nourishment for the eyes as well as the palate.

Note: In my experience, seasoning aspics with umeboshi vinegar keeps them from gelling.

Carrot Aspic

Makes 9 servings

This delightful orange-colored, molded vegetable salad lightens up and balances simple grain, bean, and vegetable fare.

Chervil is a low-growing plant which is related to parsley. Sometimes called gourmet parsley, it is sweeter and more fragrant than parsley, but has the same bright green color, and a relatively mild flavor in comparison with other herbs.

During the months that cucumberand corn are not in season, substitute more of the other vegetables.

3 cups carrot juice
1 cup water
1/3 cup agar sea vegetable flakes
1/2 cup each onion, celery, carrot, cucumber, and corn, diced small
1 tablespoon chervil, or 2 teaspoons chervil and 1 teaspoon tarragon, basil, or other herb
1 teaspoon unrefined sea salt
3 tablespoons lemon juice
9 small lettuce leaves for serving, or sprigs fresh parsley, basil, watercress, or sprouts for garnish

In a 2-quart pot, place 1 cup carrot juice, water, and agar flakes. Stir so agar soaks while you cut the vegetables. Add vegetables, herb, and salt and bring to boil, then simmer until agar completely dissolves and vegetables are cooked, about 5-10 minutes.

Turn heat off and allow to cool about 10 minutes. Add remaining carrot juice and lemon juice and transfer to 8-inch square baking dish or pretty mold. (You'll have about 5 cups of ingredients, so measure capacity of molds to determine how many are needed.) Smooth out air bubbles on surface. Aspic cools in 1 hour in the refrigerator.

Cut aspic in big heart shapes, or in squares or slices to serve on individual lettuce leaves, or simply arrange on a plate and garnish with your choice of green topping.

Nice served with a dollop of *Tofu Mayonnaise* (see page 108) flavored with a dab of horseradish paste.

Gelled Corn Pasta Salad

Makes 12 servings

1 quart water
6-inch piece kombu sea vegetable
1/3 cup agar sea vegetable flakes
1/2 cup carrot, thinly sliced
1/2 cup celery, cut in half lengthwise, then thinly crosswise
1/2 cup green onions or watercress, thinly sliced (onions on diagonal)
1/3 cup natural soy sauce
2 tablespoons apple cider vinegar
1 cup cooked corn macaroni, 1/2 cup dry

Bring water, kombu, agar, carrot, and celery to boil. Watch for foaming over. Set lid ajar and cook over low heat until agar is completely dissolved and vegetables are cooked, about 5-7 minutes. Remove kombu. Add remaining ingredients in last minute of cooking.

Transfer to a 9- or 10-inch glass pie plate you have brushed liberally with olive oil. Refrigerate until gelled, about 1 hour. Run a sharp knife around the edges and turn it over onto a serving platter. Cut in wedges and garnish to serve.

Split Pea Aspic

Makes 8 servings

I call this "pease pudding-gel" when I serve it at a meal with an Old English or Early American theme. It's actually a split pea soup which is gelled. It looks great poured into a fish-shaped mold of 3 1/4 cups capacity. For a special occasion, make both green and yellow split pea fish, and serve them side-by-side facing in opposite directions, garnished with several large sprigs of parsley.

1 cup green or yellow split peas
3 1/4 cups water (3 cups to cook peas, 1/4 cup to cook vegetables)
3-inch piece kombu sea vegetable
1/4 cup agar sea vegetable flakes
1/2 cup each carrot, celery, and onion, diced small, or part fresh corn kernels and peas
1 teaspoon thyme or savory, dried, or 2 teaspoons fresh
1/4 cup water
2 tablespoons light or white miso

Rinse split peas and place in pressure cooker with 3 cups water, sea vegetable, and agar flakes. Cover and bring to pressure, then turn heat low to cook for 1/2 hour. (No flame spreader needed.)

Meanwhile, place vegetables, herb, and water (1/4 cup) in saucepan and cook until vegetables are tender, about 5-7 minutes.

When pressure subsides, remove kombu from yellow split peas only, to retain bright yellow color. Add miso and stir vigorously to purée ingredients until smooth. (A wire whisk works well.) Add cooked vegetables and stir. Transfer to lightly-oiled mold to gel at cool room temperature, about 1 hour. Turn mold out on serving platter, or cut and serve.

To double the recipe, increase ingredients proportionately except water which should measure 5 cups.

Bean Aspic (African)

Makes 12 servings or 6 1/4 cups

This dish was inspired by one in an African cookbook. They mash the beans and season them with sautéed onions, garlic, and red pepper. I've included soy sauce instead of salt because of its superior flavor in the dish.

Black-eyed peas are an African staple, often ground raw into a flour or coarse meal as well as cooked from the fresh or dried bean. They came to the American South from Africa with the slave trade. Today Africans also use pinto, black, kidney, small red, and cranberry beans.

2 cups pinto beans
8 cups water (4 cups to soak, 4 cups to cook)
6-inch piece kombu sea vegetable
1/3 cup agar sea vegetable flakes
1 tablespoon oil (peanut, olive, corn, etc.)
2 onions, diced
2 large cloves garlic, minced
1/4 cup natural soy sauce

1/2-1 teaspoon red pepper, crushed, or
    ground cayenne pepper, to taste
    (optional)
Large sprigs parsley for garnish

Rinse, then soak beans overnight in 4 cups
water. Drain and transfer to pressure cooker
with 4 cups fresh water. Bring to a rolling
boil, then turn heat down slightly to boil for
5 minutes. Add kombu and agar, stir well to
immerse them in the water, and cover to
bring to pressure. Turn heat low and cook
for 1 hour.

Heat oil and sauté onion and garlic
until soft.

When pressure subsides, mash beans
and sea vegetable well. Add vegetables and
seasonings, stir, and cook until done, about
10 minutes. Transfer to lightly-oiled molds
or standard 8-inch square baking dish to
set, about 2 hours at room temperature, or
1 hour in the refrigerator. Transfer to nice
platter or cutting board to serve, garnished.

To double this recipe, increase ingredients proportionately, but delete 1 cup
water for cooking; i.e., for 4 cups beans,
figure 7 cups water.

Sauces, Spreads, and Dressings

It's all in the sauce. Quite true, for sauces, as well as other toppings, are the finishing touch for cooked grains, noodles, and bread, and for vegetables and salads—cooked or raw. The best sauces complement and enhance the dish with which they are served, and don't mask the subtle goodness of the ingredients. Toppings made with only the finest quality ingredients, that are simple to prepare and are not too salty, oily, or highly seasoned, are what I aspire to create.

This chapter is a compilation of all the recipes for sauces, etc., sprinkled throughout the book, plus others which only appear here. The recipes are divided into categories by the predominant ingredients. We begin with vegetable-based sauces, spreads, and dressings (either based on a vegetable purée, or on arrowroot powder or kuzu root starch for texture). These are followed by bean spreads and a gravy; creamy tofu-based sauces and dressings; nut or seed butter-based spreads and dressings; simple oil-free dressings; vinaigrettes and marinades; and flour-based gravies. Table seasonings are the delectable toasted seeds and nuts, often combined with toasted and crumbled sea vegetables, to sprinkle over a steaming bowl of rice or other grain. The chapter ends with sweet spreads and toppings.

Vegetable-Based Sauces, Spreads, and Dressings

The following recipes are based on a vegetable purée or a sauce of colorful, cooked vegetables that have been thickened with arrowroot powder or kuzu root starch.

Vegetable Sauce

Makes 2 1/4 cups

This sauce goes nicely on simply steamed vegetables such as broccoli and cauliflower as well the breakfast or brunch waffles it appears with in the menu (see page 216).

2 cups water
1/2 cup carrots, thinly sliced in flower shapes or quarter moons
3-inch piece kombu sea vegetable
2 heaping tablespoons (1/4 cup) kuzu root starch or arrowroot powder
1/4 cup cool water
3 tablespoons natural soy sauce or miso
1/2 cup green onions, thinly sliced on the diagonal

Bring 2 cups water to boil with carrots and kombu. Cook until carrots are tender, about 5 minutes. Remove kombu. Mix arrowroot or kuzu with cool water and soy sauce to dissolve, and add to pot with green onions. If using miso, dilute it in a little of the hot broth and add to pot with the thickener. Stir constantly until mixture comes to boiling point and sauce becomes thick and shiny, in about 1 minute.

*Variation: **Gingered Vegetable Sauce***
♥ Add 1/2 teaspoon fresh ginger, peeled and grated.

Mixed Vegetable Sauce

Makes 4 1/2 cups

This classic Chinese-style vegetable sauce includes much of summer's bounty. Vary ingredients to enjoy nature's harvest throughout the entire year. Great on rice or other whole grains, or pasta.

3 cups water
3-inch piece kombu sea vegetable
1 carrot, diced small
1 onion (yellow, white, or red), diced small
1/2 cup green beans or yellow wax beans and/or whole snow or sugar snap peas, thinly sliced to size of other vegetables
1/2 cup green summer squash (zucchini or patty pan), diced small
1/2 cup yellow summer squash, diced small
4 red radishes or 1/4 cup red bell pepper, diced small
1/4 cup arrowroot powder or kuzu root starch
1/4 cup cool water
4-6 tablespoons natural soy sauce
1 teaspoon ginger, freshly grated
1/4 cup almonds, toasted
1/4 cup green onion, sliced for garnish

In a 2-quart pot, bring water to boil with kombu. Add carrot, onion, and green beans and cook about 5 minutes. Add remaining vegetables and cook until tender, about 5 minutes more. Transfer vegetables to colander and set kombu aside.

Measure to see that 2 cups of broth remain and add a little water if necessary. In a small bowl, place arrowroot or kuzu in cool water and set aside. Bring broth to boil with soy sauce and ginger. Stir kuzu to dissolve and add to hot stock, stirring until mixture turns saucy and shiny, about 1 minute.

Mix sauce with vegetables and almonds. Garnish.

Season's Savory Vegetable Sauce

Makes 2 2/3 cups

This smooth sauce nicely tops about 6 cups cooked vegetables.

2 cups vegetable cooking broth or water
3-inch piece kombu sea vegetable
1/4 cup arrowroot powder or kuzu root starch (about 2 tablespoons per cup liquid)
1/4 cup cool water
4-6 tablespoons natural soy sauce

Optional sauce ingredients:

1 large clove garlic, minced
1 teaspoon ginger, freshly grated, or ginger juice, ginger root grated and squeezed
2 teaspoons red shiso leaf, freshly chopped or 1 teaspoon powdered

To prepare sauce, place broth and kombu in saucepan, with optional ingredients if desired, and bring to boil. Turn heat low and remove kombu. Thoroughly dissolve arrowroot or kuzu in cool water, and add it to pot with soysauce. Stir until mixture becomes shiny and thick, about 1 minute. Pour over cooked vegetables.

Red Sauce

Makes 2 1/2 - 3 1/2 cups

Use this sauce in any dish which normally calls for tomato sauce. It's bright and saucy without the acid qualities or the solanine found in all members of the nightshade family of vegetables (tomatoes, eggplant, peppers, and potatoes), associated with arthritis and other joint diseases. For reference, see The Nightshades and Health *by Norman F. Childers and Gerard M. Russo (see Resources).*

Carrots and/or sweet winter squashes such as sweetmeat or buttercup have the best flavors for the red sauce. (This is a nice way to use pumpkin, but the flavor is milder.) There is no need to remove the skin from soft-skinned squashes (or pumpkins), but do so from those with dark green or hard skins, after cooking.

1 pound carrots and/or winter squash, 3 cups, thinly sliced
1 small-medium beet, thinly sliced
1 1/2 cups water (1/2 cup to cook vegetables, up to 1 cup to add for proper texture)

Pressure-cook ingredients for 5 minutes. Purée in food processor, blender, or by hand in a food mill adding water to desired consistency.

To double recipe, keep water for cooking at 1/2 cup. For larger volumes, use 1 cup water to cook vegetables.

Variations: **Italian Red Sauce** ♥ Add 1 bay leaf to pressure cooker with vegetables. Remove bay leaf. Purée with 2-4 tablespoons soy sauce, miso, umeboshi vinegar, or sauerkraut juice; 1 1/2 teaspoons each basil and oregano; and a pinch of black pepper.
Carrot Marinara Sauce ♥ Heat 1-2 tablespoons olive oil in skillet and sauté

until tender 1 onion, diced small; 2 cloves garlic, minced; and 2 cups mushrooms (6 ounces), sliced. Add sauce to vegetables and cook covered 10 minutes more to blend flavors. Makes 3 cups.

Salsa Pacifica

Makes 10-12 servings or 4 1/3 - 5 1/4 cups

A mild homemade version of the standard Mexican hot pepper sauce known as Salsa Picante. The wonderful carrot-beet sauce re-places the usual tomato sauce. Serve as a dip for chips, a sauce on Mexican specialties, or a taste enhancer for simple grain and vegetable fare. Very colorful and flavorful!

Seasoned Red Sauce:

Makes 3 1/2 - 4 cups

2 1/2 cups *Red Sauce* (see preceding recipe)
1 cup water
1/2 cup apple cider vinegar
1 tablespoon cilantro, finely chopped
1 1/2 teaspoons unrefined sea salt
1 teaspoon cumin
1 teaspoon oregano
1/16 teaspoon cayenne red pepper powder
    or 1/2 teaspoon crushed red pepper
4 cloves garlic, finely chopped

Vegetables:

1/2 cup onion, diced small
1/4 cup celery, diced small
1/4 cup green pepper, diced small
1/4 cup green onion, thinly sliced
1/4 cup parsley, thinly sliced
1/4 cup cucumber, diced small

To make seasoned red sauce, mix red sauce with other ingredients.

Add vegetables to seasoned red sauce and let mixture sit in a cool place until ready to serve.

Note: When bell peppers and cucumber are out of season, substitute more of the other vegetables.

Adobe Sauce

Makes 1 1/2 - 2 cups

This sauce makes a nice filling for enchiladas (see page 82).

1 1/2 cups *Red Sauce* (see page 117)
1/2 cup water
1 tablespoon apple cider vinegar
1/4 cup onion, coarsely chopped
2 cloves garlic, coarsely chopped
1 1/2 teaspoons cilantro, optional
1/2 teaspoon cumin powder
1/2 teaspoon oregano
1/2 teaspoon crushed red pepper
1/2 teaspoon unrefined sea salt

Blend ingredients until smooth.

Carrot-Sesame Dressing

Makes 4 servings or 2 cups

2 cups water or vegetable cooking broth
2 cups carrots, sliced in 1/2-inch rounds
2 tablespoons sesame butter
2 tablespoons natural soy sauce

To make dressing, bring water or broth to boil in a 2-quart saucepan with carrots and cook until tender, 5-8 minutes. Transfer carrots to food processor with 1 cup cooking broth, sesame butter, and soy sauce. Purée until smooth. Allow to cool.

Sesame-Onion Sauce

Makes 2/3 cup

1/2 onion, cut in 1/2-inch dice
1/4 cup water
2 tablespoons sesame butter
1 tablespoon natural soy sauce
1 tablespoon parsley, minced for garnish

To make sauce, place onion and water in small saucepan and bring to boil. Slow-boil until soft, about 10 minutes. Add sesame butter and soy sauce and stir well. For large amounts, cook onions in water to barely cover. If sauce is watery, cook uncovered to thicken.

Carrot-Almond Butter Spread

Makes 8 servings or 1 - 1 1/4 cups

2 cups carrots, thinly sliced, about 1/2 pound
1/2 cup water
2 tablespoons almond butter
1 1/2 teaspoons natural soy sauce
1/4 teaspoon sea salt

Pressure-cook carrots in water for 5 minutes (or boil until tender in water to cover). Drain, reserving broth for another use. Purée carrots with remaining ingredients.

Italian Herb Paste ♥ Pesto

Makes 1 - 1 1/4 cups

Pesto is the classic Italian herb paste made from fresh basil. It is popular in France as well where it is called pistou. *Even without cheese, and just half the oil used in most recipes, this version doesn't sacrifice pesto's irresistible flavor. An undiscernable amount of soy sauce adds a depth of flavor usually derived from cheese.*

A must during the summer and early fall when basil is fresh, pesto serves as a topping for pasta, rice, cooked vegetables, salad, or in soup.

2 cups fresh basil, about 3/4-1 bunch, stems and any discolored leaves discarded, gently packed
2 large cloves garlic, chopped
1/2 cup walnuts or pine nuts, lightly toasted
2 tablespoons extra virgin olive oil
1/2 teaspoon unrefined sea salt
1 tablespoon natural soy sauce
Up to 1/4 cup water

To prepare pesto, blend ingredients until smooth, adding water last to texture desired.

For use as a sauce for pasta, dilute pesto with a little of the hot pasta cooking water, then mix with drained pasta.

Variation: **Winter Pesto** ♥ Substitute fresh parsley for fresh basil and include about 1/4 cup dried basil in the total volume. Should this pesto sit long and the dry herb absorb moisture, add a little more water or oil for texture desired.

Bean Spreads and Gravy

Lentil Paté/Lentil Loaf

Makes 10-15 servings or 5 cups

Historically, paté was made with goose liver, and more recently with chicken, beef, veal, or pork liver. The animals are force-fed so their livers became marbled and enlarged up to one-quarter of their body weight. This is gourmet?!

This luscious lentil-based paté shares the smooth texture and the gentle color and flavor of the original. It's also a good way to use up stale bread.

1 cup lentils
3 cups water
3-inch piece kombu or wakame sea
    vegetable
1 bay leaf
1 tablespoon sesame oil
1/2 onion, diced
2 large cloves garlic, minced
1 rib celery, diced
A pinch of sea salt
1/2 cup parsley, minced
2 tablespoons thyme
1/2 pound whole grain bread, 4 - 4 1/2
    cups, diced in 1/2-inch cubes
1/3 cup light miso
1/4 cup sesame tahini

Sort through lentils for stones by spreading them on a white plate. Rinse and drain lentils. Bring lentils to boil with water in pressure cooker. Simmer uncovered for 5 minutes. Add sea vegetable and bay leaf. Cover and bring to pressure. Turn heat low to cook for 1/2 hour. Or boil lentils for 1 hour.

Heat oil and sauté vegetables briefly. Cover to cook until soft, several minutes. Stir in salt, parsley, and thyme. Add bread. If it is quite dried out, sprinkle it with 1/4 cup water. Cook a couple of minutes more.

Line a loaf pan with parchment or waxed paper. Preheat oven to 350°.

When lentils come down from pressure, remove bay leaf. While still hot, purée lentils with all other ingredients and mix well. (Mixture is too dense for a blender, but a food processor, or a hand-powered food mill or ricer, work well. Return any thicker parts that stay in ricer to purée and mix in.) Transfer mixture to loaf pan, smooth surface, and bake for 1 hour.

Allow to cool 2-3 hours, then lift loaf from pan and peel off paper. Paté tastes even better after overnight aging.

Serve sliced on whole-grain bread or crackers, along with soup and salad, or on toasted bagels with red onion rings and sprouts. Or garnish whole loaf with fresh thyme or parsley sprigs.

Tempeh Party Ball Spread

Makes 8-12 servings or 1 1/3 cups

Some people say this attractive bean spread tastes more like a fish spread. The idea for it comes from the cheese balls found in gourmet shops and mail order catalogs.

8 ounces tempeh, cut in 1-inch pieces
Water
2 tablespoons wet mustard
1-2 tablespoons natural soy sauce (start
    with less); or 1/2-1 teaspoon sea salt; or
    half of each
2 tablespoons celery, finely chopped

1/4 cup green onions or chives, finely
  chopped

In a small saucepan bring tempeh to boil in
water to cover. Cook until done all the way
through, 10-15 minutes. Drain and mash or
purée tempeh with mustard and soy sauce
and/or salt. Mix in celery and half of the
green onions or chives.

  With moistened hands, shape mixture
into 2 balls and roll them in the remaining
onions. Serve surrounded with a circle of
crackers. May be made ahead of time.

Mung Bean Gravy ❤ Moong Dal *(Indian)*

Makes 6-7 servings or 3 cups

According to Martha Ballentine in Himalayan
Mountain Cookery, *mung beans are highly
regarded by the people of India where they
originated. They are used whole and split
and are cooked rather than sprouted as is
done in this country. Ballentine says they are
"especially recommended for those engaged
in spiritual practices* (who have the) *need to
maintain a lightness, alertness and clarity of
mind." Smaller than all but the tiniest azuki
beans, they require no soaking and cook up
in an hour.*

1 cup whole mung beans
5 cups water
6-inch piece kombu or wakame sea
  vegetable
1 tablespoon sesame oil
1 1/2 teaspoons ground coriander
1 teaspoon ground cumin
1/2 teaspoon ground turmeric
3 tablespoons light miso
1 tablespoon parsley, chopped

Place beans with water in pressure cooker
and bring to boil. Let slow boil 5 minutes
uncovered, then add sea vegetable, cover,
and bring up to pressure. Turn heat low and
cook for 1 hour. No flame spreader is necessary.

  Toward the end of cooking, heat oil and
fry seasonings (coriander, cumin, and turmeric) until brown, about 1/2 minute.
Transfer cooked beans, seasonings, and
miso to food mill, blender, or food processor
to purée until smooth. Texture should be
quite soupy. Return dal to pot and cook several minutes to blend flavors. Add parsley
just before serving.

  For larger amounts, such as 4 times
this recipe, measure water to 3 inches above
beans (about 13 cups water). Increase other
ingredients proportionately except oil which
may be cut in half. Makes 10 cups. Beans
will cook nicely even if pressure cooker is
3/4 full.

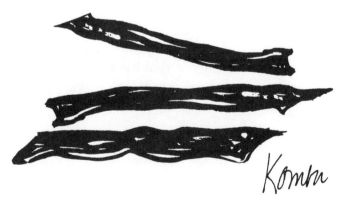

Kombu

Creamy Tofu Sauces and Dressings

Directions in the following recipes state that it's necessary to boil or steam the tofu for 2 minutes before use. This is a step I omit when I know and trust the source—e.g., our local tofu shop. But for tofu that may have travelled a long way and perhaps sat in the market for many days, the quick cooking serves as a refreshing and sanitizing agent.

Tofu is a godsend for health-conscious cooks who want to create low-fat, no-cholesterol, dairy-free dressings and sauces. Tofu's creamy quality (in both color and texture) makes these recipes sensorially satisfying like the dairy versions, and certainly as quick and easy to work with.

Indian-style Tofu "Yogurt"

Makes 1 cup

This recipe has the flavor and mouth-feel of yogurt. If you desire the lactobacillus in yogurt, be aware that it is contained in other fermented foods such as homemade pickles and miso, the fermented bean paste.

1/2 pound tofu, fresh, about 1 cup
2 tablespoons brown rice vinegar
1 teaspoon cumin
1/2 teaspoon unrefined sea salt
1/4 cup water

Boil or steam whole tofu for 2 minutes. Drain, allow to cool, then crumble tofu into blender and purée until creamy smooth with other ingredients.

Variation: For **Plain Tofu "Yogurt"** ♥ simply omit cumin.

Tofu "Sour Cream" Dressing

Makes 2/3 cup

1/2 cup *Tofu "Sour Cream"* (recipe follows)
2 tablespoons water
1 tablespoon natural soy sauce
1 tablespoon brown rice vinegar (or apple cider vinegar)
2 teaspoons extra virgin olive oil
1/8 teaspoon black pepper

Tofu "Sour Cream":

Makes 2 cups

1 pound tofu, fresh
2 tablespoons vinegar (brown rice vinegar or apple cider vinegar for Russian dishes)
1 tablespoon natural soy sauce
1/2 teaspoon unrefined sea salt
Water to proper texture, about 1/3 cup

To prepare tofu "sour cream" for dressing, boil or steam tofu for 2 minutes. Drain several minutes, then blend with other ingredients until creamy smooth. To prepare dressing, mix those ingredients well.

Tofu "Mayonnaise" Dressing

Makes little more than 1 cup

This tofu "mayonnaise" dressing is great on any salad where you would normally use regular mayonnaise such as macaroni, tempeh (a lot like chicken salad), or cole slaw.

1 cup *Tofu "Mayonnaise"* (recipe follows)
2 tablespoons dill pickle, finely chopped
2 teaspoons wet mustard
1-2 cloves garlic, minced

Tofu "Mayonnaise":

Makes 1 1/4 cups

Tofu "mayonnaise" substitutes well for regular mayonnaise as an ingredient in sandwiches and salads. Containing no eggs and very little oil, this wholesome version is very low in fat and calories, with no cholesterol. Lasts up to 3 weeks refrigerated. (If texture thickens up with refrigeration, whisk in a little extra oil or water to regain velvety smoothness.)

Most homemade mayonnaise is a mixture of oil, egg yolk, lemon juice and sometimes vinegar, mustard, salt, and pepper. The ingredients in commercial mayonnaise might also include "vegetable salad oil, whole eggs, water, sugar, natural flavors, and calcium disodium EDTA to protect flavor."

This version is simpler, and definitely more wholesome, with a delicious new flavor. Great served as a dip for artichokes.

1/2 pound tofu, fresh, soft or firm
2 tablespoons lemon juice, or 1 tablespoon
    each lemon juice and brown rice
    vinegar
2 tablespoons extra virgin olive oil
1/2-1 teaspoon unrefined sea salt
1 teaspoon wet mustard
1/8 teaspoon turmeric
Water to blend to smooth consistency, about
    2-4 tablespoons

To make tofu "mayonnaise," combine ingredients in food processor or blender and purée until creamy smooth. If tofu needs refreshing (see introductory note on page 87), boil or steam for 2 minutes, drain, and allow to cool.

To make dressing, simply combine ingredients. For large amounts, increase ingredients proportionately.

Variations: **Curried "Mayonnaise" Dressing** ❤ Use only lemon juice in tofu "mayonnaise" and add 1 teaspoon curry powder, or 1/2 teaspoon each curry and cumin powders, to dressing.

Tofu "Mayonnaise" Dressing No. 2

Makes 1 1/4 cups

This dressing accompanies the Hot Slaw *recipe on page 97.*

1/2 pound tofu, fresh
2 tablespoons lemon juice
2 tablespoons brown rice syrup
1 tablespoon brown rice vinegar
1 tablespoon oil (olive, sunflower, sesame,
    etc.)
1 teaspoon unrefined sea salt
1 teaspoon wet mustard or 1/4 teaspoon dry
    mustard powder
2 tablespoons water
1/4 teaspoon celery, caraway, or dill seeds

Boil or steam whole block of tofu for 2 minutes. Drain, allow to cool, then blend until smooth with all other ingredients. For large amounts, omit water, adding it gradually, and only if necessary for blending.

Heavy Tofu "Cream" with Herbs

Makes 1/2 cup

2 ounces tofu, fresh, about 1/3 cup
1 teaspoon natural soy sauce
1/8 teaspoon each rosemary and coriander
3 tablespoons water

Prepare by blending ingredients until smooth.

Tofu "Cheese" Sauce

Makes a little more than 1 cup

A nice filling for enchiladas (see recipe on page 82).

1/2 pound tofu, fresh
1 tablespoon apple cider vinegar
2 cloves garlic, sliced
1/2 teaspoon unrefined sea salt
Water to blend, about 2 tablespoons

Blend ingredients until smooth.

Italian White Sauce

Makes 3-4 cups

Italian White Sauce really satisfies the desire for dairy foods, especially cheese, and for rich Italian flavors.

1-2 tablespoons extra virgin olive oil
2 large onions, thinly sliced
Water
4 large cloves garlic, finely sliced

1 pound tofu, fresh
2 tablespoons natural soy sauce
1 teaspoon unrefined sea salt
1 tablespoon each basil and oregano

Heat oil in a large skillet and sauté onions briefly. Add 2 tablespoons of water and cook, stirring occasionally, until onions are almost soft, about 5 minutes. Add garlic, crumble tofu over garlic, and add soy sauce, salt, and herbs. Cover to cook for about 5 minutes more. Purée ingredients until creamy smooth, adding water to texture desired, perhaps 1/2 cup. Or blend just half the mixture for a chunkier effect.

Creamy Herb (Dill) Dressing

Makes 1 1/4 - 1 1/2 cups

There is no cheese or sour cream as in the standard version of this dressing. Great served over boiled or steamed vegetables such as broccoli or cauliflower.

1/2 pound tofu, fresh
1-2 tablespoons pickled plum (umeboshi) vinegar or natural soy sauce
1-2 tablespoons brown rice vinegar
1 tablespoon dill weed, dried, or 1/4 cup fresh, minced
1/3 - 1/2 cup water (start with less to texture desired)

To prepare dressing, boil or steam whole block of tofu for 2 minutes. Drain and allow to cool. Blend ingredients until smooth. Dressing thickens as it sits.

Variations: **Creamy Basil Dressing** ❤
Substitute fresh basil for dill.

Creamy Garlic-Dill Dressing ❤ Add 2 cloves garlic.

A nice herbal combination is 1/4 teaspoon thyme, 1/8 teaspoon rosemary, powdered, and 1 tablespoon fresh parsley, minced.

For an ***Herb Dip*** ❤ simply add less water.

Ranch Dressing

Makes 1 1/3 cups

Thanks to Steve and Donnell Campbell of Bethalto, Illinois for their creative version of a salad dressing enjoyed in the Midwest. Tofu replaces buttermilk and mayonnaise. Very popular! Dressing is delicious on rice as well.

1/2 pound tofu, 1 cup mashed, fresh
2 tablespoons green onion, finely sliced
2 teaspoons parsley, minced
1 teaspoon dill weed, dried, or 2 teaspoons fresh, chopped
1 clove garlic, pressed or sliced
2 tablespoons lemon juice
1 tablespoon natural soy sauce
1 tablespoon extra virgin olive oil
2 teaspoons pickled plum (umeboshi) paste
2 teaspoons brown rice vinegar
1/4 teaspoon white pepper
About 1/2 cup water

To prepare dressing, if tofu is not completely fresh, boil or steam whole block of tofu for 2 minutes. Drain and allow to cool.

Blend all ingredients until smooth in food processor or blender, adding water to proper consistency.

Thousand Island Dressing

Makes about 1 1/2 cups

1/2 pound tofu, fresh
2 tablespoons brown rice vinegar
2 tablespoons natural soy sauce
2 tablespoons *Red Sauce* (recipe follows)
2 tablespoons brown rice syrup
1 tablespoon sesame oil
1 tablespoon onion
2 tablespoons dill pickle, finely chopped

Red Sauce:

Makes 1/2 cup

1/2 cup carrot, finely sliced
2 tablespoons beet, finely chopped
1/2 cup water

To prepare dressing, boil or steam tofu for 5 minutes if not completely fresh. Drain and allow to cool.

Prepare red sauce by boiling ingredients in a small saucepan until soft, about 5 minutes, then purée in small container of blender. (A small amount such as this won't purée in a food processor.) Place all dressing ingredients in food processor or blender except dill pickle and purée until smooth, then fold in pickle.

Seed or Nut Butter-Based Spreads and Dressings

Basic Fresh-Ground Seed and Nut Butter Recipe

Toasted seeds and nuts make for rich-tasting spreads, companions to any whole grain bread, crackers, or rice cakes.

Sesame tahini (a dietary staple in Mediterranean and Middle Eastern cooking) is made from hulled, raw (not toasted) sesame seeds. It is not a whole food since the nutritious outer layer of the seeds has been removed. But as an occasional food, it serves as a light-colored base for creamy dressings, spreads, and sauces.

Preheat oven to 350° (or simply place seeds in oven at a cold start and turn to 350° to make the most of the fuel). Spread seeds or nuts one layer deep on baking sheet—1 cup sesame or 2 cups other nuts or seeds. Toast until they turn golden in color and you can smell their rich aroma, about 10-15 minutes. Grind them in a hand-powered steel mill or blender. (Don't use stone grinding plates—they will clog and be ruined.)

One-half cup toasted sesame seeds yields a little more than 1/3 cup sesame butter. 1/2 cup toasted walnuts yields 1/4 cup walnut butter.

Variation: For an even richer flavor, sprinkle seeds with soy sauce and return to oven for last 2 minutes of cooking, then grind.

Sesame-Miso Spread

Makes a little more than 3/4 cup

Vary seed and nut butters and misos for a great variety of flavors.

1/2 cup sesame butter (or any other seed or nut butter)
Up to 2 tablespoons brown rice miso (or any other variety) or soy sauce, to taste
1/4 cup water (optional, if texture is too thick)

Mix ingredients well. A wire whisk is helpful.
Note: Ingredients may be lightly simmered together to blend flavors further. For large groups, figure 1 1/2 tablespoons per serving.

Variation: **Nutty Miso Spread** ❤ Substitute 6 tablespoons peanut butter and 2 tablespoons almond butter for sesame butter, and a light miso for brown rice miso.

Almond-Onion Spread

Makes a little more than 3/4 cup

1/2 cup almond butter
1-2 tablespoons miso (any variety) or soy sauce
2-4 tablespoons water, less with soy sauce, more with miso (optional, if texture is too thick)
2 tablespoons green onion, thinly sliced, or yellow, white, or red onion, grated or minced

Mix together nut butter, miso, and water (if needed) until smooth. A wire whisk is helpful. Stir in onions last.

Figure 1-2 level tablespoons per serving.

Variation: **Almond-Chive Spread** ❤ Substitute chives for onions.

Japanese Plum Dressing

Makes a little more than 1 cup

2 tablespoons pickled plum (umeboshi) paste
1/2 cup almond or sesame butter
2 tablespoons onion, coarsely chopped
Water to texture desired—start with 1 cup

Blend ingredients until smooth, adding water gradually as needed.

Variation: **Japanese Plum Sauce** ❤ For a sauce with less bite, cook several minutes to neutralize the raw onion taste.

Tahini-Lime Dressing

Makes a little more than 1/2 cup

1/4 cup sesame tahini, toasted
2 tablespoons lime juice
1 tablespoon umeboshi vinegar
1 teaspoon garlic, chopped (optional)
Up to 1/4 cup water

Blend ingredients until smooth.

Walnut-Miso Dressing

Makes a little more than 1 1/2 cups

1 cup walnuts, lightly toasted (makes 1/2 cup walnut butter)
1/4 cup white miso
2 tablespoons lemon juice or brown rice vinegar, or part of each
1 cup water

Combine ingredients in blender or food processor and blend until smooth.

Orange-Shiso Dressing

Makes a little more than 3/4 cup

Shiso leaves are added to umeboshi plums in the pickling process to turn the plums red and add flavor. The combination makes for a delicious zesty taste, perfect for salad dressings. Use the leaves in the package of plums for this recipe.

1/2 cup orange juice
1/3 cup sesame tahini, toasted
1 - 1 1/2 tablespoons umeboshi vinegar (start with less)
2 teaspoons red shiso leaves, finely chopped

Blend ingredients until smooth.

Simple, Oil-free Dressings and Sauces

See the chart on page 63 for a listing of many possible combinations.

Light Lemon-Rice Vinegar Dressing

Makes 2 tablespoons

Although used in a pressed salad, this dressing is good on simply boiled or steamed vegetables.

1 tablespoon lemon juice
1 tablespoon brown rice vinegar

Mix ingredients.

2-Taste Dressing

Makes 2 tablespoons

2 tablespoons brown rice vinegar or lemon juice
2 tablespoons natural soy sauce

Mix ingredients.

3-Taste Dressing

Makes a little more than 1/2 cup

1/3 cup lemon juice
3 tablespoons natural soy sauce
1 tablespoon sesame oil, plain or toasted

Mix ingredients.

Dilled 3-Taste Dressing

Makes 1/2 cup

3 tablespoons umeboshi vinegar
3 tablespoons brown rice vinegar
2 tablespoons sesame oil
1 tablespoon fresh dill, minced, or 1 teaspoon dry

Mix ingredients. Dill weed retains its color even when dressing is mixed hours ahead of time.

Ginger Sauce

Makes 2 1/4 cups

2 teaspoons fresh ginger, peeled and grated
2 cups water
1/4 cup natural soy sauce
1/4 cup arrowroot powder or kuzu root starch

Place ingredients in small saucepan. Stir to dissolve thickener. Bring to boil, stirring gently until a sauce is formed, in several minutes.

Vinaigrette Dressings

Vinaigrette dressings usually call for more oil than vinegar and so are higher in fat than most of the following recipes. Unrefined oils are higher in quality than other commercial oils because they are processed by chemical-free techniques, yielding higher nutrition. They have good color and they taste and smell like the foods from which they were extracted. Their richer flavor necessitates less volume in dressings.

Dressings made with mild-tasting specialty oils, which are a little more highly refined, such as pale-colored walnut or almond oil, all require less vinegar than the more full-bodied oils such as extra virgin olive oil or toasted sesame oil. As a general rule, when designing your own dressings, figure 1/2-1 teaspoon dry herbs and 1/2 teaspoon salt per 1/2 cup vinaigrette. To substitute soy sauce for salt, figure 1/2 teaspoon salt equals 1 tablespoon soy sauce.

Apple Cider Vinaigrette

Makes 1/2 cup

1/4 cup apple cider vinegar
2 tablespoons apple cider or apple juice
2 tablespoons mild oil (sesame, almond, walnut, etc.)
1/2 teaspoon unrefined sea salt
1/8 teaspoon black pepper

Mix ingredients and set aside to blend flavors.

Creamy Cilantro Vinaigrette

Makes 1/2 cup

6 tablespoons sesame oil
2 tablespoons apple cider vinegar
2 tablespoons cilantro, coarsely chopped
1/2 teaspoon unrefined sea salt

Blend ingredients until frothy. This dressing is best prepared just before serving, as ingredients separate and cilantro loses its pretty green color with time.

Gingered Lemon-Soy Dressing

Makes 5 tablespoons

This dressing goes well on cooked vegetables or on ingredients which need strong seasoning, such as tofu with sprouts.

3 tablespoons natural soy sauce
2 tablespoons lemon juice or rice vinegar, or
    1 tablespoon of each
1 teaspoon toasted sesame oil
1 teaspoon ginger, peeled and grated

Mix dressing ingredients.

Gingered Vinaigrette Dressing

Makes 3 tablespoons

1 tablespoon wine vinegar
1 tablespoon brown rice vinegar
2 teaspoons sesame oil

1 teaspoon fresh ginger, peeled and grated
1/4 teaspoon unrefined sea salt

Mix dressing ingredients and let sit several minutes.

Lemon-Garlic-Mint Dressing

Makes 1/3-1/2 cup

1/4-1/3 cup lemon juice, start with less and add to taste
2 tablespoons extra virgin olive oil
1 clove garlic, minced
1 tablespoon fresh mint leaves, minced
1/2 teaspoon unrefined sea salt

Mix ingredients well.

Japanese Vinaigrette Dressing

Makes 1/2 cup

Low in oil, high in flavor, this dressing is good for salads which need a lot of flavor such as those based on tofu and/or cooked vegetables.

1/4 cup brown rice vinegar
2 tablespoons natural soy sauce
1 tablespoon Japanese sweet rice cooking wine (mirin)
2 teaspoons toasted sesame oil

Simply mix ingredients.

Sweet Poppy Seed Dressing

Makes a little less than 1/2 cup

This is a great creamy-style vinaigrette dressing.

1 teaspoon poppy seeds
1/4 cup sesame oil
2 tablespoons brown rice vinegar
1 tablespoon pure maple syrup or 2 tablespoons brown rice syrup or Japanese sweet rice cooking wine (mirin)
1 teaspoon onion
1/4 teaspoon dry mustard powder
1/4 teaspoon unrefined sea salt

Blend ingredients. If including brown rice syrup as sweetener, if necessary heat the jar in a small pot of water so syrup softens and dissolves easily when mixed with other ingredients. Stir again just before serving.

Sweet Mustard-Dill Dressing

Makes a little more than 1/2 cup

1/4 cup brown rice vinegar
2 tablespoons sesame oil
2 tablespoons pure maple syrup
1 tablespoon natural soy sauce
1 tablespoon dried dill weed or 2 tablespoons fresh, minced
2 teaspoons wet mustard

Mix ingredients and set aside to blend flavors.

Italian Herb Dressing

Makes 1/4 cup

2 tablespoons extra virgin olive oil
2 tablespoons red wine vinegar (or apple
    cider or brown rice vinegar, or part bal-
    samic vinegar)
1/4 teaspoon unrefined sea salt or 1 1/2
    teaspoons natural soy sauce
1/4 teaspoon oregano
1/8 teaspoon rosemary, powdered

Mix ingredients and allow to sit to blend
flavors.

Italian Herb Dressing No. 2

Makes 1/2 cup

1/4 cup extra virgin olive oil
1/4 cup red wine or apple cider vinegar
2 cloves garlic, minced
1 tablespoon dry basil, or 2 tablespoons
    fresh, minced, or a combination of
    Italian herbs (basil, oregano, and
    rosemary)
1 teaspoon unrefined sea salt

Mix ingredients and set aside.

Parisian Parsley Dressing

Makes 6 tablespoons

1/4 cup lemon juice, freshly squeezed,
    about 1 lemon
2 tablespoons extra virgin olive oil
1 clove garlic, minced

1/2 teaspoon parsley, minced
1/4 teaspoon unrefined sea salt

Combine ingredients, and set aside to blend
flavors.

Shiso Leaf Dressing

Makes 6 tablespoons

*This dressing is flavored with shiso leaf, the
red herb which is pickled with the salted
plums (umeboshi). It comes in the package
with the plums or in a separate package,
already dried and powdered.*

1/4 cup umeboshi vinegar
2 tablespoons toasted sesame oil
1 tablespoon red shiso leaf, chopped, or
    dried and powdered

Mix ingredients.

Variations: Substitute 2 tablespoons
soy sauce for umeboshi vinegar. Substitute
brown rice vinegar or citrus juice for part of
ume vinegar.

Tangy Orange Dressing

Makes 6 tablespoons

*Thanks to Lynn Montgomery for this tasty
recipe.*

2 tablespoons orange juice
1 teaspoon orange peel, freshly grated
2 tablespoons brown rice vinegar
1 tablespoon safflower oil
1 tablespoon sesame oil
1/4 teaspoon unrefined sea salt

Mix ingredients and allow to sit for flavors to meld.

Variation: **Gingery Orange Dressing** ❤
Add the juice of 1 tablespoon ginger, freshly grated.

Toasted Sesame Dressing

Makes 2 tablespoons

1 tablespoon toasted sesame oil
1 1/2 teaspoons natural soy sauce
1 1/2 teaspoons lemon juice or brown rice vinegar

Mix ingredients.

Marinades

Teriyaki Sauce/ Marinade

Makes 2 cups

Barbecue sauces are highly seasoned vinegar marinades, also used for basting. In this country they are based on catsup, vinegar, and mustard. With our new knowledge of the delicious tastes and nutritional qualities of Oriental seasonings such as natural soy sauce, brown rice vinegar and syrup, umeboshi plum juice, and cooking sake, we can create a variety of barbecue marinades from East and West.

1 cup natural soy sauce
1/2 cup brown rice vinegar
1/2 cup brown rice syrup or 1/4 cup pure maple syrup
1/4 cup onion, grated or minced
4 cloves garlic, crushed and minced
1 tablespoon ginger, freshly grated
1 tablespoon mustard powder

Place ingredients in a small saucepan and heat just long enough to dissolve rice syrup.

Variations: Make the following substitutions: lemon juice for vinegar; sake, mirin, or another malted grain syrup (barley malt) for part of the rice syrup; grated daikon radish or chopped green onions in place of onion; Japanese green horseradish powder (wasabi) in place of the mustard powder.

Lentil Salad Marinade

Makes a little more than 3/4 cup

This marinade is also a delightful vinaigrette dressing.

1/2 cup brown rice vinegar
1/4 cup extra virgin olive oil
2 cloves garlic, minced
4 teaspoons wet mustard
1 teaspoon lemon peel, freshly grated
1 teaspoon unrefined sea salt

Prepare marinade and set aside to blend flavors.

Red Barbecue Sauce

Makes 1 2/3 cups

Standard commercial barbecue sauces contain a multitude of sweet, spicy, and fatty ingredients. Based on catsup or chili sauce or tomato soup, they are flavored with onion and celery, white or brown sugar, vinegar and/or lemon juice, Worcestershire sauce, celery seed, chili powder, butter or margarine, salt, pepper, wet or dry mustard, paprika, cinnamon, cloves, and allspice. Here is a natural alternative using no tomatoes.

1 cup *Red Sauce* (see recipe on page 117)
1/4 cup apple cider vinegar
1/4 cup soy sauce
2 tablespoons onion, minced
2 tablespoons brown rice syrup
1 tablespoon wet mustard
1 tablespoon sesame oil
1/4 teaspoon basil
1/4 teaspoon oregano
1/4 teaspoon cumin powder
1/16 teaspoon cayenne pepper powder

Mix ingredients well.

Other marinade recipes:

Seasoned Marinades (see page 151)

Dips

Basic Dip Recipe ♥
Creamy Mustard Dip

Makes 1 cup

This basic dip recipe with its many variations is great with vegetable crudités (see page 68).

1/2 pound tofu, fresh
1 tablespoon soy sauuce
1 tablespoon brown rice vinegar
1 tablespoon wet mustard
Water, only if necessary to blend (start with
    1 tablespoon)

Boil or steam whole block of tofu for 2 minutes. Drain. Blend all ingredients until creamy smooth.

Variations: Substitute umeboshi vinegar for soy sauce, and lemon or lime juice for rice vinegar. Omit mustard and substitute other seasonings (onion or chives, garlic, herbs, horseradish, ginger, etc.). To convert dip into a salad dressing, add 1/4-1/2 cup water, and adjust seasonings to taste.

Sushi Dipping Sauce

Makes 2 tablespoons

1 tablespoon natural soy sauce
1 tablespoon water or Japanese sweet rice
    cooking wine (mirin)

To make dip sauce, simply mix ingredients. This is enough for 2 sushi rolls.

Variation: Mix in small amount of high quality prepared wasabi (Japanese green horseradish).

Buckwheat Noodle Dipping Broth

Makes 1 3/4 cups

2 cups water
3-inch piece kombu sea vegetable
1/4 cup natural soy sauce
1/2 teaspoon ginger, freshly grated, or pow-
    dered Japanese horseradish (wasabi)

To make dipping broth, bring water and kombu to boil and simmer 5 minutes. Remove sea vegetable and set aside for later use. Add soy sauce and ginger (or wasabi) to broth and simmer 1 minute more. Serve broth in separate bowls for dipping, or pour directly over deep bowls of noodles.

Variations: ❤ ***Summer Soba*** Allow both noodles and broth to cool to room temperature or chill to serve during the heat of summer. For a main dish, figure 1 1/2 cups whole wheat udon noodles with 1/2 cup broth, topped with 1 tablespoon each grated daikon and chopped green onion and 1/2 teaspoon nori flakes.

A variety of flavors come from adding other ingredients to the basic kombu stock (dashi). Cook 2 dry mushrooms 15 minutes, discard hard stem, and add enough water to equal 2 cups after cooking. Add 2-4 tablespoons sweetener such as brown rice syrup or sweet rice wine (mirin), and/or 1 tablespoon lemon juice. To further enhance taste, serve side dishes of 1/4 cup green onions, finely sliced on the diagonal; 1/2 cup grated daikon; plain or seasoned nori sea vegetable strips, finely cut; or 1-2 tablespoons nori flakes and 1-2 tablespoons toasted sesame seeds to be sprinkled on top of the noodles.

Other dip recipes:

Mexican Bean Dip (see page 149)

Daikon radish

Flour-Thickened Gravies

The general proportions for thickening flour-based gravies is 1 part flour to 5 or 6 parts liquid (water or broth).

Brown Sauce

Makes 1 cup

This is a nice quick sauce for simply-cooked vegetables or grains.

1 cup water or broth
1/4 cup whole-wheat flour
3 tablespoons natural soy sauce

Make sauce by mixing ingredients in a small saucepan. Place over high heat and stir with a wire whisk until sauce thickens, then simmer uncovered 5 minutes more.

Pistachio Gravy

Makes about 2 1/2 cups

3 tablespoons pistachio nut butter
2 cloves garlic, chopped
1 teaspoon each cumin and oregano, or 2
    teaspoons dill
3 tablespoons natural soy sauce
3/4 cup whole-wheat pastry flour, or up to
    half organic, unbleached white flour
2 - 2 1/2 cups vegetable broth or water

Purée ingredients in a food processor or blender, adding water gradually. Transfer to a 2-quart saucepan. Simmer about 5 minutes, stirring with a wire whisk.

Country Gravy

Makes 12 servings or 1 1/2 cups

Sunflower oil and an herbed, soy-flavored stock lend their rich flavors as welcome replacements for the usual high-fat gravy ingredients—meat drippings and bouillon.

2 tablespoons sunflower oil (or other kind)
1/3 cup whole-wheat pastry flour
2 cups cool water
1 tablespoon natural soy sauce
1 teaspoon unrefined sea salt
1 tablespoon fresh sage, minced, or 1 1/2
    teaspoons dried, crushed
2 tablespoons parsley, minced

Heat oil, add flour, and stir until oil is completely absorbed. Set pan aside to cool, about 15 minutes. Mix remaining ingredients except parsley and gradually add liquid to flour, stirring with a wire whisk to avoid lumping. (Gravy should be no more than 1 inch deep in pan in order for it to cook in this brief amount of time.) When all liquid is added, bring mixture to boil, stirring occasionally. Lower heat to slow boil uncovered until desired consistency is reached, 10-15 minutes. Stir in parsley in last 2 minutes of cooking.

For larger amounts, increase ingredients proportionately, but allow more time for cooking, about 1/2 hour for 4 times this recipe.

Table Seasonings

Toasted seeds and nuts, alone or mixed with toasted sea vegetables, make for an incredible array of exotic-tasting toppings for whole grains.

Basic Toasted Nuts and Seeds Recipe

Called for in recipes throughout this book, nuts and seeds add their crunchy textures and rich flavors to every item on the menu from soup to dessert. Because of their high fat content, averaging around 50%, they are best eaten as a topping or ingredient in other dishes instead of alone by more than a handful.

The macrobiotic and vegan approaches to health are definitely low-fat. In addition to being principally (macrobiotic) or completely (vegan) vegetarian, they both usually eschew dairy products and eggs. The oil used in sautéing, or that is found in a balanced way in the nuts and seeds used in cooking or at the table, fulfills the need for reasonable amounts of fat.

Any seeds or nuts (sunflower, sesame, and
    pumpkin seeds; almonds, walnuts,
    hazelnuts, peanuts, pecans, and pine
    nuts)—1 cup sesame seeds or 2 cups
    other nuts or seeds fill a standard baking sheet one layer thick
Soy sauce (1/2-1 tablespoon per cup seeds
    or nuts), optional

Preheat oven to 350°. Rinse and drain sesame seeds, and others if desired. Spread seeds or nuts one layer thick on dry baking sheet. Always check and stir after 5 minutes or when you smell the first faint aroma of the nut or seed oil being released. Bake until golden and fragrant, about 7-15 minutes, less for pecans and pine nuts, even longer if rinsed first. Allow to cool, and store in a tightly covered container until ready to use in salads, breads, desserts, etc.

For table seasonings to sprinkle on whole grains, flavor is enhanced further by drizzling (or spraying with a mister) soy sauce over seeds or nuts after about 5 minutes of baking. Stir well and return to oven to dry and finish toasting, about 2-10 minutes more.

For large groups, figure 1-2 tablespoons per serving.

Toasted Pumpkin Seeds, Native American Style

Makes 1 cup

1 cup pumpkin seeds
1 tablespoon unrefined sea salt
1 cup water

Soak seeds in salted water for 1/2-1 hour, stirring occasionally.

Preheat oven to 350°. Drain seeds and transfer to dry baking sheet. Bake until dry and golden in color, stirring after 10 minutes, about 20 minutes total. Or toast seeds in a dry skillet, stirring often.

Trail Mix

Makes little less than 1 cup

6 tablespoons sunflower seeds, toasted and
    sprinkled with soy sauce
1 tablespoon almonds, toasted
1/4 cup raisins
1/4 cup dried apples, diced

Mix ingredients well.

Variation: Add an equal volume of puffed and/or flaked cereal to mix.

Sesame Salt

Makes about 1 1/4 cups

A favorite topping for brown rice, the ratio of seeds to salt in this recipe is 16:1 or 1 cup: 1 tablespoon. The flavor is delicious, but after tasting, if you wish to cut salt down even further, figure 1-2 teaspoons sea salt per cup of seeds instead. The seeds are partially ground up to facilitate digestion, as they are so small they often end up leaving the body whole if not thoroughly chewed. The large groups I have served buffet-style consumed 1/2-1 tablespoon sesame salt per serving.

1 cup whole (unhulled) sesame seeds
1-3 teaspoons unrefined sea salt

Rinse seeds in water to cover. Pour off any stems that float to the surface, then drain.

Good quality sea salt is moist and sometimes coarse, and must be very briefly dried for easy grinding. Heat skillet and add salt. Stir until it looks dry, about 1-2 minutes over medium heat. Transfer salt to serrated ceramic mortar (called a *suribachi* in Japanese) and grind briefly with wooden pestle to pulverize, or grind in blender or food processor.

Add seeds to skillet and stir over medium heat until they taste good, are dry, or crush easily between the pressure of 2 fingers, 5-10 minutes. If seeds pop a lot, heat is too high.

Or spread seeds on a baking sheet and toast in a 350° oven for 10-15 minutes, adding salt in last few minutes of baking. Grind salt, then add seeds and grind together until half the seeds are pulverized, about 5-10 minutes. The aroma is worth the effort!

Store in a sealed container.

Variation: **Black Sesame Salt** ❤ Substitute black sesame seeds for brown, or mix.

Sesame-Parsley Sprinkles

Makes 1/3 cup

Very nice on rice, make just enough for one meal at a time so parsley is fresh.

1/4 cup *Sesame Salt* (see preceding recipe)
2 tablespoons parsley, minced

Mix ingredients.

Sesame-Sunflower Topping

Makes 3/4 cup

3 tablespoons *Sesame Salt* (see recipe on preceding page)
6 tablespoons sunflower seeds, toasted and sprinkled with soy sauce
3 tablespoons green onions, finely sliced

Mix ingredients well.

Sesame-Shiso Sprinkles

Makes 2/3 cup

1/2 cup unhulled sesame seeds, toasted and left whole or slightly ground
2 tablespoons red shiso powder, or add gradually to taste

Toast seeds in 350° oven until golden and swollen or in a skillet over medium heat, stirring often.

Mix ingredients well and store in tightly covered container. Figure 1-2 teaspoons per serving.

Note: The commercial package of sprinkles contains 3/4 cup. I usually add more shiso for greater flavor, about 1 1/2 teaspoons per package.

Variations: **Pumpkin Seed-Shiso Sprinkles, Sunflower-Shiso Sprinkles** ❤ Chop seeds, or crush with rolling pin, or grind in Japanese serrated mortar (suri-bachi), or in a blender or food processor. Proceed as above.

Sesame-Shiso-Nori Sprinkles

Makes 3/4 cup

1/2 cup sesame seeds, toasted and ground halfway
3 tablespoons red shiso powder
1 tablespoon nori sea vegetable flakes

Simply mix ingredients and store in tightly closed container.

Sea Vegetable Chips, Flakes, and Powders

Sea vegetables are the ideal way to take sea salt as it occurs in its natural state, unrefined and full of the trace elements and minerals found in the sea as well as in human blood. Even most of the sea salt sold in natural foods stores has been highly refined and consists almost exclusively of 2 elements, sodium and chloride. (See Resources.)

The kelp powder found in most natural foods stores is a combination of many varieties of sea vegetables which are harvested from the ocean. This is the food which brings most North Americans in touch with the experience of eating sea vegetables. Once you come to know the distinct qualities (flavors, textures, soaking and cooking times, and uses) of individual kinds of seaweeds, you'll want to prepare your own kelp powders.

Dulse, wakame, or kombu seaweeds are usually used in this way. I find some varieties of Japanese kombu, and wakame with hard midribs, too hard to enjoy when toasted. Wild nori (porphyra) is a domestic sea vegetable which is easily harvested, and also makes delicious baked chips, flakes, or powders. However, a little goes a long way. A full baking sheet of dried wild nori or dulse reduces to just 1/4 cup powder when pulverized.

Sea chips, flakes, and powders are delicious and easy to use. Simply sprinkle them into or over soups, grains, vegetables, or salads. Nori and dulse flakes and kombu powder are available commercially as well.

Dulse, nori, or wakame sea vegetables, dried

Preheat oven to 350°. Pull apart sea vegetables and place on baking sheet to bake until brittle, for just 3-5 minutes, or up to 10-15 minutes for wakame. Nori turns green when done. Overcooking makes for a bitter flavor.

Serve as is, suggesting that guests crush chips over their soup, grains, morning cereals, or vegetables. Or before serving, crush chips into flakes or pulverize into powder with Foley food mill, blender, or food processor. Two cups dry seaweed, baked and pulverized, yields just 1/2 cup flakes or 2 tablespoons powder. Sift wakame through strainer to remove hard pieces. Store in tightly covered container.

Seeded Sea Powders

Makes 1 - 1 1/2 cups

Toasted seeds mixed with sea vegetable flakes make incredibly tasty table seasonings, and are great ways to include sea vegetables in the diet on a daily basis. Some combinations celebrate the native seeds and seaweeds of North America. Each has its own special flavor and array of nutrients.

Two domestic sources for wild nori (and other sea vegetables) are Mendocino Sea Vegetable Company and Rising Tide Sea Vegetables. The first nori to be cultivated in the U.S. from Washington State and processed into flat sheets for sushi is available from Sound Sea Vegetables (see Granum in Resources).

2 cups dry dulse, wild nori, regular or green nori (or 3 sheets cultivated nori), or wakame, gently packed, or 1/4 cup packaged nori or dulse flakes
1 cup sunflower or pumpkin seeds
1/2-1 tablespoon natural soy sauce

Bake sea vegetables as in preceding recipe. Nori sheets may be waved over an open flame (an electric burner works too) to toast, or for large amounts, spread them out on a baking sheet to bake for 2-3 minutes.

Turn oven to 350°. Spread seeds on baking sheet and place in cold oven to toast until golden in color, 10-15 minutes, or bake as usual in hot 350° oven, checking seeds after 8 minutes. Sprinkle or spray seeds with soy sauce, stir, and return seeds to oven to toast until dry, about 2 minutes more. Instead of baking, a dry skillet may be used on stovetop, but this method demands constant attention to avoid uneven toasting.

Crush seeds with a rolling pin and mix with crumbled sea vegetable flakes, or process both to a powdery consistency in hand-powered steel mill on a loose setting, or in a blender or food processor. (Seeds will clog and ruin a stone mill.) Store in tightly covered container.

Variations: **Sunflower-Dulse Sprinkles, Wild Nori-Sunflower Sprinkles, Pumpkin Seed-Dulse Sprinkles**

(Wild) Nori-Sesame Sprinkles

Makes 2/3 cup

1 cup dry wild nori seaweed (1/4 ounce), or
    3 tablespoons nori flakes
1/2 cup *Sesame Salt* (see recipe on page
    137)

Preheat oven to 350°. Spread nori on baking sheet and bake for just 5 minutes. After it cools for a couple of minutes, crumble with fingers, checking to see if any small shells need discarding. Mix with sesame salt.
    Figure 2-3 teaspoons per serving.

Variation: Replace sesame salt with toasted sesame seeds which have been sprinkled with soy sauce (as an alternative to sea salt) before grinding.

Commercial Condiments

These particular table seasonings are favorites which are commercially available in well-stocked natural foods stores. One excellent source is Granum Inc.

Sesame-Nori-Miso Sprinkles
A combination of dried barley miso, whole toasted sesame seeds, and green nori sea vegetable flakes. Figure 1/2-1 teaspoon per serving.

Vegetable-Miso Seasoning ♥ Tekka
Root vegetables (carrot, burdock root, lotus root, and ginger root) are sautéd in sesame oil and cooked with soybean miso over a low fire for several hours until a crumbly powder is formed. Tekka is the Japanese word for "iron fire" since the seasoning is prepared in a cast iron pan and, partially for this reason, is known to be high in that mineral.

Seasoned Nori Strips
So delicious wrapped around rice, nori sheets are dipped in a mixture of soy sauce and rice syrup, seasoned with a little red pepper, then toasted and cut in strips.

Sweet Spreads and Toppings

Delicious, homemade sweet spreads and toppings are heartwarming served anytime, bringing back homespun feelings of simpler days gone by.

The difference between jams and preserves is that the fruit is cut in larger pieces for preserves. These recipes are for relatively small amounts and so are easy to prepare as each of the summer fruits come into season. Some berries have a tart taste. Enjoy them for this quality enhanced by the addition of brown rice syrup (see page 171), or really sweeten them up with pure maple syrup.

Canned fruit spreads make ideal gifts year-round. They are great as a topping for fresh bread, toast, muffins, pancakes and waffles, or puddings, or tucked inside dessert crepes and as fillings for pies and cakes. Use within a year.

One of the best benefits of making your own is that you can avoid the white sugar, corn syrup, or honey included in many commercial spreads.

Fruit spreads should be soft and spreadable enough to mound gently and stay in place on a spoon, and should not be stiff or syrupy.

Pectin is often used to enhance the texture of jams and jellies. It is a naturally occurring substance, extracted from the liquid portion of some cooked fruits, especially apples.

The first ingredient in commercial pectin is dextrose (sugar) which is added to neutralize the sour taste of citrus rinds from which it is made.

Sugarless pectins are generally made with sugar substitutes and usually have sodium benzoate added as a preservative.

One type of pectin gels with or without sweeteners, but is treated with ammonia.

The following recipes feature agar sea vegetable flakes as the gelling agent. Agar is a transparent, odorless, colorless combination of seaweeds. High in iodine, iron, and other minerals and trace elements, agar firms up jams, preserves, and jellies as it does aspics and dessert gels and puddings.

Basic Berry Jam or Preserves Recipe ♥ *Strawberry Jam*

Makes 1 - 1 2/3 cups

Canning jars with lids (optional)
1 pint basket berries (about 2 cups or 10-11 ounces strawberries, blueberries, blackberries, or red raspberries), rinsed, stems discarded, strawberries diced small or processed briefly
1/8 teaspoon unrefined sea salt
1/4-1/2 cup brown rice syrup (see page 171) or 2-4 tablespoons pure maple syrup, or half of each
2 tablespoons agar sea vegetable flakes

To prepare jars and lids for canning, first check jars for any nicks or cracks, and lids and ring bands for rust or bends. Discard if any of these exist. Bring a large pot of water to boil. Add jars and completely submerge them. Continue boiling for 15 minutes, adding lids in last 2 minutes. Turn heat off to keep hot until ready to fill. Transfer jars and lids to table with tongs.

To prepare jam/preserves, place berries in 2- or 3-quart pot and sprinkle salt over fruit. Pour in syrup and sprinkle agar flakes on top. Bring ingredients to boil over medium-low heat and stir, then simmer until flakes completely dissolve, 5-10 minutes. Stir with a spoon, or a wire whisk to break up strawberries or blueberries.

Immediately pour or spoon (sterilize spoon too) fruit into sterilized jars to within 1/4 inch of top. Wipe rim with clean cloth and screw lids on tightly. Return water to boil. Place filled jars in boiling water to completely cover, and when water resumes boiling, time for 10 minutes.

With tongs, transfer jars to dry surface to cool. You'll hear a pinging sound signifying lids have sealed. This may happen right away or in a couple of hours to overnight. The depressed center of the lid confirms sealing. Any jars that haven't sealed should be eaten soon.

Note: Some berries have hard seeds which may taste gritty. Although they are often left in, you may wish to strain some out through cheesecloth before canning. Yield is less.

Basic Stone Fruit Jam or Preserves Recipe ♥ Peach Preserves

Makes 3 half-pints or about 2 1/2 - 2 2/3 cups

3 half-pint canning jars with lids (optional)
4-5 cups ripe peaches (or nectarines, or apricots), 1 2/3 - 2 pounds, pitted and chopped small or processed briefly
1/4 teaspoon sea salt
1/2-1 cup brown rice syrup (see page 171) or 1/4-1/2 cup maple syrup, or half of each
1/4 cup agar sea vegetable flakes

Prepare according to preceding recipe for *Strawberry Jam.*

Plum Conserve

Makes 4 half-pints or 2 pints

An early American treat, conserves are chunky, jam-like combinations of 2 or more fruits mixed with nuts. Since plums have a tart sweetness, especially after cooking, this version may be sweetened further with more raisins, or with brown rice syrup (see page 171) or pure maple syrup.

4 cups plums (about 2 pounds), ripe (soft, juicy, and sweet), pitted and chopped
1 1/2 cups raisins
1 tablespoon orange peel, grated
1/4 cup agar sea vegetable flakes
1/4 teaspoon unrefined sea salt
1 cup hazelnuts or walnuts, toasted and chopped
4 half-pint or 2 pint canning jars

Place all ingredients except nuts in pot and bring to boil over medium-low heat. Cook covered until plums become very juicy, raisins are plump, and agar is completely dissolved, 5-10 minutes. Stir occasionally. Add nuts.

To can, transfer mixture to sterilized jars and proceed as in *Strawberry Jam* recipe on page 141.

Variation: Cut volume of raisins to 1 cup, substituting 1/2 cup brown rice syrup or 1/4 cup pure maple syrup for the rest of the raisins. Decrease nuts to 1/2 cup and increase agar to 1/2 cup. You may have a little extra conserve depending on which variation you choose.

Windfall Apple Sauce

Makes about 9 cups

Although the commercially prepared apple sauces and butters found in natural foods stores are great, you might want to try making your own in these updated versions of old-fashioned methods.

Windfalls are the apples that fall to the the ground after a good breeze. This velvety smooth apple sauce can be prepared by boiling or pressure-oooking.

If you have a lot of apples to process, simply cut them in half to pressure-cook. A Foley food mill (ricer) is effective in removing the core and seeds after cooking.

6 pounds apples, about 5 quarts, halved,
  cored, and cut in large chunks
1 teaspoon unrefined sea salt
1 tablespoon cinnamon (optional)
1 cup water or apple juice, or part sweetener

Be sure to cut off any bruised or dark spots on apples.

Place all ingredients in pressure cooker or pot (pressure cooker may be filled to the brim), sprinkling apples with salt and cinnamon as you go. Bring to pressure or boil, then turn heat down to cook until done, for 5 minutes in pressure cooker, 10-20 minutes in a pot, stirring occasionally. Purée in Foley, blender, or food processor.

To can apple sauce, transfer to hot sterilized canning jars and boil in water to cover for 10 minutes. (See *Strawberry Jam* recipe on page 141 for detailed instructions.)

Open Kettle Apple Butter

Makes about 5 cups

Traditional Pennsylvania Dutch style apple butter is made with fresh apples, apple cider syrup, and perhaps a little cinnamon for seasoning. Cooked down in a brass or cast iron pot over a wood fire, it was stirred with a long wooden paddle.

Use cider syrup as you would maple syrup.

9 cups *Windfall Applesauce* (see preceding
  recipe)
1 cup *Cider Syrup* (recipe follows)

Cider Syrup:

Makes 1 cup

1 quart apple cider (or juice)

To make cider syrup, boil cider in uncovered pot until texture becomes syrupy and volume decreases to 1 cup, about 1 hour over medium heat. Stir occasionally.

Place apple sauce and syrup in pot, mix, and bring to boil, then place flame spreader under pot to cook uncovered until amount decreases to about half the original volume. This occurs in 5-8 hours. Stir every half hour.

Variation: **Oven Apple Butter** ❤ For long, slow, even cooking which you don't have to tend, make apple butter by placing uncovered pot in 225° oven until volume decreases by about half, about 8 hours or overnight.

Sesame-Maple Spread

Makes a little less than 1 cup

1/2 cup sesame butter (unhulled, not
    tahini)
1/2 cup pure maple syrup

Mix ingredients well.

"Caramel" Spread

Makes 1 cup

*This sweet spread has a taffy-like texture
when it cools.*

1/2 cup barley malt
1/2 cup sunflower butter
1 teaspoon natural soy sauce
1 teaspoon vanilla

In a small saucepan, heat ingredients
together, mixing well.

Strawberry Sauce

Makes 3 cups

2 pints (baskets) strawberries
3 tablespoons arrowroot powder or kuzu
    root starch
1/2 cup apple juice
1/4 teaspoon sea salt
1/4 cup brown rice syrup

Rinse whole strawberries in a bowl of cool
water, drain, then pinch off and discard
stems. Place arrowroot or kuzu and 1/4 cup
juice in a small bowl and set aside. Place
berries in cooking pot and sprinkle them
with salt. Pour rice syrup and remaining 1/4

cup juice over berries. Bring to boil over
medium heat and continue to cook until berries are tender, about 5 minutes, stirring occasionally. Stir thickener, turn heat low, and
add it to the pot. Carefully stir until a thick,
shiny sauce forms, about 30 seconds.

Blueberry Topping

Makes 2 3/4 cups

2 tablespoons arrowroot powder or kuzu
    root starch
1 1/2 cups apple juice
2 tablespoons pure maple syrup
1/2 teaspoon vanilla
Pinch of unrefined sea salt
2 cups blueberries

Place arrowroot or kuzu in small bowl with
1/2 cup juice, syrup, vanilla, and salt. Bring
remaining juice to boil in a 2-quart saucepan. Add berries and when they have released their juice, in about 2 minutes, stir
kuzu mixture and add to pot. Stir over medium heat until mixture changes from chalky
to clear and shiny, about 1 minute.

Sweet and Simple Sauce

Makes 1 cup

1 cup apple juice
2 tablespoons pure maple syrup
1/2 teaspoon vanilla
1/8 teaspoon each cinnamon and nutmeg
Few grains sea salt
Zest of 1/4 orange, lemon, or lime
1 1/2 tablespoons arrowroot powder or kuzu
    root starch

Place ingredients in saucepan. Stir to
dissolve thickener. Bring to boil, stirring

constantly, until a thick sauce forms, in a couple of minutes.

Watermelon Syrup

Makes 2 cups

Watermelon syrup makes a bright red and very sweet accent to any dessert. The process is somewhat similar to making old-fashioned open kettle apple butter.

Pulp of 12-pound watermelon, seeded

Purée watermelon pulp in Foley food mill, blender, or food processor. A 12-pound watermelon yields about 14 cups purée. Transfer to very large pot (the larger and heavier the pot, the faster syrup cooks) and bring to boil, then simmer uncovered over medium-low to medium heat until thick, 3-4 hours, stirring occasionally. Syrup thickens further as it cools.

Hot Cinnamon Syrup

Makes 6 tablespoons

5 tablespoons malted barley syrup
1 tablespoon water (optional, only if syrup is very thick even after heating)
1/4 teaspoon cinnamon

To prepare syrup, heat ingredients together in a 1-quart pot, and mix well.

Almond "Milk," Almond "Cream," and Toasted Almond Sprinkles

Makes little more than 1 cup "milk" and "cream," and 2/3 cup sprinkles

1/2 cup almonds
3/4 cup water
3/4 cup apple juice
1 tablespoon arrowroot powder or kuzu root starch
1 tablespoon agar sea vegetable flakes
1/4 teaspoon almond extract
1/4 teaspoon vanilla

To prepare almond "milk," purée nuts alone until finely pulverized. Gradually add water and juice and continue to purée. Pour through 2 thicknesses of cheesecloth laid in a strainer. Twist cloth and squeeze through as much "milk" as possible.

To prepare almond "cream," place arrowroot or kuzu in a small bowl and pour enough of the measured almond "milk" over kuzu to barely cover it. Transfer remaining almond "milk" to 1-quart pot with agar flakes. Bring to boil, then simmer until agar dissolves. Stir thickener and add to pot with extracts. Stir quickly while cooking until mixture becomes thick, in a matter of seconds.

To make toasted almond sprinkles, spread ground almond pulp on baking sheet and bake at 250° until golden, stirring a couple of times during cooking, about 40 minutes. Store for future use.

Tofu "Whipped Cream"

Makes 2 1/4 cups

Absolutely fresh tofu is a necessity here or the flavor will be chalky.

1 pound tofu, fresh
1/4 cup pure maple syrup
1 tablespoon vanilla
Few grains unrefined sea salt
2 tablespoons-1/2 cup water, only if necessary to blend

Blend ingredients until creamy smooth.

I usually do not boil the tofu for this topping, as boiling tends to make it firm up. If you do boil tofu ahead, store "cream" in blender and whip it up again just before serving.

For large amounts, mix all ingredients except water, then add it gradually until desired consistency is reached. Less will be needed.

Crumb Topping

1 tablespoon corn oil
1/2 cup whole-wheat pastry flour
1 tablespoon pure maple syrup

Drizzle oil over flour. Mix, then rub between palms. Next work in syrup.

Sprinkle over top of pie or other dessert in last 10 minutes of baking. Or spread on baking sheet to prepare separately for sprinkling over puddings or other unbaked desserts. Bake until golden, about 8 minutes at 400°.

Beans and Soyfoods

Basic Small Bean Recipe

Makes 8 servings

No soaking is necessary for these small beans.

2 cups split peas, lentils, navy, azuki, or
　　mung beans
4-5 cups water, more for navy, azuki, or
　　mung beans
6-inch piece kombu sea vegetable
Vegetables—your choice, cut bite-size
　　(optional)
2-4 tablespoons natural soy sauce or miso,
　　or 1-2 teaspoons unrefined sea salt, or
　　half of each
Parsley, chives, or green onion tops, minced
　　for garnish (optional)

Place beans, water, and sea vegetable in
pressure cooker or pot. Pressure-cook for
20-30 minutes for split peas or lentils, and
1 hour for navy beans, azuki, or mung
beans. (No pre-boiling or flame spreader is
necessary.) Or pot cook beans until done,
adding water when necessary.

　　When pressure subsides, add chopped
vegetables if included, and cook until done,
then add soy sauce, or miso dissolved in a
little hot bean broth, or salt. Simmer very
gently 3 minutes more. For a saucier consistency, stir beans vigorously with a wire
whisk before adding vegetables.

　　To double this recipe, use 1/2 cup less
water to cook beans, i.e., 7 1/2 cups. For
larger amounts, add water to 2 inches above
beans instead of calculating quantity by
multiplying, which would result in too much
water and mushy beans.

Basic Large Bean Recipe

Makes 8 servings

2 cups chickpeas, black beans, pinto beans,
　　etc.
2 quarts (8 cups) water (4 cups to soak, 4
　　cups to cook)
6-inch piece kombu sea vegetable
Vegetables—your choice, cut bite-size
　　(optional)
2-4 tablespoons natural soy sauce or 1-2
　　teaspoons unrefined sea salt, or half of
　　each
Parsley, chives, or green onion tops, minced
　　for garnish (optional)

Sort through, rinse, and soak beans at least 8 hours or overnight in 4 cups water. Drain and reserve soaking water for house plants, garden, or compost. Place beans and 4 cups fresh water in pressure cooker or pot and boil vigorously uncovered for 5 minutes to allow initial gas to escape in the form of bubbles or foam. Scrape off and discard foam or stir it back in. Add sea vegetable and pressure-cook for 1 hour. No flame spreader is necessary.

Or boil beans until tender, 2-3 hours, adding water if necessary. Add chopped vegetables if included, and soy sauce and/or salt (and other seasonings if included), and cook several minutes longer.

For a saucier consistency with a richer flavor as for a stew, remove 1 cup bean broth (save for soup stock), and stir beans vigorously with a wire whisk before adding other ingredients. Cook uncovered over medium-low heat until vegetables are cooked and proper consistency is reached, 15-30 minutes longer, stirring occasionally. Or simply leave the broth in, cooking beans longer.

To double this recipe, use 2 cups less water to cook beans, i.e., 6 cups. To cook larger amounts, increase all ingredients proportionately except water which should cover beans by 1 inch for both soaking and cooking.

Chili Beans ❤
White Bean Chili

Makes 7-8 servings

The Hopi use a small white bean which is similar to the navy bean to make their chili. The women prefer fresh over dry beans because they cook quicker, and use various colored string beans including kidney and pinto. The vines and pods (as well as corn cobs and sage brush) are burned for use as culinary ashes. High in minerals, ash water is added to cornmeal in various preparations.

Native Americans served beans in boiled squash halves. See recipe on page 70.

Makes 4 - 5 3/4 cups, depending on type
of bean and whether soaked or not

2 cups black, pinto, kidney, small or dark
    red, pink, or navy beans
8-9 cups water (4 cups to soak, 4-5 cups to
    cook, more for navy beans which
    require no soaking)
6-inch piece kombu sea vegetable
1 bay leaf
1 onion, diced
2-4 cloves garlic, minced
1/4 cup natural soy sauce; or 2 tablespoons
    soy sauce and 1 teaspoon sea salt; or to
    retain natural color of light beans such
    as navy, 1/4 cup white miso or 2 tea-
    spoons sea salt, or half of each
1-2 teaspoons oregano, or to taste
1-2 teaspoons cumin, or to taste
1/4 teaspoon cayenne pepper powder, or
    1/2 teaspoon crushed red pepper (chili),
    or to taste

Sort through beans for stones or small chunks of dirt, then rinse and drain them. To prepare beans other than navy, soak in water overnight. Drain and place in pressure cooker with 4 cups fresh water. Bring to boil and cook uncovered for 5 minutes, then add kombu and bay leaf and cover to bring to pressure. Turn heat low to cook for 1 hour.

For navy beans, eliminate soaking. Bring beans to boil with 5 cups water and proceed according to *Basic Small Bean Recipe* on page 147.

When pressure subsides, remove bay leaf. Remove kombu to retain clear white color of beans if desired, or allow kombu to dissolve into beans. Add remaining ingredients and cook covered (but not under pressure) until onions are soft, stirring occasionally, about 10 minutes.

If a thicker consistency is desired, remove 1 cup broth and/or mash or stir beans with a wire whisk before adding vegetables. For a thinner consistency, add a little more water.

For larger amounts, such as 8 cups beans, add only enough cooking water to cover beans by 2 inches, about 12 cups water.

Variations: Sauté onion and garlic in 1-2 tablespoons olive oil for richer flavor.

Mexican Black Bean Chili ♥

Before the Spaniards came to Mexico, the Aztecs relied on corn, beans, and chilies as dietary staples as did the native Americans in North, Central, and South America. With the Spanish conquest came new foods—rice, olive oil, and wine. Today chili beans still go well with rice and corn tortillas, or with whole-wheat bread, balanced with a vegetable dish and/or a salad.

Chili or hot red pepper is native to tropical America. It is related to the tomato and shares that plant's short growing season. Because of its hot, irritating, and highly stimulating qualities, chilies are not used extensively in wholesome everyday cooking. It seems appropriate, however, to enjoy this spice in moderation in those international dishes where it has always appeared.

Chilies vary in pungency. Some are very hot, causing irritation to the hands of the pickers. The sun-dried fruits are shredded, or ground as with cayenne pepper. Chili powder is a blend of chili pepper, cumin seed, oregano, garlic, and sometimes salt, coriander, allspice, and cloves as well. (Paprika is a European pepper which is large and mild.)

Proceed as above featuring black beans and including 1/4 cup soy sauce.

Pinto Bean Chili ♥

Proceed as above featuring pinto beans. Substitute 2 teaspoons chili powder blend for garlic, oregano, cumin, and cayenne. People are most familiar with pintos and so I chose them for the chili dish at a Mexican dinner I catered for 300 people.

Mexican Bean Dip ♥

Purée chili while hot. Serve with tortilla chips or crackers.

Texas Chili ♥

This Tex-Mex chili variation contains wheatmeat in place of meat and a red sauce made from carrots and beets instead of tomatoes (see page 117). Crispy serving suggestion: top with a few corn chips.

Follow preceding recipe, featuring kidney beans. Include 1 cup wheatmeat (see page 49), chopped, and decrease soy sauce to 3 tablespoons since there is some in the wheatmeat. Include 1/2 cup *Red Sauce* (see recipe on page 117).

When beans are done, partially mash them with sea vegetable. Add remaining ingredients including red sauce and stir well, then cook covered until onions are tender and flavors well blended, about 10 minutes. Stir occasionally.

Bean Burritos

Makes 6

6 whole wheat tortillas or chapatis (store-bought or see page 41)
3 cups *Refried Beans* (recipe follows)

Refried Beans ❤ Frijoles Refritos:

Makes 8 servings or 4 - 5 1/2 cups, less with black and pinto beans

In Mexican homes, market eating stalls, and restaurants, there is always a big pot of boiled beans in the kitchen cooking all day, from which is taken enough for frying at each meal. Commercial refried beans usually contain beans, water, lard, sugar, and salt. I find olive oil works well here as it has the same rather musty quality that lard has without the animal fat. Rich...delicious!

2 cups beans (black, pinto, kidney, or pink)
2 quarts (8 cups) water (4 cups to soak, 4 cups to cook)
6-inch piece kombu sea vegetable
1 bay leaf
2 tablespoons extra virgin olive oil
2 tablespoons natural soy sauce
1 teaspoon unrefined sea salt
1 tablespoon cilantro, chopped

Sort through, rinse, and drain beans. Soak 8 hours or overnight in 4 cups water. Drain, reserving soaking water for house or garden plants. Transfer beans to pressure cooker and add 4 cups fresh water. Bring to boil and allow to boil for 5 minutes uncovered. Add kombu and bay leaf, cover, and bring to pressure. Turn heat low to cook for 1 hour for excellent texture and taste.

In a large skillet, heat oil. Add beans and their broth. Remove bay leaf and add soy sauce, salt, and cilantro. Mash the beans as they cook, uncovered, over medium-low heat until they appear somewhat dry, about 10 minutes. Beans may seem watery at first, but will become thick and saucy. (To hasten process, when pressure comes down, stir beans vigorously with a wire whisk.)

For large amounts, soak beans in water to cover by 2 inches. Drain. Transfer beans to pressure cooker, add fresh water to cover beans by 2 inches.

To freshen tortillas, steam for 1/2 minute or place in hot skillet long enough that they become warm but not crisp, about 15 seconds on each side.

To assemble burritos, place 1/3-1/2 cup beans along center of each tortilla and fold sides over. Serve seam side down. For large amounts, figure 1 1/2 burritos per serving.

Other bean recipes:

Chickpea-Lentil Soup ❤ Haraira *(Moroccan)* [see page 7]
Mung Bean Gravy ❤ Moong Dal *(Indian)* [see page 121]
Lentil Paté or Loaf (see page 120)
Split Pea Aspic (see page 112)
Bean Aspic (African) [see page 112]
Corn-Bean Pie (see page 80)

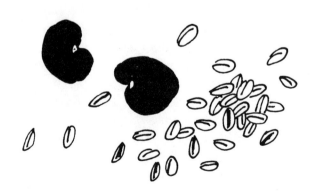

Soyfoods: Tofu and Tempeh

Tofu Cutlets

Makes 2-4 servings

Tofu cutlets have become reliable standbys in many vegetarian homes. Quick and easy bean foods, they are marinated very briefly, then broiled, baked, pan fried, or barbecued for a protein dish that satisfies even the most confirmed meat eaters. Make enough for tomorrow's lunch (cutlets are great tucked in sandwiches, burgers, or pocket pitas with all the fixins': tofu mayonnaise, mustard, lettuce, and sprouts), or cut in small pieces for adding to vegetable dishes, salads, or as a flavorful topping for whole grains.

Use leftover marinades to season sauces for grains or vegetables, or in soup or beans.

1/2 pound tofu, firm, cut in 1/2-inch
    slices
1 cup natural soy sauce
Toasted sesame or other oil

Marinate tofu in soy sauce for 2-3 minutes. The marinating time is short because the marinade is full-strength, undiluted soy sauce. Strain soy sauce back into bottle, or if seasonings have been added (see variations), pour into a separate bottle. Tofu absorbs 1-2 tablespoons soy sauce.

Bake cutlets at 400° until golden, about 20 minutes. Or broil for 7-15 minutes—less in a hot broiler, more from a cold start. Or pan fry for 10-15 minutes. Either way, turn cutlets over half way through cooking for even browning, if desired.

Variations: **Seasoned Marinades** ❤
Add one or more seasonings to soy sauce for a full range of flavors: garlic (2 large cloves, crushed or minced); fresh ginger or horseradish (2 teaspoons, grated); onion (1/4 cup, grated or minced); wet mustard (1/2 cup); Japanese horseradish powder [wasabi] (1-2 tablespoons); 1/4 cup fresh herbs or 1 tablespoon dried herbs.

Mexican Marinade ❤ Include 1 tablespoon cumin powder and 1 teaspoon oregano. Garlic and lime juice are other possible variations here.

Try combinations such as **Lemon-Garlic Tofu** ❤. Figure 1/2 cup each soy sauce and lemon juice and 2 large cloves garlic, crushed or minced. Marinate twice as long.

Tofu Teriyaki

Makes 5-6 servings

Barbecues are occasions when meals are turned into social gatherings. Whether they are easy lunches on the patio, picnics in the park around the grill, summer evening cookouts, or sumptuous Sunday brunches, barbecues provide relaxation and enjoyment. Colorful grain and vegetable dishes, salads, fresh fruit desserts, and seasonal beverages round out the meal.

Barbecue sauces are highly seasoned vinegar marinades, also used for basting. In this country they are based on catsup, vinegar, and mustard. With our new knowledge of the delicious tastes and nutritional qualities of Oriental seasonings such as natural soy sauce, brown rice vinegar and syrup, umeboshi vinegar, and cooking sake (mirin), we can create a variety of barbecue marinades from East and West.

Much evidence has come out relating charred food (usually meat) to cancer. To enjoy grilled food on occasion, be sure to cook it so it is done all the way through, but not blackened on the outside.

Brochettes or kabobs may be baked or broiled instead of barbecued. Great served over brown rice with a little of the marinade drizzled over all.

1 pound tofu, fresh, not soft, cut in 1/2-inch slabs
1 1/2 cups *Teriyaki Sauce/Marinade* (recipe follows)

Teriyaki Sauce/Marinade:

Makes 2 cups

1 cup natural soy sauce
1/2 cup brown rice vinegar
1/2 cup brown rice syrup or 1/4 cup pure maple syrup
1/4 cup onion, grated or minced
4 cloves garlic, crushed and minced
1 tablespoon ginger, freshly grated
1 tablespoon dry mustard powder

To prepare teriyaki sauce, place ingredients in a small saucepan and heat just long enough to dissolve rice syrup.

Preheat oven to 350°. (Tofu may be barbecued or broiled as well.) Marinate tofu for 15 minutes. Transfer to lightly-oiled baking sheet and cook for 15-20 minutes, turning once halfway through if desired.

Sauce variations: Make the following substitutions: lemon juice for vinegar; sake, mirin, or another malted grain syrup (barley malt) for part of the rice syrup; grated daikon radish or chopped green onions in place of onion; Japanese green horseradish powder (wasabi) in place of the mustard powder.

Brown Rice or Noodles with Teriyaki Vegetables ♥ Use leftover teriyaki sauce in kuzu-thickened sauces for serving over vegetables, tempeh, rice or noodles.

In a small saucepan, combine 1/4 cup teriyaki sauce with 1 cup cool water and thickener (2 level tablespoons arrowroot powder or 1 heaping tablespoon kuzu root starch). Bring to boil and stir well until a thick sauce forms, about a minute. Makes 1 1/4 cups. Mix sauce with 4-5 cups cooked vegetables.

Homestyle Bean Curd with Peanuts in Ginger Sauce

Makes 6 servings

Homestyle bean curd is simply boiled tofu, but prepared in this way, it pleases every time. To the Chinese, a plentiful crop of peanuts and sunflower seeds, known as "passing time foods," shows that the condition of life is improving because they were able to spend their energies on growing these little luxuries in addition to staple foods.

Makes 3 1/4 cups
1 pound bean curd (tofu), fresh and firm, cut in 1-inch cubes
Water
1/4 cup peanuts, toasted
3 green onions, tops cut in 1-inch lengths, whites set aside

Ginger Sauce:

Makes 2 1/4 cups
2 teaspoons fresh ginger, peeled and grated
2 cups water
1/4 cup natural soy sauce
1/4 cup arrowroot powder or kuzu root starch

Boil tofu in water to cover for 10 minutes and drain.

Place sauce ingredients in small saucepan. Stir to dissolve thickener. Bring to boil, stirring gently until a sauce is formed, in several minutes. Add peanuts and green onions to sauce and cook over low heat one minute more.

Gently transfer tofu to serving bowl. Pour sauce over tofu to serve.

Other tofu recipes:

Creamy Mustard Dip (see page 68)
Scrambled Tofu (see page 218)
Fresh Corn Soufflé (see page 81)
French Onion Quiche ❤ Quiche Alsacienne (see page 81)
Tofu Enchiladas (see page 82)

Braised Tempeh

Makes 3-4 servings

So delicious and easy, this dish has become a regular at our house.

1 tablespoon toasted sesame oil
8 ounces tempeh, sliced in half to make 2 thin, 1/2-inch thick slabs, then quartered to make 8 pieces; or cut in 1/2-inch slices
1 tablespoon natural soy sauce
1-4 tablespoons water, more for thick kinds

In a skillet, heat oil over medium-low heat, then lay tempeh slabs or slices side-by-side. Mix soy sauce and water and pour over tempeh. Cover to cook about 5 minutes, then turn tempeh over and cover to cook until done, about 5 minutes more.

For large amounts, when stove top space is valuable, oven-braise tempeh. Preheat oven to 400°. On a baking sheet, prepare tempeh as above, simply increasing ingredients proportionately. Cover with foil and bake for 15 minutes, then turn tempeh, cover again, and cook 10 minutes longer. Remove cover to cook 5 minutes more.

Tempeh Cutlets ❤
Tempeh Sandwiches and Burgers

Garlic and coriander are used as seasonings here because they are historically cooked with tempeh in its country of origin, Indonesia.

Makes 4

Tempeh Cutlets:

1/4-1/2 cup water (less for dense, smaller slab of tempeh, more for lighter, larger slab tempeh)
2 tablespoons natural soy sauce
1 large clove garlic, minced
1 teaspoon powdered coriander (optional)
8-ounce package tempeh, cut in 4 sandwich-size slabs or rounds, about 1/2-inch thick

All the fixins' for Tempeh Sandwiches or Burgers:

8 slices whole-grain bread, plain, toasted, or steamed to soften; or 2 pita pocket breads, cut in half, then steamed to soften; or 4 burger buns
1/2 cup *"Tofu Mayonnaise"* (see recipe on page 123)

1/3 cup wet mustard and/or natural catsup
4 lettuce leaves
1/3 cup sauerkraut or dill pickles, thinly
    sliced, or part of each
1/2 cup alfalfa sprouts or cucumber, thinly
    sliced in rounds (optional)

Place water, soy sauce, garlic, and coriander if included in skillet or pan of appropriate size to hold tempeh slabs side-by-side. Add tempeh. Bring to boil, then simmer covered until liquid is absorbed and tempeh is cooked all the way through, 10-15 minutes, turning tempeh over after 5 minutes.

Serve cutlets as a side dish or as filling for sandwiches or burgers with all the fixins'.

Seasoning variation: Omit coriander. Include 1 tablespoon lemon juice, 1/4 teaspoon dry herbs (a combination of thyme and basil is nice), and 1/2 teaspoon sesame oil.

Barbecued Tempeh Cutlets in Pocket Pitas

Makes 4 servings

These sandwiches are great for picnic outings or for a meal at home or to go. Tempeh prepared this way has a rich, satisfying flavor. It may be barbecued, broiled, or baked. Baking is easiest for very large groups.

8 ounces tempeh, cut in 4 pieces, 1/2 inch
    or less in thickness
1 cup *Red Barbecue Sauce* (recipe follows)
2 large whole-wheat pita pocket breads

1/2 cup *"Tofu Mayonnaise"* (see page 123)
4 lettuce leaves
Red onion, very thinly sliced in rounds
Cucumber, very thinly sliced in rounds

Red Barbecue Sauce:

Makes 1 2/3 cups

Standard barbecue sauces are based on ketchup or chili sauce or tomato soup, flavored with onion and celery, white or brown sugar, vinegar and/or lemon juice, Worcestershire sauce, celery seed, chili powder, butter or margarine, salt, pepper, wet or dry mustard, paprika, cinnamon, cloves, and allspice. Try this tasty natural foods variation.

1 cup *Red Sauce* (see page 117)
1/4 cup apple cider vinegar
1/4 cup natural soy sauce
2 tablespoons onion, minced
2 tablespoons brown rice syrup
1 tablespoon wet mustard
1 tablespoon sesame oil
1/4 teaspoon basil
1/4 teaspoon oregano
1/4 teaspoon cumin
1/16 teaspoon cayenne pepper powder

To prepare barbecue sauce, mix ingredients well.

Marinate tempeh in barbecue sauce for 1/2 hour.

Preheat barbecue grill, broiler, or oven while you prepare sandwich fixins'. Cut each pita bread in half. Steam bread about 2 minutes to soften and prevent crumbling with handling. Spread a tablespoon of tofu "mayonnaise" on each inner side and fill each pocket with lettuce and rounds of red onion and cucumber.

Barbecue tempeh, covered, for 5-7 minutes on each side, turning just once. To broil tempeh, cook on first side until toasted,

about 8 minutes, then turn it over, spoon
over a little more sauce, and cook 8 minutes
more. To bake, cook for 15 minutes at 450°,
then turn cutlets over, baste generously,
and bake 15 minutes more. Add cutlets to
pocket sandwiches.

Other tempeh recipes:

Tempeh Party Ball Spread (see page 120)
Hiziki-Vegetable Sauté with Tempeh (see
    page 85)

Pickles and Relishes

Nutritional Qualities

Natural, homemade pickles add pleasure at mealtime with their tangy taste, crunchy texture, and color. Versatile, they may be served as a side dish or snack, or in sandwiches or salads. They are a rich source of enzymes, lactobacilli, and other live microorganisms which develop during curing, including vitamin B12. The human digestive system needs a beneficial balance of these substances to maintain strong, healthy intestines for assimilation of other foods, to synthesize vitamins, lower cholesterol, and to inhibit the growth of undesirable bacteria and the overgrowth of yeast such as Candida.

According to Ballentine in *Diet and Nutrition*, locally produced strains of bacteria grown on food apparently are able to produce antibiotic substances in the intestines. These are probably responsible for regulating bowel microbes, subduing those which are undesirable.

Food which is fermented is predigested like vegetables that have had the cell walls broken down with cooking. But with naturally fermented, fresh pickles, the living enzymes normally destroyed by cooking remain intact. Best of all, cultured vegetables add zing to meals with flavors ranging from mellow-sour to zesty tart.

Homemade pickles, unlike most commercial ones, are not pasteurized. The same holds true for other fermented vegetarian foods of high quality such as miso, soy sauce, and tempeh. They have the same desirable qualities of fermentation found in yogurt and aged cheese, but without the cholesterol and saturated fat. Grains and fruit are the principal ingredients used in the fermentation process of making sourdough bread and unpasteurized beer and wine.

History

A fondness for pickled products always has been characteristic of people in many places throughout the world. The history of fermented vegetables extends so far into antiquity that no precise time can be established for its origin. Presumably, it was observed that when vegetables flavored with salt or salt brine were packed tightly in a vessel, they changed in character but remained appetizing and nutritious.

The Chinese may have been the first to preserve vegetables by a fermentation process. When the Emperor Ch'in Shih Huang Ti was constructing the Great Wall of China in the 3rd century B.C., a portion of the workers' rations consisted of a fermented mixture of vegetables—possibly cabbages, radishes, turnips, cucumbers, beets, and whatever other vegetable materials were available.

The Tartars under Genghis Khan are sometimes credited with introducing fermented vegetables to Europe, but there is little doubt that these methods of preserving vegetables were introduced there much earlier. Pliny's writings mentioned spiced and preserved cucumbers. They were a delicacy enjoyed by Caesar's legions; Emperor Tiberium ate pickles regularly; and Cleopatra is said to have delighted in eating them.

The first pickles were most likely packed in brine solutions, not only because dry salt withdrew insufficient water from the vegetable pieces or chunks, but also because the use of brine would permit settling out of sand and other insolubles in the impure salt of the time. Dry salting (pressing with salt) was a later development of the art. In general, cucumbers, olives, and other vegetables in large pieces are cured in a brine solution while shredded or chopped cabbage is dry-salted in making sauerkraut.

Pickles are a significant part of the diet of Far Eastern peoples, Europeans, and Americans today; it is estimated that at least 75% of American families eat fermented vegetable products at least once a week. In Korea a blend of pickled mixed vegetables *(kimchi)* is second only to rice in feeding the population. In Europe and America, cucumber pickles, sauerkraut, and olives have become the favorites, although pickled onions, cauliflower, peppers, and others are enjoyed, especially mixed.

According to Pederson in *Microbiology of Food Fermentations* on which much of this information is based, environmental factors important in the fermentation of vegetables

consist essentially of a suitable salt concentration, the establishment of anaerobic (air-free) conditions, proper temperature, cleanliness, and the presence of suitable lactic acid bacteria. Trimming and cleaning, but not scrubbing, are essential for removing extraneous microorganisms. Of course, chemical-free, organic vegetables are the best choice.

Sufficient salt or salt brines must be added to withdraw liquid from the vegetable and to deter softening, but the salt content must be kept low enough to allow a rapid initiation of the fermentation in order to produce acid rapidly and to reduce oxygen. Some pickles are ready in just an hour. Others require a few days or weeks and may be stored in the refrigerator for several seasons.

Quick Cucumber Dill Pickles

Makes 1 1/4 cups

2 cups cucumber, 3/4 pound or 1 medium cuke or 2-4 lemon cucumbers, peeled if skin is waxed or bitter tasting, thinly sliced
1 teaspoon sea salt (1/2 teaspoon per cup soft vegetables or greens)
1/2 teaspoon dried dill weed or seeds or 1 1/2 teaspoons fresh, minced

Rub cucumber slices with salt and mix in dill. Press with plate and weight or in a small pickle press for at least 1 hour. Drain and taste. If flavor is too salty, rinse pickles in water and squeeze. Serve or refrigerate.

Variation: Prepare other vegetables such as cabbage in the same way. Squeeze out excess liquid before serving.

Quick Carrot-Daikon Pickles

Makes 1 1/4 cups

1 cup carrot, grated
1 cup daikon, grated
2 green onions, thinly sliced
2 teaspoons sea salt (1 teaspoon per cup root
   vegetables)

Prepare as in preceding recipe. Notice the strong daikon flavor softens with time. If pickles taste too salty, rinse briefly in cool water.

Variation: Substitute turnip or red radish for daikon.

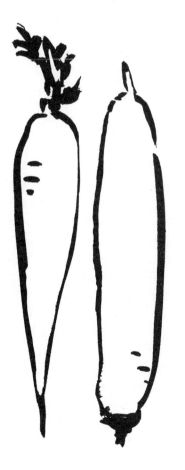

Sauerkraut

Cabbage has always had a special place in the diet as an adjunct to making other foods more agreeable and digestible, as well as for its own taste and nutritional value. Drawings and carvings from Ancient Egypt depict cabbages placed on temple altars as offerings worthy of the gods. Greek doctors used cabbage as a general cure for illnesses, and it was a common vegetable in both Greek and Roman gardens. Cato, in a manuscript written about 200 B.C., lauds cabbage as the most important vegetable the Romans had under cultivation. From then until 450 A.D. it was the principal plant used in the Roman Empire for the treatment of disease.

The fact that early accounts describe solid, white-headed varieties indicates that cabbage must have been domesticated for a long time in order to have undergone the extensive modification from wild to cultivated types. Although cabbage is native to many parts of Europe, its use as a cultivated vegetable in Northern Europe is attributed to the Romans.

The term *sauerkraut* is the combination of two words: *sauer* meaning sour and *kraut* meaning greens or plant. The word is originally German, but the assertion so often made that cabbage in the form of kraut is of Germanic origin is not substantiated. These peoples were nomadic when they first came in contact with the Romans toward the beginning of the Christian era.

The best known sauerkraut story revolves around Captain Cook who discovered the Hawaiian Islands. Kraut was part of his sailors' daily rations, and its vitamin C content is attributed with keeping the sailors scurvy-free.

Homemade sauerkraut has a fresh, sharp taste. Sauerkraut is literally acid cabbage. In the beginning, sauerkraut differed markedly from that prepared at present. Among the earliest forerunners were whole or broken cabbage leaves, dressed and served, or packed in vessels, with sour wine or vinegar. Gradually the sour liquids were entirely replaced by salt, and a spontaneous fermentation occurred. In the 1600s the Germans, in order to prepare a food for winter, cut the cabbages, loosened them, placed shreds in layers with salt, juniper berries, spice, barberries, and pepper roots. Each layer was pressed firmly for better contact and a salt brine was added.

Cabbage was the only ingredient used due to the health characteristics ascribed to it and the plentiful supply. Other related vegetables were added later: cauliflower in about 1600, then Brussels sprouts, and broccoli at about 1700. By the late 1700s, the Dutch *zoorkool* was the first sauerkraut to be manufactured by methods similar to those used today.

Proper temperature is one of the important elements of successful sauerkrauting. Cool, dry days or a cool room temperature (60-72°) is best. Heat (over 75-80°) and humidity may cause the cabbage to sour before it ferments.

Unfortunately, today's commercial sauerkraut, no matter how simple the ingredients, is pasteurized by cooking the kraut in the jar to extend shelf life. This process kills the valuable enzymes and bacteria for which sauerkraut and other pickles are known.

The brine from kraut, particularly that made from red cabbage, has a pink wine color and is relished in Europe as an appetizer. The juice from freshly fermented sauerkraut is sprightly effervescent and far superior to that from canned kraut.

Unless sauerkraut is prepared carefully with clean vegetables, the correct amount of salt evenly distributed in the kraut, and the mixture packed tightly, properly covered, and stored at the appropriate temperature, the quality will be inferior. Salt withdraws water and nutrients from the vegetable tissue. The nutrients furnish the substrate for growth of the lactic acid bacteria. Salt, in conjunction with the acids produced by fermentation, inhibits the growth of undesirable microorganisms and delays enzymatic softening of the tissue. A satisfactory salt concentration favors the growth of the various lactic acid bacteria in their natural sequence and yields a kraut with the proper salt-acid balance.

Insufficient salt results in softening of the tissue and yields a product lacking in flavor. Too much salt delays the natural fermentation and may result in a harsh flavor, darkening of color, or growth of pink pigment-producing microorganisms. 1.0-2.5% salt by weight is the proper amount for reliable dry salt pickling. The following recipe calls for 1.5%. Microorganisms can't grow in an environment with a solution above 3.5% salt. The uniform distribution of salt is fully as important as the amount of salt used.

Contact with the air permits growth of yeasts and molds on the vegetable surfaces and generally results in softening, darkening, and development of undesirable flavors and odors. It also destroys the lactic acid. Many methods have been tried to exclude air, including the use of tight wooden covers, weights (plate and stone), cloth, papers, oil coatings, and others. The general use today of plastic sheets in commercial pickling and plastic baggies for home pickling—both filled with water to provide weight and thus keep the vegetable submerged in the brine— has proven to be the most effective technique.

I have used this method with great success. However, there may be dangers to this practice as chemicals in the plastic may leach into the brine. Two other alternatives along this line are biodegradable plastic bags made from recycled plastic which supposedly breaks down into harmless organic powder, and cellophane bags.

According to a spokesperson for the Coalition for Recyclable Waste (*Vegetarian Times*, November 1988), biodegradable plastic is made by mixing conventional plastic resins with a biodegradable product such as starch. The theory is that microbes first consume the starch and then the remaining plastic particles, but the plastic industry has just begun to test it. Meanwhile, plastics often include toxic metal ingredients, such as cadmium and mercury, that can be hazardous to human health. Recycled plastics are not considered safe to use with food products.

Cellophane bags are made with a thin, flexible, transparent cellulose material made from wood pulp. However, chemicals are used in the process and a company spokesperson advised against using cellophane in pickling.

Thanks to Linda Redfield, a former biochemist turned organic gardener with an interest in all traditional fermented foods, for her help in understanding the pickling process.

Fresh Sauerkraut

Makes 3 quarts or 4 3/4 pounds

5 pounds green and/or red cabbage, about 7
   quarts, very thinly sliced, or shredded by
   hand or in a food processor, including
   core
2 1/2 tablespoons sea salt (1.2 ounces)
1 gallon ceramic crock

To determine proper amount of salt, multiply weight of cabbage in ounces (80 ounces in this case, or 5 times 16 ounces) by 1.5% or .015. Result is 1.2 ounces sea salt, or about 1 1/4 - 1 1/2 teaspoons salt per cup cabbage. (Moist, granular salt may be used, or you may wish to briefly dry roast it in a skillet and grind it before measuring. 1/3 cup wet yields 1/4 cup dried and ground.)

Rinse and drain cabbage. Trim and discard discolored portions of leaves or stem. Cut finely with a knife, or shred with a grater or food processor. Better still, invest in a cabbage shredder or slicer (see Resources).

Mix cabbage and salt in a large bowl before transferring to crock, working salt into cabbage by hand, distributing evenly. Every time you add a layer of cabbage to crock, press down firmly with palms or fists. (Some people pack cabbage with a potato masher, wooden mallet, or baseball bat.) This step helps to expel air and to start juices flowing.

Wipe sides of crock clean. Place 2 or 3 layers of outer cabbage leaves on top of shredded cabbage to completely cover surface. Cabbage leaves have bacteria on them that help activate the fermentation. Place a glass pie plate or a round casserole dish on top of the cabbage leaves. Plate should be slightly smaller than the size of the crock.

Place a weight on top of plate that is heavy enough (4-5 pounds) to bring brine barely over the cabbage in 8 hours. A large jar of grains, beans, or water, or a rock or brick work well. Cover crock with a plastic bag and tie it closed around crock with a string.

When pickling is complete, throw away the outer cabbage leaves along with any moldy, discolored kraut on top.

After one day, check the water level. Enough liquid should have been drawn out of the cabbage to cover it, but not the plate. Adjust weight. Store in a dark place at cool room temperature, 68-70°. (I keep a thermometer next to the crock.)

Fermentation takes 1-2 weeks and is indicated by the formation of gas bubbles. Taste mixture every other day or so to experience the changes. Sauerkraut should smell and taste good. If any mold forms on the brine around edges, scrape it off and discard it.

When no bubbles rise and kraut tastes right, fermentation has ended. Or, use a pH paper as described in the introductory comments to the section on brine pickles which follows. A ratio between 3.3 and 3.7 indicates kraut is ready.

Kraut and brine may be transferred to clean jars and stored in the refrigerator for several months.

Variations: Red cabbage gives a vibrant, deep pink color to the kraut. A beautiful light pink results from the combination of green and red cabbages.

Add ingredients for a variety of flavors such as caraway, dill, celery, or anise seeds; seaweeds such as dulse; and other vegetables such as carrot (a Russian addition), onion, garlic, and daikon.

Brine Pickles

There is much pleasure and a homey feeling to be derived from the sight of glass jars filled with colorful vegetables and seasonings in their brine.

Bulky and whole vegetables and those with a low water content are usually placed in a salt brine solution for fermentation. In the U.S. pickles prepared from cucumbers and olives are by far the most prevalent fermented, cured, and preserved products. In Asia, blends of vegetables are more popular. They serve them with the staple rice gruel (congee), as a side dish, and even cooked into meals.

Nearly all vegetables, whether leafy, tuberous, or those containing seeds, provide sufficient nutrients for the growth of lactic acid bacteria. In the Orient, great quantities of vegetables are raised and preserved for future use by fermentation. Radishes, turnips, Chinese cabbage, cabbage, and other Brassicas (mustard greens, etc.), peppers, onions, leeks, cucumbers, watercress, dandelion greens, asparagus, bean sprouts, and in some preparations, seaweed, fish, and even nuts are added. Rice bran, miso, soy sauce, and even amazake is used in the vegetable blends prepared in Japan. Seasonings vary from ginger and red peppers to garlic and coriander seeds.

Europeans include sliced carrots, beets, turnips, radishes, chard, cauliflower, Brussels sprouts, mustard leaves, celery, lettuce, green beans, fresh peas, and other vegetables. Jerusalem artichoke is one of the wild plants reported to have been used in the past. While red onion and red radish are pretty displayed in the jars at first, they lose most of their color during fermentation, turning the brine (and cauliflower) light pink.

Typical pickling seasonings contain

whole ingredients which vary from dill seeds alone or with garlic, to mustard seeds with bay leaves and fresh horseradish. Commercial combinations may include some or all of the following: whole mustard, dill, caraway, coriander, or cardamom seeds; cinnamon, allspice, ginger, turmeric, or mace; bay leaves, black and/or red chili pepper, or horseradish.

Water quality is important here as chemicals in tap water, including chloride and fluoride, may kill organisms, beneficial and otherwise. This may be a reason for the lack of vitamin B12 today in fermented foods traditionally known for this nutrient such as miso and tempeh.

According to scientific research, brine pickles are most effectively fermented in a brine of 3-5% salt. During fermentation, the brine becomes increasingly cloudy for the first few days due to growth of bacteria, and gases are released with foaming. Later, if the brine is not covered to exclude air, a filmy yeast growth will often occur on the surface. More than one growth of this scum yeast is undesirable since the yeasts utilize the lactic acid, neutralize the brine, and make possible the growth of other microorganisms. Softening may result. Without yeast growth, the lactic acid bacteria normally settle onto the pickles and to the bottom of the container.

Pickling takes about 1-2 weeks. One way to know if the fermentation period is over is to dip a piece of pH paper (scale 3.0 to 5.5— see Resources) in brine. If it reads between 3.3 and 3.7, fermentation is complete. Pickles may be stored in the refrigerator or the traditional farmhouse root cellar for months where the curing process continues.

Brine Pickles

To determine proper amount of salt brine solution (3% salt), figure salt by weight and water by volume, i.e. 3 ounces (weight) of salt for every 100 ounces (volume) water.

As an example of calculation, for 8 cups water (64 ounces), multiply by .03 to figure ounces in salt. 64 X .03 = 1.92 ounces salt or 4 tablespoons dry, finely ground sea salt. This breaks down to about 1 1/2 teaspoons salt per cup water.

The procedure for preparing the following 3 recipes is described after the last one.

Brine Pickles with Fennel

Makes 3 quarts

Fennel adds a wonderful, refreshing taste to this colorful batch of pickles.

1/3 cup sea salt (2.4 ounces)
2 1/2 quarts (10 cups or 80 ounces) water
1 pound broccoli, 5-8 cups or 1 large bunch, tough ends discarded, cut in half crosswise, large flowerets cut in half lengthwise, stems thinly sliced, leaves left whole
1/2 pound cauliflower, 2 1/2 - 3 cups or 1/2 small head, flowerets cut in half, stems and leaves sliced
1/2 pound carrots, 2 cups or 2 carrots, cut in half lengthwise, then in thin diagonals
2 cups fennel (or anise), thinly sliced, or 4 ribs celery, cut in half lengthwise, then in diagonals, including leaves
1-gallon jar and 1-quart jar

Herbed Green Bean, Carrot, and Onion Pickles

Makes 2 quarts

2 tablespoons plus 2 teaspoons sea salt (1.5 ounces)
1 1/2 quarts (6 cups or 48 ounces) water
1 pound green beans, or half yellow wax beans, stem end trimmed, 4-5 cups
2 carrots, thinly sliced in matchsticks or julienne
1 onion, thinly sliced in rounds
2 large cloves garlic or 1 clove elephant garlic, thinly sliced
1 fresh sprig rosemary
5 fresh sprigs tarragon
1/2 gallon jar or 2 quart jars

Boone's Brine Pickles

Makes 5 quarts

The original version of these pickles by Rebecca Boone appeared in the Rebecca Boone Cook Book. *These favorite and cherished recipes were handed down to elder citizens of Boonesborough, Kentucky by their forefathers, direct descendants of Daniel Boone and other pioneers in 1775. I added the pickling seasonings and the choice of cucumbers over gherkins for easier availability.*

1/3 cup sea salt (2.4 ounces)
2 1/2 quarts (10 cups or 80 ounces) water
1/2 head white cabbage (any kind will do), about 1 pound or 6-8 cups, cut in wedges held together by a little of the core or cut in 1 1/2-inch squares, core thinly sliced
1 cauliflower, 1 1/2 pounds or 8 cups, "pulled to pieces" (separated into flowerets, large flowerets cut in half; greens and core, sliced)
10 French beans (green beans), trimmed and cut in half on the diagonal
1 dozen pearl onions, peeled, or 1/2 yellow onion, diced large
1 dozen gherkins or 3 medium cucumbers, cucumbers quartered lengthwise and cut across in thirds or 3-inch pieces
1 stick horseradish, finely sliced or grated (optional)
2 tablespoons pickling seasonings (1 tablespoon per quart water), optional
1-gallon jar and 1-quart jar

To make brine solution, mix salt in water until it dissolves. If you need more, mix water and salt in same proportions.

Gently pack vegetables and seasonings in glass jars. Pour brine solution to barely cover ingredients. Submerge vegetables by placing a small plate or teacup on top of them. Cover jar with plastic bag tied with a string to keep air out.

Taste periodically to determine when pickles are ready to enjoy, in 7-14 days. Refrigerate.

Bread and Butter Pickles

Makes 10 servings or 2 1/2 cups

This is the most common pickled product prepared from fresh vegetables in the U.S. today—both in the home and commercially. It is not fermented, and is therefore classified as a quick pickle because it includes vinegar. Both a high-quality vinegar and sweetener are included in this version.

Thanks to Steve and Donnell Campbell.

1 tablespoon unrefined sea salt
3 cups water
1 cucumber, thinly sliced in rounds
1 onion, very thinly sliced in rounds, rounds separated
1/3 cup brown rice vinegar
1/3 cup brown rice syrup
1/2 cup water
1/2 teaspoon mustard seeds
1/4 teaspoon celery seeds
1/4 teaspoon turmeric

Bring salted water to boil, then pour it over cucumber and onion to sit until onions have lost their bite and are translucent, about 2 1/2 - 3 hours.

At end of soaking time, place remaining ingredients in small saucepan and heat together to dissolve the sweetener. Drain pickles and pour warm dressing over them. Let stand to absorb flavors, at least until mixture has cooled, before serving. Flavor heightens over time. Refrigerate.

Relishes

A relish is a savory or spicy condiment which is not fermented, and is therefore not a true pickle. It is prepared with vinegar or another tangy ingredient such as lemon juice.

Corn Relish

Makes 9 servings or 3 1/4 cups

A new version of an early American relish, this colorful side dish has a refreshing zesty zing. Easy to make, I like to can it to serve at Thanksgiving and for Christmas gift giving.

1/2 cup onion
1/2 cup celery
1/2 cup green bell pepper
1/2 cup red bell pepper
2 cups fresh corn kernels, yellow or part white
1/2 cup apple cider vinegar
1/2 cup apple juice
1 1/2 teaspoons mustard powder
1 teaspoon sea salt
1/2 teaspoon celery seed

Dice vegetables to size of corn. Place all ingredients, except bell peppers, in a 2-quart pot. Bring to boil, then slow boil covered for 5 minutes, stirring occasionally. Add bell peppers in last 2 minutes of cooking to preserve color. Allow to cool, then drain just before serving.

May be preserved by canning (see pages 141 and 142) or refrigerate.

Gingered Apple-Raisin Relish ♥ Chutney (Indian)

Makes 10-12 servings or 2 cups

This lively chutney may be prepared with raw or cooked fruit. Traditionally, chutney was stone-ground, but an electric blender works wonders nowadays.

1 cup raisins
3 cups apples (3 large apples), diced
1/2 teaspoon unrefined sea salt
1/8 teaspoon cayenne pepper
1 tablespoon ginger, freshly grated
1/2 cup lemon juice

To cook fruit, place raisins in pan and top with apples. Sprinkle with seasonings, add juice, and bring to boil, then simmer covered until somewhat tender, 5-10 minutes. Stir occasionally.

Cooked or raw, blend all ingredients into a coarse paste. Consistency should be mushy, but not watery. Refrigerate.

Ginger root

Commercially Available Japanese Pickles

Daikon Radish Rice Bran Pickles ♥ Takuan

Takuan, daikon radish pickled in rice bran *(nuka)* and sea salt, is one of the most important and traditional of all Japanese pickles. They were first developed by a Zen monk named Takuan. Apparently, after the cooks refined brown rice into white rice for the nobles, the Buddhist monks used the leftover bran to make pickles.

Rich in enzymes, B vitamins (particularly B1, niacin, and B12 which dissolve from the bran), and lactobacilli, the flavor is strong and refreshing. Linoleic acid and vitamin E, which work together in the body to reduce cholesterol, are also abundant in rice bran.

The best brands available are made of organically grown daikon, rice bran, and sea salt.

Unfortunately, they are pasteurized briefly (5 minutes at 185° F/85° C) to kill certain pathogens and to prevent the package from bursting. Apparently, few B vitamins are lost in the process.

The radishes are sun-dried to soften them before pickling. They are made in the fall once the weather has become consistently cool, as cold weather kills undesirable bacteria. Light takuan are removed in about 3 months, after becoming amber colored, sweet and juicy. Darker takuan are left to pickle over a winter, or up to 3 years, in earthenware crocks for a dark, compact, chewy pickle.

Amazake Daikon Pickles

Sweet, light, and white in color, these pickles are so pleasing, it's hard to stop eating them! They are made of organic daikon radish which has been sun-dried, then pickled in sea salt and organic brown rice amazake (sweet fermented brown rice nectar) for 3 months. The volume of salt is considerably lower than other pickles, making refrigeration necessary. Made in Japan by 3 generations of the Kitani family, amazake daikon pickles are sold only by Goldmine Natural Food Co. (see Resources).

Daikon Radish

Sushi Pickles

Sushi Pickles are served on their own, as a garnish, or in sushi rolls.

Sushi Ginger contains fresh ginger root pickled in rice vinegar, shiso leaves, and sea salt, and sometimes contains umeboshi vinegar.

Sushi Daikon contains daikon radish, soy sauce, and licorice.

Standard commercial versions, as opposed to ones found in natural foods shops, also contain sugar, coloring, and preservatives.

Pickled Plums (Umeboshi)

Umeboshi (pronounced oo-may-BOW-shi), meaning salt-pickled plum, are the bright red Japanese pickled plums with the unsurpassed tart-bitter-sour-salty taste. They are enjoyed for their seemingly endless culinary uses and their medicinal values in Oriental folk medicine.

Japanese plums are the fruit of the East Asian tree *Prunus Mume* which is in fact a species of apricot. Historically, they were grown only in China, Taiwan, and Japan.

On about February 15, during the coldest, bleakest season of the year, the plum trees all come into full, fragrant bloom. Plum-blossom-viewing festivities have been recorded since A.D. 730. Travellers come from far and wide to witness the spectacle of delicate, snow-white or pink blossoms. With their 5 petals, they are one of the most popular subjects for Chinese and Japanese painters and poets, along with bamboo and pine.

In Japan, ume trees are cultivated primarily on the sunny hillsides in Wakayama Prefecture, south of Osaka.

Whereas we in the West pick both apricots and plums when they are ripe for eating, the Japanese pick ume when they are still green and firm. Japanese plum trees are now being grown in parts of North America—New Orleans, Washington State, and California—being made into umeboshi by small-scale farmers and producers.

In May or June the plums are harvested. They are layered with sea salt equal in weight to 20% of the weight of the plums. Then they are topped with large clean stones as pressing weights. During the next 2 weeks to 2 months, beneficial lactic acid bacteria produce an essential fermentation that imparts flavor and nutritional factors. The salt draws out juice (plum vinegar or *ume su*) from the plums.

In late July and August, during the

warmest and driest season, the plums are set out to dry in the sun for 3-7 days, and are set back to soak in the brine each night.

Next, shiso leaves (*aka shiso* in Japanese, *aka* meaning red to distinguish from green or *ao shiso* which is used fresh in sushi and other dishes) are added. These are known in English as beefsteak or perilla leaves. A little of a previous batch's juice is added, turning the umeboshi a beautiful deep red, imparting a lovely aroma and flavor. The mixture is weighted for 12-18 months. The plums are then returned to the vats with fresh shiso leaves for a minimum of 20 days to 2-6 months pickling. With age, the original highly saline, yet citric, pickling solution becomes more and more alkaline, changing in taste from acidic to sour.

Shiso leaves look similar to mint leaves, although much larger. They contain a natural preservative called perilla-aldehyde which is documented to have over 1,000 times the strength of synthetic preservatives used in foods. It is this element which preserves the rice in rice balls that have umeboshi in their centers and which, when ingested, helps clear the intestinal tract of undesirable bacteria.

Beginning in August, the plums are ready to eat. However, taste and medicinal qualities improve over a year as the salt mellows with time. In a hands-on workshop he gave on making fermented foods, Naburo Muramoto (author of *Healing Ourselves* and *Natural Immunity—Insights on Diet and AIDS*) told us of 100-year-old umeboshi in Japan.

Nowadays some companies use plums grown and processed with the aid of artificial chemicals, red chemical dyes, refined salt, and short or artificial aging methods. The best umeboshi are made from organic plums, organic shiso leaves, and fully mineralized sea salt. A small number of Japanese food-crafters continue to produce them and they are distributed throughout the world by conscientious natural foods/macrobiotic importers.

The use of umeboshi dates back more than 4000 years in ancient China. About 1500 years ago, the ume plum tree was introduced to Japan from China as a medicinal food, believed to have been transported to Japan in 530 A.D. by Buddhist monks. The Chinese smoked and dried the plums to preserve them. The earliest Japanese records of salt plums date back to a medical text from 984 A.D. Since then, their reputation as a food that promotes long life and good health has steadily grown.

The Japanese method for preserving the plums developed further during the 16th century when the Tokugawa Shogun came to power. The samurai, Japan's warrior class, used umeboshi to prevent food poisoning as other preservation techniques were limited. When they were forced to drink muddy water on their travels, they took umeboshi to ward off stomach distress. They also believed it kept them from running short of breath. Its use as a food item spread shortly thereafter when the samurai became more powerful than the noble class.

Today in Japan salt plums are used as a favorite seasoning for rice, rolled in sushi or small bits eaten in with each bite of rice. To serve plums as a condiment with rice, first soak them in water for 5 minutes to remove exterior salt, if necessary or desired. Many Japanese make a point of enjoying a salt plum each morning as preventive medicine or for "the morning after."

There are 3 different forms of the pickled plum used in cooking. The whole plums, a smooth paste or purée made from pitted umeboshi (great for spreading on corn-on-the-cob), and the red liquid or brine formed during the pickling process. It is drawn off and sold as umeboshi vinegar.

Today's natural cook uses all forms of umeboshi in grain and vegetable dishes as well as in dressings, sauces, dips, and soups, and as a pickling ingredient for vegetables. Its pleasing, tangy flavor may be used in place of lemon juice or vinegar to impart acidic and preserving qualities, and in place of salt, soy sauce, or miso as a salt seasoning.

Another food derived from the umeboshi-making process is pickled shiso leaves. Large ones are spread and packed flat to maintain their shape. These are used to wrap sushi or rice balls. Others are sun-dried and ground into a powder, or minced. They are used as an iron-rich seasoning which is delicious sprinkled on foods.

Another condiment is made from powdered pickled shiso leaves mixed with other seasonings such as toasted sesame seeds and crumbled nori.

Umeshoban is a paste made from umeboshi, natural soy sauce, and concentrated twig tea. It is used to make a savory broth.

Finally, for information on plum extract, see page 201.

In the early days, there were no scientific studies demonstrating the plums' medicinal benefits, such as curing food poisoning, stomach trouble, and removing chemical toxins. They simply worked and people passed the knowledge on verbally. We now have a wealth of evidence regarding their efficacy.

A healthy person's blood stays at the slightly alkaline level of ph 7.3. More acidic blood hosts infections and viruses. This condition is evidenced by emotional symptoms such as irritability or hypersensitivity. Physical symptoms include headaches, dizziness, stiff shoulders, and insomnia, and more serious sickness such a stomach cancer or

diabetes. The blood turns acidic with over-consumption of meat, eggs, sweets, alcohol, and refined grains (white rice and white bread), and from too much stress. Known in Japan as "the king of alkaline foods," umeboshi quickly helps restore the desirable acid/alkaline balance in the bloodstream.

Umeboshi contain 5% citric acid or natural vitamin C, which gives the tart-sour flavor. It makes umeboshi a strong alkalizing agent, assisting the body in discharging lactic acid which accumulates in the system when we eat the acidic foods mentioned above. The strong alkalinity works well to combat fatigue, a tendency to cold, cough, fever, diarrhea and constipation, dysentery, upset stomach, muscle cramps, headache, hangover, motion sickness, and jet lag. When travelling, just half a plum a day for prevention (2 plums a day during times of sickness) works wonders.

Umeboshi contain picric acid, which stimulates the liver and kidneys to remove harmful material from the bloodstream and intestinal tract. Rich in enzymes, they are a natural aid to digestion.

According to natural foods researcher and writer, Rebecca Theurer Wood ("Rescue Remedy—The Amazing Japanese Plum, *Macromuse* Dec. 1987/Jan. 1988), "A common food craving during pregnancy is pickles. The craving may be a sign of a lack in the woman's blood of adequate calcium for the developing fetus. The sour flavor draws calcium from her teeth and bones to make it available to the baby. This explains the old adage, 'Every pregnancy costs a tooth.' The citric acid of ume heightens calcium retention from our foods. In addition, ume is a superior source of readily assimilable calcium. Many women enjoy ume (particularly the extract form—see page 201) as a remedy for morning sickness and as an agent to aid in the absorption of calcium." Wood also adds herpes to the long list of health problems ume helps to balance.

Research shows the anti-bacterial effects of umeboshi as it acts as a blood cleanser and food detoxifier. According to Professor Otaka at Hirosaki University, scientists discovered that ume acts as an antibiotic to stop the growth of dysentery, typhoid and colon bacilli, and staphylococci.

A Tokyo University scientist, Professor Akiya reported that radioactive strontium 90, which is easily absorbed into the bones, chemically combines with the citric acid in ume products and is excreted from the body. After the bombing of Hiroshima, the use of umeboshi and other fermented food products led to an increase in red blood cell formation among survivors.

Umeboshi really does fulfill the Hippocratic adage, "Let food be your medicine, and your medicine be your food."

Desserts

This chapter progresses from the simplest fresh fruit desserts to fruit juice-sweetened gelatins and puddings, and on to fresh fruit pies and other pastries such as cobblers, crisps, and cakes. It ends with several kinds of cookies.

As an ingredient in desserts, salt serves to neutralize the acid quality in fruit, bringing out its sweetness. Salt also draws out the delicious fruit juices during cooking.

For a choice in sweeteners, *Mitoku, Sweet Cloud, and Tree of Life are the only brands of brown rice syrup I recommend.*

Fresh Fruit Desserts

Fresh Fruit Kabobs

Makes 4 servings

This dessert is as quick as it is attractive.

8 pieces cantaloupe, cut in 1-inch cubes
8 pieces honeydew melon, cut in 1-inch
    cubes
4 strawberries, rinsed and stems discarded
4 slices kiwi fruit, peeled with a small, sharp
    knife, then cut in 1/2-inch rounds
4 8- or 9-inch bamboo or wooden skewers

Artfully arrange fruit on skewers to serve. One possible arrangement is: cantaloupe-honeydew-strawberry-kiwi-cantaloupe-honeydew.

Melon topped with Watermelon Syrup

Makes 4 servings

I chose this fresh melon dessert as the finale to a Native American dinner because I read in Hopi Cookery that the Hopi enjoy cantaloupe and muskmelon. The watermelon syrup makes a bright red and very sweet accent which, although probably Japanese in origin, seems just right here. The process is somewhat similar to making old-fashioned open kettle apple butter (see page 143).

4 slices cantaloupe or muskmelon
1/4-1/2 cup *Watermelon Syrup* (recipe
    follows)

Watermelon Syrup:

Makes 2 cups
Pulp of 12-pound watermelon, seeded

Purée watermelon pulp in Foley food mill, blender, or food processor. A 12-pound watermelon yields about 14 cups purée.

Transfer to very large pot (the larger and heavier the pot, the faster syrup cooks) and bring to boil, then simmer uncovered over medium-low to medium heat (higher heat for heavier pot) until thick, 3-4 hours, stirring occasionally. Syrup thickens further as it cools.

To serve, place a dollop of syrup in the center of each slice of melon.

Cantaloupe

Gels and Puddings

Did you know that the old reliable Knox gelatin is made of ground-up horse and/or cow's hooves and bones? Animal tissue is boiled in water to obtain the glutinous substance that forms the basis for gelatins and glue.

Natural gels based on sea vegetables have the same texture as the Jell-O you grew up with. The seaweeds are processed into an odorless, colorless, and tasteless form by an ancient method of freeze-drying. Agar, also known as kanten in Japanese, is the name of the substance used to make gelatins or aspics.

Agar comes in 4 forms—flakes, strips, granules, or bars—however, here I've used flakes because they are most widely available and very easy to use. The general rule is 1-3 tablespoons agar flakes per cup of liquid to be gelled. Agar gels in 1-2 hours, shorter in the refrigerator, longer at room temperature. The higher volume of agar is needed for gels which will be whipped for a frothy texture; which contain many ingredients; or which must be gelled unrefrigerated in hot weather. Even after gelling, agar-based gels can be reheated and gelled again. So, if your gelatin comes out too hard, just reboil it with additional juice and chill. If it's too soft, reboil with additional agar and chill.

These recipes all fit a standard 8-inch square baking dish of 2-quart capacity. If a mold is used, be sure to oil it lightly before filling.

Select quality juices; unfiltered and organic are best. Juices made from fruits or vegetables are highly concentrated foods (1 cup of apple juice contains the juice of 3 apples without the fiber). Therefore, for a lighter effect and taste, especially for children whose tastebuds (and sweettooths) are just being established, dilute juice with water, 1/4 or more of the total volume.

A minimal amount of salt is included in the recipes to enhance and balance the sweet taste.

Basic Gel Recipe ♥
Apple Gel with Toasted Walnut Sprinkles

Makes 9 servings

1 quart (4 cups) apple juice
1/3 cup agar sea vegetable flakes
1/4 teaspoon unrefined sea salt
1/2 cup walnuts, toasted and chopped for garnish

Place juice, agar, and salt in 2-quart saucepan and bring to boil. Watch to avoid foaming over. Simmer until agar completely dissolves, about 2-5 minutes. Transfer to baking dish or lightly-oiled mold to gel, about 2 hours at room temperature, or half the time in the refrigerator. Garnish with a sprinkling of nuts to serve.

Variations: Substitute other fruit juices for apple (apple-boysenberry, black cherry, etc.) and other nuts for walnuts (almonds, hazelnuts, etc.). Add 1/2 teaspoon each vanilla and finely grated lemon rind, or 1 teaspoon ginger juice, freshly grated and squeezed.

Add seasonal fruits such as sliced apricots or melon balls to pot to cook about 1 minute before transferring mixture to dish for gelling.

Strawberry-Apple Gel ♥ Add a 1-pint basket of strawberries, rinsed and sliced, to pot during last 30 seconds of cooking.

Minty Apple-Raisin Gel ♥ Substitute 1 1/2 cups mint tea for part of apple juice, or just add 1 teaspoon dry peppermint leaves, crushed, to juice with agar and salt. When agar is dissolved, strain out leaves. Add 1/2 cup raisins and return just to boil, then transfer to dish or mold to gel. Garnish with sprigs of fresh mint.

Jelly Berry Bo

Makes 9 servings

Thanks to a natural foods chef with a sense of humor, Flip, formerly of Heartwood Institute, Garberville, California, for the name of this recipe, a simple variation of the basic apple gel.

1 quart apple juice
1/3 cup agar sea vegetable flakes
1/4 teaspoon unrefined sea salt
2 cups mixed berries (blueberries, strawberries [quartered], raspberries, and blackberries)
1 teaspoon lemon juice
1/2 teaspoon lemon rind, fresh grated

Bring juice, agar flakes, and salt to boil, then simmer until agar completely dissolves, about 2-5 minutes. Add berries, lemon juice, and rind to pot during last few seconds of cooking. Transfer to 2-quart, 8-inch square baking dish to gel.

Fruit-Filled Cantaloupe Cups

Makes 4-8 servings

This light and easy summer dessert has a full palette of colors.

2 cantaloupes, halved and seeds discarded
1 cup apple juice
2 level tablespoons agar sea vegetable flakes
Several grains unrefined sea salt
1 cup mixed fresh fruit (seedless red and/or
   green grapes, tiny watermelon balls,
   and berries such as blueberries, blackberries, or raspberries)
4-8 fresh mint sprigs (optional)

Cut a flat spot on the bottom of each cantaloupe half so it sits upright. In a small pot,
bring juice to boil with agar and salt and
simmer until agar dissolves completely,
about 2-5 minutes.

Fill cantaloupe cups with fruit and pour
hot liquid over fruit to fill cups. Place mint
sprigs along edge of cups (just 1 if cups will
be left whole, or 2—1 at each side—if cups
will be cut in half again after gelling) for 8
small wedge-shaped servings. Gel sets up in
1/2 hour at room temperature.

Mocha Gelatina

Makes 5-9 servings,
less if whipped after gelling

*This Italian variation of a basic apple gel has
a rich flavor plus a frothy texture if blended.
Use more agar for gels which are to be
whipped, 2 tablespoons per cup of liquid.*

1 quart apple juice
1/3-1/2 cup agar sea vegetable flakes, more
   if gel will be blended
1/4 cup almond butter
2 tablespoons carob powder, sifted
2 tablespoons instant grain "coffee" powder
2 tablespoons pure maple syrup
1/4 teaspoon unrefined sea salt
1/4 cup almonds, toasted and chopped or
   ground, for garnish
Edible flowers such as nasturtiums for
   garnish

Place first **7** ingredients in 3-quart saucepan
and stir to moisten agar. Bring to boil, then
simmer until agar dissolves completely, in 5
to 10 minutes. Pour through a strainer into
a standard 8-inch square baking dish or another appropriate container. Press through
any solids. Refrigerate for an hour or allow
to set up at cool room temperature.

Cut in squares to serve or blend gel until creamy smooth, then pour into individual
serving cups. Garnish.

Other gel recipes:

Basic Berry Jam or Preserves Recipe ❤
   Strawberry Jam (see page 141)
Basic Stone Fruit Jam or Preserves Recipe ❤
   Peach Preserves (see page 142)
Plum Conserve (see page 142)

Fresh Fruit Pudding-Gels

The idea of combining 2 gelling agents, agar sea vegetable flakes with either arrowroot powder or kuzu root starch, each with its own textural quality, leads to a smooth and creamy pudding with the refreshing lightness of a gel. Very quick and easy to prepare and with endless creative possibilities, these desserts have become favorites for their terrific "mouth feel."

Pudding-gel recipes may be changed into gels and vice versa. For example, to obtain a firmer gelled texture, substitute more agar for the arrowroot or kuzu. Remember when working with kuzu that it should not be stirred to dissolve in cool water until just before adding to the pudding. Otherwise, it settles into a hard lump which takes a bit longer to stir.

For variety, add fresh seasonal fruits to hot mixture to cook about a minute before allowing to gel.

Thanks to Carol Connell for introducing this technique to me.

Pear Pudding-Gel with Kiwi Fruit and Hazelnuts

Makes 5 servings or 3 1/2 - 3 2/3 cups

1 quart pear juice (or another fruit juice)
1/4 cup arrowroot powder or kuzu root
    starch
1/4 cup agar sea vegetable flakes
1/4 teaspoon unrefined sea salt
1 pear, quartered lengthwise, cored, and
    thinly sliced crosswise

1/2 cup hazelnuts, toasted, skins rubbed off
    and discarded, nuts chopped for gar-
    nish
5 thin slices kiwi fruit for garnish

Place 1/2 cup of the juice with the thickener in a small bowl and set aside.

Bring to boil remaining pear juice with agar and salt. Simmer until agar completely dissolves, about 2 minutes.

Mix thickener to dissolve it and add to hot liquid with pear slices. Stir until color becomes clear and boiling resumes, about 1 minute more.

Pour into individual serving bowls and allow to gel, about 1 1/2 hours at room temperature or 45 minutes in the refrigerator. Garnish with a sprinkling of nuts and a slice of kiwi fruit on top.

Cherry Pudding-Gel

Makes 6 servings

This wonderful dessert goes very nicely with a Hazelnut Heart Cookie (see page 187) tucked in the side of each serving.

1 quart cherry-apple cider or cherry juice
1/4 cup arrowroot powder or kuzu root
    starch
1/4 cup agar sea vegetable flakes
1/4 teaspoon unrefined sea salt
1 cup cherries, pitted
1 teaspoon vanilla
1 teaspoon cinnamon
6 whole cherries with stems, for garnish

Place 1/2 cup of the juice with the arrowroot or kuzu in a small bowl and set aside. Bring to boil remaining juice with agar flakes and salt. Simmer until agar completely dissolves. Mix thickener and add to hot liquid with cherries, vanilla, and cinnamon. Stir until color becomes clear and dark and ingredients start to boil, about a minute more. Allow to gel in pot or individual serving bowls, then serve garnished with a whole cherry with its stem on.

Strawberry Pudding with Toasted Almonds

Makes 6 servings

1 quart strawberry-apple juice blend
1/4 cup arrowroot powder or kuzu root starch
1/4 cup agar sea vegetable flakes
1/4 teaspoon unrefined sea salt
1/2 pint (half a basket) strawberries, thinly sliced
1/2 cup almonds, toasted and chopped

Place 1/2 cup juice with arrowroot or kuzu in a small bowl and set aside. Bring to boil remaining juice, agar, and salt. Simmer until agar completely dissolves. Stir thickener and add to hot liquid. Stir until color becomes clear and boiling resumes, about 1 minute more. Add strawberries to cook about 30 seconds.

Pour mixture into individual serving bowls and allow to gel. Garnish with a sprinkling of nuts.

Peachy Pudding-Gel with Toasted Walnuts

Makes 5 servings

A delicious ending to a meal on a hot summer's day.

1 quart peach juice or a natural blend of juices featuring peach
1/4 cup arrowroot powder or kuzu root starch
1/4 cup agar sea vegetable flakes
1/4 teaspoon unrefined sea salt
1 peach, thinly sliced or chopped (optional)
1/2 cup walnuts, toasted and chopped for garnish

Place 1/2 cup of the juice with arrowroot or kuzu in a small bowl and set aside.

Bring to boil remaining juice, agar, and salt. Simmer until agar completely dissolves.

Stir thickener and add to hot liquid. Stir until color becomes clear and boiling resumes, about 1 minute more. Add peach pieces if included.

Pour into individual serving bowls or 8-inch square baking dish and allow to gel. Garnish with a sprinkling of nuts.

Variation: **Blueberry-Peach Pudding** ❤
Add 1 cup blueberries to pot in last minute of cooking, just enough to soften them slightly. Omit walnuts. Instead top pudding with *Tofu "Whipped Cream"* (see page 184) and a sprinkling of nutmeg.

Russian Pudding ❤ Gurievskaya Kasha

Makes 10 servings

The favorite Russian dessert according to an out-of-print cookbook written by a Russian immigrant, this version must be every bit as delicious as the original which contains lots of eggs and sugar.

1 cup whole-wheat pastry flour
2 1/2 cups water
1/2 teaspoon unrefined sea salt
1/2 cup brown rice syrup (see page 171)
1/4 teaspoon vanilla extract
1/4 teaspoon almond extract
1 cup fresh or dried fruit, cooked and
    chopped, or preserves
1/4 cup raisins
1/2 cup walnuts or pecans, toasted and
    crushed
1/2 teaspoon cinnamon for dusting surface

In a saucepan, mix flour, water, and salt with a wire whisk. Bring to boil, stirring often to avoid sticking. Add sweetener and stir well. Turn heat low, place flame spreader under pot, and simmer covered for 1/2 hour. Stir in extracts.

Pour half of hot pudding into small, oiled pie pan or another oven-proof container. Sprinkle on a layer of the fruit and nuts, then pour the rest of the pudding over that. Smooth out the surface and sprinkle with cinnamon. Allow to cool somewhat to gel.

To reheat pudding before serving, place it in a 350° oven for 1/2 hour. Cut into wedges to serve.

Fresh Fruit Pies

"Simple as pie." Fresh fruit pies are always popular with old friends, as well as newcomers to low-fat, low- or no-sweetener desserts made from natural ingredients.

To glaze crust, mix 2 tablespoons brown rice syrup with 1 tablespoon water or juice. Brush mixture on crust and return to oven for the last 5 minutes of baking.

Award-Winning Strawberry Pie

Makes 10 servings

This pie won first prize in the Specialty Division of our Senior Resource Center's Million Dollar Dessert Contest, held at the Humboldt County (California) Fair. It's a simpler variation of the American Berry Pie (Strawberry-Blueberry Pie) *recipe in my previous cookbook,* American Macrobiotic Cuisine.

Daniel Boone's wife Rebecca comments in a cookbook attributed to her that good old Aunt Jemima always used a cup of sugar in her strawberry pie. This version of the bright red treat is satisfying to the eye as well as the palate, and without the side effects of highly refined white sugar.

Basic Single Crust Pastry:

1 1/2 cups whole-wheat pastry flour
1/4 teaspoon unrefined sea salt
1/4 cup light vegetable oil (canola oil, etc.,
    or part corn oil)
1/4-1/2 cup apple juice or water; or 2 tablespoons sweetener (brown rice syrup or
    pure maple syrup) and water to texture
    desired

Filling:

3 pints strawberries
1/2 teaspoon unrefined sea salt
1/2 cup brown rice syrup (see page 171)
1/2 cup agar sea vegetable flakes
1 sprig fresh mint for garnish (optional)

Preheat oven to 400°. To prepare pastry, mix dry ingredients. Work in oil, then juice, or sweetener and water. Knead quickly to make dough smooth, soft, and pliable. Add more flour if necessary. Roll dough out and transfer it to a lightly-oiled, 9-inch pie pan. Crimp edges and bake until edges are barely golden, 10-15 minutes. Allow crust to cool slightly before filling.

Roll out any extra dough for crackers after sprinkling seeds, crushed nuts, herbs, or other seasonings on the surface. Cut with a knife, pastry wheel, or cookie cutters and bake along with crust until golden around the edges, 8-10 minutes.

To prepare filling, rinse strawberries by placing them in a bowl of cool water and rinsing them quickly. Pinch off stems after rinsing so none of the flavorful juice is lost in the water.

Place whole strawberries in saucepan and sprinkle with salt. Pour rice syrup over berries and sprinkle agar flakes over all. Cover pan and bring to boil, then simmer until agar is completely dissolved, about 15 minutes. Strawberries are so full of liquid (about 1/2 cup comes out) that no added liquid is necessary as long as you keep the heat at medium-low. Stir several times.

Pour filling into prebaked crust. Allow to gel at room temperature or in a refrigerator. To garnish pie, place fresh mint sprig in center of pie after it has partially gelled.

Glaze crust if desired (see page 177).

Blueberry-Peach Pie

Makes 10 servings

This pie is made in the early American way using a little flour to absorb the flavorful fruit juices and act as the thickening agent. (Arrowroot powder substitutes well for flour.)

Filling:

4 large or 6 medium peaches, thinly sliced, about 1 1/2 pounds or 5 cups
1/3 cup whole-wheat pastry flour or arrowroot powder
1/4 cup sweetener (brown rice syrup—see page 171—or pure maple syrup, or part of each), optional
1/2 teaspoon cinnamon
1/2 teaspoon nutmeg
1/2 teaspoon unrefined sea salt
1 basket blueberries (or others such as red raspberries, strawberries, etc.) [one 12-ounce dry pint basket of blueberries contains 2 - 2 1/2 cups]

Double Crust Pastry (top and bottom):

3 cups whole-wheat pastry flour; or up to half the volume of organic, unbleached white flour
1/2 teaspoon unrefined sea salt
1/2 cup light vegetable oil (canola oil, etc., or part corn oil)
1/2-1 cup apple juice or water; or 1/4 cup sweetener (brown rice syrup or pure maple syrup) and water to texture desired

Preheat oven to 400°.

To prepare filling, combine ingredients adding berries last.

To make pastry, mix dry ingredients. Work in oil, then liquid. Knead briefly. Roll out half of dough between sheets of waxed paper, or on a floured surface or pastry cloth. Transfer to lightly-oiled, 9-inch pie pan. Roll out other half of dough for top pastry.

To assemble pie, transfer filling to pie and pat down. Cover with top pastry. Pinch edges together. Tear off excess dough and shape edges. Cut one or more designs in top pastry with cookie cutter or knife for steam vents after it has been transferred to pie. (Roll out extra dough and cut with a knife, a pastry wheel for wavy edges, or cookie cutters for rolled cookie-crackers. Bake until golden around the edges, about 10 minutes, while pie bakes.)

Cover pie with aluminum foil and tuck around sides. Bake until fruit becomes quite juicy and sauce is clear instead of chalky in color, 45-60 minutes. Remove foil. Glaze crust if desired (see page 177). Return pie to oven until top browns, about 10 minutes more. Let cool to set, at least 1 hour.

Variation: **Fresh Peach Pie** ♥ Omit berries and substitute 1/2 pound more peaches, 2 pounds in all.

Basic Stone Fruit Pie Recipe ♥
Nectarine Crumb Pie

Makes 10 servings

Filling:

2 pounds nectarines (or other stone fruits: peaches, apricots, or cherries), ripe, thinly sliced, 4 - 5 1/2 cups
1/4 cup whole-wheat pastry flour or arrowroot powder
1/4 teaspoon unrefined sea salt
1/4 cup brown rice syrup

Crumb Topping:

1/2 cup whole-wheat pastry flour
1 tablespoon light vegetable oil, ie. canola
1 tablespoon pure maple syrup
Single Crust Pastry (see page 177)

Preheat oven to 400°.

To prepare filling, combine fruit with flour and salt. Drizzle sweetener over fruit and mix well.

To prepare crumb topping, mix flour with oil. Add sweetener and rub mixture between palms.

To make pastry, mix ingredients and stir to form a smooth dough. Add a little more flour if necessary. Roll dough out between sheets of waxed paper or on a floured surface or pastry cloth, then transfer it to a lightly-oiled, 9-inch pie pan. Tear off excess dough and shape edges.

To assemble pie, transfer filling to pie and pat down. Sprinkle topping over all. Cover pie with aluminum foil and tuck around sides. Bake until fruit becomes juicy and bubbly, 30-45 minutes, then remove foil. Glaze crust if desired (see page 177). Return pie to oven until top browns, about 10 minutes more.

Let cool to set, at least 1 hour.

Peaches 'n Almond "Cream" Tart

Makes 8-10 servings

Single Crust Pastry (see page 177)

*Almond "Milk," Almond "Cream," and Toasted
Almond Sprinkles:*

Makes little more than 1 cup "milk"
and "cream," and 2/3 cup sprinkles

*A great substitute for regular or even tofu
"whipped creams." (Tofu, since it derives
from a bean, high in protein, doesn't lend
itself to combination with fruits which are
high in natural sugars.)*

1/2 cup almonds
3/4 cup water
3/4 cup apple juice
1 tablespoon arrowroot powder or kuzu root
    starch
1 tablespoon agar sea vegetable flakes
1/4 teaspoon almond extract
1/4 teaspoon vanilla extract

Filling and Glaze:

Makes 2/3 cup glaze

2 cups apple juice
1/8 teaspoon unrefined sea salt
4 peaches, 1 1/4 - 1 1/2 pounds, halved and
    pitted
2 tablespoons agar sea vegetable flakes
1/8 teaspoon cinnamon
1/4 teaspoon almond extract
1/4 teaspoon vanilla extract
Almond "Cream"

Preheat oven to 400°.

To prepare pastry, mix flour and salt.
Work in oil, then liquid. Knead briefly to
form a soft, smooth dough. Add a little more
flour if necessary. Roll out on floured surface and transfer to lightly-oiled, 9-inch tart
pan. Trim dough to 1 inch over edges and
fold inwards toward center of pastry. Form
attractive edges and bake until golden,
about 10-15 minutes.

Glaze pastry if desired (see page 177).
Set aside to cool.

To prepare almond "milk" for almond
"cream," place almonds in food processor or
blender and purée until nuts are finely pulverized. Add water and juice and continue to
purée. Pour through 2 thicknesses of
cheesecloth laid in a strainer. Twist cloth
and squeeze through as much almond "milk"
as possible.

To prepare almond "cream," place arrowroot or kuzu in a small bowl and pour
enough of the measured almond "milk" over
kuzu to barely cover it. Transfer remaining
almond "milk" to 1-quart pot with agar
flakes. Bring to boil, then simmer until agar
dissolves. Stir thickener to dissolve it and
add to pot with extracts. Stir quickly while
cooking until mixture becomes thick, in a
matter of seconds. Transfer "cream" to pie
shell to cover bottom. Allow to cool while you
prepare the peaches.

In a 3-quart saucepan bring juice to boil
with salt. Add peaches in 2 batches, skin
side down, and allow to cook until just tender, about 3 minutes each batch. Remove
from pan and peel off skin. Save cooking
juice. Slice peach halves and layer them in 2
concentric circles on top of almond "cream."

To make glaze, bring 1 cup of the peach
cooking juice to boil with agar flakes and
cinnamon and simmer until agar dissolves,
about 2 minutes. Add extracts. Pour about
1/4 cup over peaches to fill in the spaces in
between them. Pie sets up in about 20 minutes. Beautiful!

Note: Although not used in this dish, to
make toasted almond sprinkles, spread
ground almond pulp on baking sheet and

bake at 250° until golden, stirring a couple of times during cooking, about 40 minutes. Store for future use.

Almond Pudding Pie with Tofu "Whipped Cream" Topping

Makes 10 servings

This always-pleasing dessert is so simple to prepare, it's ideal for large groups.

2 1/2 cups cool water
1 cup whole-wheat pastry flour
1/4 teaspoon unrefined sea salt
1/2 cup almonds, toasted and crushed or
    chopped
1/2 cup pure maple syrup (or part brown
    rice syrup)
1/2 teaspoon almond extract
3/4 cup *Tofu "Whipped Cream"* for topping
    (recipe follows)

Tofu "Whipped Cream":
Makes 2 1/3 cups
Absolutely fresh tofu is a necessity here or the flavor will be chalky.

1 pound tofu, fresh
1/4 cup pure maple syrup
1 tablespoon vanilla
2 tablespoons water, only if necessary to
    blend
Few grains unrefined sea salt

To prepare pudding pie filling, add cool water to flour in pan, a little at a time, stirring constantly to prevent lumping. (A wire whisk is helpful.) Add salt and bring to boil over high heat, stirring often. Cover, place a flame spreader under pot, and simmer for 1/2 hour.

Sprinkle almonds over sides and bottom of liberally-oiled pie plate. Add syrup and extract to pot in last few minutes of cooking. Stir, then pour mixture into pie plate to gel, about 1 hour.

To prepare tofu "whipped cream," simply blend ingredients until creamy smooth. Spoon a dollop on top of each serving of pie.

Pastries

Bramble Berry Cobbler

Makes 8 servings

Historically cobblers were made in various ways. Rebecca Boone, Daniel's wife, topped hers with a pie- or cookie-dough type crust. Biscuit doughs like this one were also used. Nowadays, fresh fruit desserts which are topped or mixed with rolled oats or granola, such as the Easy Fresh Fruit Crisp *recipe which follows, are also called cobblers or crumbles.*

Bramble berries—such as red or black raspberries, boysenberries, or nectarberries—grow on prickly shrubs related to roses. Red raspberries are especially dramatic here but strawberries and even loganberries taste great too.

Filling:

6 cups bramble berries (raspberries, black-
    berries, or boysenberries)
1/3 cup arrowroot powder
1/4 teaspoon unrefined sea salt
1/2 cup brown rice syrup

Cobbler Topping:

1/2 cup whole-wheat pastry flour
1/2 cup organic, unbleached white flour
1 1/2 teaspoons non-aluminum baking
    powder, ie. Rumford's
1/8 teaspoon unrefined sea salt
3 tablespoons light vegetable oil, ie. canola
2 tablespoons brown rice syrup (see page
    171)
2 tablespoons pure maple syrup
1/2 teaspoon vanilla
1/2 cup soymilk (I prefer Edensoy Original),

or a little less Rice Dream beverage, or apple juice

Preheat oven to 400°.

To prepare filling, quickly rinse berries by immersing them in a bowl of cool water. Drain. Gently mix berries with arrowroot powder and salt. Transfer to a 2-quart baking dish and drizzle sweetener over fruit.

To prepare cobbler topping, mix dry ingredients. Work in oil. Heat jar of syrup for a more pourable consistency if necessary. Mix in remaining ingredients.

Spoon batter on top of fruit, leaving a portion of fruit exposed in the center to check for doneness.

Bake until fruit is bubbling and topping is golden, about 30 minutes. Check to see that center is cooked through. You will notice the exposed berries in the center-top of the cobbler change from dry and chalky to shiny and juicy.

Brush surface with oil and return cobbler to oven to bake 5 minutes more.

Variation: **Raspberry-Peach Cobbler** ❤
Substitute 3 peaches, 2 cups or 10 ounces, thinly sliced, for 1 basket of berries.

Easy Fresh Fruit Crisp ❤
Peach Crisp

Makes 8 servings

This modern version of a traditional American favorite includes store-bought granola and apple juice for a quick seasonal fruit dessert. See my first cookbook, American Macrobiotic Cuisine, *for a homemade granola recipe (Nutty Granola, page 89).*

6 peaches, pitted and diced, 5 1/2 - 6 cups
    (or equivalent amount apples, apricots,

nectarines, cherries, etc.)
1 tablespoon cinnamon or part nutmeg
3 cups maple-nut granola with raisins
1-2 cups apple juice (less for peaches, more
    for apples)

Preheat oven to 400°. Lightly brush a 2-quart baking dish with oil. Mix fruit with cinnamon and 2 cups granola, and transfer to baking dish. Sprinkle remaining granola on surface and pour juice over all. Cover with aluminum foil and bake until center is cooked, about 40 minutes. Uncover and return to oven to bake until top is dry and golden, 5-10 minutes more.

Blueberry Buckle

Makes 9 servings

This early American dessert is quite similar to a cobbler with the addition of a cake-like pastry bottom.

It is said that Blueberry Buckle originated in Alaska where blueberries grow easily. Other berries substitute nicely.

Filling:

1 scant pint blueberries (2 cups)
1/8 teaspoon unrefined sea salt

Cake bottom and cobbler topping: Prepare double the cobbler topping for *Bramble Berry Cobbler* recipe on the preceding page.

Preheat oven to 400°.
    To prepare filling, rinse, drain, and mix berries with salt. (If strawberries are used, cut them in quarters.)
    Prepare both cake bottom and cobbler topping. Pour half batter to cover the bottom of a lightly-oiled, 8-inch square baking dish

or the equivalent.
    Distribute berries evenly over bottom cake layer. If necessary, add a little flour to remaining batter to make it spoonable. Distribute evenly over berries. Bake until golden, about 25 minutes. Brush surface with oil and return to oven for 5 minutes more.

Apple-Nut Cake

Makes 8-12 servings

1 cup whole-wheat pastry flour
1 cup organic, unbleached white flour
1 tablespoon non-aluminum baking
    powder
1 teaspoon each cinnamon and nutmeg
1/2 teaspoon cloves
1/4 teaspoon unrefined sea salt
1/3 cup canola oil or part corn oil
1/3 cup brown rice syrup (see page 171) or
    barley malt syrup
1/3 cup pure maple syrup
1 teaspoon vanilla
1/2 cup soymilk
1 cup apple, chopped small
1 cup walnuts, toasted and chopped

Preheat oven to 400°.
    Mix dry ingredients. Work in oil, then gently stir in sweeteners, vanilla, and soymilk. Line a 2-quart baking dish with parchment or waxed paper and oil the sides. Transfer batter to baking dish and sprinkle apple and walnuts on top to cover the surface.
    Bake until cake tests done and appears quite golden, about 30 minutes. Brush edges of cake with oil and bake 5 minutes more.
    Apple cake is quite nice served with a double recipe for *Sweet and Simple Sauce* (see page 185).

Strawberry Shortcake

Makes 6-12 servings

Most shortcake recipes call for white flour, sugar, milk, cream, butter, salt, and baking powder. Commercial shortcake contains sugar and corn syrup, flour, eggs, salt, leavening agents (baking soda, sodium acid pyrophosphate, and/or sodium bicarbonate), and artificial flavor and color.

Baking powder is a manufactured leavening agent which may be harmful to the intestines when taken regularly. It is believed by some to kill intestinal flora. However, for quickbreads such as biscuits, or cakes like the sponge cakes used for shortcake, it makes a world of difference, fulfilling the expectation of a familiar light texture. For healthy people, it seems appropriate to include it occasionally if desired.

Aluminum-free baking powder is the best kind to choose. It contains calcium acid phosphate, bicarbonate of soda, and corn starch. Figure 1 1/2 teaspoons baking powder per cup flour when designing your own recipes.

Try raspberry, peach, and pear shortcakes too, in addition to the variations here. A special pan called a shortcake plaque is available. Fill cups 3/4 full. This recipe makes 6-8 individual cakes in 15-20 minutes.

Shortcake:

1 cup cornmeal
1 cup whole-wheat pastry flour
1 cup organic, unbleached white flour
1 1/2 tablespoons aluminum-free baking powder
1/2 teaspoon unrefined sea salt
1/2 cup canola or light corn oil
1/2 cup brown rice syrup (see page 171)
1/2 cup pure maple syrup
1 teaspoon vanilla
1 cup soymilk

Strawberry Sauce:

Makes 3 cups

2 pints (baskets) strawberries
1/4 teaspoon unrefined sea salt
1/4 cup brown rice syrup
1/2 cup apple juice
3 tablespoons arrowroot powder or kuzu root starch

Tofu "Whipped Cream":

Makes little more than 1 cup

1/2 pound tofu, fresh
2 tablespoons pure maple syrup
1 1/2 teaspoons vanilla
Few grains unrefined sea salt
Water to blend, up to about 1/4 cup

Preheat oven to 400°. To prepare shortcake, mix dry ingredients. Stir in oil, then gently mix in remaining ingredients. Batter should be thick, but pourable.

Transfer to an oiled, 8-inch square baking dish you have lined with parchment or waxed paper. Bake until golden, about 30 minutes.

To prepare sauce, rinse whole strawberries in a bowl of cool water, drain, then pinch off and discard stems. Place arrowroot or kuzu and 1/4 cup juice in a small bowl and set aside. Place berries in cooking pot, sprinkle with salt, and pour rice syrup and remaining 1/4 cup juice over berries. Bring to boil over medium heat, and continue to cook until berries are tender, about 5 minutes, stirring occasionally. Stir thickener, turn heat low, and add it to the pot. Carefully stir until a thick, shiny sauce forms, about 30 seconds.

To make tofu "whipped cream," simply blend ingredients until creamy smooth. I usually do not boil the tofu for this topping as boiling tends to make it firm up. If you do boil it ahead, store "cream" in blender and whip it up again just before serving. For large amounts, mix all ingredients except water, then add it gradually until desired consistency is reached. Less will be needed.

Let cake and sauce cool at least 1/2 hour before serving. Cut cake in 6, 9, or 12 squares or wedges to serve. Pour sauce over each serving of cake, and a dab of tofu "whipped cream" over sauce.

Blueberry Corncake ❤ *This early New England favorite is the perfect treat for an evening in July.* Add 1 1/2 cups blueberries to shortcake batter. Transfer to 2 pans. Prepare the following topping.

Blueberry Topping:

Makes 2 3/4 cups

2 tablespoons arrowroot powder or kuzu root starch
1 1/2 cups apple juice
2 tablespoons pure maple syrup
1/2 teaspoon vanilla
Pinch of unrefined sea salt
2 cups blueberries

To prepare topping, place arrowroot or kuzu in small bowl with 1/2 cup of the juice, syrup, vanilla, and salt. Bring remaining juice to boil in a 2-quart saucepan. Add berries and when they have released their juice, in about 2 minutes, stir thickener mixture and add to pot. Stir over medium heat until mixture changes from chalky to clear and shiny, about 1 minute. Serve hot over cake.

Plum Corncake (or Peach, Nectarine, or Apricot Corncakes) ❤ Omit strawberry sauce and tofu "whipped cream." Include 5 plums (or other large stone fruits: peaches, nectarines, or apricots, less if fruits are very large), halved and pits discarded. Follow

shortcake recipe, then lay plum halves, cut side down, on cake in rows, 3 by 3 in a square dish. Bake as usual. Prepare the sauce which follows if desired. Cut squares around plums to serve. Drizzle sauce in a line across each serving.

Sweet and Simple Sauce:

Makes little less than 1 cup

1 cup apple juice
2 tablespoons pure maple syrup
1/2 teaspoon vanilla
1/8 teaspoon each cinnamon and nutmeg
Few grains unrefined sea salt
Zest of 1/4 orange, lemon, or lime
1 1/2 tablespoons arrowroot powder or kuzu root starch

Place ingredients in saucepan. Stir to dissolve thickener. Bring to boil, stirring constantly, until a thick sauce forms, in a couple of minutes.

Blueberries

Coconut Rice Cake

Makes 9-10 servings

Native to South Africa, the ingredients in this dessert show Indian and English influences. Although the original recipe didn't call for baking, it improves flavor and texture considerably.

1/4 teaspoon unrefined sea salt
2 cups water
1 cup long grain brown rice
2 cups shredded coconut, toasted
1/2 cup brown rice syrup
1 teaspoon cinnamon
1/4 teaspoon cardamom seeds, crushed or
    ground
1/4 teaspoon distilled rose water (optional)

In a small saucepan, bring salted water to boil. Rinse and drain rice, add to boiling water, and return to boil. Cook for 1 hour over low heat. Place flame spreader under pot after 1/2 hour.

Toast coconut in a large skillet over medium heat, stirring often, until lightly brown, about 3-5 minutes.

Preheat oven to 350°.

When rice is done, transfer it to a mixing bowl and toss with coconut. Heat but don't boil remaining ingredients to soften syrup. Mix ingredients well with a wire whisk. Add to rice and coconut, and mix well. Transfer to lightly-oiled 8-inch square baking dish or a pie pan and smooth surface. Bake for 20 minutes, and allow to cool at least 1/2 hour before serving.

For larger amounts, such as 3 times this recipe, simply multiply ingredients proportionately except water. Figure 1 1/2 cups water per cup dry rice.

Cookies

Sweet Rice Cookies

Makes about 1 dozen

East coast macrobiotic teacher Murray Snyder created the original version of this favorite cookie recipe in 1971. Thin and crunchy and free of any concentrated sweeteners, they are sold in natural foods stores in Boston and New York today.

1 cup sweet brown rice flour or regular short grain brown rice flour
1 cup rolled oats
1/4 teaspoon unrefined sea salt
1/4 cup sesame seeds, toasted
1/4 cup sunflower seeds, toasted
1/2 cup raisins
1/4 cup light vegetable oil such as canola, or part corn oil
1 cup apple juice

Preheat oven to 400°.

Mix dry ingredients. Stir in oil, then juice. Let batter sit for a minute for grains to absorb moisture.

Transfer heaping tablespoonfuls of batter to lightly-oiled baking sheet, or one lined with parchment paper. Thinly flatten dough with the back of a fork into 3-inch rounds. Bake until fully golden on edges and bottom, 15-20 minutes.

Variation: **Giant Sweet Rice Cookies**
♥ For dramatic variation, make cookies about 6 inches round. Makes 4-6, less with 1/2 cup dough per cookie, more with 1/3 cup dough per cookie.

Hazelnut Heart Cookies

Makes about 1 dozen

Served with the Cherry Pudding-Gel *on page 175, the crunchy quality of these cookies contrasts nicely with the creamy texture of the pudding.*

1/2 cup hazelnuts, toasted, skins rubbed off and discarded, finely chopped
1 cup whole-wheat pastry flour
1/2 teaspoon non-aluminum baking powder (optional, for a slightly flakier texture)
1/8 teaspoon unrefined sea salt
2 tablespoons light vegetable oil (canola or part corn)
1/3 cup sweetener (brown rice syrup, barley malt syrup, or sorghum syrup; or 3 tablespoons one of these malted grain syrups combined with 2 tablespoons pure maple syrup)
1/2 teaspoon vanilla
Apple juice to texture desired, about 1 tablespoon

Preheat oven to 350°.

Mix dry ingredients. Work in oil, then add remaining ingredients. Knead briefly to form a smooth dough. Roll out to 1/8- or 1/4-inch thickness.

Cut out heart shapes as close to each other as possible. Transfer to lightly-oiled baking sheet or one lined with parchment paper. Bake until lightly toasted around the edges, 7-8 minutes for thinner cookies, 10-15 minutes for thicker ones.

Sesame-Oat Squares

Makes 2 dozen

This delicious cookie recipe was developed by my husband, Patrick, and his brother Shawn.

These cookies (and wheatmeat burgers) were the hottest selling items in our small food business.

2 cups sesame seeds, toasted
3 cups rolled oats
3 cups whole-wheat pastry flour
1 teaspoon unrefined sea salt
3/4 cup light vegetable oil (sesame, canola, or part corn oil)
1/2 cup pure maple syrup
3/4 cup brown rice syrup
2 tablespoons vanilla

Preheat oven to 350°. Toast sesame seeds by spreading them evenly on a baking sheet and baking them until they crush easily between two fingers and they no longer have a raw taste, 5-10 minutes.

   Mix oats, flour, seeds, and salt. In a separate bowl, mix remaining ingredients. Mix dry and wet ingredients together. Add a little apple juice if mixture doesn't hold together when squeezed.

   Transfer mixture to an unoiled baking sheet with 1-inch-high sides. Press firmly with moistened hands to fill sheet evenly. Smooth top with a rolling pin and edges with a rubber spatula, dipping implements in water if they stick to dough.

   Bake for 20 minutes, then cut cookies into 24 squares, 4 on the short end by 6 on the long end. Return cookies to oven to bake 10 minutes more. Cutting before cookies are completely cooked is easier than afterwards when they tend to crumble. Let cool to serve.

Raisin-Spice Cookies

Makes 1 dozen

Thanks to Susan Marelich for these delectable cookie creations which are so low in fat.

2/3 cup whole-wheat pastry flour
2/3 cup barley flour
2/3 cup oat flour
2 teaspoons cinnamon
1/2 teaspoon nutmeg
1/2 teaspoon allspice
1/4 teaspoon cloves
1/4 teaspoon ginger
1/4 teaspoon unrefined sea salt
1/4 cup corn oil
2/3 cup raisins
1/4 cup barley malt
1/4 cup apple juice
1 teaspoon vanilla

Preheat oven to 350°.

   Combine flours, spices, and salt. Rub in oil with fingers. Add raisins. Mix remaining ingredients and add to flour mixture to form dough.

   Divide dough into 12 portions, about 3 tablespoons each. Transfer to lightly-oiled baking sheet and flatten to 1/4-inch thick with moistened fingers or fork. Bake for 15-20 minutes.

Lemon-Poppy Seed Cookies

Makes 1-2 dozen

Another wonderful cookie recipe from Susan Marelich.

1 1/2 cups whole-wheat pastry flour
1/2 cup sweet brown rice flour
4 teaspoons poppy seeds, toasted
1/4 teaspoon unrefined sea salt
3 tablespoons corn oil
1/4 cup lemon juice
1/4 cup brown rice syrup
2 tablespoons pure maple syrup
2 teaspoons lemon rind, freshly grated

Glaze:

1 1/2 teaspoons pure maple syrup
1 1/2 teaspoons corn oil

Preheat oven to 350°.

Toast poppy seeds in a hot skillet, stirring occasionally, until a pleasant aroma rises, about 2 minutes, or bake them when oven reaches temperature for about 5 minutes.

Mix flour, seeds, and salt together. Rub oil into flours with fingers.

Mix remaining ingredients and add to flour to form dough. Roll dough out on a lightly-floured surface to a generous 1/4-inch thickness, for 1 dozen 2 1/2-inch round shapes, or roll out thinly for 2 dozen 2-inch heart-shaped cutout cookies. Cut out shapes and transfer to lightly-oiled baking sheet. Prick surfaces with a fork in several places. Mix glaze ingredients and apply using fingers or pastry brush.

Bake for 10-12 minutes. Cookies harden as they cool.

Gazelle's Horn Cookies ♥ Kab el Ghzal (Moroccan)

Makes 1 dozen

These Moroccan crescent-shaped pastries are stuffed with a sweet, cinnamon-flavored almond paste. Fragrant waters such as orange flower water and rose water are used in wealthy Moroccan homes for their aromatic qualities much as one uses vanilla. Apparently, 7 pounds of buds or blossoms make 1 gallon of the fragrant waters.

A simpler variation of the original recipe follows.

Almond Paste:

Makes little less than 1/2 cup

1/2 cup almonds, toasted
2 tablespoons pure maple syrup
1/4 teaspoon cinnamon

Pastry:

1 cup whole-wheat pastry flour
2 tablespoons pure maple syrup
1/8 teaspoon unrefined sea salt
2 tablespoons corn oil
1/2 teaspoon orange flower water (optional)
2 tablespoons water

Almond paste is better made from scratch than with almond butter because the latter is often too soft to hold its shape. (If you do find thick, rather dry almond butter, substitute 1/4 cup for all the almonds.) Place almonds in food processor and blend until powdery. Add remaining ingredients and blend until well mixed. Divide paste in 12 portions of equal size and roll them in short (2-3 inches) cylinders with tapered ends.

Preheat oven to 350°.

For pastry, mix dry ingredients, then add remaining ingredients and stir to form a smooth dough. Divide dough in 2 equal portions. Between sheets of waxed paper or on a floured surface, roll out one section long and thin, about 2 1/2 inches wide. Place 6 cylinders end-to-end lengthwise along dough, then fold dough over, and cut between cylinders. Trim with the zigzag edge of a pastry wheel. With your fingers, bend cookies into gazelle's horn shapes (see illustration). Transfer to lightly-oiled cookie sheet or one lined with parchment paper. Repeat.

Roll out extra dough for plain rolled cookies. Bake cookies until barely golden around edges and on bottom, 15-20 minutes. For a shinier surface, after baking steam cookies in a steamer basket for several minutes. Or brush with a glaze mixture of 1 tablespoon each brown rice syrup and water after 10 minutes of baking. Return to oven.

Variation: **Almond Spiral Cookies** ♥
Thanks to Lynn Montgomery for this simpler shape variation.

Roll dough to a rectangle, 12 inches x 6 inches. Trim edges. Spread paste on pastry with a knife dipped in water and roll up the long edge. Seal by wetting edge furthest from you. Cut in 1-inch sections.

Candy

Nutty Carmelcorn ♥
Macrojax

Makes 5-7 servings or 5 1/2 - 7 1/2 cups

Have you ever examined the ingredients on a box of Cracker Jacks or Poppycock? The former contains sugar, corn syrup, popcorn, peanuts, molasses, corn oil, salt, and soy lecithin, while the latter has popcorn, almonds, pecans, corn syrup, brown sugar, partially hardened vegetable oil (cottonseed, coconut, palm, or soy), and salt.

Try this great alternative! Serve it for dessert, as a Halloween treat, or bring it picnicking or hiking.

8 cups popped corn (1/2 cup popcorn yields 10-11 cups popped)
1/4 cup each almonds, peanuts, and either walnuts or hazelnuts, toasted (skins removed from hazelnuts after toasting)
1/4 cup raisins
1/2 cup brown rice syrup

Preheat oven to 350°.

Place all ingredients in a large bowl and pour sweetener over them. If syrup does not pour easily, heat jar in a pan of boiling water to soften it. This is a must or you'll crush the popcorn trying to mix ingredients.

With moistened hands, mix well so syrup lightly covers all. This is sticky business, so keep remoistening your hands and work quickly.

Transfer mixture to generously-oiled baking sheet and spread out to a single layer. Bake for 8-10 minutes, and not a minute more or syrup may burn. Let cool to harden, about 5 minutes, before removing with spatula.

Soak baking sheet in hot water to remove crusty sweetener, about 5 minutes.

Variations: Substitute puffed or flaked cereals, or crumbled rice cakes, for part of the popcorn.

Ethnic Vegetable Dessert

Latin American Squash in Hot Cinnamon Syrup

Makes 4 servings

My husband and I enjoyed this sweet and simple dessert on our travels in Central America. In Costa Rica, it is considered the national dessert, known as "maza-morra." They prepare it without the cornmeal base whereas their Guatemalan neighbors do include it. Barley malt syrup substitutes nicely for the brown sugar or molasses they use.

2 1/2 cups winter squash such as butternut, halved lengthwise, seeded, then cut in 1 1/2-inch chunks

Sweet Cornmeal Mush:

Makes 1 1/3 cups

1 1/2 cups water
2 tablespoons barley malt or pure maple syrup
Few grains sea salt
1/2 cup cornmeal

Hot Cinnamon Syrup:

Makes 6 tablespoons

5 tablespoons malted barley syrup
1 tablespoon water (optional, only if syrup is very thick even after heating)
1/4 teaspoon cinnamon

To prepare cornmeal, in a 1-quart pot, bring 1 cup water to boil with syrup and salt. Mix cornmeal with remaining 1/2 cup water and add to boiling water. Stir, and when boiling resumes, place flame spreader under pot and simmer covered for 20 minutes, stirring occasionally.

Skin may be left on butternut squash. Steam squash chunks until soft, about 15-20 minutes. Or for richer flavor, bake squash at 450°, halved lengthwise, cut side down, until tender, 20-30 minutes.

To prepare syrup, heat ingredients together in a 1-quart pot and mix well.

To serve, spoon cornmeal into individual serving plates or bowls and spread it out as a base for 1 or 2 chunks of squash. Just before serving, drizzle hot syrup over squash.

Beverages

Mild Herb Teas

Alfalfa, Blackberry, Blueberry, Raspberry, Strawberry, Camomile, Comfrey, Mullein, Nettle, Red Clover, etc.

Makes 4 servings

These herb or leaf teas are all prepared in the same way. Figure 2 teaspoons dry leaves (and flowers in camomile and red clover teas) per cup of water. They are delicious served hot or cool.

1 quart (4 cups) water
8 teaspoons dry herb tea (2 teaspoons per cup water) or a little less than 3 level tablespoons

Bring water to boil, then turn heat off, and add herb. Stir to completely submerge, then cover to steep for 5-10 minutes, or to desired strength. Strain and serve.

Notes: All tea ingredients may be used more than once with a pinch of fresh tea added to enhance flavor. To save time when preparing teas for large groups and to avoid a last minute time crunch, whenever you have the time, bring water to boil, turn heat off, and stir in tea ingredients to completely submerge. Allow to steep 10 minutes, and strain. Reheat when ready to serve.

If desired, sweeten with brown rice syrup (1 tablespoon per cup tea for large amounts). See the next recipe for an herbal sweetener.

Mild Herb Tea with Sweet Herb ♥ Stevia

Makes 4 servings

Stevia (Stevia Rebaudiana Bertoni), also known as sweet herb or leaf, has a dark green leaf with an amazingly sweet flavor. Natives of Paraguay in South America have used the wild herb as a sweetener in drinks and foods for over a century. The Japanese have imported it from Paraguay and Brazil since the 1970s, and have conducted extensive research on its properties, safety, and effectiveness as a natural sweetener. Studies in both countries show stevia has beneficial (and no negative) effects on persons with hypoglycemia. With 25 times the sweetness of sugar, you'll find that a little sweet herb goes a long way.

1 quart water
8 teaspoons dried herb tea (2 teaspoons per cup water), or a little less than 3 level tablespoons
1/2 teaspoon sweet herb (stevia) [1/8 teaspoon per cup water]

Bring water to boil. Turn heat off, add herbs, and stir to completely submerge. Cover to steep 5-10 minutes or to taste. Strain and serve.

Thyme Tea

Makes 4 servings

Thyme tea is enjoyed by the French. They like its pleasing flavor and feel it's good for the lungs and intestines. Among herbalists, thyme tea is commonly used in the treatment of bronchial problems, but they caution that it not be used over a long period of time. Thyme tea contains 2.5% thyme oil and 10% tannic acid.

1 quart water
2 teaspoons thyme, dried, or 4 teaspoons fresh

Bring water to boil, then turn heat off, and add herb. Stir to moisten, then cover to steep for 10 minutes. Strain and serve.

Sweet Peppermint Tea

Makes 4 servings

Grown extensively in herb gardens in this country and in Europe, Mexicans call this popular herb "yerba buena" meaning good herb. Brewed in combination with regular tea and sweetened, it is one of Morocco's staple beverages. Peppermint tea serves as an alternative for people used to sweet tea who are making the transition to more balanced, mellow drinks.

1 quart water
8 teaspoons dried peppermint leaves (2 teaspoons per cup water), or a little less than 3 tablespoons
Up to 1/4 cup brown rice syrup or 1 teaspoon sweet herb (stevia)

Bring water to boil. Turn heat off, stir in peppermint and sweetener, and let steep for 10 minutes. Strain and serve.

Dixie Mint Tea

Makes 4 servings

A unique, southern-style mint tea.

1 quart water
2 tablespoons twig tea (see page 196)
2 tablespoons brown rice syrup
2 teaspoons fresh orange rind, finely chopped or grated
2 tablespoons mint leaves, dried, or 1/4 cup fresh
1 tablespoon orange juice

Bring water to boil. Turn heat low and add twig tea, sweetener, and orange rind. Simmer for 10 minutes. Turn heat off, add mint and juice, and steep 10 minutes more. Strain. Serve warm or cool with a sprig of fresh mint or a thin slice of orange.

Licorice Root Tea

Makes 4 servings

1 quart water
2 teaspoons licorice root, sliced, shredded, or crushed and dried
1 tablespoon twig tea (optional), see next page

Bring water to boil. Turn heat low, add licorice root and twig tea if included, and simmer 10 minutes. Strain and serve. Tea becomes sweeter the longer it sits.

Oriental Herb Tea ❤ Mu

Makes 4 servings

Mu tea is a beverage composed of either 9 or 16 Oriental herbs. Mu #16 was designed by George Ohsawa, the Japanese natural healer, philosopher, and macrobiotic leader, as a very well-balanced beverage, especially for women. Meanings for the Japanese word "mu" range from unique to infinity, emptiness, nothingness, or complete balance.

Although it's said that Mu #9 was not prescribed by Ohsawa, it is still quite popular. It contains peony root, cinnamon, Japanese parsley root, hoelen, licorice, peach kernel, ginger root, Japanese ginseng, and rehmannia. Mu #16 contains all the ingredients in #9 plus mandarin orange peel, cnicus, atractylis, cypress, cloves, coptis, and moutan.

Both kinds have a mild to rich, sweet flavor (sweetness comes naturally from the licorice root and cinnamon bark), *depending on strength of preparation. Both are served as is, hot or cool, and may be brewed with apple juice or cider for a festive winter beverage.*

1 quart water
1-2 mu tea bags or 4-8 teaspoons loose tea

Bring water to boil, turn heat low, add tea, and simmer 10 minutes. Flavor becomes richer as tea sits.

Variation: **Mu Tea with Licorice Root** ❤ Add extra licorice root for a more noticeable mild sweet taste. Figure 1 teaspoon mu tea and 1/2 teaspoon licorice root, dried and shredded, or 1 slice dried root per cup of water. Bring to boil and simmer for 10 minutes. Flavor is best, sweeter and richer, after tea sits awhile. Strain and serve. May be reheated.

Twig Teas

Twig Tea

Makes 4 servings

Twig tea is called "kukicha," its Japanese name, and is often incorrectly referred to as "bancha" which means green leaf tea. Since tea is one of the most heavily chemicalized crops in Japan and worldwide, purchase only organic twig tea.

Most of the caffeine in tea is found in the leaves, not the twigs. For this reason, as well as the fine flavor, it is preferred. Because some people are sensitive to the traces of caffeine in twig tea, I often reserve it for serving early in the day.

1 quart water
4-8 teaspoons twig tea (1-2 teaspoons per
      cup water)

Bring water to boil, turn heat low, add twigs and stir to submerge. Cover to simmer gently for 10 minutes to extract the flavor from the twigs. Strain and serve.

Twigs can be reused up to 4 times with a pinch of fresh tea added each time.

Sun Tea

Makes 4 servings

Sun tea may be made with any herb tea as well as with twig tea. Twig tea bags are used here because the twigs have been pulverized, and thus release their flavor more quickly. The taste of sun tea is refreshing and slightly different from boiled or steeped tea, perhaps because it is infused by the sun's energy, light, and warmth.

1 quart water
2 twig tea bags or 1/4 cup loose twig tea

Place water and tea in a glass container. Loosely cover with cheesecloth, and set outdoors in a sunny spot until tea is of desired strength, for 4 or more hours. Strain and serve.

Twig Tea with Toasted Brown Rice

Makes 4 servings

This tea is called "genmai kukicha" or "genmai cha" in Japanese, as "genmai" means brown rice.

1 quart water
1/4 cup twig tea with toasted brown rice
      (1 tablespoon per cup water)

To make your own, figure equal amounts of brown rice and twig tea. Rinse, then toast raw rice in dry skillet until golden and crispy, about 5 minutes. Mix with twigs and store in a sealed container in a cool, dry, dark place as for other dry foods.

Bring water to boil, turn heat low, add tea and stir to submerge. Simmer for 10 minutes. Strain and serve.

Evening Tea with Lemon or Apple Slice

Makes 4 servings

It's a Russian custom to serve tea with a slice of lemon or apple in it, or with a tablespoonful of jam or preserves! According to one cookbook written by a Russian immigrant, their evening tea is taken at 10 P.M. and midnight.

1 quart water
2 tablespoons twig tea (1 1/2 teaspoons per cup water)
4-8 slices lemon or apple

Bring water to boil, turn heat low, add twigs, and cover to simmer gently 10 minutes. Strain and serve with a slice of lemon or apple in each cup.

Indian Tea ♥ Chai

Makes 4 servings

This flavorful specialty beverage is also known as Yogi tea.

1 quart water
8 teaspoons twig tea (2 teaspoons per cup of water, or a little less than 3 level tablespoons)
2 cardamom pods, pods discarded, seeds crushed
6-inch stick cinnamon, broken
4 whole cloves
1 tablespoon malted grain syrup (brown rice syrup or barley malt) or pure maple syrup
1/2 teaspoon ginger, freshly grated
1/4 cup soymilk

Bring all ingredients to boil, except soymilk (as boiling causes curdling), and simmer covered for 10 minutes. Turn heat off, then add soymilk. Strain and serve.

Grain Teas and "Coffees"

Toasted Corn Tea

Makes 4 servings

My favorite tea, it has an enticing aroma and a soothing flavor. Korean produced, it is available in Oriental markets, or make your own.

1 quart water
1/4 cup toasted corn (1 tablespoon per cup of water)

Bring water to boil, turn heat low, and add toasted corn to simmer 10 minutes. Strain and serve.

To make your own toasted corn, dry roast one cup whole, dry kernels of yellow grain corn in a skillet. Kernels become light to dark golden brown over medium heat in about 8-15 minutes. Stir often to avoid scorching. For large amounts or an easier method requiring no stirring, spread corn on a baking sheet and toast in a 350° oven until golden; same amount of time.

Toasted Barley Tea

Makes 4 servings

Known as "mugicha" in Japanese ("mugi" means barley and "cha" means tea), this beverage is made with unhulled barley. It is easily found in Japanese markets, or can be made at home by the method described for corn tea. Always served cool during the summer in Japan.

1 quart water
8 teaspoons toasted barley, or a little less than 3 tablespoons total (2 teaspoons per cup water)

Bring water to boil, turn heat low, add barley and simmer for 10 minutes. Strain and serve.

Grain "Coffee," Instant and Brewed

Makes 4 servings

There are many cereal grain beverages on the market today. Their popularity continues to grow as people discover their dark color, rich aromas, and flavors similar to coffee— although they contain no coffee or caffeine. Barley "coffees" are made from barley which has been hulled, dark-roasted, and ground, coarsely for brewing or finely for instant versions. Other grain "coffees" are made from roasted rye and wheat, and sometimes contain roots such as chicory, dandelion, or beet, the latter for sweetness.

Yannoh is the name of the original instant coffee substitute created by George Ohsawa and the early proponents of macrobiotics. Japanese yannoh is a lightly-toasted blend of ground azuki beans, red peas, black soybeans, brown rice, and dandelion root. Another version, from the Lima Company in Belgium, contains barley, rye, chicory, and wild acorns.

1 quart water
4-8 teaspoons grain "coffee," instant powder
    or granules (1-2 teaspoons per cup wa-
    ter, depending on strength desired)

For instant variety, add boiling water to measured amount powder in cup, or add powder to pot for larger amounts. Stir and serve.

    For granules, bring water to boil and turn heat low. Add granules to pot gradually to avoid foaming over and stir in. Cover to simmer very gently 10 minutes. Strain and serve.

    Variation: **Lemon Espresso-Style Grain "Coffee"** ❤ Figure 2 teaspoons to 1 level tablespoon grain "coffee" per cup water for this very tasty brew. Cut lemon peel in 4 to 8 long, thin strips. Twist and place a strip on the bottom of each cup before pouring hot espresso-style "coffee."

Cool Summer Drinks

Any tea is refreshing served chilled at picnic outings or on any hot afternoon.

Cool Apple Tea

Makes 1 serving or 1 cup

1/3-1/2 cup apple juice or cider (less for
    milder sweet flavor)
2/3-1/2 cup water
1 teaspoon mild herb or twig tea or 4 fresh
    mint leaves

Bring juice and water to boil. For fresh or dried mild herb teas, turn heat off, stir in tea to completely submerge, and cover to steep for 5-10 minutes. For twig tea, add and continue to simmer 5 minutes. Either way, strain and transfer to refrigerator to cool before serving.

    Variation: **Cool Lemon Tea** ❤ Figure 2 teaspoons mild herb tea, 1/8 teaspoon sweet herb (stevia), and 1/2 teaspoon lemon juice per cup water.

Fruit-Tea Fizz

Makes 1 serving or 1 cup

1/2 cup fruit juice
1/4 cup twig tea
1/4 cup carbonated mineral water

Chill ingredients and mix just before serving.

Variation: Make fruit juice ice cubes with a grape or berry in each one. Some ice cube trays come in shapes such as hearts or stars.

Black Cherry Soda

Makes 4 servings or 1 quart

Also called spritzers or sparklers, an endless array of refreshing sodas can be made by varying flavored mineral waters (with lime, lemon, or orange) and juices.

When making natural sodas, avoid club soda as it contains carbonated tap water and sodium salts.

2 1/2 cups carbonated mineral water
1 1/2 cups black cherry juice
Lemon or lime juice to taste (optional)
Cherries with stems, 1 per serving (optional)

Chill ingredients. Mix and serve with one cherry in each glass.

Lemonade

Makes 5 servings or 5 1/4 cups

Lemonade is made from fruit juice, water, and a sweetener. (Pink lemonade is artificially colored.) This delicious version is easy to make for an occasional treat on hot summer days. Maple syrup is the best sweetener to use here for flavor and ease in dissolving.

1 quart water
1 cup lemon juice, freshly squeezed
1/4 cup pure maple syrup

Mix ingredients and chill to serve.

Variations: **Limeade** ❤ Substitute fresh lime juice for lemon. **Orangeade** ❤ Substitute 2 cups fresh orange juice for the lemon juice. Makes 6 1/4 cups.

Ginger Ale

Makes 4 servings or 4 1/3 cups

1 quart carbonated mineral water, chilled
3 tablespoons pure maple syrup
4 teaspoons ginger juice (ginger freshly grated and squeezed)
2 teaspoons lemon juice

Mix ingredients and serve.

"Medicinals"

Miso Tea

Makes 1 serving or 1 cup

Quick nourishment for busy mornings, miso tea is a light miso broth containing no other ingredients.

1 cup water
Miso to taste, about 1 teaspoon to 1 level tablespoon depending on strength desired

Bring water to boil. In a separate bowl, dissolve miso in a little of the hot water, then return it to pot and simmer gently 2 minutes. Another way to add miso is to place it in a small strainer and hold it in the hot water, pressing miso through with a spoon.

Plum Tea

Makes 1-2 servings or 1 cup

Plum extract, also called ume extract or baini-ku ekisu, is made from Japanese plums which are picked green, crushed, and pressed to extract the juice. It is then cooked about 24 hours to form a tart, concentrated syrup. Plum concentrate is said to have 30 times the strength of the pickled plum (ume-boshi). It contains no salt, unlike the pickled plum. According to Japanese folk medicine, as well as scientific studies, it shares the same healing qualities (see pages 167-170), plus some.

Ume extract has the ability to absorb and neutralize several hundred times its weight in acid.

In the mid 1920s, it was first produced on a commercial basis. At that time the Japanese army and navy officially used it as an antiseptic and as a guard against food poisoning, dysentery, and other illnesses.

Other uses include prevention of skin disease, anemia, frigidity, impotence, and premature aging.

The plum extract also works in ridding persons of constipation as well as diarrhea. It increases or decreases bacterial action when necessary to re-establish order and proper bowel movements. It has both the capacity to suppress breeding of bacteria in the small intestines that leads to diarrhea, or to promote bacterial development to increase fine movements to aid bowel movements.

Pregnant women particularly suffer from constipation due to the lack of natural fine muscle movements in the lower abdomen. The problem increases as the pressure from the newly forming fetus increases. An organic acid called catechuic acid is necessary to generate fine movements in the bowels, and it is contained in high amounts in umeboshi and plum extract.

Several other food products were developed in the 1960s and 70s from ume extract. Small balls or granules are formed from the concentrate and brown rice flour. (See Soken Trading Co. in Resources.) Others are made from equal parts of the extract and flour from jinenjo, the wild mountain root with health-giving properties of its own. (See Eden Foods in Resources.) Jinenjo has 28 times more diastase enzyme than the healthful daikon radish, and is thought to be beneficial to the kidneys and liver. Balls may be swallowed like pills.

Ideal any time of day, plum tea's sour taste, when taken in the morning, straightens you up to start the day right.

1 cup water or tea
1/4 teaspoon ume plum extract

Bring liquid to boil. Pour into individual cup (s) and stir in plum extract.

Ume-Kuzu Morning Tea with Ginger

Makes 2 servings or 2 cups

This beverage combines the healing qualities of the umeboshi plum (see pages 167-170), with kuzu's abilities to soothe and strengthen the intestines and stomach. A colorless, odorless, and tasteless thickening agent, kuzu root starch is wonderful in Chinese-style sauces, and puddings as well. I like to make this tea thicker by doubling the amount of kuzu.

A similar beverage is used in Japan. There it is taken on New Year's morning (and many other times as well) to insure a strong and illness-free year.

1 tablespoon kuzu root starch
2 cups cool water or twig tea
2 teaspoons pickled plums (umeboshi), torn in small pieces or mashed, or umeboshi paste
2 teaspoons natural soy sauce
1 teaspoon ginger juice, freshly grated and squeezed

Mix kuzu with a little of the liquid and set aside. Bring remaining ingredients to boil, then add kuzu-water mixture and stir until beverage becomes clear and slightly thick.

Bean and Nut "Milks"

These beverages make great replacements for cow's milk to pour over hot or cold cereals and as an ingredient in dessert toppings. They also appear in the Breakfasts section on pages 213-215.

Sweet Soymilk

Makes 1 cup

1 cup soymilk
2 teaspoons maple syrup or 4 teaspoons brown rice syrup

Amazake-Soymilk

Makes 1 cup

3/4 cup soymilk
1/4 cup plain amazake (see page 242)

To prepare sweet soymilks, simply mix ingredients. If brown rice syrup is used, gently heat it with soymilk to dissolve.

To sweeten, change proportions to 2/3 soymilk:1/3 amazake, or 1/2 soymilk:1/2 amazake.

Sweet Nut "Milk"

Makes 3 1/2 - 4 cups

Almonds and hazelnuts have the best flavors for "milks," fresh and slightly sweet—and the whitest hue, even with the skins left on. (Sunflower and sesame seeds both taste quite raw with a rather strong flavor. Sunflower gives a grey color to the "milk" whereas sesame gives a tan color. They are best reserved for use in gravies where further cooking is required.)

1 cup raw almonds or hazelnuts
1 quart water
2-4 tablespoons pure maple syrup (2 teaspoons-1 tablespoon per cup nut milk)
1 teaspoon vanilla (about 1/4 teaspoon per cup nut milk)

To prepare sweet nut "milk," blend nuts or seeds alone until completely pulverized, then gradually add water and blend a little longer. Strain through 2 thicknesses of cheesecloth, wrapping cloth around nut pulp and squeezing tightly to extract the white liquid. Add maple syrup and vanilla.

For even whiter almond "milk," blanch almonds by pouring 2 cups boiling water over nuts and letting them sit for 2 minutes. Drain, and remove almond skins by pressing almond between fingers. (This process doesn't work with hazelnuts.)

Reserve pulp to toast for use in morning oatmeal (1/4 cup pulp to 1 cup oatmeal and 2 tablespoons raisins is delicious!), cookies, breads, or crunch or crumble toppings.

Variation: **Apple-Almond "Milk"** ❤
Sweeten almond "milk" with fresh apple instead of a concentrated sweetener. In food processor or blender add 1 apple per quart almond "milk." Yields 5 cups.

Oat "Milk"

Makes 7 - 7 1/2 cups

Made from cooked whole oats, this sweetened milk-like beverage is based on grains instead of beans or nuts with their higher protein and fat contents. However, it's a little more time-consuming to prepare, and isn't as clear in texture.

1 cup whole oats
10 cups water
Few grains unrefined sea salt
1/2 cup brown rice syrup or 1 large apple, cored and diced (optional)

To prepare plain oat "milk," pressure-cook first 3 ingredients for 1 hour (no flame spreader needed), then purée in Foley food mill (also known as a ricer). Strain oat "milk" to smooth out texture. Clean out pressure cooker valve as oats tend to foam up into it.

For a mildly sweet flavor, pressure-cook apple with oats. I personally prefer the flavor of brown rice syrup. If necessary, heat jar so it pours easily, then add to oat "milk" at end.

Breakfasts

For an endless variety of quick-cooking breakfasts, hot morning cereals can't be beat. They have the same comforting nature as the cream of wheat or cream of rice we all became used to as children, but with fuller flavor and richer nutrient value from the whole grains. Processed (highly milled) cereals are synthetically enriched with nutrients lost in processing, but not all are added back in. Whole-grain cereals—preferably made from organically-grown grains—are naturally balanced sources of fiber, vitamins, and minerals.

Freshly-ground flour tastes the best and offers the most sustenance, making the investment in a good grain mill worthwhile, but a large variety of whole-grain flours is available in natural food stores. Some stores even grind the flour on-the-spot, making it as fresh as home-ground.

For any hot morning cereal, people who are used to sweeter breakfasts may want to substitute apple juice for all or part of the water, or add chopped dried fruit or raisins, or a little sweetener (brown rice syrup, barley malt, pure maple syrup, or sorghum). Serve as is or substitute amazake (sweet rice nectar), sweetened soymilk, or nut "milk" for those still wanting milk on their cereals.

See pages 213-215 for recipes.

For the creamiest hot cereal with the least amount of effort in the morning, get in the habit of soaking flour or cracked grain overnight.

Different kinds of flour require different amounts of liquid to achieve a cereal with a smooth and creamy texture. These recipes serve as a starting-off point. Take note of how you would prefer your cereal (thicker or thinner in texture, flour plain or toasted before cooking, etc.), and then change it to your taste the next time you make it. As a general rule, the ratio of flour to water is 1:3, and for amounts above 2 cups flour, the amount of water decreases to 1 : 2 1/2, or 2 cups flour to 5 cups water.

For very large volumes, calculate amounts at a ratio of 1 part flour to 2 parts water, then add more water if necessary. It's easier to thin down a cereal than to thicken it up. Allow 1 hour cooking time.

The amount of salt is up to 1/8 teaspoon per cup of grain—just the same as for other grains such as rice, bread, or pastries.

Soak pot in water immediately after cooking cereal so bottom crust peels or scrubs off easily.

Basic Hot Morning Cereal Recipe ❤
Hot Hazelnut Cereal

A simple variation on the cream of wheat theme, this cereal may be made with whole-wheat flour or, for a chewier texture, with cracked wheat. Incredibly sweet when flour is freshly ground.

Makes 2 servings or 2 1/4 - 2 1/2 cups,
less with cracked wheat, more with flour

2 tablespoons hazelnuts, toasted, skins
    rubbed off, nuts coarsely chopped
1 cup whole-wheat (bread or pastry) flour or
    cracked wheat
3 cups water
1/8 teaspoon unrefined sea salt

Makes 4 servings or 4-5 cups

1/4 cup hazelnuts, toasted, skins rubbed
    off, nuts coarsely chopped
2 cups whole-wheat (bread or pastry) flour
    or cracked wheat
5 cups water
1/4 teaspoon unrefined sea salt

To toast hazelnuts, spread on baking sheet and place in cold oven. Set temperature to 350° and cook until skins darken and nuts are golden in the center when broken in half, about 15 minutes. Or bake just 8-10 minutes in a hot (preheated) oven.

To make your own flour or cracked wheat, 1 cup wheat berries yields 1 1/2 cups flour or 1 1/4 cups very coarsely ground cracked wheat, sifted.

Soak flour or cracked grain in enough of the measured amount of water to cover overnight, about half the volume or 1 1/2 - 2 cups. Gradually add the water to the flour, whisking to work out any lumps. (No-soak method follows.) In the morning, bring remaining water and salt to boil in a 2- or 3-quart saucepan. Add soaked grains and return to boil, stirring to avoid sticking or lumping. A flat-bottom wooden spoon and/or a wire whisk are helpful. Turn heat to low and cook until soft, about 5-15 minutes, less with flour, more with cracked grains. Stir 2-3 times during cooking and add nuts in last several minutes to retain crunch.

For cereal which has not been pre-soaked: gradually add half the water to flour in a bowl to form a smooth batter. Bring remaining water with salt to boil, then add cereal batter. Bring to boil, stirring often, then turn heat low to cook until soft, 15-30 minutes, less for flour, more for cracked grain, placing a flame spreader under pot after 15 minutes. Stir 2-3 times during cooking.

For larger amounts than those stated above, figure 1 cup grain (flour or cracked) to 2 cups water. (The 1:3 proportion often makes larger amounts of cereal too watery. However, when it is needed, it is stated in the recipes.) Soak flour in enough of the measured water to cover. In the morning, bring the remaining water to boil with the salt. Add the soaked cereal and proceed as usual. This method saves time and effort spent waiting for a large volume of cereal to come to a boil, requiring constant stirring. It also lessens the chance of the cereal burning at the bottom of the pot.

Figure 1 - 1 1/2 cups cooked cereal per serving.

Rye and Wheat Cereal

Rye and Wheat Cereal is delicious with toasted sunflower seeds (see recipe on page 136). It has a naturally sweeter taste than any of the other cereals.

Makes 2 servings or 2 1/2 cups

1/2 cup rye flour
1/2 cup whole-wheat flour
3 cups water
1/8 teaspoon unrefined sea salt

Makes 4 servings or about 5 1/2 cups

1 cup rye flour
1 cup whole-wheat flour
5 cups water
1/4 teaspoon unrefined sea salt

Follow directions in preceding *Basic Cereal Recipe.*

Rice Cream

Makes 3 servings or 3 1/2 cups

The natural, whole grain version of that childhood standby cream of rice, rice cream is a favorite morning cereal because of its white color, smooth texture, and balanced flavor. Rice cream is enhanced with a sprinkling of just about any table seasoning or with a drizzle of soy sauce.

1 cup brown rice flour, toasted
4 cups water
1/8 teaspoon unrefined sea salt

In a dry skillet, lightly toast rice until you can smell its grainy aroma, about 3-5 minutes. This step brings out an added depth of flavor and may be done either before or after rice is ground into flour.

Proceed according to directions for *Basic Cereal Recipe* on preceding page.

Tibetan Barley Cereal ♥ Tsampa

Makes 2 servings or 2 2/3 cups

Tsampa is eaten by travellers in both Mongolia and Tibet. The original version is a paste made from barley flour with tea leaves, yak butter, salt, and soda.
This simplified variation is tasty garnished with a sprinkling of any table seasoning.

1 cup barley flour, toasted
3 cups water
1/8 teaspoon unrefined sea salt

In a dry skillet, lightly toast barley flour to bring out flavor. Proceed according to directions for *Basic Cereal Recipe* on preceding page.

Whole-Wheat 'n Amaranth Cereal

Makes 2 servings or 2 1/2 cups

Because of its unique but pleasant taste, amaranth seems to please most when prepared in combination with other, milder grains. The relatively high cost due to the great distance it travels from its source (until it is grown closer commercially) is another reason to enjoy this ancient grain in small quantities. For historical information, see page 55.
If amaranth flour is unavailable in your natural foods store, make your own with a grain mill, or if you don't have one, lightly toast amaranth seeds in a dry skillet before

grinding in the small container of a blender, 1/4 cup at a time.

3/4 cup whole-wheat flour
1/4 cup amaranth flour
1 tablespoon amaranth seeds, lightly
    toasted
3 cups water
1/8 teaspoon unrefined sea salt or 3/4 tea-
    spoon natural soy sauce
2 tablespoons sunflower seeds, toasted and
    sprinkled with soy sauce (see page 136)

Proceed according to directions in *Basic Cereal Recipe* on page 206. Add sunflower seeds just before serving to maintain the crunchy texture.

    Variation: **Corn and Amaranth Morning Cereal** ❤ Substitute corn flour or meal for wheat.

Pantry Porridge

Makes 2 servings

This cereal makes use of all those tiny bits of flour or flakes left over from making baked goods or cereals. Of course it tastes different every time, so take note of the ingredients in an especially tasty version. Sprinkle with your choice of table seasoning.

1 cup combination flours and/or flakes
2-3 cups water (less for flakes, more for
    flours)
1/8 teaspoon unrefined sea salt

Proceed according to directions in *Basic Cereal Recipe* on page 206.

Soft Millet Morning Cereal

Makes 2-3 servings or 3 1/2 - 4 1/2 cups

1 cup millet
1/8 teaspoon unrefined sea salt
4-5 cups water
1 teaspoon sesame oil (optional)

Rinse millet by swishing it in a bowl of cool water. Drain.

    If a richer flavor is desired, toast millet in a dry or lightly-oiled skillet over medium heat until a pleasing aroma rises and millet dries out somewhat, 5-8 minutes.

    Bring salted water to boil in a 2- or 3-quart pot. Add millet to boiling water and when boiling resumes, turn heat low to cook covered until millet is soft, about 1/2 hour. Delicious with *Pumpkin Seed-Shiso Sprinkles* (see page 138).

    For large amounts, such as 60 servings, the millet to water ratio drops to 1:3.

Steel-Cut Oats

Makes 2-3 servings or 2 2/3 cups

Steel-cut oats are whole oat groats which have been sliced in 2-3 pieces with a steel blade. No heat is used in the process, thus nutrients are preserved. Cooked steel-cut oats have a wonderful texture, both creamy and chewy at the same time. Great with Sunflower-Dulse Sprinkles *(see page 139).*

1 cup steel-cut oats
3 cups water
1/8 teaspoon unrefined sea salt

Proceed as in *Basic Cereal Recipe* on page 206.

For large amounts, increase all ingredients proportionately. The 1 part grain to 3 parts water ratio holds true here even for large volumes.

3-Grain Cereal

Makes 2-3 servings or 2 2/3 cups

This cracked grain porridge is made from whole grains which have been very coarsely ground and then sifted to remove the fine particles of flour. Texture is chewier as a result. Nice with toasted seeds sprinkled with soy sauce (see recipe on page 136).

Follow *Basic Cereal Recipe* on page 206, substituting a combination of three cracked grains for wheat. Choose cracked wheat, oats (steel-cut), corn (grits or polenta), cracked barley, brown rice, millet, or rye. The first 3 combine nicely and are widely available.

Breakfast Grits

Makes 2-3 servings or 2 3/4 cups

A breakfast favorite! Commercial corn grits and polenta appear to be processed in the same way nowadays, but historically there were different methods. Whole corn is coarsely ground and sifted.

After cereal is cooked, further variations include pan frying after cooking (fried grits), or spreading grits in bowl or baking dish to gel, then slicing and frying (see Scrapple recipe on page 218).

Cereal:

1 cup corn grits or polenta
3 cups water
1/8 teaspoon unrefined sea salt

Topping:

1 teaspoon natural soy sauce
1 teaspoon corn oil or toasted sesame oil

Prepare according to *Basic Cereal Recipe* on page 206. To serve, drizzle a little soy sauce, or a combination of soy sauce and oil, over grits, 1/4-1/2 teaspoon per serving.

For large amounts, simply multiply ingredients proportionately.

Variation: To serve, drizzle a little sweetener (such as pure maple or a malted grain syrup, heated) over top of grits.

Grain-Bean-Seed Cereal ♥ Kokkoh

Kokkoh is a delicious, nutritionally well-rounded blend of toasted and freshly-ground grains, beans and seeds. The original recipe was reportedly created by George Ohsawa, the founder of present-day macrobiotics, according to traditional Oriental folk medicine. Widely used as an infant cereal, kohkoh is actually an easy-to-digest food for children of all ages.

Use kokkoh's combination of ingredients in soups, sauces, or cracker recipes as well. Other recipe variations range in ingredients from simply sweet and short grain brown rices to more elaborate versions in which oats and sesame seeds, or wheat, millet, barley, soybeans, seaweed, and sunflower seeds are added.

Nice toppings for this cereal are vegetable-miso seasoning (tekka) or a drizzle of soy sauce.

Dry Kohkoh Mix:

Makes 1 2/3 cups dry mix

1/2 cup short grain brown rice
1/2 cup sweet brown rice
1/3 cup whole oats
1/4 cup azuki beans
1 tablespoon sesame seeds

Hot Kokkoh Cereal:

Makes 3 servings or 3 2/3 cups

1 cup *Dry Kohkoh Mix*, ground
4 cups water
1/8 teaspoon unrefined sea salt

Makes 4 servings or 5 1/2 cups

2 cups *Dry Kokkoh Mix*, ground
6 cups water
1/4 teaspoon unrefined sea salt

In a large skillet, lightly toast ingredients together over medium-high heat. Stir often until a nice aroma rises and color becomes slightly golden, about 5-10 minutes. Transfer to a large bowl to cool briefly, about 5 minutes, then grind finely.

Prepare cereal according to directions in *Basic Cereal Recipe* on page 206.

Variations: Add a 3-inch piece of kombu for extra minerals.

Infant's "Milk" and Baby Food ♥
Leave mixture whole and pressure-cook 1 cup with 10 cups water for 1 hour, or boil for 1 1/2 hours. Strain for about 7 cups liquid. Pureé for baby food, adding less water as baby's need for soft food diminishes with age.

Oatmeal

Oatmeal is a breakfast food everyone is familiar with, so it's an easy one to recommend for people making the transition from high-fat and sugar-laden breakfasts to more nourishing high-fiber fare.

When rolled oats are made, after the groats are split from the outer hull they are steam-heated and passed between rollers. Quick-cooking varieties are made by cutting the groats into smaller pieces before steaming and rolling.

Some studies have shown that the type of fiber in oatmeal helps lower cholesterol levels. The October, 1986 issue of *Vegetarian Times* reported that people on a low-fat diet further reduced their cholesterol levels by 2.7 percent when they began eating 2 ounces (3/4 cups dry weight) of oatmeal daily, according to researchers at the Northwestern University Medical School's Department of Community Health and Preventive Medicine.

The ratio of flakes to water is 1:2 for both small and large amounts. Pre-soaking is unnecessary with flaked cereals but makes sense when you're in a hurry or cooking large quantities. The consistency will be very creamy and cooking time reduced to merely heating it up.

Since dulse was historically served along with oats in Scotland and Ireland, a table seasoning such as *Sunflower-Dulse Sprinkles* (see recipe on page 139), is tasty and appropriate today also. For a sweeter taste, omit sprinkles and pour a little sweetened soy or nut "milk" or sweet rice nectar (amazake) over oatmeal (see recipes on pages 214 and 215).

Makes 1-2 servings or 2 cups

1 cup oat flakes
2 cups water
1/8 teaspoon unrefined sea salt

Makes 2-3 servings or about 3 1/2 cups

2 cups oat flakes
3-4 cups water
1/4 teaspoon unrefined sea salt

Bring ingredients to boil in a 2- or 3-quart saucepan, then turn heat low and cover until done, about 10 minutes. When using a small pot, keep the lid ajar to prevent oats from foaming over.

For large amounts, bring salted water to boil first before adding rolled oats. This step saves time spent stirring while waiting for cereal to come to boil, and guards against sticking. Stir occasionally. Figure about 1-1 1/2 cups per serving.

Oatmeal with Rice

Makes 2 servings or 2 1/2 cups

Follow preceding *Oatmeal* recipe, adding 1/2 cup cooked rice to 1 cup oat flakes. No extra liquid is needed.

Oatmeal with Raisins

Makes 2 servings or 2 1/4 cups

Follow *Oatmeal* recipe on preceding page, adding 1/4 cup raisins. Stir a couple of times during cooking to prevent raisins from sinking and sticking to the bottom of the pot.

Variation: Substitute other dried fruit for raisins. Soak fruit until reconstituted in water to cover, cut it in small pieces, and use sweet soaking liquid in cooking cereal.

Oatmeal with Granola

Makes 1-2 servings or 1 2/3 cups

A sweet variation on the oatmeal theme, granola may be added to other cereals as well.

3/4 cup oat flakes
1/4 cup granola (sweetened with pure maple or malted grain syrup, or concentrated fruit juice), 1 tablespoon set aside for garnish
2 cups water
1/8 teaspoon unrefined sea salt

Prepare as regular oatmeal (see recipe on preceding page). Sprinkle a little granola on top of each serving.

Variations: **Oatmeal with Trail Mix or Muesli** ❤ Substitute trail mix (any combination of nuts, seeds, raisins, and/or currants) or muesli for granola. To toast trail mix so the nuts and seeds have a richer flavor, spread entire mix on baking sheet and bake just 5 minutes at 350°. In this brief amount of time, raisins and/or currants won't burn. Makes 2 cups cooked cereal.

Hot Muesli Morning Cereal

Muesli (from the German word for "mix") is a combination of grain flakes, nuts, seeds, and fruit. It originated in Switzerland with

Dr. Maximillian Bircher-Brenner. Muesli is often soaked overnight in a cool or hot liquid, to be eaten in the morning. This is also a nice way to prepare it in hot weather, or for a snack or when camping. Cooking it like oatmeal makes for a warming, creamy breakfast cereal.

Muesli Mix:

Makes about 4 cups

2 cups rolled oats
1 cup rolled wheat (or other grain flakes
    such as rye, barley, or millet)
1/4 cup sunflower seeds (or pumpkin
    seeds), toasted
1/4 cup hazelnuts (or other nuts such as
    walnuts, almonds, or pecans), toasted
    and coarsely chopped
1/4 cup dried apples, finely chopped
1/4 cup raisins

Hot Muesli Cereal:

Makes 2 cups or 2 servings

1 cup *Muesli Mix*
2 cups liquid (water, mild herb or twig tea,
    diluted juice, or soy or nut "milk" [see
    recipes on pages 213-215])
1/8 teaspoon unrefined sea salt

Combine ingredients for muesli mix and store in a tightly sealed jar.
    Prepare as oatmeal on page 210.

Variations: **Summer Muesli** ❤ Prepare as usual. When serving, top cereal with fresh fruit in season such as strawberries, blueberries, grapes, melon balls, or apple cubes.
    Cool Muesli ❤ Soak ingredients overnight in your choice of liquid. Muesli is ready to eat in the morning without cooking.

Brown Rice for Breakfast

An easy and nourishing breakfast is made by pouring hot miso soup (or tea as is done in Japan) over leftover rice.

Soft Breakfast Rice

Makes 3-4 servings or about 4 1/4 - 4 2/3 cups, less if pressure-cooked, more if boiled

In Hong Kong and China, soft white rice is standard breakfast fare. Called congee, *it is served by street vendors and in fancy hotel restaurants with small amounts of savory toppings.*
    Soft rice goes well topped with sesame salt and plain or seasoned nori sea vegetable strips, or Wild Nori-Sunflower Sprinkles *(see page 139), or with cubes of marinated and baked tofu (see page 151).*

1 cup short grain brown rice
5 cups water
1/8 teaspoon unrefined sea salt

Rinse, drain, and toast rice in a dry skillet if desired, 5-8 minutes. Soak rice overnight in pressure cooker or 3-quart pot if time allows. In morning, add salt and bring to pressure or boil, then cook over low heat for 45 minutes-1 hour, less with pressure cooking, more with boiling. Stir well and serve.

    Variation: **Whole Rice Cream** ❤ is the main food recommended for people on a healing diet. It is the most easily digestible grain dish because it is made from whole grain rice (instead of flour) which is pressure-cooked and puréed, the latter step serving to remove the fibrous part of the bran layer.

Follow *Soft Breakfast Rice* recipe, then purée in a Foley food mill (also called a ricer) or by straining and squeezing through several thicknesses of cheesecloth. Makes 2-3 servings or 3 cups cereal cream and 1 cup pulp. Great with sesame salt, vegetable miso seasoning (tekka), or a drizzle of soy sauce. (Reserve fibrous part for baked goods or feed to pets mixed with fish [for cats] or natural pet food.)

Steamed Rice

Simply steam leftover cooked rice in a steamer basket over water, or place in pot with 1/4 inch water and simmer until heated all the way through, 5-10 minutes. Stir to break up lumps. If a bamboo steamer basket is used, line it with cheesecloth to keep rice from falling through slats.

Dry Cereals

There are a growing number of high quality, ready-to-eat dry cereals on the market today. Their light textures are especially attractive in the warm months when a hearty breakfast just doesn't sound good. Enjoy them plain as a crunchy snack as well.

Be sure to read the labels. Ingredients should be easy to identify—simply flakes or puffed whole cereal grains. Some cereals contain sweeteners as well. Good quality barley malt, rice syrup, pure maple syrup, or fruit juice are best. There should be no questionable ingredients such as other forms of sugar (corn syrup, etc.), leavening agents such as yeast or baking powder, artificial flavor and color, or preservatives. Added vitamins and minerals are undesirable as their concentrated nature throws off the natural balance of the whole food.

"If not milk, what do I put on top of my cereal?"

These nourishing breakfasts with their honest whole-grain flavors stand on their own without further enhancement. However, for people who really feel they must have a white, milk-like liquid to pour over their cereals, soymilk, almond or hazelnut "milks," oat "milk," or sweet rice nectar (*amazake*—see page 242) are wonderful substitutes for cow's milk. For anyone who has been raised on corn flakes or oatmeal with milk and fresh fruit or raisins for breakfast, the new high-quality cereals served with these "new" beverages and a little fruit are a satisfying breakfast treat. Recipes follow. Diluted fruit juice is another sweet cereal topping.

Dairy products in general are excluded as an everyday item in a health-giving approach to food. Fat content may be high.

Factory-farmed cows often lead horrible lives in tiny indoor pens where hormones, antibiotics, and other chemicals are a standard part of their feed. Most of the world's people are allergic to cow's milk and more and more Westerners are finding their runny noses disappear when they eliminate dairy products. It doesn't seem that human beings even need the milk of another species in the animal kingdom after being weaned from mother's milk.

Dry Cereals with Fresh Fruit and Toppings

Makes 1 serving

1 1/2 cups whole grain flakes, puffs, or other dry breakfast cereal
Several slices and/or whole pieces seasonal fresh fruit (peaches, strawberries, red raspberries, blueberries, etc.) or 1 teaspoon raisins
3/4-1 cup *Sweet Soymilk, Amazake-Soymilk, or Sweet Nut "Milk"* (recipes follow)

Sweet Soymilk

Makes 1 cup

1 cup soymilk
2 teaspoons maple syrup or 4 teaspoons brown rice syrup

Mix ingredients. If brown rice syrup is used, gently heat it with soymilk to dissolve.

Amazake-Soymilk

Makes 1 cup

3/4 cup soymilk
1/4 cup plain amazake (see page 242)

Mix ingredients.
To sweeten, change proportions to 2/3 soymilk:1/3 amazake, or 1/2 soymilk:1/2 amazake.

Sweet Nut "Milk"

Makes 3 1/2 - 4 cups

Almonds and hazelnuts have the best flavors of all the nuts, fresh and slightly sweet, and the whitest hue, even with the skins left on. (Sunflower and sesame seeds both taste quite raw, with a rather strong flavor. Sunflower gives a grey color to the milk whereas sesame gives a tan color. They are best reserved for use in gravies where further cooking is required.)

1 cup raw almonds or hazelnuts
1 quart water
2-4 tablespoons pure maple syrup (2 teaspoons-1 tablespoon per cup nut "milk")
1 teaspoon vanilla (about 1/4 teaspoon per cup nut "milk")

To prepare sweet nut "milk," blend nuts or seeds with 1 cup water until completely pulverized, then add remaining 3 cups water and blend a little longer. Strain through 2 thicknesses of cheesecloth, wrapping cloth around nut pulp and squeezing tightly to extract the white liquid. Add maple syrup and vanilla.

For even whiter almond "milk," blanch almonds by pouring 2 cups boiling water over nuts and letting them sit for 2 minutes. Drain, and remove almond skins by pressing almond between fingers. (This process doesn't work with hazelnuts.) Both are quite white without the blanching process.

Reserve pulp to toast for use in morning oatmeal (1/4 cup pulp to 1 cup oatmeal and 2 tablespoons raisins is delicious!), cookies, breads, or crunch or crumble toppings. Spread pulp on baking sheet to bake at 250° until golden and dry, 40 minutes-1 hour, stirring occasionally.

Variation: **Apple-Almond "Milk"** ❤
Sweeten almond "milk" with fresh apple instead of a concentrated sweetener. Add to food processor or blender 1 apple (cored, and peeled, if desired) per quart almond milk. Yields 5 cups.

Oat "Milk"

Makes 7 - 7 1/2 cups

Made from cooked whole oats, this sweetened milk-like beverage is based on grains instead of beans or nuts with their higher protein and fat contents. However, it's a little more time-consuming to prepare, and isn't as clear in texture.

1 cup whole oats
10 cups water
Few grains unrefined sea salt
1/2 cup brown rice syrup or 1 large apple, cored and diced (optional)

To prepare plain oat "milk," pressure-cook first 3 ingredients for 1 hour (no flame spreader needed), then purée in Foley food mill (also known as a ricer). Strain oat "milk" to smooth out texture. Clean out pressure cooker valve as oats tend to foam up into it.

For a mildly sweet flavor, pressure-cook apple with oats. I personally prefer the flavor of brown rice syrup. Heat syrup jar so it pours easily, then add to oat "milk" at end.

Variation: **Amazake-Oat "Milk"** ❤
Mix oat "milk" with amazake for a sweeter beverage.

Waffles

Waffles are reliable, easy-to-make breakfast or brunch foods. Almost any whole-grain flour or combination turns out well-shaped, delicious waffles. Waffles don't require whole-wheat bread flour with its high gluten content, sourdough starter, or commercial leavening agents to make them rise. Pastry wheat flour makes for smoother waffles than bread wheat flour.

The general recipe is equal parts flour and liquid. A little more liquid makes for lighter, crisper waffles, less liquid makes denser, softer waffles.

My favorite waffle iron is a stove top, cast-iron model shaped in 5 hearts which makes one 7- inch flower-shaped waffle. Old electric waffle irons are frequently found in thrift shops and at garage sales. Oftentimes all that's required is a new cord from your local hardware store. Belgian waffle irons have generous indentations in them to hold syrupy toppings.

For a crispy snack, toast leftover waffles in toaster or oven.

Whole-Grain Waffles with Vegetable Sauce

Makes 4-8 small-medium waffles
or 2 large Belgian waffles

Batter:

Makes 3 cups

2 cups whole-wheat pastry flour
2 - 2 1/4 cups water
2 tablespoons oil (optional)
1/4 cup carrot, grated
1/4 cup green onion, finely sliced
1/4 teaspoon unrefined sea salt or 1 1/2
    teaspoons natural soy sauce

Vegetable Sauce:

Makes 2 1/4 cups

2 cups water
1/2 cup carrots, thinly sliced in flower
    shapes or quarter moons
3-inch piece kombu sea vegetable
2 heaping tablespoons (1/4 cup) arrowroot
    powder or kuzu root starch
1/4 cup cool water
3 tablespoons natural soy sauce or miso
1/2 cup green onions, thinly sliced on the
    diagonal

To make batter, mix flour and water and let sit overnight if time allows. In morning, add remaining ingredients and stir well. As flour texture varies, you may need to add a little more water for a good batter consistency. If waffles are dense, batter is too thick.

Brush iron with oil before preheating so it will permeate iron, preventing batter from sticking. Add batter to hot waffle iron to cook over medium heat until done, about 10-15 minutes, or 5-7 minutes each side for irons which must be turned over on a stove burner. Oil irons between each waffle or, if well-seasoned, every other one.

To prepare sauce, bring 2 cups water to boil with carrots and kombu. Cook until carrots are tender, about 5 minutes. Remove kombu. Mix arrowroot or kuzu with cool water and soy sauce, and add to pot with green onions. If using miso, dilute it in a little of the hot broth and add to pot with thickener. Stir constantly until mixture comes to boiling point and sauce becomes thick and shiny, in about 1 minute. Volume allows for extra sauce.

Variation: **Gingered Vegetable Sauce**
❤ Add 1/2 teaspoon fresh ginger, peeled and grated, to sauce. This sauce may also be served on simply steamed vegetables such as broccoli and cauliflower.

Mochi Waffles

These are the easiest waffles to make, especially for large groups. Preparation time is minimal because all that's required is cutting the mochi. Cooking time is fast, 5-10 minutes, and irons are clean after serving since no batter is used.

Mochi is sweet brown rice which has been cooked, pounded, and then dried in slabs to cook up quickly for a fast whole-grain food or snack. For more information, see *Good Morning Miso Soup with Mochi* recipe on page 2. For breakfast, hard mochi melts and puffs to take on the shape of the waffle iron, and then becomes barely crisp on the outside. Great served hot as is or spread with sweet or savory nut butter spreads. See recipes for *"Caramel," Sesame-Miso,*or *Sesame-Maple Spreads* on pages 144, 126, and 144 respectively. Other possible toppings include apple cider jelly, apple butter, jam, or maple syrup. Enjoy!

Mochi
Vegetable oil to brush waffle iron

Cut sweet rice cakes (mochi) to half their thickness (horizontally, all they way through so they are about 1/4 inch thin and will cook quickly). Place slabs side-by-side on hot, oiled waffle iron, breaking 1 or 2 pieces in half to fill in the gaps. As mochi melts it will fill in the small blank spots. Cook 2-5 minutes on each side in stove top cast-iron waffle irons, depending on brand, or just 5 minutes in electric irons, or until lid easily pulls away from bottom. Serve hot.

For large groups, serve as freshly made as possible, or put waffles in 200° oven to keep warm.

Breads and Muffins

Breads and muffins are traditional breakfast fare in this country and in many other parts of the world. See the following recipes in other sections of this cookbook.

Steamed Whole-Grain (Sourdough Sesame) Bread with Sesame-Miso and Sesame-Maple Spreads (see page 34 for bread recipe, and 126 and 144 for spread recipes)
Whole Grain Toast with Homemade Fruit Spreads (see page 31 for bread recipe and 141-143 for spread recipes)
Fruit 'n Nut Muffins with Apple Butter Spread (see page 34 for muffin recipe and 143 for spread recipe)

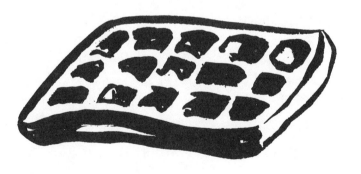

Other Breakfast Foods

Early American Scrapple

This southern breakfast dish is made from cornmeal mush which is cooked with wheatmeat and sage, and then poured into a loaf pan to set overnight. In the morning, it is sliced and fried. Wheatmeat substitutes for pork, and corn oil for bacon drippings.

Scrapple may be served in place of bread or cereal, alone or with a little malted grain sweetener (barley malt or brown rice syrup) or maple syrup drizzled over it.

Makes 6-9 servings

2 cups cornmeal
4 cups water
1/4 teaspoon sea salt
1 cup *Wheatmeat* (see page 49), finely
    chopped
2 teaspoons dried sage, crumbled, or 4 tea-
    spoons fresh sage, finely chopped
Corn oil
Natural soy sauce (optional)

Place cornmeal, water, and salt in pan and bring to boil, stirring often to keep from lumping. Add wheatmeat and sage and stir well. When mixture returns to boil, turn heat low to cook covered for 10-15 minutes. Stir occasionally.

Transfer mush to corn-oiled bread pan to set. Mush measures 2 1/2 inches deep in standard bread pan. Soak cooking pot in water immediately so bottom crust peels off easily, 1/2 hour or longer (overnight) depending on pan.

When ready to serve, cut loaf in 1/2- to 1-inch slices. Loaf is easiest to cut when turned out of pan onto cutting board to slice from softer bottom side. Heat a little corn oil in skillet over medium heat. Fry scrapple on both sides until golden brown and crisp, about 5 minutes each side. For even greater flavor, drizzle a little soy sauce, about 1/8 teaspoon, over each slice of scrapple before turning it over. Figure 2 or 3 slices per serving.

For large amounts, bake scrapple on oiled baking sheet in 350° oven for 1/2 hour, turning and drizzling with soy sauce halfway through.

Scrambled Tofu

Makes 2-3 servings

What sets this recipe apart from others is blending the tofu with the turmeric for scrambled "eggs" which look yellow all the way through. The yellow color increases as tofu cooks. Scrambled tofu is great served with bread or toast, muffins, mochi, or over rice.

2 large shiitake mushrooms, dried or fresh
    (optional)
1/2 pound tofu, fresh
1/8-1/4 teaspoon turmeric
1 tablespoon natural soy sauce; or 2 table-
    spoons white miso; or 1 1/2 teaspoons
    soy sauce and 1/4 teaspoon sea salt
Up to 1/4 cup water or shiitake cooking
    broth, only if necessary to blend
1 tablespoon sesame oil, plain or toasted
1 teaspoon nori or dulse sea vegetable flakes
    (store-bought or see recipe on page 138)
1/4 cup green onions or 1 tablespoon
    chives, finely sliced and gently packed

If including dried shiitake mushrooms, bring them to boil in water to cover and cook until tender, about 20 minutes. Save cooking broth to use in place of water. Cut off and discard hard stems. Thinly slice tops. Simply slice fresh mushrooms.

Blend tofu, turmeric, and seasonings (soy sauce/miso/or salt) until smooth. Add water or shiitake mushroom cooking broth, if needed to blend.

In a small skillet, heat oil. Add fresh mushrooms if included and sauté briefly. Add tofu puree, sea vegetable flakes, and boiled shiitake if included. Cook uncovered over medium-low heat until proper consistency is reached, about 10 minutes, stirring and scraping bottom of pan with spatula occasionally. Add green onions or chives near end of cooking.

For large amounts, cook tofu in batches, no deeper than 3/4 inch for speed in cooking, about 15 minutes.

Other breakfast foods:

Good Morning Miso Soup with Mochi
   (see page 2)

Listing of Recipes by Chapter

Soups 1-14

Miso Soups 1-8
    Basic Miso Soup Recipe; Savory Miso Soup; Good Morning
        Miso Soup with Mochi 1-2
    Vegetable Soup ❤ *Sopa de Verduras* 3
    Peasant's Cabbage Soup 3
    Corn Miso Soup 3
    Escarole-Arame Soup 4
    Oriental Vegetable Soup 4
    Cream of Celery Soup 5
    Summer Squash Soup 5
    Cucumber Soup 5
    Soup Paysanne; Mexican Vegetable Soup with Cornmeal
        Dumplings, Hominy, or Wheatballs ❤ *Sopa Juliana con*
        Albondigas; Mexican Clear Broth Soup with
        Vegetables ❤ *Caldo* 6
    Hominy Soup ❤ *Pozole* 7
    Chickpea-Lentil Soup ❤ *Haraira* (Moroccan) 7
    The Stone Soup Story 8

Broths 8-11
    Consommé 8
    Vegetable Cutout Consommé 8
    Vegetable Cutout Soup 9
    Light Lemon-Miso Broth with Garlic Toasts 9
    Hot and Sour Soup (Chinese) 10

Stews 11-12
    African Skillie Stew 11
    Biscuit-Topped Savory Stew; Hearty Harvest Stew 12

And More Soups 13
    Fresh Pea Soup with Mint 13
    Sauerkraut Soup 13

Grains, Breads, and Pasta 15-58

Brown Rice 16-25
    Varieties of Brown Rice 16-18
        Short or Medium Grain Brown Rice 16
        Long Grain Brown Rice; Brown Basmati Rice; Wild
            Rice; Shaped Rice 17
        Quick-Cooking Brown Rice 17
        Baked Rice for North Americans 18

    Rice with Other Grains 18-19
        Brown Rice and Barley 18
        Bulgur Rice 18
        Long Grain with Wehani Red Rice 19

Rice with Vegetables 19-25
    Rice with Mixed Vegetable Sauce.. 19
    Rice with Fresh Greens 20
    Red Herb Rice 20
    Ume Plum Rice with Red Radish, Italian Broadleaf
        Parsley, and Red Herb Sprinkles 20
    Easy Rice Pilaf... 21
    Rice with Fresh Corn and Pumpkin Seeds 21
    Long Grain-Wehani Rice Blend with Fresh Corn;
        Country Wild Rice Blend with Fresh Corn 21
    Ranch Rice.. 22
    Summer Sushi 22
    Cucumber-Rice Rolls; Inside-out Sushi;
    Half-size Sushi Rolls... 23
    Romaine-Rice Rolls 24
    California Rolls... 24
    Jambalaya (Southern) 25

Wheat 26-51
  Naturally Leavened Bread 26-38
    History; Quality; Ingredients; Basic Cookware;
        The Starter; Basic Recipe 26-33
    Steamed Bread... 33
    Garlic Toasts.. 33
    Croutons... 33
    Sourdough Sesame Bread 34
    Onion Bread, Onion-Herb Bread or Muffins......................... 34
    Muffins: Carrot-Nut Muffins; Fruit 'n Nut Muffins 34
    Country French Bread ❤ *Baguettes*; Crusty Italian
    Bread; Small Sandwich Baguettes ❤ *Petit Pain*;
    New Orleans-Style French Bread; Seeded French
    Bread; Garlic Bread... 35
    Anise-Scented Barley Bread (Moroccan)............................... 36
    Black Bread 36
    Shaped Breads... 37
    Green Onion Flat Bread.. 37
    Pita Pocket Bread 37
    Freeform-Style Country French Bread and
        Crusty Italian Bread... 38
    Breadsticks: Sesame Breadsticks; Mexi-Sticks.................... 38

  Quick Breads..38-41
    Skillet Cornbread; Carrot Cornbread 38
    Tequezquite-Leavened Cornbread, Corn Sticks,
        and Mini-Muffins 39
    Biscuits; Toasted Sesame Biscuits; Dropped
        Biscuits 40
    Chapatis 41
    Tortillas.. 41

  Pasta...Oodles of Noodles..43-49
    Spaghetti and Wheatballs; Carrot Marinara Sauce........... 43
    Buckwheat Noodles with Dipping Broth; Summer
        Soba 44

Noodles with Season's Savory Vegetable Sauce;
Easy Dinner Rice with Summer
Vegetable Sauce 45
Noodle Sushi.. 46
Vegetable Fried Noodles; Vegetable Fried Rice.............. 47
Quick and Easy Noodle-Vegetable Delight...................... 48
Wheatmeat 49
Couscous 50
Couscous; Moroccan Couscous 50
Bulgur.. 51
Bulgur with Fresh Corn and Pumpkin Seeds;
Cracked Wheat 51

Millet...52
Baked Millet Kasha (Russian) 52

Corn..52-54
Homemade Hominy and Masa; Whole Corn Thumbprint
Dumplings 52
Cornmeal Mush ❤ *Fufu* (African); African Millet Meal
Porridge; Hopi Finger Bread... 53

Oats 54

Barley 54

Amaranth.. 54

Quinoa..56-57
Quinoa 56
Quinoa with Bulgur... 57

Simple to Sumptuous Vegetable Dishes
Simple to Sumptuous Vegetable Dishes......................59-86
Quick-Boiled Vegetables.. 59-65
Basic Recipe for:
Oil-Free,Quick-Boiled/Parboiled/Blanched Greens (or Combined
Vegetables); Blanched Cabbage with Escarole, Endive, and Carrot;
Blanched Chinese Cabbage and Red Onions;
Blanched Mustard Greens and Bean Sprouts;
Collard Greens with Toasted Pumpkin Seeds;
Season's Greens with Kernel Corn 59-61
Cooking Greens Chart 62
Quick-Boiled Greens (or Other Vegetables) with 1-, 2-, or
3-Taste Dressings; Chart... 63
Veggie Sticks 64
Blanched Broccoli, Carrot, and Summer Squash 64
Blanched Greens with Carrots and Shiitake Mushrooms.......... 64
Corn on the Cob with Pickled Plum (Umeboshi) 65
Corn Baked in the Husk.. 65

Steamed Vegetables 66-67
    Basic Steamed Vegetables Recipe.. 66
    Steamed Cabbage Wedges 66
    Simply Steamed Vegetables with Ume Vinegar 66
    Broccoli and Cauliflower with Ume-Rice Vinegar Dressing
        and Toasted Sesame Seeds... 67

Simmered Vegetables 67
    Red and Green Shiso Cabbage; Shiso-Simmered Kohlrabi...... 67

Specialty Vegetable Dishes 68-71
    Vegetable Crudités with Creamy Mustard Dip (Basic Dip
        Recipe); Spring Crudité Platter 68
    Vegetables with Italian Herb Paste ❤ *Pesto*; Winter Pesto 69
    Acorn Squash Cups filled with White Bean Chili 70
    Patty Pan Squash with Sesame-Onion Sauce; Nutty Miso
        Stuffed Patty Pan 70

Simple to Savory Ethnic Sautés 71-77
    Basic Onion Family-Greens Sauté Recipe; Shallot-Kale
        Sauté; Shallot-Savoy Sauté; Season's Greens Sautéd
        with Fresh Mushrooms; Garlic-Greens Sauté;
        Garlic-Mushroom-Greens Sauté 71
    Onions and Greens (Native American) 72
    Yellow Summer Squash Sauté 73
    Green Vegetable Gumbo (Southern) 73
    Millet "Mashed Potatoes" with Country Gravy;
        Millet "Mashed Potato" Casserole............................. 74
    Chinese Mixed Vegetables in Brown Sauce 75
    Seasoned Vegetables ❤ *Tagine* (Moroccan) 76
    Vegetables, North Indian Style 76
    Stroganoff (Russian); Tempeh Stroganoff 77

Main Dish Casseroles and Pies 78-84
    Mixed Baked Squash, Southern Style 78
    Vegetable Pot Pie 78
    Garden Vegetable Pie in Pistachio Pastry 79
    Corn-Bean Pie 80
    Fresh Corn Soufflé... 81
    French Onion Quiche ❤ *Quiche Alsacienne*;
        Red Onion Quiche 81
    Tofu Enchiladas 82
    Lasagna.. 83

Sea Vegetable Dishes 84-86
    Green Beans and Arame.. 84
    Arame with Chives... 84
    Hijiki with Fresh Corn 85
    Sesame Hijiki; with 3-Taste Dressing 85
    Hijiki-Vegetable Sauté with Tempeh.. 85

Salads

Fresh Vegetable Salads.. 88-95
      Salad with Apple Cider Vinaigrette................................... 88
      Salad with Ranch Dressing.. 88
      Garden Salad with Dulse and Tahini-Lime Dressing 89
      Garden Vegetable Salad with Walnut-Miso Dressing 89
      Garden Patch Salad with Creamy Herb (Dill) Dressing;
          Herb Dip 90
      Green Salad with Creamy Cilantro Vinaigrette 90
      Tossed Green Salad with Orange-Shiso Dressing 90
      Mixed Green Salad with Toasted Sesame Dressing................ 91
      Mixed Green-Sprout Salad with Thousand Island Dressing..... 91
      Salad with Sweet Poppy Seed Dressing 92
      Chinese Cabbage and Watercress Salad with Japanese
          Plum Dressing; Bok Choy-Alfalfa Sprout Salad 92
      Creamy Cucumber Salad ❤ *Raita*; Plain Tofu "Yogurt" 93
      Marinated Cucumbers and Onions ❤
          Bread and Butter Pickles... 94
      Salsa Salad 95
      Hard Bread Salad ❤ *Panzanella*.....................................95

Pressed Vegetable Salads...96
      Quick Pressed Salad with Light Lemon-Rice Vinegar
          Dressing... 96
      Nappa Cabbage and Red Radish Pressed Salad................... 96

Cooked Vegetable Salads... 97-101
      Hot Slaw... 97
      Chef's Salad with Carrot-Sesame Dressing......................... 98
      Cooked Vegetable Salad with Tofu "Sour Cream" Dressing 98
      Moroccan Carrot Salad.. 99
      Cooked Vegetable Salad with Parisian Parsley Dressing 99
      Vegetables Vinaigrette ❤ Boiled Vegetable Salad with
          Tangy Orange Dressing; Gingery Orange Dressing 100

Whole Grain and Vegetable Salads..101-102
      Basic Grain and Vegetable Salad ❤ Barley and Sweet Corn
          Salad; Rice and Sweet Corn Salad 101
      Bulgur Wheat Salad ❤ *Tabouli*...................................... 102

Pasta Salads 103-105
      Pasta Primavera 103
      Arame-Cucumber-Noodle Salad with Shiso Leaf Dressing 104
      Hot Italian Pasta Salad 104

Bean Salads 105-108
      Marinated Lentil and Wild Land and Sea Greens Salad;
          Marinated Lentil Salad in Pita 105
      Fiesta Bean Salad.. 106

Mandarin Summer Salad... 107
Tempeh Salad; Curried Tempeh Salad; Macaroni Salad 107

Sea Vegetable Salads..109-110
Mim's Arame Salad.. 109
Hijiki, Corn, and Tofu Salad 109
Sea Palm-Sprout Salad 110

Aspics/Gelled Salads...111-113
Carrot Aspic 111
Gelled Corn Pasta Salad 111
Split Pea Aspic.. 112
Bean Aspic (African) 112

Sauces, Spreads, and Dressings
....115-146
Vegetable-Based Sauces, Spreads, and Dressings................................116-119
Vegetable Sauce; Gingered Vegetable Sauce.............................. 116
Mixed Vegetable Sauce 116
Season's Savory Vegetable Sauce 117
Red Sauce; Italian Red Sauce; Carrot Marinara Sauce 117
Salsa Pacifica... 118
Adobe Sauce... 118
Carrot-Sesame Dressing 118
Sesame-Onion Sauce.. 119
Carrot-Almond Butter Spread 119
Italian Herb Paste ❤ *Pesto*; Winter Pesto.................................. 119

Bean Spreads and Gravy..120-121
Lentil Paté/Lentil Loaf 120
Tempeh Party Ball Spread 120
Mung Bean Gravy ❤ *Moong Dahl* (Indian) 121

Creamy Tofu Sauces and Dressings 122-125
Indian-style Tofu "Yogurt"; Plain Tofu "Yogurt".......................... 122
Tofu "Sour Cream" Dressing; Tofu "Sour Cream" 122
Tofu "Mayonnaise" Dressing; Tofu "Mayonnaise";
    Curried "Mayonnaise" Dressing 122
Tofu "Mayonnaise" Dressing No. 2 123
Heavy Tofu "Cream" with Herbs 124
Tofu "Cheese" Sauce.. 124
Italian White Sauce 124
Creamy Herb (Dill) Dressing; Creamy Basil Dressing;
    Creamy Garlic-Dill Dressing; Herb Dip 124
Ranch Dressing... 125
Thousand Island Dressing 125

Seed or Nut Butter-Based Spreads and Dressings 126-127
Basic Fresh-Ground Seed and Nut Butter Recipe......................... 126
Sesame-Miso Spread; Nutty Miso Spread 126
Almond-Onion Spread; Almond-Chive Spread............................. 126, 127
Japanese Plum Dressing... 127

Tahini-Lime Dressing 127
Walnut-Miso Dressing 127
Orange-Shiso Dressing 127

Simple, Oil-free Dressings and Sauces 127
Light Lemon-Rice Vinegar Dressing 127
2-Taste Dressing 127
3-Taste Dressing 127
Dilled 3-Taste Dressing... 127
Ginger Sauce 127

Vinaigrette Dressings 129-132
Apple Cider Vinaigrette... 129
Creamy Cilantro Vinaigrette.. 129
Gingered Lemon-Soy Dressing 129
Gingered Vinaigrette Dressing 129
Lemon-Garlic-Mint Dressing 130
Japanese Vinaigrette Dressing 130
Sweet Poppy Seed Dressing 130
Sweet Mustard-Dill Dressing 130
Italian Herb Dressings 1 and 2 131
Parisian Parsley Dressing 131
Shiso Leaf Dressing 131
Tangy Orange Dressing; Gingery Orange Dressing 131
Toasted Sesame Dressing 132

Marinades 132-133
Teriyaki Sauce/Marinade 132
Lentil Salad Marinade... 133
Red Barbecue Sauce... 133

Dips 134-135
Basic Dip Recipe ❤ Creamy Mustard Dip.. 134
Sushi Dipping Sauce 134
Buckwheat Noodle Dipping Broth 134

Flour-Thickened Gravies.. 135-136
Brown Sauce 135
Pistachio-Miso Gravy 135
Country Gravy.. 136

Table Seasonings 136-140
Basic Toasted Nuts and Seeds Recipe 136
Toasted Pumpkin Seeds, Native American Style 137
Trail Mix... 137
Sesame Salt; Black Sesame Salt 137
Sesame-Parsley Sprinkles... 138
Sesame-Sunflower Topping... 138
Sesame-Shiso Sprinkles; Pumpkin Seed-Shiso Sprinkles;
         Sunflower-Shiso Sprinkles 138
Sesame-Shiso-Nori Sprinkles... 138

Sea Vegetable Chips, Flakes, and Powders.................................. 138
Seeded Sea Powders; Sunflower-Dulse Sprinkles: Wild
        Nori-Sunflower Sprinkles; Pumpkin Seed-Dulse Sprinkles............ 139
(Wild) Nori-Sesame Sprinkles... 140
Commercial Condiments.. 140

Sweet Spreads and Toppings...141-146
Basic Berry Jam or Preserves Recipe ❤ Strawberry Jam 141
Basic Stone Fruit Jam or Preserves Recipe ❤ Peach
        Preserves... 142
Plum Conserve 142
Windfall Apple Sauce... 143
Open Kettle Apple Butter; Cider Syrup; Oven Apple Butter 143
Sesame-Maple Spread 144
"Caramel" Spread 144
Strawberry Sauce 144
Blueberry Topping 144
Sweet and Simple Sauce... 144
Watermelon Syrup... 145
Hot Cinnamon Syrup 145
Almond "Milk," Almond "Cream," and Toasted Almond
        Sprinkles... 145
Tofu "Whipped Cream" 146
Crumb Topping 146

Beans and Soyfoods..147-156
Beans 147-150
Basic Small Bean Recipe 147
Basic Large Bean Recipe.. 147
Chili Beans ❤ White Bean Chili; Mexican Black Bean
        Chili; Pinto Bean Chili; Mexican Bean Dip; Texas Chili 148
Bean Burritos; Refried Beans... 150

Soyfoods: Tofu and Tempeh...151-155
Tofu Cutlets; Seasoned Marinades; Mexican Marinade;
        Lemon-Garlic Tofu... 151
Tofu Teriyaki; Brown Rice or Noodles with Teriyaki
        Vegetables.. 151
Homestyle Bean Curd with Peanuts in Ginger Sauce 152
Braised Tempeh... 153
Tempeh Cutlets; Tempeh Sandwiches and Burgers................................ 153
Barbecued Tempeh Cutlets in Pocket Pitas 154

Pickles and Relishes...157-170
Pickles 157-165
Nutritional Qualities; History... 157
Quick Cucumber-Dill Pickles.. 158
Quick Carrot-Daikon Pickles 159
Sauerkraut... 159
        Fresh Sauerkraut... 161

Brine Pickles.. 162
    Brine Pickles with Fennel 163
    Herbed Green Bean, Carrot, and Onion 164
    Boone's Brine Pickles 164
Bread and Butter Pickles 165

Relishes 165-166
    Corn Relish 165
    Gingered Apple-Raisin Relish ♥ *Chutney* (Indian).......... 166

Commercially Available Japanese Pickles 166-170
    Daikon Radish Rice Bran Pickles ♥ *Takuan*....................166
    Amazake Daikon Pickle.. 167
    Sushi Pickles.. 167
    Pickled Plum (Umeboshi) 167

Desserts...171-192

Fresh Fruit Desserts 171
    Fresh Fruit Kabobs.. 171
    Melon topped with Watermelon Syrup............................. 171

Gels and Puddings 172-177
    Basic Gel Recipe ♥ Apple Gel with Toasted Walnut
        Sprinkles; Strawberry-Apple Gel; Minty
        Apple-Raisin Gel... 173
    Jelly Berry Bo.. 173
    Fruit-Filled Cantaloupe Cups 174
    Mocha Gelatina 174
    Pear Pudding-Gel with Kiwi Fruit and Hazelnuts............. 175
    Cherry Pudding-Gel... 175
    Strawberry Pudding with Toasted Almonds...................... 176
    Peachy Pudding-Gel with Toasted Walnuts;
        Blueberry-Peach Pudding 176
    Russian Pudding ♥ *Gurievskaya Kasha*...........................177

Fresh Fruit Pies 177-181
    Award-Winning Strawberry Pie 177
    Blueberry-Peach Pie; Fresh Peach Pie 178
    Basic Stone Fruit Pie ♥ Nectarine Crumb Pie.................. 179
    Peaches 'n Almond "Cream" Tart...................................... 180
    Almond Pudding Pie with Tofu "Whipped Cream" Topping...................... 181

Pastries..182-186
    Bramble Berry Cobbler; Raspberry-Peach Cobbler 182
    Easy Fresh Fruit Crisp ♥ Peach Crisp 182
    Blueberry Buckle.. 183
    Apple-Nut Cake 183
    Strawberry Shortcake; Blueberry Corncake; Plum
        Corncake (or Peach, Nectarine, or Apricot Corncakes)................. 184
    Coconut Rice Cake 186

Cookies 187-190
    Sweet Rice Cookies; Giant Sweet Rice Cookies 187
    Hazelnut Heart Cookies 187
    Sesame-Oat Squares 187
    Raisin-Spice Cookies 188
    Lemon-Poppy Seed Cookies 188
    Gazelle's Horns Cookies ❤ *Kab el Ghzal* (Moroccan);
        Almond Spiral Cookies 189

Candy 190
    Nutty Carmelcorn ❤ Macrojax 190

Ethnic Vegetable Dessert 191
    Latin American Squash in Hot Cinnamon Syrup.................................. 191

Beverages 193-204

Mild Herb Teas 193-195
    Alfalfa, Blackberry, Blueberry, Raspberry, Strawberry,
        Camomile, Comfrey, Mullein,
           Nettle, Red Clover, etc. 193
    Mild Herb Tea with Sweet Herb ❤ *Stevia*...193
    Thyme Tea.. 194
    Sweet Peppermint Tea 194
    Dixie Mint Tea 194
    Licorice Root Tea 195
    Oriental Herb Tea ❤ *Mu*; Mu Tea with Licorice Root 195

Twig Teas 196-197
    Twig Tea 196
    Sun Tea.. 196
    Twig Tea with Toasted Brown Rice 196
    Evening Tea with Lemon or Apple Slice 197
    Indian Tea ❤ *Chai*..197

Grain Teas and "Coffees" 198-199
    Toasted Corn Tea.. 198
    Toasted Barley Tea 198
    Grain "Coffee," Instant and Brewed; Lemon Espresso-Style
        Grain "Coffee" 198

Cool Summer Drinks 199-200
    Cool Apple Tea; Cool Lemon Tea 199
    Fruit-Tea Fizz 199
    Black Cherry Soda... 200
    Lemonade; Limeade; Orangeade 200
    Ginger Ale 200

"Medicinals" 201-202
    Miso Tea.. 201
    Plum Tea 201
    Ume-Kuzu Morning Tea with Ginger 202

Bean and Nut "Milks".. 202-203
    Sweet Soymilk 202
    Amazake-Soymilk 202
    Sweet Nut "Milk"; Apple-Almond "Milk" 203
    Oat "Milk"; Amazake-Oat "Milk" 203

Breakfasts...205-219

Hot Morning Cereals...205-212
    Basic Hot Morning Cereal Recipe ❤ Hot Hazelnut Cereal 206
    Rye and Wheat Cereal... 207
    Rice Cream... 207
    Tibetan Barley Cereal ❤ *Tsampa* 207
    Whole-Wheat 'n Amaranth Cereal; Corn and Amaranth
        Morning Cereal... 207
    Pantry Porridge.. 208
    Soft Millet Morning Cereal 208
    Steel-Cut Oats... 208
    3-Grain Cereal... 209
    Breakfast Grits.. 209
    Grain-Bean-Seed Cereal ❤ *Kokkoh* 209
    Oatmeal 210
    Oatmeal with Rice 211
    Oatmeal with Raisins... 211
    Oatmeal with Granola, Trail Mix, or Muesli.................. 211
    Hot Muesli Morning Cereal; Summer Muesli; Cool Muesli 211

Brown Rice for Breakfast 212-213
    Soft Breakfast Rice; Whole Rice Cream 212
    Steamed Rice 213

Dry Cereals... 213-215
    Dry Cereals with Fresh Fruit and Toppings.................. 214
    Sweet Soymilk 214
    Amazake-Soymilk 214
    Sweet Nut "Milk"; Apple-Almond "Milk" 214
    Oat "Milk"; Amazake-Oat "Milk" 215

Waffles 216-217
    Whole Grain Waffles with Vegetable Sauce; Gingered
        Vegetable Sauce 216
    Mochi Waffles 217

Breads and Muffins... 217

Other Breakfast Foods 218-219
    Early American Scrapple 218
    Scrambled Tofu 218

Menus

At almost every public meal, I serve two grains (a whole grain such as brown rice or quinoa, and a cracked grain such as whole-grain bread or pasta) to ensure variety and enjoyment, and for festive occasions. Vegetables and in many cases soup, salad, and dessert are also included.

For healthful everyday cooking when time is at a premium, simplify the menus by choosing just 1 or 2 items, say a whole-grain dish and a vegetable. Beans or quick-cooking soyfoods might be included once or twice a day. Always put the grains (and beans) on first, and prepare side dishes while they cook. It might be convenient to cook grains and beans twice a week and bake bread once a week.

The "quick and easy" menus can be prepared in 20 minutes depending on what you have on hand.

Most of the quick and easy menu items do not appear in the other menus. The longer menus were prepared in under 5 hours by 2-8 cooks for 25-150 guests.

Breakfasts aren't included in the menus because they are listed fully in their own chapter. Very few desserts are included in the quick and easy menus because, if you're in a hurry, they aren't an essential menu item.

MENU PLAN

Soup
Whole Grains
Table Seasoning
Vegetables
Beans
Salad
Pickle
Dessert
Beverage

QUICK AND EASY MENU PLAN

Whole Grains
Vegetables
Beans or Soyfoods
    (one or two times daily)

Quick and Easy
Lunch and Dinner Menus

Brown Rice with
  Sesame Salt
Hijiki-Vegetable
  Sauté with
  Tempeh
Quick-Boiled Greens
  with 1- Taste
  Dressing

Baked Mochi Puffs
  with Sushi
  Dipping Sauce
Sautéd Vegetables

Vegetable Soup
Sourdough Sesame
  Bread

Vegetable Fried
  Rice

Easy Dinner Rice with
  Vegetable Sauce
Apple Gel with
  Toasted Walnut
  Sprinkles

Brown Rice
Red Onion Quiche
Mixed Vegetables
  with 2-Taste
  Dressing
  (lime-soy)

Quick and Easy
  Noodle-Vegetable
  Delight

Long Grain Brown
  Rice
Chili Beans
Season's Greens
  Sautéd with Fresh
  Mushrooms

Tempeh Sandwich
Blanched Greens
Giant Sweet Rice
  Cookies

Rice and Vegetable
  Rolls ❤ Sushi
Blanched Watercress
  with 3-Taste
  Dressing

Moroccan Couscous
Steamed Vegetables

Pasta with Sesame-
  Onion Sauce
Steamed Broccoli
Fresh Peach Pie

Bulgur with
  Vegetables
Lemon-Garlic Tofu
Sea Palm-Sprout
  Salad

Vegetable Fried
  Noodles
Pressed Salad

Basic Miso Soup
Shaped Rice with
  Table Seasoning
Shallot-Kale Sauté

Buckwheat Noodles
  in Broth
Braised Tempeh
Quick-Boiled Collard
  Greens

quick and easy menus, continued

Fettucini-Style
  Whole-Grain Pasta
  (Brown Rice Udon
  Noodles) with
  Italian White
  Sauce
Blanched Nappa
  Cabbage

Macaroni Salad
Long Grain Wehani
  Rice Blend with
  Fresh Corn
Sesame Salt
Bok Choy and
  Carrots

Consommé
Onion-Herb Muffins
Boiled Red Kale with
  Carrot Flowers and
  2-Taste Dressing
  (Vinegar-Soy)

Whole-Wheat Udon
  Noodles with
  Teriyaki
  Vegetables

Quinoa
Vegetables
  Vinaigrette
Lentils

Millet
Curried Tempeh
  Salad
Quick-Boiled
  Mustard Greens

Escarole-Arame Soup
Small Baguettes ❤
  Petite Pain
Nut Butter Spread
Vegetable Crudités
  with Herb Dip

Soup Paysanne
Crusty Italian Bread
Brine Pickles with
  Fennel

Country Wild Rice
  Blend with Toasted
  Sunseeds
Garlic-Greens Sauté
Bok Choy-Alfalfa
  Sprout Salad
  (Vinegar-Miso)

Mexican Clear Broth
  Soup
Cornmeal
  Mini-Muffins
Refried Beans
Broccoli with 2-Taste
  Dressing
  (Lemon-Soy)

Whole-Grain
  Couscous
Broccoli and Carrots
  with Season's
  Savory Vegetable
  Sauce
Sea Palm-Sprout
  Salad

Steamed Bread with
  Hazelnut Butter
Spring Crudité Platter
  with Creamy Dill
  Dip

Rice and Sweet Corn
  Salad
Fresh Fruit

Festive Lunch and Dinner Menus

Corn Miso Soup
Quinoa with Bulgur
Pacific Wild Nori Sea
    Vegetable Flakes
Garden Vegetable Pie
    in Pistachio Pastry
Mixed Green-Sprout
    Salad with
    Thousand Island
    Dressing
Raisin-Spice and
    Lemon-Poppy Seed
    Cookies
Toasted Corn Tea

Carrot Cornbread
Steamed Vegetables
    with Ume Vinegar
Salad with Sweet
    Poppy Seed
    Dressing
Fresh Sauerkraut
Fruit-Filled
    Cantaloupe Cups
Red Clover Tea

Long Grain with
    Wehani Red Rice
Sesame Salt
Quick-Boiled
    Cabbage and Kale
Split Pea Aspic
Hijiki with Fresh
    Corn
Quick Pressed Salad
    with Light Lemon-
    Rice Vinegar
    Dressing
Pear Pudding-Gel
    with Kiwi Fruit
    and Hazelnuts
Comfrey Tea

Bulgur Rice with
    Sunflower
    Sprinkles
Hijiki-Vegetable
    Sauté with
    Tempeh
Naturally Leavened
    Bread with Sesame
    Butter
Red and Green Shiso
    Cabbage
Award-Winning
    Strawberry Pie
Alfalfa Leaf Tea

Vegetable Cutout
    Soup
Bulgur Wheat Salad
    ♥ *Tabouli*
Blanched Greens with
    Carrots and
    Shiitake
    Mushrooms
Medium Grain Brown
    Rice with Pumpkin
    Seed-Dulse
    Sprinkles
Sesame Hijiki
Strawberry Shortcake
Twig Tea with Toasted
    Brown Rice

Summer Squash
    Soup
Brown Basmati Rice
    with Pumpkin
    Seeds
Season's Greens with
    Kernel Corn
Tofu Cutlets
Garden Salad with
    Dulse and
    Tahini-Lime
    Dressing
Daikon Radish-Rice
    Bran Pickles ♥
    Takuan
Cherry Pudding-Gel
    with Hazelnut
    Heart Cookie
Sun Tea

festive menus, continued

Noodles with
  Season's Savory
  Vegetable Sauce
Braised Tempeh
Arame with Chives
Nappa Cabbage and
  Red Radish
  Pressed Salad
Nettle Tea with Sweet
  Herb ❤ *Stevia*

Cream of Celery Soup
Brown Rice and
  Barley with
  Sesame-Sunflower
  Topping
Gelled Corn Pasta
  Salad
Chinese Cabbage and
  Watercress Salad
  with Japanese
  Plum Dressing
Green Beans and
  Arame
Quick Carrot-Daikon
  Pickles
Raspberry Leaf Tea
  with Brown Rice
  Syrup

Easy Rice Pilaf
Baguettes with Lentil
  Paté
Carrot Aspic
Broccoli and
  Cauliflower with
  Ume-Rice Vinegar
  Dressing and
  Toasted Sesame
  Seeds
Thyme Tea

Short Grain Rice with
  Sesame-Parsley
  Sprinkles
Mim's Arame Salad
Onion Bread with
  Carrot-Almond
  Butter Spread
Shiso Simmered
  Kohlrabi
Quick Cucumber-Dill
  Pickles
Blueberry-Peach Pie
Twig Tea

Summer Soba
Hijiki, Corn, and Tofu
  Salad
Blanched Collard
  Greens
Pink Sauerkraut
Toasted Barley Tea

Tempeh Sandwich
Chef's Salad with
  Carrot-Sesame
  Dressing
Ume Plum Rice with
  Red Radish, Italian
  Broadleaf Parsley,
  and Red Herb
  Sprinkles
Blueberry Corncake
Twig Tea with
  Toasted
  Brown Rice

festive menus, continued

Cucumber Soup
Mexi-Sticks
Corn-Bean Pie
Medium Grain Brown
  Rice with Toasted
  Almonds
Patty Pan Squash
  with Sesame-
  Onion Sauce
Greens with 1-Taste
  Dressing
Herbed Green Bean,
  Carrot, and Onion
  Pickles
Jelly Berry Bo
Strawberry Leaf Tea

Whole-Grain Bread
  with Almond-
  Onion Spread
Blanched Cabbage
  with Endive,
  Escarole, and
  Carrots
Rice with Fresh
  Greens
Sesame-Shiso
  Sprinkles
Alfalfa Leaf Tea

Quick and Easy
  Noodle-Vegetable
  Delight
Rice with Sesame Salt
Garden Vegetable
  Salad with
  Walnut-Miso
  Dressing
Mellow Mullein Tea

Brown Rice with
  Mixed Vegetable
  Sauce
Noodle Sushi
Corn Baked in the
  Husk
Blanched Chinese
  Cabbage and Red
  Onions
Daikon-Rice Bran
  Pickles ❤ *Takuan*
Toasted Corn Tea

Short Grain Brown
  Rice with Wild
  Nori-Sesame
  Sprinkles
Tempeh Salad
Blanched Bok Choy
Yellow Summer
  Squash Sauté
Amazake Daikon
  Pickles
Twig Tea

Buckwheat Noodles
  with Dipping Broth
Kohlrabi with 2-Taste
  Dressing
Red Herb Rice
Mixed Green Salad
  with Toasted
  Sesame Dressing
Alfalfa Leaf Tea with
  Sweet Herb

Light Lemon-Miso
  Broth with Garlic
  Toasts
Pressure-Cooked
  Short Grain Brown
  Rice with Sesame
  Salt
Fiesta Bean Salad
Quick-Boiled Kale
Dill Pickles
Peachy Pudding-Gel
  with Toasted
  Walnuts
Toasted Corn Tea

Picnic Menus

Arame-Cucumber-
   Noodle Salad with
   Shiso Leaf
   Dressing
Vegetable Crudités
   with Creamy
   Mustard Dip
Onion Bread with
   Spread
Nutty Carmelcorn ❤
   Macrojax
Watermelon
Ginger Ale

Pasta Primavera
California Rolls
Corn on the Cob with
   Pickled Plum
   (Umeboshi)
Sesame-Oat Squares
Lemonade

Summer Sushi
Rice Cakes with
   Tempeh Party Ball
   Spread
Blanched Mustard
   Greens and Bean
   Sprouts
Veggie Sticks
Plum Corncake
Fruit-Tea Fizz

Marinated Lentil
   Salad in Pita
Bulgur with Fresh
   Corn and Pumpkin
   Seeds
Blanched Broccoli,
   Carrot, and
   Summer Squash
Red Sauerkraut
Fresh Fruit
Cool Lemon Tea

Cucumber-Rice and
   Romaine-Rice
   Rolls
Tofu Teriyaki
Tossed Green Salad
   with Orange-Shiso
   Dressing
Fresh Fruit Kebabs
Cool Apple Tea

Barley and Sweet
   Corn Salad
Barbecued Tempeh
   Cutlets in Pocket
   Pitas
Trail Mix
Assorted Melon Slices
Black Cherry
   Soda

American Regional Menus

NATIVE AMERICAN

Country Wild Rice
Blend with Fresh
Corn
Onions and Greens
with Toasted
Pumpkin Seeds,
Native American-
Style
Acorn Squash Cups
filled with White
Bean Chili
Melon topped with
Watermelon Syrup
Toasted Corn Tea

EARLY AMERICAN

Peasant's Cabbage
Soup
Vegetable Pot Pie
Millet "Mashed
Potato" Casserole
Baked Rice with
Sunflower-Dulse
Sprinkles
Garden Patch Salad
with Creamy Dill
Dressing
Corn Relish
Blueberry Buckle
Red Clover Tea

Hearty Harvest Stew
A Basket of Breads:
Onion Bread,
Carrot-Nut
Muffins, and
Sesame
Breadsticks
Salad with Apple
Cider Vinaigrette
Boone's Brine Pickles
Bramble Berry
Cobbler
Blackberry Leaf Tea

MIDWESTERN

Biscuit-Topped
Savory Stew
Quick-Cooking
Brown Rice with
Toasted Sunflower
Seeds
Salad with Ranch
Dressing
Bread and Butter
Pickles
Apple-Nut Cake
Alfalfa Leaf Tea

SOUTHERN

Jambalaya
Green Vegetable
Gumbo
Alison's Skillet
Cornbread
Mixed Baked Squash,
Southern Style
Easy Fresh Fruit
Crisp
Dixie Mint Tea

TEXAS RANCH HOUSE

Ranch Rice
Texas Chili
Hot Slaw
Cornmeal
Mini-Muffins
(Tequesquite-
Leavened)
Dill Pickles
Nectarine Crumb Pie
Alfalfa Leaf Tea

Ethnic Menus

MEXICO

Vegetable Soup ❤ *Sopa de Verduras*
Tofu Enchiladas
Long Grain Brown Rice with Sesame Salt
Green Salad with Creamy Cilantro Vinaigrette
Mint Tea

Hominy Soup ❤ *Posole*
Brown Rice ❤ *Arroz Integral*
Mexican Black Bean Chili
Tortillas
Collard Greens with Toasted Pumpkin Seeds ❤ *Pepitas*
Salsa Pacifica
Camomile Tea

Mexican Vegetable Soup with Cornmeal Dumplings
Bean Burritos
Long Grain Brown Rice with Sesame Salt
Blanched Kale
Salsa Salad
Latin American Squash in Hot Cinnamon Syrup
Camomile Tea

INDIA

Brown Basmati Rice with Mung Bean Gravy ❤ *Moong Dahl*
Vegetables, North Indian Style
Chapatis
Creamy Cucumber Salad ❤ *Raita*
Gingered Apple-Raisin Relish ❤ *Chutney*
Indian Tea ❤ *Chai*

CHINA

Hot and Sour Soup
Long Grain Brown Rice ❤ *Mifan*
Chinese Mixed Vegetables in Brown Sauce
Green Onion Flat Bread
Homestyle Bean Curd with Peanuts in Ginger Sauce
Licorice Root Tea

Oriental Vegetable Soup
Vegetable Fried Noodles
Long Grain Brown Rice with Sesame Salt
Blanched Bok Choy
Mandarin Summer Salad
Sweet Rice Cookies
Mu Tea with Licorice Root

FRANCE

Consommé
French Onion Quiche ❤ *Quiche Alsacienne*
Seeded French Bread with Hazelnut Butter
Cooked Vegetable Salad with Parisian Parsley Dressing
Strawberry Pudding with Toasted Almonds
Grain "Coffee"

Vegetable Cutout Consommé
Fresh Corn Soufflé
Country French Bread ❤ *Baguettes* with Almond-Chive Spread
Boiled Vegetable Salad with Tangy Orange Dressing
Peaches 'n Almond "Cream" Tart
Grain "Coffee"

ITALY

Spaghetti and
Wheatballs with
Carrot Marinara
Sauce
Steamed Vegetables
with Italian Herb
Paste ❤ *Pesto*
Garlic Bread
Almond Pudding Pie
with Tofu
"Whipped Cream"
Topping
Grain "Coffee"

Soup Paysanne
Lasagna
Medium Grain Rice
with Sesame Salt
Broccoli Spears
Hard Bread Salad ❤
Panzanella
Mocha Gelatina
Lemon Espresso-
Style Grain
"Coffee"

Hot Italian Pasta
Salad
Long Grain Brown
Rice with Sesame
Salt
Blanched Nappa
Cabbage
Grain "Coffee"

SOVIET UNION

Sauerkraut Soup
Mushroom Stroganoff
Baked Millet Kasha
Cooked Vegetable
Salad with Tofu
"Sour Cream"
Dressing
Black Bread
Russian Pudding ❤
*Gurievskaya
Kasha*
Evening Tea with
Lemon or Apple
Slice

MOROCCO

Chickpea-Lentil Soup
❤ *Haraira*
Seasoned Vegetables
❤ *Tagine*
Couscous
Anise-Scented Barley
Bread
Moroccan Carrot
Salad
Gazelle's Horns
Cookies ❤ *Kab el
Ghzal*
Sweet Peppermint
Tea

AFRICA

Fresh Pea Soup with
Mint
Cornmeal Mush ❤
Fufu
African Skillie Stew
Bean Aspic
Coconut Rice Cake
Twig Tea

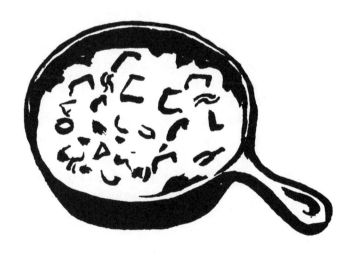

Glossary of Food Terms

Agar sea vegetable flakes—Also known as *kanten* in Japanese, agar is a gelling agent made from a combination of red seaweeds. Odorless, colorless, tasteless, and calorie free, agar is one way to get the full array of minerals from sea vegetables. Agar comes in 4 forms—flakes, strips, granules, and bars.

According to Jan and John Belleme in *Cooking with Japanese Foods* (East West Health Books, 1986), "Kanten is harvested and processed only in the coldest winter months. After the seaweed is cooked, it is allowed to harden into a dense gelatin, then cut into squares and spread on mats to freeze-dry naturally. Over a period of about 10 days, moisture in the gelatin freezes at night and forms ice on the surface, then thaws during the day, until all the moisture is gone and only the light, flaky bars of pure kanten remain. Kanten flakes are produced by simply shredding the bars...."

Agar dissolves when boiled several minutes in a liquid. It sets up upon cooling, about 1 hour in the refrigerator, and may be reheated.

I make gels, aspics, puddings, pie fillings, jams, preserves, and jellies with agar instead of gelatin which is made from the hooves and bones of cows and horses. The animal tissue is boiled in water to obtain the glutinous substance that forms the basis for gelatins and glue.

Amazake—A sweet, fermented brown rice nectar, amazake is used as a sweetener or sweet beverage. It is not a refined sweetener, but is concentrated and naturally sweet from the fermentation process. Cooked sweet or regular brown rice is incubated with rice koji for about 8 hours in which time the enzymes in the koji break down the complex starches in the rice, converting them to simpler sugars. Originally from Japan, it is now made in this country as well. Rich in natural sugars and enzymes, amazake's effect on the body may be milder than honey and maple syrup.

Arame sea vegetable—Arame comes in thin brown strands that have been shredded from a wide-leaf sea grass. It is a good introductory sea vegetable as it's quick and easy to cook and has a very mild taste.

Arrowroot—Arrowroot is a white powder derived from a topical tuber. It is used as a thickener in the same volume and weight as kuzu root starch (see next page); it has a very slightly milder gelling capacity. Natives in the British Virgin Islands consider arrowroot to be as healing as the Japanese do kuzu. At half to one-quarter the price of kuzu, arrowroot is a desirable choice.

Brown rice syrup—This is a natural sweetener made from soft cooked rice. The rice has been mixed with sprouted and malted rice or barley. The enzymes in the malted grain convert the complex carbohydrates in the rice to natural sugars. The sweet mash is strained and the liquid cooked down to a thick, sweet syrup. Its effect on the body's blood sugar balance is milder than honey and maple syrup because the more complex sugars in brown rice syrup, called maltoses, are digested more slowly. See page 171.

Brown rice vinegar—This is a mild-tasting vinegar based on whole grain brown rice instead of fruit as in cider or wine vinegars. Very pleasing in vinaigrette and other dressings.

The best rice vinegar should contain only brown rice, rice koji, and water, and should be naturally fermented for about 1 year. Brown rice vinegar has a higher amino acid content than other naturally-brewed vinegars. It neutralizes lactic acid buildup in the body.

Avoid distilled vinegar, also called white or grain vinegar, which is highly refined.

Hijiki sea vegetable—Hijiki's black strands are especially high in calcium and iron. Its flavor is stronger than arame, but becomes quite delicious with increased familiarity. For a mild-tasting hijiki dish, do not use the soaking water in cooking; save it to dilute with water for house plants.

Koji—Koji is grain inoculated with the *Aspergillus* mold. It is used in the fermentation of soy sauce, miso, sake, amazake, and mirin. Koji supplies enzymes to break down the complex structure of beans and grains into readily digestible amino acids, fatty acids, and simple sugars.

Kombu sea vegetable—A kelp, kombu is the thickest sea vegetable and is used for making soups, broths, and sauces, and in cooking beans. Kombu contains the natural form of MSG and is therefore a flavor enhancer. It also imparts minerals and a pleasing, mild flavor. In broths, it is removed before serving as it is still too firm to be consumed. It may be used more than once this way, then cut and cooked with a pot of vegetables. In beans, kombu dissolves with cooking and may be whisked into the beans for a creamy texture. Kombu helps to soften the beans and makes them easier to digest.

Kombu contains laminine, an amino acid which helps reduce tension. It is also known to lower cholesterol and relieve water retention.

Kuzu root starch—Kuzu is a thickening agent that is also medicinal. Kuzu comes in white chalky chunks. It is extracted by a labor-intensive process from the roots of the kuzu (kudzu) vine. The starch comes from Japan although the plant grows abundantly in the southern part of this country where it was introduced as a highway beautification project (which went wild).

Kuzu is odorless, colorless, and tasteless. It dissolves in cool water and thickens upon boiling for making wonderful puddings, beverages, or Chinese-style sauces. Soothing and strengthening to the intestines and stomach, kuzu helps create an alkaline blood condition necessary for restoring and maintaining health. It is also good for colds.

Kuzu starch is produced by a chemical-free method, whereas many chemicals are used in the processing of the most popular thickener, cornstarch. See *The Book of Kudzu* by William Shurtleff and Akiko Aoyagi (Avery Publishing Group, 1985) for more information.

Mirin—This Japanese sweet rice cooking wine is used to add a delicate sweet flavor to broths and dressings. It balances the flavors of soy sauce, miso, and vinegar.

High-quality mirin contains only sweet rice, rice koji (which may not be listed), and water. It is naturally brewed like good sake (rice wine). The alcohol quickly evaporates with cooking, leaving only the sweet taste.

Miso—Miso is the fermented soybean paste made from soybeans and salt and usually a grain such as barley or brown rice. Koji is the fermenting agent. Dark misos are aged longer than light misos, up to 3 years. They have a higher salt content and proportionately more soybeans than light misos. Light misos have a sweeter flavor.

Today's innovative North American miso masters make miso with a wide variety of grains and beans such as corn or chickpeas. The best misos are made from organic ingredients and are aged by natural processes. They are not pasteurized.

In revising or designing recipes, miso replaces the flavors from meat and salt. Added to hot water or broths, light misos make a light chicken-style bouillon, and dark misos make beef-like stocks. Miso is a savory ingredient in dips, dressings, spreads, and casseroles.

In addition to tasting delicious, miso has several health-promoting qualities. It boosts the immune system and is known to detoxify the bloodstream of pollution, radiation, and nicotine. (See *The Book of Miso* by William Shurtleff and Akiko Aoyagi.)

Miso contains lactic acid and enzymes to aid digestion. Scientific studies show Japanese people who regularly drink miso soup suffer significantly less from some forms of cancer and heart disease.

Mochi—The Japanese name for pounded sweet rice, store-bought mochi is a quick and easy to prepare whole-grain food. Traditionally made in Japan, it is now made in America and sold in natural foods stores. Mochi is made from a special short grain brown rice known as sweet brown rice, more glutinous in nature than regular brown rice. Since the rice has been precooked by steaming—and then mashed or pounded into a dense mass before being dried in slabs—it needs only to be baked, broiled, pan-fried, or boiled briefly. Baked mochi puffs up into a chewy cake with a crisp crust. Mochi waffles are a great breakfast or snack.

Natural soy sauce—Natural soy sauce, also called *shoyu* in Japanese, is made from whole soybeans, wheat, and salt which are aged together without chemicals according to time-honored practices. After 1-2 year's fermentation, the thick solution is pressed to extract the dark liquid. Since high quality soy sauce accounts for less than 1% of Japan's production, natural soy sauce may be purchased only in natural foods stores.

Natural soy sauce has a very attractive, rich flavor which substitutes nicely for salt and meat flavors when converting recipes.

Nori seaweed—This is a mild-tasting sea vegetable that has been dried and pressed into thin sheets. It is used to wrap around rice for sushi or rice balls, or as a healthy snack food. Regular nori requires toasting before eating, but sushi nori comes toasted.

Domestic nori (both wild and cultivated) is available dried in its natural state or pressed into sheets.

Green nori comes in flakes to be sprinkled on grains, vegetables, or salads for a mineral-rich topping.

Pickled Plum (Umeboshi)—The bright pink Japanese plum which has been fermented with salt and shiso leaves, umeboshi is a wonderful flavoring agent for vegetables, especially cabbage and other greens. It is superb rubbed on fresh corn in place of butter and salt, and it adds its zesty taste and preservative qualities to cooked brown rice. See pages 167-170 for more specific information.

Red shiso leaf or powder—The mineral-rich leaf which imparts the brilliant red color to the umeboshi plum, shiso contains a natural preservative with 1,000 times the strength of synthetic preservatives used in foods. Shiso leaf may be cut and used fresh to flavor dips and dressings, or in cooking to flavor vegetables and broths; it may also be used in rice balls or sushi. Shiso can also be purchased dried and powdered.

Sea Palm—A sea vegetable that grows on the northern Pacific Coast of the United States, sea palm has a mild flavor and cooks up quickly. Its delightful noodle-like strands are delicious in salads; with other vegetables and pasta; or oven-toasted and served as is or ground into a powder with toasted seeds to sprinkle on top of grains.

Sea Vegetables—The most mineral-rich foods on the planet, sea vegetables are fast becoming part of many a natural cook's repertoire. In addition to calcium and iron, they also contain vitamins, protein, and trace elements that are often lacking in root and green leafy vegetables because of soil demineralization.

According to a McGill University study, sea vegetables contain sodium alginate, a substance which binds with strontium 90 and other toxins such as lead, and excretes them from the body. Research at John Hopkins University found that kelp has a stable iodine that replaces 80% of the iodine in radiation.

Add sea vegetables to salads, soups, stews, and land vegetable dishes. See listings for agar, arame, kombu, hijiki, nori, sea palm, and wakame.

Shiitake mushrooms—The second most popular mushroom in the world, next to the button mushroom, shiitake contain far more nutrients. They are sold both fresh and dried. Shiitake grow on oak logs naturally or by cultivation. In comparison, button mushrooms are grown in a hothouse with a lot of chemical applications. Organic button mushrooms are rarely available.

Most commercially available dried shiitake are from Japan, Korea, and China, but small-scale growers are appearing in this country as well.

According to *Cooking with Japanese Foods*, cooked shiitake are "a concentrated medicine for the treatment of flu, heart disease, high blood pressure, obsesity, and problems related to sexual dysfunction and aging." According to *Mushrooms as Health Foods* by Dr. Kisaku Mori (Japan Publications, 1974, out of print), shiitake also aid in the treatment of cancer, excess cholesterol, gallstones, hyperacidity and stomach ulcers, diabetes, vitamin deficiencies (including vitamin B12, and anemia.

The rich flavor of shiitake mushrooms adds depth to soups, broths, gravies, and vegetable dishes.

Shiso—See Red Shiso Leaf or Powder.

Soba—Buckwheat noodles are called soba in Japanese. They are made from buckwheat flour alone or with varying amounts of whole-wheat flour. Some varieties are combined with wild mountain yam, called *jinenjo soba*; with green tea for *cha soba*; or with green mugwort herb for *yomogi soba*.

Somen—These are a very delicate, thin, varmicelli-like Japanese wheat pasta often served cool in summertime.

Suribachi—The ceramic mortar from Japan with a serrated surface for grinding seeds or mixing sauces. The suribachi comes with a wooden pestle called a *suricogi*.

Sweet Herb—Also known as sweet leaf or *stevia*, sweet herb is a dark green leaf which imparts a very sweet taste to beverages or foods. Natives of Paraguay in South America have used the wild herb as a sweetener for over a century. The Japanese have imported it from Paraguay and Brazil since the 1970s, and have conducted extensive research on its properties, safety, and effectiveness as a natural sweetener. Stevia has completely beneficial effects on persons with hypoglycemia. It contains 25 times the sweetness of sugar.

Tamari—Wheat-free soy sauce, tamari was originally produced as a by-product of the miso-making process, although now it is also made on its own. It is thicker and more expensive than natural soy sauce, and is used in Japanese cuisine for special dip sauces.

Tempeh—Fermented soybean cake; the protein backbone of Indonesia as tofu is in Asia. The whole beans are cooked and inoculated with a bacteria that binds the beans together. Tempeh has a cheese-like taste and texture, and must be cooked before eating.

Toasted Sesame Oil—An exquisite oil used for its rich taste and fragrance, toasted sesame oil is made from whole sesame seeds that are first toasted, then pressed to extract the oil.

A small amount of toasted sesame oil enhances dressings, sauces, and vegetable dishes. Combined with a milder tasting, light oil such as plain sesame oil, it is delicious in fried rice or noodles, or any sautéd dishes.

Tofu—Tofu, or soybean curd, is made from soybeans which are soaked, then blended and strained. Only the soymilk is used to make tofu so it is not a whole food like tempeh. In traditional tofu, the "milk" is gelled by cooking with *nigari*, a sea salt derivative. Calcium chloride is used commercially. Tofu has a clean, mild flavor. It absorbs flavors well and is therefore normally served with a savory broth or sauce, or seasoned before, during, or after cooking.

Blended smooth for a creamy texture and appearance, it's very useful in salad dressings and sauces. Indispensable for the vegetarian cook in creating new recipes free of cheese or cream.

Dried tofu from Japan keeps indefinitely and has a pleasant chewy texture when soaked, then cooked in a flavorful broth or stew.

Udon—Japanese pasta which looks like fettucini, udon comes in whole-wheat or brown rice versions (as well as the common white flour variety).

Umeboshi—See Pickled Plum.

Unrefined sea salt—This salt differs from regular sea salt in that it is hand-harvested and air-dried. It contains all the minerals and trace elements found in the ocean. Regular sea salt is the same as commercial salt without the anti-caking agents and other additives. It is highly refined, containing 99.9% of one mineral, sodium chloride. (See Resources for unrefined seasalt.)

Wakame sea vegetable—The standard soup sea vegetable, varieties of wakame differ in taste and texture. It is delicious in salads, or toasted dry and crushed for a mineral-rich table seasoning.

Alaria is the North American sea vegetable most like Japanese wakame, although it usually calls for a somewhat longer cooking time.

Wasabi—Japanese horseradish root which is also dried and powdered for use as a paste. The best wasabi powder contains 60% pure Japanese horseradish and 40% regular horseradish and is naturally green in color.

Whole-wheat flour—This flour is made from winter or spring wheat which is high in gluten for breadmaking.

Whole-wheat pastry flour—This flour is made from a completely different wheat berry than bread wheat. It is tan-colored and low in gluten, therefore more appropriate for use in pastries.

Resources...Food for the Mind & Body

We find the true expression of the word "gourmet"—the finest quality foods made by craftspeople committed to purity and tradition—in the natural foods movement of today. The spirit that motivates these pioneers to work with nature in the creation of these foods is one of respect and brotherhood with humanity and the earth, and a positive outlook in troubled times. Their foods may cost a little more, but the quality and subsequent health benefits to our planet and its inhabitants makes them worth it.

Products from the companies listed below are available by mail order directly, or through your local natural food or health food store or coop. Write or call them for their informative catalogues or to find the nearest places where their products are sold. If outlets do not exist, you may wish to become a distributor for your area.

Sources are current as of 1994.

American Brown Rice
Organically grown

●LUNDBERG FAMILY FARMS, P.O. Box 369, Richvale, CA 95974, (916) 882-4551
●SOUTHERN BROWN RICE, P.O. Box 185, Weiner, AR 72479, (501) 684-7341
●LONE PINE, P.O. Box 416, Carlisle, AR 72024, (501) 552-3217

American Miso
Made with organic grains and beans, pure water, and real sea salt; unpasteurized

●SOUTH RIVER MISO CO., South River Farm, Conway, MA 01341, (413) 369-4057
●AMERICAN MISO CO., Great Eastern Sun, 92 McIntosh Rd., Asheville, NC 28806, (800) 334-5809
●GREAT LIFE PRODUCTS, 581 F North

Twin Oak Valley Rd., San Marcos, CA 92069, (619) 471-2637. Miso, soy sauce, and apriboshi
●JUNSEI YAMAZAKI, 4192 Road S., Orland, CA 95963. Also umeboshi

American Wildcrafted Sea Vegetables

●MAINE SEAWEED CO., P.O. Box 57, Steuben, ME 04680. Summer camp for seaweed harvesting.
●MAINE COAST SEA VEGETABLES, RR 1, Box 78, Franklin, ME 04634, (207) 565-2907
●MENDOCINO SEA VEGETABLE CO., 20400 Orr Springs Rd., Comptche, CA 95427, (707) 937-2050
●OCEAN HARVEST SEA VEGETABLE CO., P.O. Box 1719, Mendocino, CA 95460, (707) 937-1923
●RISING TIDE SEA VEGETABLES, P.O. Box 1914, Mendocino, CA 95460, (707) 964-5663
●SOUND SEA VEGETABLES (See GRANUM INC. listing on next page); sheets of domestic (Washington State) cultivated nori; Canadian kombu; and New Brunswick dulse

Macrobiotic Food Companies

These companies import or distribute the highest quality natural foods from Japan, and were the first to introduce them to consumers beginning in the late 1960s: soy sauce, tamari, miso, umeboshi products, oils and vinegars, Japanese noodles, sea vegetables, wheatmeat, pickles, candies, chips, dried foods (wheat gluten [fu], shiitake mushrooms, daikon, lotus root, tofu), whole grain sweeteners, teas and grain "coffees," cookware and utensils, etc. Mail order is available to individuals where noted.

●GRANUM, INC., 2901 N.E. Blakeley St., Seattle, WA 98105, (206) 525-0051. Mitoku products

●GREAT EASTERN SUN, 92 McIntosh Rd., Asheville, NC 28806, (800) 334-5809. Mitoku products under Emperor's Kitchen label

●EDEN FOODS, 701 Tecumseh Rd., Clinton, MI 49236, (313) 973-9400. Japanese natural food products imported from The Muso Co. and sold under the Eden label; also Lima Belgium and their own prepared foods

●MOUNTAIN ARK TRADING CO., 120 S. East Ave., Fayetteville, AR 72701, (800) 643-8909. Mail order, featuring organically grown food staples

●MACROBIOTIC COMPANY OF AMERICA, 799 Old Leicester Hwy., Asheville, NC 28806, (800) 438-4730

●GOLDMINE NATURAL FOOD CO., 3419 Hancock St., San Diego, CA 92110, (619) 296-8536 or (800) 475-3663. Food (including the Ohsawa America line) and lifestyle products. Mail order.

●OAK FEED STORE, 2911 Grand Ave., Coconut Grove, FL 33133, (305) 448-7595. Mail order

●NATURAL LIFESTYLE SUPPLIES, 16 Lookout Dr., Asheville, NC 28804, (800) 752-2775. Mail order

Naturally-Leavened Bread
Traditional European sourdough bread, yeast-free; contains organic, stone-milled grains, pure water, and unrefined sea salt; mail order

●BALDWIN HILL BAKERY, 15 Baldwin Hill Rd., Phillipston, MA 01331, (508) 249-4691

●PONCE BAKERY, 116 W. 12th St., Chico, CA 95926, (916) 891-8354

●PACIFIC BAKERY, 514 S. Hill St., Oceanside, CA 92054 (P.O. Box 950, 92049), (619) 757-6020

●FRENCH MEADOW BAKERY, 2610 Lyndale Ave. S., Minneapolis, MN 55408

Wheat

●WHEAT MONTANA, P.O. Box 4778, Helena, MT 59604, (800) 535-2798.

Unrefined Sea Salt

●GRAIN AND SALT SOCIETY, P.O. Box DD, Magalia, CA 95954, (916) 873-0294. Celtic sea salt; cellophane bags for storing bread

●GREAT LIFE PRODUCTS, 581 F. North Twin Oak Valley Rd., San Marcos, CA 92069, (619) 471-2637. Muramoto's Balanced Minerals Sea Salt

●NORSOUTH PRODUCTS, Box 12412, Prescott, AZ 86304, (602) 776-8364. Si Salt from Southern California.

Pure Water

●MULTI-PURE water filtration system—For information, purchase, or distributorship write East West Center, 1122 M St., Eureka, CA 95501, or call (707) 445-2290

Other Food Sources

●ARROWHEAD MILLS, INC., Box 2059, Hereford, TX 79045, (806) 364-0730

●WESTBRAE NATURAL FOODS, P. O. Box 48006, Gardena, CA 90248, (310) 886-8200. Organic, American-made, Japanese-style pastas

●WALNUT ACRES, Penns Creek, PA 17862, 1-800-433-3998. Organic foods, mail order

●NEW WAVES OF GRAIN AMARANTH CO., P.O. Box 2325, Ft. Collins, CO 80522

●HARDSCRABBLE ENTERPRISES, HC 71, Box 42, Circleville, WV 26804, (304) 358-2921. Dried shiitake mushrooms, growing kits, and dehydrators

●ADOBE MILLING CO., INC., P.O. Box 596, Dove Creek, CO 81324, (303) 677-2620. Native American (Anasazi) and heirloom bolita beans

●WARREN CREEK FARM, 1264 Warren Creek Rd., Arcata, CA 95521. Organic heirloom beans including speckled bayo.
●MAYWAY TRADING CO., 1338 Cypress St., Oakland, CA 94607, (510) 208-3113. Chinese herb company that also carries sweet herb (stevia).

Cabbage Shredder

●Austrian slicer with stainless steel blades cuts large quantities of cabbage. Available from Johnny's Selected Seeds, Foss Hill Rd., Albion, ME 04910, (207) 437-9294

Cellophane Bags

●See Grain and Salt Society on page 248.

pH Paper

●pH paper is white paper colored with a dye and used to test for chemical acidity or alkalinity. Refer to the side of the box for exact number or range or colors desired. One source is LAB-PRO Inc., 1290 Anvilwood Ct., Sunnyvale, CA 94089, (408) 745-0222

Periodicals

●*Natural Health, The Guide to Well-Being*, P.O. Box 57320, Boulder, CO 80320-7320, (617) 232-1000
●*Vegetarian Times*, Box 570, Oak Park, IL 60303-0570, (708) 848-8100
●*Vegetarian Gourmet*, 2 Public Ave., Montrose, PA 18801, (717) 278-1984
●*Macrobiotics Today*, 1511 Robinson St., Oroville, CA 95965, (916) 533-7702
●*MacroChef*, 243 Dickinson St., Philadelphia, PA 19147, (215) 551-1430
●*Spectrum—The Wholistic News Magazine*, 61 Dutile Rd., Laconia, NH 03246, (603) 528-4710
●*San Francisco Chronicle*, 901 Mission St.,

San Francisco, CA 94119, (415) 777-1111. The *Chronicle* won an award for the third best food section in the country. Full of informative food articles and inspiring recipes, a great love for fresh food is expressed here.
●*Good Medicine*, Physicians Committee for Responsible Medicine, P.O. Box 6322, Washington, DC 20015, (202) 686-2210

Books and Articles—Mentioned in the Text or Recommended

●*Shopper's Guide to Natural Foods* by East West Journal Editors, Avery Publishing Group, 1987
●*The Whole Foods Encyclopedia* by Rebecca Wood, New York, 1988
●*Cooking with Japanese Foods, A Guide to the Traditional Natural Foods of Japan* by Jan and John Belleme, East West Natural Health Books (17 Station St., Brookline, MA 02146), 1986
●*The Book of Miso*, Ballentine, 1981
●*The Book of Tofu*, Ten Speed Press, 1983
●*The Book of Tempeh*, Soyfoods Center (see Organizations listings), 1979
●*The Book of Kudzu—A Culinary and Healing Guide* by William Shurtleff and Akiko Aoyagi, Avery Publishing Group, 1985
●*Mushrooms as Health Foods* by Dr. Kisaku Mori, Japan Publications, 1974 (out of print)
●*The Mysterious Japanese Plum: Its Uses for Healing, Vigor and Long Life* and *Traditional Herbs for Natural Healing* by Kosai Matsumoto II, Woodbridge Press, 1978 (both out of print)
●*Don't Drink Your Milk!* by Frank A. Oski, M.D., Teach Services, Rt. 1, Box 182, Brushton, NY 12916, (800) 367-1844
●*Diet and Nutrition, A Holistic Approach* by Rudolph Ballentine M.D., Himalayan Publications, Honesdale, PA, 1978
●*McDougall's Medicine, A Challenging Second Opinion* by John McDougall, M.D., 1985, New Win Publishers, Inc., 1986

●*Food and Healing* by Annemarie Colbin, Ballentine Books, 1986

●*Diet for a New America—How Your Food Choices Affect Your Health, Happiness, and the Future of Life on Earth* by John Robbins, Stillpoint Publishing, Walpole, NH, 1987

●*American Macrobiotic Cuisine* by Meredith McCarty, Turning Point Publications, 1986

●*The Self-Healing Cookbook* by Kristina Turner, Earthtones Press, P.O. Box 441, Vashon Island, WA 98070

●*Himalayan Mountain Cookery* by Martha Ballentine, Himalayan Publications, Honesdale, PA, 1976

●*Hopi Cookery* by Juanita Tiger Kavena, The University of Arizona Press, 1981

●*Rebecca Boone Cook Book* by Bertha Barnes, Route 5, Richmond, KY 40475

●*Microbiology of Food Fermentations* by Carl Pederson, AVI Publishing Company, 1979

●*Sea Salt's Hidden Powers—How to Tell Its Integrity and Use It Correctly* by Jacques de Langre, Happiness Press, P.O. Box DD, Magalia, CA 95954

●*The Nightshades and Health* by Norman F. Childers and Gerard M. Russo; and *Arthritis—The Nightshades, Aging and Ill Health* by Norman F. Childers PhD, Arthritis Nightshades Research Foundation, 3906 NW 31st Place, Gainesville, FL 32606, (904) 372-5077 Informative newsletter too.

●STEVIA (sweet herb) information source: International Federation of Diabetes, Seventh Congress held in Buenos Aires, August 1970, reported in International Congress Series no. 209, Amsterdam; and Brazilian Society for the Progress of Science, 28th Congress reported in Ciencia e Cultura, Vol. 29, [5], page 599.)

Organizations

●THE KUSHI FOUNDATION, P.O. Box 390, Becket, MA 01223, (413) 623-5703. Live-in study center for macrobiotics founded by Michio and Aveline Kushi

●GEORGE OHSAWA MACROBIOTIC FOUNDATION and VEGA STUDY CENTER, 1511 Robinson St., Oroville, CA 95965, (916) 533-7702. Live-in study center and publishing company founded by Herman and Cornellia Aihara

●THE SOYFOODS CENTER, William Shurtleff, P.O. Box 234, Lafayette, CA 94549, (510) 283-2991. Information on soyfoods; author of the *Books of Miso, Tofu, Tempeh, and Kudzu*. Also: how to start businesses in the production of these foods, and world's largest bibliographic database on soyfoods

●PHYSICIANS COMMITTEE FOR RESPONSIBLE MEDICINE. Organization representing 3,000 M.D.s who believe diet and lifestyle are one's first line of defense from and treatment of disease. See listing for the periodical, *Good Medicine.*

●ARTHRITIS NIGHTSHADES RESEARCH FOUNDATION. Organization dedicated to informing the public about the connection between the nightshade family of foods and arthritis. See periodical listing for *The Nightshades and Health.*

●FOOD FIRST—THE INSTITUTE FOR FOOD AND DEVELOPMENT POLICY, 145 9th St., San Francisco, CA 94103, (415) 864-8555. A nonprofit research and education center dedicated to investigating and exposing the root causes of hunger, environmental destruction, and rapid population growth. Founded by Frances Moore Lappé, author of *Diet for a Small Planet*, and food policy analyst Joseph Collins in 1975

●EARTHSAVE FOUNDATION, 706 Frederick St., Santa Cruz, CA 95062-2205, (408) 423-4069. Based on the work of John Robbins in *Diet for a New America*, this organization educates people about the dietary link to environmental degradation, encouraging sound nutrition, conservation of resources, and sustainable agriculture.

Cooking FRESH...and Fast

Preserving precious time is a major intention in most people's lives these days. Short order meals are easy to make, and simple fare needn't be boring. With a little forethought to menu planning, a quick-cook inventory list, and as little as 15-30 minutes, satisfying meals are assured. You'll avoid the canned and frozen food trap, convenient on a once-in-awhile basis, but devoid of the energy inherent in fresh foods.

The tendency to schedule too many things sometimes overshadows the knowledge that good health is a priority for a full life uninterrupted by sickness. And the enjoyment of cooking can bring a feeling of renewal to the mind as well as the body.

The benefits derived from relaxation and visualization techniques work when applied to menu planning; a little time spent "seeing" simple meals ahead of time saves time spent in frustration later when under pressure to perform—times when everyone's hungry, the cook's feeling hypoglycemic, a bit frantic, and totally uncreative. Once you've developed a repertoire, habit takes over and you'll feel capable of preparing easy whole meals on the spot.

Make it a practice to have one complete, balanced meal per day, at least 4 or 5 days a week. This means having soup; a grain dish; a bean dish (prepared with a little sea vegetable); a leafy greens and a root and/or ground vegetable (squash) dish; a table seasoning (a condiment to sprinkle on the grains to enhance flavor); and a beverage. Include dessert if you want it and time allows. Fermented foods such a miso in the soup (or in a sauce or dressing for vegetables or a salad) and sauerkraut or other pickles are worthwhile including on a regular basis as well.

See the 30 quick-cook menus that follow and take vegetarian or macrobiotic cooking classes whenever possible to see how others prepare appealing meals...pronto!

For times when you want a really light meal, a simple vegetable-miso soup served alone or with bread, resteamed rice, quick-baked or pan-fried mochi, rice cakes, or crackers suffices. Or try noodles topped with sliced and steamed carrots and broccoli or leafy greens and a broth or dressing.

Or make delicious one-pot lunches or dinners: Begin by sautéing or stir-frying onion, garlic, and a root vegetable, then add sliced greens and a little water. Cover to cook until tender, about 5 minutes, adding leftover cooked grain last. Season with soy sauce and steam until grains are warm.

In warm weather, assemble a simple whole-meal salad featuring pre-cooked (or leftover) rice or millet, or a freshly made quick-cooking grain such as whole-grain pasta, bulgur, quinoa, or couscous. Add chopped celery, green onions, watercress, grated carrot and/or red radish, and an easy dressing. For more variety, add cooked beans or prepared tofu or tempeh cutlets, store-bought or made ahead. Serve the dish warm with cooked vegetables during colder times of the year.

Include leftover vegetables and cooking broths in tomorrow's soup. Make it easy on yourself.

Even with a hectic schedule, there's time to cook brown rice, beans, and bread. Rice may take 45-60 minutes to cook, but this is easily planned for anytime one is at home doing other things. Beans that require presoaking may be left all day or overnight to be pressure-cooked like the rice. (Or choose the no-soak, quick-cooking beans:

lentils, split peas, navy beans, azukis, or mung beans; or soyfoods such as tofu or tempeh.) Even naturally leavened bread takes just 3-6 hours from start to finish—time easily spent doing other things while the dough rises and then bakes. Prepare enough of these foods to last for more than one meal.

Time-saving tips

•Keep a clean, efficient kitchen.
•Shop twice a week for fresh produce and other ingredients on your checklist of staples. Include enough inventory for 3-4 meals.
•Plan regular meals to avoid blood sugar problems and cravings.
•Don't undertake too much. Know you can satisfy simply. Good food is good food whether a lot or a little time is spent in preparation. Success depends on using the finest ingredients and first-rate recipes.
•Do the dishes you know best; repeat your successes. Save experiments or more elaborate meals for leisurely times when you're feeling fresh, clear, and enthusiastic.
•Begin with the dish that takes longest to prepare so everything is done at the same time. If including a baked dish such as a quiche or pie, allow time for it to bake and then cool to set up. Bake dishes at the same time such as a sweet winter squash, a casserole, bread, and seeds or nuts for a table seasoning or as part of a dessert.
•Always try to have cooked brown rice or another whole grain on hand. In a cool kitchen, cooked rice may be left out covered with a mat or cotton cloth so it breathes and stays fresh for 3 days. Refrigerate only if the room is warm, and reheat before serving to revive texture and taste. With the grain prepared ahead of time, rounding out a meal with vegetables, and perhaps beans, a sauce, and/or a table seasoning (such as sesame salt or toasted seeds or nuts becomes easy.
•Prepare enough food at dinnertime for the next day's lunch for work or school.

•Develop simple preparation techniques.
•Cut vegetables in similar sizes for even cooking. Thinly sliced vegetables cook more quickly than larger cutting styles. Vary cutting styles for visual appeal.
•Use time-saving cooking techniques:

Cover pot while water comes to boil and during cooking. The trapped steam cuts down on cooking time.

Don't preheat the oven. Place ingredients in the oven just as you turn on the heat so none is wasted.

Use a pressure cooker to prepare beans or root vegetables.
•When serving, take a moment to garnish and present food attractively. A creative natural foods cook is a healthful gourmet. She or he realizes that elegant simplicity in food presentation is satisfying to the aesthetic sense, especially with quickly prepared meals. My husband often says "Wow! This is better than any restaurant!" to the simplest dish of pasta heaped high with 2 or 3 colorful vegetables and tofu or tempeh. If I've quick-boiled everything, I dress it (liberally for him) with a little oil mixed with soy sauce.

Or I sauté onion, sometimes with garlic and ginger, and season it with soy sauce, then mix this with the pasta and vegetables. If no greens are included with the pasta, I garnish the dish with a sprinkling of chopped parsley or green onion, or several sprigs of watercress. (Parsley grows profusely in a backyard or windowsill garden.) I quick-boil greens such as kale or broccoli, and serve them separately with a dressing of lemon juice or brown rice vinegar alone or mixed with a little soy sauce or umeboshi vinegar.

Simple...delicious!
•Rice and bean burritos, tofu or tempeh burgers or sandwiches, or stuffed pita pocket breads make nice quick fare.
•Develop a repertoire of 5 fast meals that taste great and look clear and colorful. Learn several easy dressings to enhance flavor and avoid boredom.

Measurements to remember

●Measure recipe ingredients in this book to level teaspoons, tablespoons, or cups.
●Figure up to 1-2 tablespoons miso per cup soup broth, more with white miso, to taste.
●Figure 1 tablespoon soy sauce per cup water for savory consommés or broths; 2 tablespoons per cup for stronger-flavored sauces for grains, noodles, or vegetables.
●Figure 2 tablespoons (1 heaping tablespoon) kuzu root starch or arrowroot powder per cup water or seasoned broth for Chinese-style sauces. Dissolve in cool water.
●To substitute soy sauce, miso, or umeboshi (paste or vinegar) for salt, figure 1/2 teaspoon salt equals 1 tablespoon of the others.

Quick-cook inventory

Keep this list handy, and check it off for restocking at your natural foods store or coop. Choose organic ingredients whenever possible.

Whole grains and whole-grain products

●Millet
●Buckwheat
●Quinoa
●Quick-cooking brown rice
●Mochi (sweet brown rice cakes)
●Pasta
●Breads, including pita pocket bread, chapatis, and tortillas (whole-wheat or corn)
●Cracked wheat
●Bulgur
●Couscous
●Polenta
●Oatmeal and other cereals
●Whole-wheat bread and pastry flours
●Wheatmeat
●Popcorn

Fresh vegetables, fruits, and seasonings

●Greens (including broccoli, lettuces, and sprouts)
●Onions, carrots, and other roots or tubers
●Squashes, green beans or peas, and other seasonal vegetables
●Apples, pears, and other seasonal fruits
●Garlic, ginger, fresh herbs, lemon and lime

Quick-cooking sea vegetables

●Nori, dulse, sea palm, arame, wakame, ocean ribbons, kombu for broths and beans

Quick-cooking beans and soyfoods

●Lentils, split peas, navy beans, azukis, and mung beans
●Tofu and tempeh

Miscellaneous seasonings/condiments

●Unrefined sea salt
●Miso
●Natural soy sauce or tamari
●Umeboshi (pickled plum) products
●Brown rice vinegar
●Sweet rice cooking wine (mirin)
●Oils (extra virgin olive, plain and toasted sesame, etc.)
●Mustard, natural catsup, and horseradish or wasabi
●Dried herbs, spices, and flavorful seeds
●Olives
●Pickles (sauerkraut, brine, daikon, etc.)
●Toasted nuts and seeds (almonds, hazelnuts, and walnuts; sunflower, sesame, and pumpkin seeds), and nut and seed "butters"
●Apple butter or sauce, and fruit jams
●Dried fruit (raisins/currants, apples, etc.)
●Natural sweeteners (brown rice syrup, barley malt, and pure maple syrup)
●Healthfully prepared foods: soups (instant miso soup, etc.), spaghetti sauce, beans, and salsa

Index

A

Acorn Squash Cups filled with White Bean Chili, 70
Adobe Sauce, 118
African Millet Meal Porridge, 53
African Skillie Stew, 11
Agar sea vegetable flakes, 172, 242
Skillet Cornbread, 38
Almond-Chive Spread, 127
Almond-Onion Spread, 126
Almond Pudding Pie with Tofu "Whipped Cream" Topping, 181
Almond Spiral Cookies, 189
Amaranth, 54
Amazake Daikon Pickles, 167
Amazake, 242
Amazake-Oat "Milk," 202
Amazake-Soymilk, 202
Anise-Scented Barley Bread, 36
Apple Cider Vinaigrette, 129
Apple Gel with Toasted Walnut Sprinkles, 173
Apple-Nut Cake, 183
Arame-Cucumber-Noodle Salad, 104
Arame with Chives, 84
Award-Winning Strawberry Pie, 177
Apple-Almond "Milk," 203
Arame Sea Vegetable, 242
Arrowroot powder, 242
Avocado, 24

B

B12, 2, 157, 163, 166, 245
Baguettes, 35
Baked Millet Kasha, 52
Baked Rice, 18
Baking powder, 184
Barbecued Tempeh, 154
Barley, 18, 54, 101
Barley and Sweet Corn Salad, 101
Basic Berry Jam or Preserves Recipe, 142
Basic Dip Recipe, 134
Basic Fresh-Ground Seed and Nut Butter Recipe, 127
Basic Grain and Vegetable Salad, 101
Basic Large Bean Recipe, 147
Basic Miso Soup Recipe, 1
Basic Small Bean Recipe, 147
Basic Stone Fruit Jam or Preserves Recipe, 142
Bean Burritos, 150
Bean Spreads and Gravy, 120-121
Basic Stone Fruit Pie, 179

Basic Toasted Nuts and Seeds Recipe, 136
Bean Aspic, 112
Beans, 147-150
  Basic Large Bean Recipe, 147
  Basic Small Bean Recipe, 147
  Bean Burritos, 150
  Chili Beans, 148
    Mexican Black Bean Chili, 148
    Pinto Bean Chili, 148
    Texas Chili, 148
    White Bean Chili, 148
  Mexican Bean Dip, 149
  Refried Beans, 150
Beans and Soyfoods, 147-156
Beverages, 193-204
  Bean and Nut "Milks," 202-203
    Amazake-Oat "Milk," 202
    Amazake-Soymilk, 202
    Apple-Almond "Milk," 203
    Oat "Milk," 203
    Sweet Nut "Milk," 203
    Sweet Soymilk, 202
  Cool Summer Drinks, 199-200
    Black Cherry Soda, 200
    Cool Apple Tea, 199
    Cool Lemon Tea, 199
    Fruit-Tea Fizz, 199
    Ginger Ale, 200
    Lemonade, 200
    Limeade, 200
    Orangeade, 200
  Grain "Teas" and "Coffees," 198-199
    Grain "Coffee," Instant and Brewed, 198
    Lemon Espresso-Style Grain "Coffee," 198
    Toasted Barley Tea, 198
    Toasted Corn Tea, 198
  Medicinals, 201-202
    Miso Tea, 201
    Plum Tea, 201
    Ume-Kuzu Morning Tea with Ginger, 202
  Mild Herb Teas, 193-195
    Dixie Mint Tea, 194
    Licorice Root Tea, 195
    Mild Herb Tea with Sweet Herb, 193
    Mu Tea with Licorice Root, 195
    Oriental Herb Tea, 195
    Sweet Peppermint Tea, 194
    Thyme Tea, 194
  Twig Teas, 196-197
    Evening Tea with Lemon or Apple Slice, 197
    Indian Tea, 197

    Sun Tea, 196
    Twig Tea, 196
    Twig Tea with Toasted Brown Rice, 196
Biscuit-Topped Savory Stew, 12
Biscuits, 40
Black Bread, 36
Black Cherry Soda, 200
Blueberry Buckle, 183
Blueberry Corncake, 184
Blueberry Peach Pie, 178
Blueberry-Peach Pudding, 176
Blueberry Topping, 144
Boiled Vegetable Salad, 100
Bok Choy-Alfalfa Sprout Salad, 92
Bonita fish flakes, 2
Boone's Brine Pickles, 164
Braised Tempeh, 153
Bramble Berry Cobbler, 182
Bread and Butter Pickles, 165
Breads, 26-38
  Anise-Scented Barley Bread, 36
  Baguettes, 35
  Basic Cookware, 29
  Basic Recipe, 31
  Black Bread, 36
  Breadsticks, 38
    Mexi-Sticks, 38
    Sesame, 38
  Country French Bread, 35
    New Orleans-Style, 35
    Seeded French, 35
  Croutons, 33
  Crusty Italian Bread, 35
  Freeform-Style, 38
  Garlic Bread, 35
  Garlic Toasts, 33
  Green Onion Flat Bread, 37
  History, 26
  Ingredients, 29
  Muffins, 34
    Carrot-Nut, 34
    Fruit 'n Nut, 34
  Pita Pocket Bread, 37
  Quality, 27
  Quick Breads, 38-40
    Skillet Cornbread, 38
    Biscuits, 40
    Carrot Cornbread, 38
    Chapatis, 41
    Corn Sticks, 39
    Mini-Muffins, 39
    Tequezquite-Leavened Cornbread, 38
    Tortillas, 41
  Shaped, 37
  Sourdough Sesame Bread, 34
  Starter, 30
  Steamed, 33
Breads and Muffins, 217

Breakfast Grits, 209
Breakfasts, 205-219
  Breads and Muffins, 217
  Brown Rice for Breakfast,
    212-213
    Soft Breakfast Rice, 212
    Steamed Rice, 213
  Dry Cereals, 213-215
  Early American Scrapple, 218
  Hot Morning Cereals,
    205-212
    Basic Recipe, 206
    Breakfast Grits, 209
    Corn and Amaranth
      Morning Cereal, 207
    Grain-Bean-Seed Cereal,
      209
    Hot Hazelnut Cereal, 206
    Kokkoh, 209
    Muesli, 211
    Oatmeal, 210-211
    Pantry Porridge, 208
    Rice Cream, 207
    Rye and Wheat Cereal, 207
    Soft Millet Morning
      Cereal, 208
    Steel-Cut Oats, 208
    3-Grain Cereal, 209
    Tibetan Barley Cereal, 207
    Whole-Wheat 'n Amaranth
      Cereal, 207
  Scrambled Tofu, 218
  Waffles, 216-217
    Mochi Waffles, 217
    Whole-Grain Waffles with
      Vegetable Sauce, 216
Brine Pickles, 162
Broccoli and Cauliflower, 67
Broccoli, Carrot, and Summer
  Squash, 64
Brown Basmati Rice, 17
Brown Rice, 16-25
  Rice with Other Grains,
    18-19
    Brown Rice and Barley, 18
    Bulgur Rice, 18
    Long Grain with Wehani
      Red Rice, 19
  Rice with Vegetables, 19-25
    California Rolls, 24
    Country Wild Rice Blend
      with Fresh Corn, 21
    Cucumber-Rice Rolls, 23
    Easy Dinner Rice with
      Summer Vegetable
      Sauce, 45
    Easy Rice Pilaf, 21
    Half-size Sushi Rolls, 23
    Inside-out Sushi, 23
    Jambalaya, 25
    Long Grain-Wehani Rice
      Blend with Fresh Corn,
      21
    Ranch Rice, 22
    Red Herb Rice, 20
    Rice with Fresh Corn
      and Pumpkin Seeds, 21
    Rice with Fresh Greens, 20
    Rice with Mixed Vegetable

    Sauce, 19
    Romaine-Rice Rolls, 24
    Summer Sushi, 22
    Ume Plum Rice, 20
    Vegetable Fried Rice, 47
  Varieties of, 16-18
    Baked Rice, 18
    Brown Basmati Rice, 17
    Long Grain Brown Rice, 17
    Quick-Cooking, 17
    Shaped, 17
    Short or Medium Grain, 16
    Wild Rice, 17
Brown Rice and Barley, 18
Brown Rice for Breakfast,
  212-213
Brown Rice Syrup, 242
Brown Rice Vinegar, 242
Brown Sauce, 135
Buckwheat Noodle Dipping
  Broth, 134
Buckwheat Noodles with
  Dipping Broth, 44
Bulgur, 51
  Bulgur with Fresh Corn and
    Pumpkin Seeds, 51
Bulgur Rice, 18
Bulgur Wheat Salad, 102
Bulgur with Fresh Corn and
  Pumpkin Seeds, 51
Buttermilk, 125

C

Cabbage with Escarole, Endive,
  and Carrot, 60
Calcium, 170
California Rolls, 24
"Caramel" Spread, 144
Carrot-Almond Butter Spread,
  119
Carrot Aspic, 111
Carrot Cornbread, 38
Carrot Marinara Sauce, 117
Carrot-Nut Muffins, 34
Carrot-Sesame Dressing, 118
Cereals, 205-215
Chapatis, 41
Cheese, 124, 157
Chef's Salad with Carrot-
  Sesame Dressing, 98
Cherry Pudding-Gel, 175
Chickpea-Lentil Soup, 7
Chili Beans, 148
Chinese Cabbage and Red
  Onions, 60
Chinese Cabbage and
  Watercress Salad with
  Japanese Plum Dressing, 92
Chinese Mixed Vegetables in
  Brown Sauce, 74
Cider Syrup, 143
Coconut Rice Cake, 186
Collard Greens with Toasted
  Pumpkin Seeds, 61
Commercial Condiments, 140
Consommé, 8
Cooked Vegetable Salad with
  Parisian Parsley Dressing, 99

Cooked Vegeable Salad with
  Tofu "Sour Cream" Dressing,
  98
Cookies, 187-190
Cooking Greens Chart, 62
Cool Apple Tea, 199
Cool Lemon Tea, 199
Corn, 52-54
  African Millet Meal Porridge,
    53
  Cornmeal Mush, 53
  Hominy, 52
  Hopi Finger Bread, 53
  Masa, 52
  Skillet Cornbread, 38
  Tequezquite-Leavened
    Cornbread, Cornsticks,
    and Mini-Muffins, 39
  Whole Corn Thumbprint
    Dumplings, 52
Corn and Amaranth Morning
  Cereal, 207
Corn Baked in the Husk, 65
Corn-Bean Pie, 80
Corn Miso Soup, 3
Cornmeal Mush, 53
Corn on the Cob with Pickled
  Plum, 65
Corn Relish, 165
Cornsticks, 39
Country French Bread, 35
Country Gravy, 136
Country Wild Rice Blend with
  Fresh Corn, 21
Couscous, 50
  Moroccan Couscous, 50
Cracked Wheat, 51
Cream, 124
Cream of Celery Soup, 5
Creamy Basil Dressing, 124
Creamy Cilantro Vinaigrette,
  129
Creamy Cucumber Salad, 93
Creamy Garlic-Dill Dressing,
  124
Creamy Herb (Dill) Dressing,
  124
Creamy Mustard Dip, 134
Croutons, 33
Crumb Topping, 146
Crusty Italian Bread, 35
Cucumber-Rice Rolls, 23
Cucumber Soup, 5
Curried "Mayonnaise"
  Dressing, 122

D

Daikon Radish Rice Bran
  Pickles (Takuan), 166
Dairy products, 122-125,
  213-214
Desserts, 171-192
  Candy, 190
    Macrojax, 190
  Cookies, 187-190
    Almond Spiral, 189
    Gazelle's Horns, 189
    Hazelnut Heart, 187

Lemon-Poppy Seed, 188
Raisin-Spice, 188
Sesame-Oat Squares, 187
Sweet Rice, 187
Ethnic Vegetable Dessert, 191
Fresh Fruit Desserts, 171
Fresh Fruit Kabobs, 171
Melon topped with
Watermelon Syrup, 171
Fresh Fruit Pies, 177-181
Almond Pudding Pie with
Tofu "Whipped Cream"
Topping, 181
Award-Winning Strawberry
Pie, 177
Basic Stone Fruit Pie, 179
Blueberry-Peach Pie, 178
Fresh Peach Pie, 178
Nectarine Crumb Pie, 179
Peaches 'n Almond "Cream"
Tart, 180
Gels and Puddings, 172-177
Apple Gel with Toasted
Walnut Sprinkles, 173
Basic Gel Recipe, 173
Blueberry-Peach Pudding,
176
Cherry Pudding-Gel, 175
Fruit-Filled Cantaloupe
Cups, 174
Jelly Berry Bo, 173
Minty Apple-Raisin Gel,
173
Mocha Gelatina, 174
Peachy Pudding-Gel, 176
Pear Pudding-Gel with Kiwi
Fruit and Hazelnuts, 175
Russian Pudding, 177
Strawberry-Apple Gel, 173
Strawberry Pudding with
Toasted Almonds, 176
Pastries, 182-186
Apple-Nut Cake, 183
Blueberry Buckle, 183
Blueberry Corncake, 184
Bramble Berry Cobbler, 182
Coconut Rice Cake, 186
Easy Fresh Fruit Crisp, 182
Peach Crisp, 192
Plum Corncake, 184
Raspberry-Peach Cobbler,
182
Strawberry Shortcake, 184
Dilled 3-Taste Dressing, 127
Dips, 134-135
Dixie Mint Tea, 194

E

Early American Scrapple, 218
Easy Dinner Rice with Summer
Vegetable Sauce, 45
Easy Fresh Fruit Crisp, 182
Easy Rice Pilaf, 21
Eggs, 218
Escarole-Arame Soup, 4
Ethnic Vegetable Dessert, 191
Evening Tea with Lemon or
Apple Slice, 197

F

Fiesta Bean Salad, 106
Fish, 2, 44
Food combining, 180
French Bread, 35
French Onion Quiche, 81
Fresh Corn Soufflé, 81
Fresh Fruit Kabobs, 171
Fresh Green, Red, or Pink
Kraut, 161
Fresh Pea Soup with Mint, 13
Fresh Peach Pie, 178
Fruit-Filled Cantaloupe Cups,
174
Fruit 'n Nut Muffins, 34
Fruit-Tea Fizz, 199

G

Garden Patch Salad with
Creamy Herb (Dill) Dressing,
90
Garden Salad with Dulse and
Tahini-Lime Dressing, 89
Garden Vegetable Pie in
Pistachio Pastry, 79
Garden Vegetable Salad with
Walnut-Miso Dressing, 90
Garlic Bread, 35
Garlic-Greens Sauté, 71
Garlic-Mushroom-Greens
Sauté, 71
Garlic Toasts, 33
Gazelle's Horns Cookies, 189
Gelled Corn Pasta Salad, 111
Gelling agents, 172, 242, 243
Ginger Ale, 200
Ginger Sauce, 127
Gingered Apple-Raisin Relish,
166
Gingered Lemon-Soy Dressing,
129
Gingered Vegetable Sauce, 116
Gingered Vinaigrette Dressing,
129
Gingery Orange Dressing, 131
Glossary, 242-246
Good Morning Miso Soup with
Mochi, 2
Grain-Bean-Seed Cereal, 209
Grain "Coffee," Instant and
Brewed, 198
Grains, Breads, and
Pasta, 15-58
Amaranth, 54
Barley, 54
Brown Rice, 16-25 (see
Brown Rice)
Corn, 52-54 (see Corn)
Millet, 52 (see Millet)
Oats, 54
Quinoa, 56-57 (see Quinoa)
Wheat, 26-51
Bulgur, 51 (see Bulgur)
Couscous, 50 (see
Couscous)
Cracked Wheat, 51
Naturally Leavened Bread,

26-33 (see Breads)
Pasta, 43-49 (see Pasta)
Wheatmeat, 49
Gravies, 135-136
Green Beans and Arame, 84
Green Onion Flat Bread, 37
Green Salad with Creamy
Cilantro Vinaigrette, 90
Green Vegetable Gumbo, 73
Greens, 59-64
Greens with Carrots and
Shiitake Mushrooms, 64

H

Half-size Sushi Rolls, 23
Hard Bread Salad, 95
Hazelnut Heart Cookies, 187
Hearty Harvest Stew, 12
Heavy Tofu "Cream" with Herbs,
124
Herb Dip, 124
Herbed Green Bean, Carrot,
and Onion Pickles, 164
Herb Teas, 193
Hijiki, 243
Hijiki, Corn, and Tofu Salad,
109
Hijiki-Vegetable Sauté with
Tempeh, 85
Hijiki with Fresh Corn, 85
Homestyle Bean Curd with
Peanuts in Ginger Sauce, 152
Hominy, 52
Hominy Soup, 7
Hopi Finger Bread, 53
Hot and Sour Soup, 10
Hot Cinnamon Syrup, 145
Hot Hazelnut Cereal, 206
Hot Italian Pasta Salad, 104
Hot Slaw, 97

I

Indian-style Tofu "Yogurt," 122
Indian Tea (Chai), 197
Inside-out Sushi, 23
Italian Herb Dressings 1 and 2,
131
Italian Herb Paste (Pesto), 119
Italian Red Sauce, 117
Italian White Sauce, 124

J

Jam, 141
Jambalaya, 25
Japanese Plum Dressing, 127
Japanese Vinaigrette, 130
Jelly Berry Bo, 173

K

Kale, 3
Kelp, 243
Koji, 243
Kokkoh, 209
Kombu sea vegetable, 1, 243
Kuzu root starch, 243

L

Lasagna, 83
Latin American Squash in Hot
    Cinnamon Syrup, 191
Lemon Espresso-Style Grain
    "Coffee," 198
Lemon-Garlic-Mint Dressing,
    130
Lemon-Garlic Tofu, 151
Lemon-Poppy Seed, 188
Lemonade, 200
Lentil Loaf, 120
Lentil Paté, 120
Lentil Salad Marinade, 133
Licorice Root Tea, 195
Light Lemon-Miso Broth, 9
Light Lemon-Rice Vinegar
    Dressing, 127
Limeade, 200
Long Grain Brown Rice, 17
Long Grain-Wehani Rice Blend
    with Fresh Corn, 21
Long Grain with Wehani Red
    Rice, 19

M

Macaroni Salad, 107
Macrobiotics, i-ii
Mandarin Summer Salad, 107
Marinated Cucumbers and
    Onions, 94
Marinated Lentil Salad, 105
Masa, 52
Mayonnaise, 108, 123, 125
Medium Grain Brown Rice, 16
Menu Planning, 232
Menus, 232-241
Mexican Bean Dip, 149
Mexican Black Bean Chili, 148
Mexi-Sticks, 38
Melon topped with Watermelon
    Syrup, 171
Mild Herb Tea with Sweet Herb,
    193
Milk, 202-203
Millet, 52
    Baked Millet Kasha, 52
    Millet "Mashed Potato"
        Casserole, 74
    Millet "Mashed Potatoes," 74
Mim's Arame Salad, 109
Minerals, 1, 245
Mini-Muffins, 39
Minty Apple-Raisin Gel, 173
Mirin, 243
Miso, 1, 243
Miso Tea, 201
Mixed Baked Squash, Southern
    Style, 78
Mixed Green Salad with
    Toasted Sesame Dressing, 91
Mixed Green-Sprout Salad with
    Thousand Island Dressing, 91
Mixed Vegetable Sauce, 116
Mocha Gelatina, 174
Mochi, 2, 217, 244
Mochi Waffles, 217

Moroccan Carrot Salad, 99
Moroccan Couscous, 50
MSG, 243
Muesli, 211
Muffins, 34
Mung Bean Gravy, 121
Mustard Greens and Bean
    Sprouts, 61
Mu Tea with Licorice Root, 195

N

Naturally Leavened Bread,
    26-33
Natural soy sauce, 244
Nappa Cabbage and Red Radish
    Pressed Salad, 96
Nectarine Crumb Pie, 179
New Orleans-Style French
    Bread, 35
Nightshades, 117
Noodle Sushi, 46
Noodles with Season's Savory
    Vegetable Sauce, 45
Nori seaweed, 244
Nori-Sesame Sprinkles, 140
Nutty Carmelcorn (Macrojax),
    190
Nutty Miso Spread, 126
Nutty Miso Stuffed Patty Pan,
    70

O

Oatmeal, 210-211
Oat "Milk," 203
Oats, 54, 208, 210
Onions and Greens, 72
Open Kettle Apple Butter, 143
Orangeade, 200
Orange-Shiso Dressing, 127
Oriental Herb Tea, 195
Oriental Vegetable Soup, 4
Oven Apple Butter, 143

P

Pantry Porridge, 208
Parisian Parsley Dressing, 131
Pasta, 43-49
    Buckwheat Noodles with
        Dipping Broth, 44
    Hot Italian Pasta Salad, 104
    Noodle Sushi, 46
    Noodles with Season's
        Savory Vegetable Sauce, 45
    Pasta with White Fish in
        Carrot Marinara Sauce, 43
    Quick and Easy Noodle-
        Vegetable Delight, 48
    Spaghetti and Wheatballs, 43
    Summer Soba, 44
    Vegetable Fried Noodles, 47
Pasta Primavera, 103
Pasta with White Fish in Carrot
    Marinara Sauce, 43
Patty Pan Squash with Sesame-
    Onion Sauce, 70
Peach Crisp, 192

Peaches 'n Almond "Cream"
    Tart, 180
Peach Preserves, 142
Peachy Pudding-Gel, 176
Pear Pudding-Gel with Kiwi
    Fruit and Hazelnuts, 175
Peasant's Cabbage Soup, 3
Pectin, 141
Pesto, 119
Pickled Plum (Umeboshi),
    167-170, 244
Pickles, 157-165
    Bread and Butter Pickles,165
    Brine Pickles, about, 162
        Herbed Green Bean, Carrot,
            and Onion Pickles, 164
        Boone's Brine, 164
        with Fennel, 163
    History, 157
    Japanese Pickles, about,
        166-170
        Amazake Daikon, 167
        Daikon Radish Rice Bran
            (Takuan), 166
        Pickled Plum (Umeboshi),
            167
        Sushi, 167
    Nutritional Qualities, 157
    Quick Carrot-Daikon, 159
    Quick Cucumber-Dill, 158
    Sauerkraut, 159
        Fresh Green, Red, or Pink
            Krauts, 161
Pinto Bean Chili, 148
Pistachio Gravy, 135
Pita Pocket Bread, 37
Plain Tofu "Yogurt," 122
Plum Conserve, 142
Plum Corncake, 184
Plum extract, 201
Plum Tea, 201
Potato, 74, 117
Pregnancy, 170
Preserves, 141
Pumpkin Seed-Dulse Sprinkles,
    139
Pumpkin Seed-Shiso Sprinkles,
    138

Q

Quiche, 81
Quiche Alsacienne, 81
Quick-Boiled Greens with 1-,
    2-, or 3-Taste Dressings, 63
Quick Breads, 38-40
Quick and Easy Noodle-
    Vegetable Delight, 48
Quick Carrot-Daikon Pickles,
    159
Quick cooking, 232
Quick-Cooking Brown Rice, 17
Quick Cucumber-Dill Pickles,
    158
Quick Pressed Salad with
    Light Lemon-Rice Vinegar
    Dressing, 96
Quinoa, 56-57
    Quinoa with Bulgur, 57

R

Raisin-Spice Cookies, 188
Ranch Dressing, 125
Ranch Rice, 22
Raspberry-Peach Cobbler, 182
Red and Green Shiso Cabbage, 67
Red Barbeque Sauce, 133
Red Herb Rice, 20
Red Onion Quiche, 81
Red Sauce, 117
Red shiso leaf or powder, 168, 244
Refried Beans, 150
Relishes, 165-166
  Corn Relish, 165
  Gingered Apple-Raisin Relish, 166
Rice and Sweet Corn Salad, 101
Rice Cream, 207
Rice with Fresh Corn and Pumpkin Seeds, 21
Rice with Fresh Greens, 20
Rice with Mixed Vegetable Sauce, 19
Romaine-Rice Rolls, 24
Russian Pudding, 177
Rye and Wheat Cereal, 207

S

Salad with Ranch Dressing, 88
Salad with Sweet Poppy Seed Dressing, 92
Salads, 87-114
  Aspics/Gelled Salads, 111-113
    Bean Aspic, 112
    Carrot Aspic, 111
    Gelled Corn Pasta Salad, 111
    Split Pea Aspic, 112
  Bean Salads, 105-108
    Fiesta Bean Salad, 106
    Mandarin Summer Salad, 107
    Marinated Lentil Salad, 105
    Tempeh Salad, 107
  Cooked Vegetable Salads, 97-101
    Boiled Vegetable Salad, 100
    Chef's Salad with Carrot-Sesame Dressing, 98
    Cooked Vegetable Salad with Parisian Parsley Dressing, 99
    Cooked Vegetable Salad with Tofu "Sour Cream" Dressing, 98
    Hot Slaw, 97
    Moroccan Carrot Salad, 99
    Vegetables Vinaigrette, 100
  Fresh Vegetable Salads, 88-95
    Bok Choy-Alfalfa Sprout Salad, 92

Chinese Cabbage and Watercress Salad with Japanese Plum Dressing, 92
Creamy Cucumber Salad (Raita), 93
Garden Patch Salad with Creamy Herb (Dill) Dressing, 90
Garden Salad with Dulse and Tahini-Lime Dressing, 89
Garden Vegetable Salad with Walnut-Miso Dressing, 89
Green Salad with Creamy Cilantro Vinaigrette, 90
Hard Bread Salad, 95
Marinated Cucumbers and Onions, 94
Mixed Green Salad with Toasted Sesame Dressing, 91
Mixed Green-Sprout Salad with Thousand Island Dressing, 91
Salad with Ranch Dressing, 88
Salad with Sweet Poppy Seed Dressing, 92
Salsa Salad, 95
Tossed Green Salad with Orange-Shiso Dressing, 90
  Pasta Salads, 103-105
    Arame-Cucumber-Noodle Salad, 104
    Hot Italian Pasta Salad, 104
    Macaroni Salad, 107
    Pasta Primavera, 103
  Pressed Vegetable Salads, 96
    Nappa Cabbage and Red Radish Pressed Salad, 96
    Quick Pressed Salad with Light Lemon-Rice Vinegar Dressing, 96
  Sea Vegetable Salads, 109-110
    Hijiki, Corn, and Tofu Salad, 109
    Mim's Arame Salad, 109
    Sea Palm-Sprout Salad, 110
  Whole-Grain and Vegetable Salads, 101-102
    Barley and Sweet Corn Salad, 101
    Basic Grain and Vegetable Salad, 101
    Bulgur Wheat Salad, 102
    Rice and Sweet Corn Salad, 101
    Tabouli, 102
Salsa Pacifica, 118
Salsa Salad, 95
Salt, 15, 29, 246
Sauces, Spreads, and Dressings, 115-146

Bean Spreads and Gravy, 120-121
  Lentil Paté, 120
  Mung Bean Gravy, 121
  Tempeh Party Ball Spread, 120
Creamy Tofu Sauces and Dressings, 122-125
  Creamy Basil Dressing, 124
  Creamy Garlic-Dill Dressing, 124
  Creamy Herb (Dill) Dressing, 124
  Curried "Mayonnaise" Dressing, 122
  Heavy Tofu "Cream" with Herbs, 124
  Herb Dip, 124
  Indian-style Tofu "Yogurt," 122
  Italian White Sauce, 124
  Plain Tofu "Yogurt," 122
  Ranch Dressing, 125
  Thousand Island Dressing, 125
  Tofu "Cheese" Sauce, 124
  Tofu "Mayonnaise," 122
  Tofu "Mayonnaise" Dressing, 122
  Tofu "Sour Cream," 122
  Tofu "Sour Cream" Dressing, 122
Dips, 134-135
  Basic Dip Recipe, 134
  Buckwheat Noodle Dipping Broth, 134
  Creamy Mustard Dip, 134
  Mexican Bean Dip, 149
  Sushi Dipping Sauce, 134
Flour-Thickened Gravies, 135-136
  Brown Sauce, 135
  Country Gravy, 136
  Pistachio-Miso Gravy, 135
Marinades, 132-133
  Lentil Salad Marinade, 133
  Red Barbecue Sauce, 133
  Teriyaki Sauce/ Marinade, 132
Oil-free Dressings and Sauces, 127
  Dilled 3-Taste Dressing, 127
  Ginger Sauce, 127
  Light Lemon-Rice Vinegar Dressing, 127
  3-Taste Dressing, 127
  2-Taste Dressing, 127
  White Miso Vinaigrette, 96
Seed or Nut Butter-Based Spreads and Dressings, 126-127
  Almond-Chive Spread, 127
  Almond-Onion Spread, 126
  Basic Fresh-Ground Seed and Nut Butter Recipe, 126
  Japanese Plum Dressing, 127

Nutty Miso Spread, 126
Orange-Shiso Dressing, 127
Sesame-Miso Spread, 126
Tahini-Lime Dressing, 127
Walnut-Miso Dressing, 127
Sweet Spreads and Toppings, 141-146
 Basic Berry Jam or Preserves Recipe, 141
 Basic Stone Fruit Jam or Preserves Recipe, 142
 Blueberry Topping, 144
 "Caramel" Spread, 144
 Cider Syrup, 143
 Crumb Topping, 146
 Hot Cinnamon Syrup, 145
 Open Kettle Apple Butter, 143
 Oven Apple Butter, 143
 Peach Preserves, 142
 Plum Conserve, 142
 Sesame-Maple Spread, 144
 Strawberry Jam, 141
 Strawberry Sauce, 144
 Sweet and Simple Sauce, 144
 Tofu "Whipped Cream," 146
 Watermelon Syrup, 145
 Windfall Apple Sauce, 143
Table Seasonings, 136-140
 Basic Toasted Nuts and Seeds Recipe, 136
 Commercial Condiments, 140
 Sea Vegetable Chips, Flakes, and Powders, 138
 Pumpkin Seed-Dulse Sprinkles, 139
 Pumpkin Seed-Shiso Sprinkles, 138
 Seeded Sea Powders, 139
 Sesame-Parsley Sprinkles, 138
 Sesame Salt, 137
 Sesame-Shiso-Nori Sprinkles, 138
 Sesame-Shiso Sprinkles, 138
 Sesame-Sunflower Topping, 138
 Sunflower-Dulse Sprinkles, 139
 Sunflower-Shiso Sprinkles, 138
 Toasted Pumpkin Seeds, Native American Style, 137
 Trail Mix, 137
 (Wild) Nori-Sesame Sprinkles, 140
 Wild Nori-Sunflower Sprinkles, 139
Vegetable-Based Sauces, Spreads, and Dressings, 116-119
 Adobe Sauce, 118
 Carrot-Almond Butter Spread, 119

Carrot Marinara Sauce, 117
Carrot-Sesame Dressing, 118
Gingered Vegetable Sauce, 116
Italian Herb Paste, 119
Italian Red Sauce, 117
Mixed Vegetable Sauce, 116
Pesto, 119
Red Sauce, 117
Salsa Pacifica, 118
Season's Savory Vegetable Sauce, 117
Sesame-Onion Sauce, 119
Winter Pesto, 119
Vegetable Sauce, 116
Vinaigrette Dressings, 129-132
 Apple Cider Vinaigrette, 129
 Creamy Cilantro Vinaigrette, 129
 Gingered Lemon-Soy Dressing, 129
 Gingered Vinaigrette Dressing, 129
 Gingery Orange Dressing, 131
 Italian Herb Dressings 1 and 2, 131
 Japanese Vinaigrette, 130
 Lemon-Garlic-Mint Dressing, 130
 Parisian Parsley Dressing, 131
 Shiso Leaf Dressing, 131
 Sweet Mustard-Dill Dressing, 130
 Sweet Poppy Seed Dressing, 130
 Tangy Orange Dressing, 131
 Toasted Sesame Dressing, 132
Sauerkraut, 159-161
Sauerkraut Soup, 13
Savory Miso Soup, 2
Scrambled Tofu, 218
Seasoned Red Sauce, 118
Seasoned Vegetables (Moroccan), 76
Season's Greens Sautéd with Fresh Mushrooms, 71
Season's Greens with Kernel Corn, 61
Season's Savory Vegetable Sauce, 117
Sea palm, 244
Sea Palm-Sprout Salad, 110
Sea salt, 15, 29, 246
Sea vegetables, 1, 138-140, 245
Sea Vegetable Chips, Flakes, and Powders, 138
Seeded French Bread, 35
Seeded Sea Powders, 139
Seeds. toasted, 136
Sesame Breadsticks, 38
Sesame Hijiki; with 3-Taste Dressing, 85
Sesame-Maple Spread, 144

Sesame-Miso Spread, 126
Sesame-Oat Squares, 187
Sesame-Onion Sauce, 119
Sesame-Parsley Sprinkles, 138
Sesame Salt, 137
Sesame-Shiso-Nori Sprinkles, 138
Sesame-Shiso Sprinkles, 138
Sesame-Sunflower Topping, 138
Shallot-Kale Sauté, 71
Shallot-Savoy Sauté, 71
Shaped Rice, 17
Shiitake mushroom, 245
Shiso, 91, 168, 244
Shiso Leaf Dressing, 131
Shiso-Simmered Kohlrabi, 67
Short Grain Rice, 16
Skillet Cornbread, 38
Soba, 44, 245
Soft Breakfast Rice, 212
Soft Millet Morning Cereal, 208
Somen, 245
Soufflé, 81
Soups, 1-14
 Broths, 8-11
  Consommé, 8
  Hot and Sour Soup, 10
  Light Lemon-Miso Broth, 9
  Vegetable Cutout Consommé, 8
  Vegetable Cutout Soup, 9
 Miso Soups, 1-8
  Basic Miso Soup Recipe, 1
  Chickpea-Lentil Soup, 7
  Corn Miso Soup, 3
  Cream of Celery Soup, 5
  Cucumber Soup, 5
  Escarole-Arame Soup, 4
  Good Morning Miso Soup with Mochi, 2
  Hominy Soup, 7
  Oriental Vegetable Soup, 4
  Peasant's Cabbage Soup, 3
  Savory Miso Soup, 2
  Summer Squash Soup, 5
  The Stone Soup Story, 8
  Vegetable Soup, 3
 Other Soups, 13
  Fresh Pea Soup with Mint, 13
  Sauerkraut Soup, 13
 Stews, 11-12
  African Skillie Stew, 11
  Biscuit-Topped Savory Stew, 12
  Hearty Harvest Stew, 12
Sourdough Sesame Bread, 34
Soyfoods, 151-155
 Tempeh, 153-154
  Barbecued Tempeh, 154
  Braised Tempeh, 153
  Tempeh Cutlets, for Sandwiches and Burgers, 153
 Tofu, 151-152
  Homestyle Bean Curd with Peanuts in Ginger Sauce, 152

Lemon-Garlic Tofu, 151
   Tofu Teriyaki, 151
Soy sauce, 1, 244
Spaghetti and Wheatballs, 43
Spinach, 92
Split Pea Aspic, 112
Spring Crudités Platter, 68
Steamed Bread, 33
Steamed Cabbage Wedges, 66
Steamed Rice, 213
Steamed Vegetables, 66
Steel-Cut Oats, 208
Stevia, 123
Stone Soup Story, 8
Strawberry-Apple Gel, 173
Strawberry Jam, 141
Strawberry Pudding with
   Toasted Almonds, 176
Strawberry Sauce, 144
Strawberry Shortcake, 184
Stroganoff, 77
Summer Soba, 44
Summer Squash Soup, 5
Summer Sushi, 22
Sunflower-Dulse Sprinkles,
   139
Sunflower-Shiso Sprinkles,
   138
Sun Tea, 196
Suribachi, 245
Suricogi, 245
Sushi, 22-24
   California Rolls, 24
   Cucumber-Rice Rolls, 23
   Half-size Sushi Rolls, 23
   Inside-out Sushi, 23
   Romaine-Rice Rolls, 24
   Summer Sushi, 22
Sushi Dipping Sauce, 134
Sushi Pickles, 167
Sweet and Simple Sauce, 144
Sweeteners, 242, 243
Sweet herb, 123, 245
Sweet Mustard-Dill Dressing,
   130
Sweet Nut "Milk," 203
Sweet Peppermint Tea, 194
Sweet Poppy Seed Dressing,
   130
Sweet Rice Cookies, 187
Sweet Soymilk, 202

T

Table Seasonings, 136-140
Tabouli, 102
Tahini-Lime Dressing, 127
Tamari, 245
Tangy Orange Dressing, 131
Tempeh, 245
Tempeh Cutlets for Sandwiches
   and Burgers, 153
Tempeh Party Ball Spread, 120
Tempeh Salad, 107
Tempeh Stroganoff, 77
Tequezquite-Leavened
   Cornbread, Corn Sticks,
   and Mini-Muffins, 38
Teriyaki Sauce/Marinade, 132

Texas Chili, 148
Thousand Island Dressing, 125
3-Grain Cereal, 209
3-Taste Dressing, 127
Thyme Tea, 194
Tibetan Barley Cereal, 207
Toasted Barley Tea, 198
Toasted Corn Tea, 198
Toasted Pumpkin Seeds, Native
   American Style, 137
Toasted Sesame Dressing, 132
Toasted sesame oil, 246
Tofu, 87, 122-125, 180, 246
Tofu "Cheese" Sauce, 124
Tofu Enchiladas, 82
Tofu "Mayonnaise," 122-123
Tofu "Mayonnaise" Dressing,
   122
Tofu "Sour Cream," 122
Tofu "Sour Cream" Dressing,
   122
Tofu Teriyaki, 151
Tofu "Whipped Cream," 146
Tomato, 117
Tortillas, 41
Tossed Green Salad with
   Orange-Shiso Dressing, 90
Trail Mix, 137
Twig Tea, 196
Twig Tea with Toasted Brown
   Rice, 196
2-Taste Dressing, 127

U

Udon, 246
Umeboshi, 167-169
Ume-Kuzu Morning Tea with
   Ginger, 202
Ume Plum Rice, 20
Unrefined sea salt, 15, 29, 246

V

Vegetable Crudités, 68
Vegetable Cutout Consommé, 8
Vegetable Cutout Soup, 9
Vegetable Dishes, 59-86
   Casseroles and Main Dish
      Pies, 78-84
      Corn-Bean Pie, 80
      French Onion Quiche, 81
      Fresh Corn Soufflé, 81
      Garden Vegetable Pie
         in Pistachio Pastry, 79
      Lasagna, 83
      Lentil Loaf, 120
      Mixed Baked Squash,
         Southern Style, 78
      Red Onion Quiche, 81
      Tofu Enchiladas, 82
      Vegetable Pot Pie, 78
   Quick-Boiled Vegetables,
      59-65
      Basic Recipe, 59
      Broccoli, Carrot, and
         Summer Squash, 64
      Cabbage with Escarole,
         Endive, and Carrot, 60

      Chinese Cabbage and Red
         Onions, 60
      Collard Greens with
         Toasted Pumpkin Seeds,
         61
      Cooking Greens Chart, 62
      Corn Baked in the Husk,
         65
      Corn on the Cob with
         Pickled Plum
         (Umeboshi), 65
      Greens with Carrots and
         Shiitake Mushrooms, 64
      Mustard Greens and Bean
         Sprouts, 61
      Quick-Boiled Greens
         with 1-, 2-, or 3-Taste
         Dressings; Chart, 63
      Season's Greens with
         Kernel Corn, 61
      Veggie Sticks, 64
   Sea Vegetable Dishes, 84-86
      Arame with Chives, 84
      Green Beans and Arame,
         84
      Hijiki-Vegetable Sauté
         with Tempeh, 85
      Hijiki with Fresh Corn, 85
      Sesame Hijiki; with
         3-Taste Dressing, 85
   Simmered Vegetables, 67
      Red and Green Shiso
         Cabbage, 67
      Shiso-Simmered Kohlrabi,
         67
   Sautéed Vegetables, 71-77
      Basic Onion Family-Greens
         Sauté Recipe, 71
      Chinese Mixed Vegetables
         in Brown Sauce, 75
      Garlic-Greens Sauté, 71
      Garlic-Mushroom-Greens
         Sauté, 71
      Green Vegetable Gumbo, 73
      Millet "Mashed Potatoes";
         Millet "Mashed Potato"
         Casserole, 74
      Onions and Greens, 72
      Seasoned Vegetables, 76
      Season's Greens Sautéed
         with Fresh Mushrooms,
         71
      Shallot-Kale Sauté, 71
      Shallot-Savoy Sauté, 71
      Stroganoff, 77
      Tempeh Stroganoff, 77
      Vegetables, North Indian
         Style, 76
   Specialty Vegetable Dishes,
      68-71
      Acorn Squash Cups
         filled with White Bean
         Chili, 70
      Nutty Miso Stuffed Patty
         Pan, 70
      Patty Pan Squash with
         Sesame-Onion Sauce, 70
      Spring Crudités Platter, 68
      Vegetable Crudités, 68

Vegetables with Italian
    Herb Paste (Pesto), 69
    Winter Pesto, 69
Steamed Vegetables, 66-67
    Basic Recipe, 66
    Broccoli and Cauliflower,
    67
    Steamed Cabbage Wedges,
    66
Vegetable Fried Noodles, 47
Vegetable Fried Rice, 47
Vegetable Pot Pie, 78
Vegetable Sauce, 116
Vegetable Soup, 3
Vegetables, North Indian
    Style, 76
Vegetables Vinaigrette, 100
Vegetables with Italian Herb
    Paste (Pesto), 69
Vegetarianism, i
Veggie Sticks, 64
Vinegar, 242

W

Wakame sea vegetable, 246
Walnut-Miso Dressing, 127
Wasabi, 22, 246
Water, 29, 163
Watermelon Syrup, 145
Wehani rice, 19
Wheat, 26-51
Wheatmeat, 49
Whipped cream 146, 180, 181
White Bean Chili, 148
Whole Corn Thumbprint
    Dumplings, 52
Whole-Grain Waffles with
    Vegetable Sauce, 216
Whole-wheat flour, 29, 246
Whole-Wheat 'n Amaranth
    Cereal, 207
Whole-wheat pastry flour, 246
(Wild) Nori-Sesame Sprinkles,
    140
Wild Nori-Sunflower
    Sprinkles, 139
Wild Rice, 17
Windfall Apple Sauce, 143
Winter Pesto, 69, 119

Y

Yeast, 28
Yogurt, 93, 151